The Assault on Privacy

The As

sault on Privacy

Computers, Data Banks, and Dossiers

Arthur R. Miller

Ann Arbor
The University of Michigan Press

DEPRIVACY

Although we feel unknown, ignored
    As unrecorded blanks,
Take heart! Our vital selves are stored
    In giant data banks,

Our childhoods and maturities,
    Efficiently compiled,
Our stocks and insecurities
    All permanently filed,

Our tastes and our proclivities,
    In gross and in particular,
Our incomes, our activities
    Both extra- and curricular.

And such will be our happy state
    Until the day we die
When we'll be snatched up by the great
    Computer in the sky.

—Felicia Lamport
(reprinted from *Look*)

Foreword

In *The Assault on Privacy: Computers, Data Banks, and Dossiers,*
Professor Miller has produced an alarming account of the impact information practices are having on our society and on our
liberties. This eminently readable book reflects the disciplined
research and the unique insights that are the distinctive trade-
mark of an accomplished legal scholar. Equally as important are
the value judgments he imparts as one thoughtful American
concerned with the preservation of liberty in a free society. With
unusual brilliance and clarity the author warns of computer
technology's inherent threat to privacy and individual constitutional rights. He carefully documents the most important
political and economic changes caused by burgeoning private
and official data programs, by changing communications techniques, and by rapid new developments in computer hardware
and software.

Professor Miller's analysis of those changes and of the inade-
quacies of the present law governing them is vital to those of us
who still believe that man's most cherished possession is individual
liberty and who view privacy and political freedom as the most
precious of liberties in this age of cybernetics. His proposals for
reasserting control over the "information power" bestowed by the
new technology offer timely, creative, and pragmatic approaches
to this grave threat to freedom. This book should shame some
government and industry executives into exercising more self-
restraint. It may also encourage lawmakers to take a second look
at any legislation they enact which might condone any unnecessary invasions of privacy. More important, however, is the fact
that it should bestir all Americans to claim their constitutional
legacy of personal privacy and individual rights and to demand
an end to abuses of computer technology before the light of
liberty is extinguished in our land.

December, 1970   Senator Sam J. Ervin, Jr.
Chairman, United States Senate
Subcommittee on Constitutional Rights

Preface and Acknowledgments

The genesis of this book can be traced to a telephone call I received during the fall of 1966 from Dr. James G. Miller, then Director of the University of Michigan's Mental Health Institute and currently Vice President for Academic Affairs of Cleveland State University. He asked what I am sure he thought was a relatively straightforward and easily answered question: What are the legal consequences of computerizing copyrighted materials? On closer inquiry I discovered that Dr. Miller was exploring the possibility of using computer technology to develop a national, multi-media information network, that would electronically integrate our colleges and universities, eventually providing each of them a comprehensive and easily accessible pool of scholarly works and educational services. He subsequently sought to breathe life into this idea by promoting the formation of an organization called the Interuniversity Communications Council (EDUCOM).

As a legal technician who has spent much of his career wallowing in the minutiae of courtroom procedure, I found the problem both exciting and frustrating. Indeed, although I had taught and studied copyright law for several years, I could not unearth anything in the existing statutes and judicial decisions that would provide definitive answers to the many questions that spring to mind when one begins to consider the implications of computerization on the country's copyright regime and, more broadly, its potential effect on the media through which artistic and intellectual works are now presented to the public. And the more I delved into the subject the more I felt overwhelmed by the realization that my legal training would have to be augmented by a heavy dose of learning in the various disciplines bearing on information science. Perhaps more importantly, as time went on I became aware of the profound effect computer technology is certain to have on numerous facets of the law—antitrust policy, communications regulation, courtroom procedure and judicial administration, legal education, and individual privacy. The copyright conundrum, it became apparent, was only the tip of the iceberg.

The computer-privacy question came to the fore during the Great Debate in 1967 over the proposed National Data Center. Apparently because of some of my writings and public statements on the proposed Copyright Revision Bill's failure to take adequate account of the new information technologies, the staff of the Senate Subcommittee on Administrative Practice and Procedure, chaired at that time by Senator Edward V. Long of Missouri, asked me to testify about the effect computers may have on individual privacy in contemporary life. Since that first appearance before a congressional subcommittee I have slowly been devoured by the issue, although I must confess that because of the inherent fascination of problems of interrelating law and technology I have done little to avoid this detour from my more traditional research activities. No doubt my preoccupation with the subject partially reflects a concern over the legal profession's occasional reluctance to seek out interdisciplinary solutions for current social problems.

But the reader should not be misled. I do not claim to be anything other than a lawyer; I admit to being unschooled in computer science, and I am at best a dabbler in such fields as computer assisted legal instruction and machine based legal research systems. Whatever insights I have gained into the implications of modern information technology since 1966 I attribute to my exposure to (and the patience of) such people as Colonel Andrew A. Aines, Executive Secretary of the Committee on Scientific and Technical Information (COSATI) of the Executive Office of the President, Jordan J. Baruch, formerly President of EDUCOM and now a member of the Harvard Business School faculty, J. C. R. Licklider and Carl Overhage of the Massachusetts Institute of Technology, and James G. Miller, whom I already have mentioned.

Therefore this volume, which incorporates the thoughts and views I have formulated during the past few years relating to personal privacy in the computer age, has been made possible by the encouragement I have received from these people and from the staffs of the Senate Subcommittee on Administrative Practice and Procedure, the Senate Subcommittee on Constitutional

Rights, particularly from Miss Marcia J. MacNaughton, the Senate and House Subcommittees on Financial Institutions, Charles Witter of Congressman Cornelius E. Gallagher's office, and G. Russell Pipe, who formerly was an aide to Congressman Jackson E. Betts. I also have received considerable enlightenment from my coworkers on the Census Bureau's Decennial Census Review Committee, the COSATI Panel on the Legal Aspects of Information Systems, and the National Academy of Science's Project on Computer Data Banks, which is under the directorship of Professor Alan F. Westin of Columbia University.

Having said this, I acknowledge being most deeply in the debt of a series of University of Michigan Law School student research assistants who have worked with me during the past three years. The first of them, Barry B. Boyer, of the class of 1969, gathered much of the documentation that appears in the notes, provided numerous substantive suggestions, and assisted in collecting, revising, and elaborating many of my past expressions on the subject of computers and privacy. Upon his graduation these tasks were assumed by John J. Berry, III, of the class of 1970, whose work on Chapter V was particularly helpful, and upon his departure by Mary Kay Kane, of the class of 1971, who performed valiantly during the final preparation of this book. An additional note of appreciation is extended to Frederick W. Lambert, of the class of 1969 for his valuable research assistance. As is customary in these matters, however, I reserve to myself full credit for any and all heresies that appear in the pages that follow.

Arthur R. Miller

December, 1970

Contents

Prologue

Information Technology—A Study of Good and Evil

All myths directly or indirectly go back to the myth of Paradise; and the technical productivity man is witnessing seems to have spurred a proliferation of myths. Psychologists and sociologists have observed the appearance of new myths; and many theories have been advanced to account for this return of man to the sacred world. But such explanations are unsatisfactory because they lack a material basis. That material basis is, in fact, the enormous technical progress of the modern world. This progress restores to man the supernatural world from which he had been severed, an incomprehensible world but one which he himself has made, a world full of promises that he knows can be realized and of which he is potentially the master. He is seized by sacred delirium when he sees the shining track of a supersonic jet or visualizes the vast granaries stocked for him. He projects this delirium into the myth through which he can control, explain, direct, and justify his actions . . . and his slavery.

However, as it is said in England, "you get nothing for nothing, and not much for sixpence." In spite of leisure and abundance, supposing that leisure and abundance come in the way men expect them, there is a great difference between this state and Paradise. The difference has to do with the cost. The old dream that has tempted man from the beginning, the medieval legend of the man who sells his soul for an inexhaustible purse, which recurs with an enticing insistence through all the changes of civilization, is perhaps in process of being realized, and not for a single man but for all. I say *perhaps*. Modern man never asks himself what he will have to pay for his power. *This* is the question we ought to be asking.

—Jacques Ellul, *The Technological Society*
(paper ed., 1964), 191–93

When historians come to write the story of our time, they may well characterize it as the Age of Cybernetics. Surely one of the most significant aspects of this period is the technological revolution centered around a species of machine we call "the computer," a revolution that is dramatically increasing man's capacity to accumulate, manipulate, retrieve, and transmit knowledge.

1

Without this resource we would be unable to enjoy the fruits of contemporary society's information explosion or to reap the full benefits of our capacity to thrust a rocket to the moon and the planets beyond.

A number of contemporary prophets have predicted that the new information technologies eventually will prove to be as significant to mankind as was the invention of movable type.[1] As seers such as Sir Arthur Clarke and Marshall McLuhan perceive the future, information will not be recorded or conveyed in the form of alphabetical imprints or pictures in a book but rather as holes in punch cards, magnetic fields on tapes or discs, electrical impulses moving through the memory core of a computer, and, perhaps, radiations generated in vats of complex chemicals.

Although claiming no gift of clairvoyance, I too can foresee a time when today's brick-and-mortar library will be obsolete. Our primary source of knowledge will be electronic information nodes or communications centers located in our homes, schools, and offices that are connected to international, national, regional, and local computer-based data networks. Through these systems will come the newspapers and magazines of the future, the literature and arts of the world, and the intellectual achievements of society. Much of the recorded experience of mankind literally will be at our fingertips. The day also will come when children learn to operate a computer terminal even before they begin to write. It seems inevitable that typewriterlike consoles, light pencils, and television cathode-ray tubes will join crayons, building blocks, and modeling clay in the kindergarten of the future.

This book is about certain aspects of our increasingly electronic way of life. It will not simply catalog the great strides being taken in the computer world or goggle over the predictions and projections of the scientific community's enthusiasts. Rather, its aim is to explore some of the ways in which information technology is altering basic patterns in our daily life and to evaluate the responses being made by the law, government, industry, and other institutions to the new forms of data handling.

All too often we fall prey to the fallacy that computers live in their own self-contained world, functioning independently and beyond the control of man. In our awe over the pinpoint accuracy of the voyages of Apollo 11 and Apollo 12 to the moon, let us not forget that humans programmed the computers that gave us an unremitting stream of data about those flights, dictated the character of the data that would be recorded and analyzed, and made their own decisions based on the mass of information stored in the electronic behemoths. Because of the canonization of astronauts Aldrin, Armstrong, and Collins, few people remember that it was Stephen G. Bales, a young guidance officer at the Manned Space Center in Houston, who at the critical point in Apollo 11's landing recognized that the onboard computer system was not functioning, quickly referred to the information available to him in Houston, almost 300,000 miles away from the descending spacecraft, and made the decision that Eagle was on target for a landing in the Sea of Tranquillity. In many ways, this example of the relationship between man and machine, as well as the way disaster was averted on the ill-fated flight of Apollo 13, more accurately reflects the reality of our electronic way of life than does the popular image projected by Hal, the neurotic but domineering computer in *2001: A Space Odyssey*.

In spite of the successful adjustment man has made to the machine in many contexts, it would be foolish not to recognize that the transition to an electronic way of life is bound to be accompanied by abrasive dislocations, as almost all significant deviations from traditional life styles have been. Already there is a growing awareness of the effects that certain applications of the computer may have on that elusive value we call "personal privacy." In the past the very ponderousness of movable-type technology inhibited man's urge to collect and preserve information about his peers and thereby served to limit the amount of data that was recorded about an individual. But many people have voiced concern that the computer, with its insatiable appetite for information, its image of infallibility, and its inability to forget anything that has been stored in it, may become the heart of a surveillance system that will turn society into a transparent world in which our homes, our finances, and our associations will be bared to a wide range of casual observers, including the morbidly curious and the maliciously or commercially intrusive.[2] These fears have been exacerbated by the clarion call in certain quarters for the establishment of a National Data Center, by the emergence of surveillance data systems as well as computer-based credit-reporting services, and by the hypnotic attraction for electronic record-keeping being exhibited throughout government, industry, and academe.

A brief recital of a few of the blessings and blasphemies of the new technology makes the computer-privacy dilemma abundantly clear. In various medical centers, doctors are using computers to monitor physiological changes in the bodies of heart patients in the hope of isolating those alterations in body chemistry that precede a heart attack. The quest, of course, is to provide an "early warning system" so that treatment is not delayed until the actual heart attack, which often renders the patient moribund for all practical purposes. But on the opposite side of the ledger, the same electronic sensors that can warn us of an impending heart attack can be used to locate us, track our movements, and measure our emotions and thoughts.

Returning to the positive, some information specialists have suggested providing everyone with a birth number to identify him for tax, banking, education, social security, military, and various other purposes. This would be done in conjunction with the computerization of a wide range of individualized records and their reorganization by birth number. The goal is to eliminate much of the existing multiplicity in record-keeping while at the same time expediting the business of society. There are other valuable payoffs as well. For example, if a person falls ill while away from home, a local doctor could use the patient's birth number to retrieve his medical history and drug reactions from a central medical data bank. But there are risks. The identification number given us at birth might become a leash around our necks and make us the object of constant monitoring through a womb-to-tomb computer dossier. Similarly, the administrative conveniences provided by the high degree of information centralization made possible by widescale use of computers would give those who control the recordation and preservation of personal data an ability to influence our lives, which, if abused by misleading disclosures, might make the so-called "credibility gaps" between governmental statements and reality look like bidding misunderstandings at the bridge table.

It is all too easy to think of the dangerous aspects of the technology as problems for a future generation. The unpleasant truth is that many of the present applications of computer science constitute a potential or actual threat to personal privacy. A description of one such application will illustrate how the uses of the technology can intrude upon the individual. The August 20, 1969, issue of *Computerworld* contained the following story by writer Joseph Hanlon:

> Little Rock, Ark.—A national data bank with records of 300,000 migrant children is being set up here. . . .
>
> The system is designed to aid the rapid placement of children in school. Using a Wats [Wide Area Telephone Service] line, a school official will be able to call the Little Rock center free of charge and get the school and health records of the child. With this system, "the child can be placed immediately," according to Joe Miller [no relation to the author], newly appointed director of the Data Bank for Migrant Children.
>
> When asked who had access to the data, Miller replied: "Well, I suppose anyone." Asked if there were any restrictions on the use of the data, he said: "Well, I wouldn't think so."
>
> None of the information in the data bank could be used in a derogatory way, Miller said. Personal information, such as questions about the family and their moral habits, has been excluded, he explained.
>
> But he said that the file contained an "extensive record of tests and health information, including the child's "strong and weak points" in school.
>
> The data bank is being set up by the federal programs division of the Arkansas Department of Education under a $426,150 grant from the U.S. Office of Education. School and health records of 300,000 children of migrant farm workers will be stored . . . at the University of Arkansas Medical Center. . . .
>
> Data will come from files of "record-transfer forms" maintained by the 47 state directors of migrant education. Beginning this fall, copies of these files will be mailed to Little Rock for keypunching and insertion into the data bank. . . .
>
> According to Miller, the data bank can be updated each time the child moves.

Apparently concerned by the lack of attention being paid to the privacy of the migrant children, reporter Hanlon followed up the story and in the October 1 issue of *Computerworld* he wrote:

> ...At a Sept. 5 meeting, the Committee on student record transfer of the National Conference of Directors of Migrant Education issued a policy statement that said: "The information disseminated . . . will be available to the U.S. Office of Education and state educational agencies. State educational agencies . . . will be responsible for safeguarding the information received to protect personal privacy. State educational agencies are encouraged to use the same regulations and procedures followed in disseminating other academic and school health records information in their respective states."

> Joe Miller, director of the data bank, said that he interpreted the statement to mean that state educational agencies could release information only to schools, and not to private parties. But Lee Lopez, California director of migrant education and chairman of the committee on student record transfers, said that California would release information from the files to anyone who had access to individual school records.

> In particular, Lopez said that he would release information to persons identifying themselves as prospective employers, and that he would include derogatory information such as negative character traits. "I'm sure this information would be given out to prospective employers," he emphasized.

> . . . .

> Information will be entered into the data bank through a standardized "uniform migrant student transfer form." The form includes normal questions such as academic achievement on standardized tests, physical health, vaccinations, etc. It also includes results of IQ tests and psychological tests and may include comments such as "short attention span." But the form does not have provision for general personal remarks or deprecatory comments such as "lazy."

No doubt an efficient computerized information system of this type will enable school and health officials throughout the country to integrate the children of migrant workers into their educational programs effectively and perhaps upgrade the schooling and health treatment generally accorded these children. However, the United States Office of Education and the University of Arkansas apparently do not appreciate that they are presiding over a data bank containing quantities of highly personal and potentially damaging information that is likely to be preserved until long after the purposes for its collection have ceased to exist. If Joe Hanlon's stories accurately reflect the level of sensitivity and thoughtfulness of those who will control and have access to this data bank, what we are witnessing is the construction of an information time-bomb that may have a disastrous impact on children who already are among society's most disadvantaged. These well-meaning do-gooders are unaware of the destructive capability of recorded remarks such as "short attention span" when read ten years later or the possible injury that might be caused by giving the results of an untrustworthy psychological test to a corporate employer or a government official.

Other concerns become apparent on reflection. How reliable is some of the information that will be preserved? After all, we do not have anything that approaches uniform evaluation standards in the nation's primary and secondary schools. Thus, it is unreasonable to assume that everyone who might see a pupil's record can accurately interpret the significance of a remark by a teacher in Modesto, California, that the child "does not play well with others," or "fails to work to his capacity," or is "inattentive." Nor can we be certain of the legitimacy of the reactions of all teachers, especially those who are not trained to handle and have had no experience with the special problems of migrant children.

In the past there was a limited risk that subjective appraisals by individual teachers would be widely circulated. Now, with missionary zeal our well-intentioned information handlers are ready to offer their files "to anyone who had access to individual school records" as well as to "prospective employers." Unless someone begins to give extensive and careful attention to the nature of the data to be recorded, the procedures for insuring their accuracy, the length of time they should be preserved, and the rules regarding those who may have access to the data or the right to augment or change them, there is every possibility that the system ultimately will do more harm than good.

Avowedly, this volume has been written with a bias. I am one who believes that although the new information technology has enormous long-range beneficial consequences for society, we must be concerned about the axiom—so frequently verified since the industrial revolution—that man must shape his tools lest they shape him. The computer is not simply a sophisticated indexing machine, a miniaturized library, or an electronic abacus with a gland condition; rather, it is the keystone of a new communications medium that eventually will have global dimensions and enormous impact on our lives and those of generations yet to come. Thus, it would be highly simplistic to examine the computer-privacy issue from the perspective of a particular machine operating in a federal office building, in the headquarters of one of the nation's major industrial complexes, or in the recesses of a great university. On the contrary, there is a strong similarity between the difficulties that gave rise to the complex and multi-faceted regulation of the airlines, railroads, radio, and television and the problems that already are generating pressure for the regulation of computer transmissions and facilities in both the public and private sectors. It is against the template provided by past experiences in the communications field that the question of protecting individual privacy in the computer age will be examined.

At points my tone may sound antagonistic and some of my judgments may appear harsh. To avoid any confusion on the point, it should be made clear that I do not oppose the development and utilization of the information technologies and I do recognize that to gain the advantages offered by the computer we will have to strike new balances that may affect individual privacy. Moreover, lest some think that I have cast my net too wide, I am aware that the vast majority of information systems, data banks, and computer applications pose no threat to privacy whatsoever for the simple reason that they do not involve information about individuals. But that proposition is not inconsistent with another—those information systems, data banks, and computer applications that do relate to people bear close watching.[3] The lesson to be learned from the current ecological crisis, which dawns on us only after years of indifference to the wanton soiling of our natural habitat, is that we cannot continue to spawn new generations of computers or to stockpile huge stores of personal data without anticipating and guarding against deleterious side effects on our way of life.

I
The Cybernetic Revolution

In each insurance company, in every bank and store,
Are filing clerks and billing clerks and typists by the score;
The work that all these people do will one day disappear
In ERMA[1] systems tended by a lonely engineer.
                    (But they'll never mechanize me—not me!
                    Said Charlotte, the Louisville harlot.)
While former auto workers try to fill their empty days,
The automated auto plant will turn out Chevrolets;
With automatic pilots landing jet planes on the strip,
The present men who guide them will not need to take the trip.
                    (But how can they automate me? Goodness me!
                    Asked Millie, the call girl from Philly.)
Who'll keep the inventory up, who'll order the supplies
Of paper towels, linens, iron pipe, or railroad ties?
Executives now do this with a steno and a phone,
But big computers soon will make decisions all alone.
                    (They cannot cybernate me, tee hee!
                    Laughed Alice, the hooker from Dallas.)
Machines will teach our children how to read and add and spell;
Because they've lots of patience, they will do it very well.
If business men and managers are not on the alert,
Their functions will be taken on by CPM[2] and PERT.[3]
                    (I'll never be coded in FORTRAN[4]—wheee!
                    Cried Susie, the Hackensack floozie.)
CHORUS OF CHARLOTTE, MILLIE, ALICE, AND SUSIE
The future will be like the past despite all dire foreseeings;
We stoutly shall defend the human use of human beings.

[1] Electronic Recording and Machine Accounting.
[2] Critical Path Method.
[3] Program Evaluation and Review Technique.
[4] Formula Translation.

—S. I. Hayakawa, "Solemn Thoughts on the
Second Industrial Revolution," 23
ETC: A Review of General Semantics 7–8
(1966) (footnotes in original)

1. The New Technology

[I]t should be realized that as soon as the borders of electronic intelligence are passed, there will be a kind of chain reaction, because the machines will rapidly improve themselves. In a very few generations—*computer* generations, which by this time may last only a few months—there will be a mental explosion; the merely intelligent machine will swiftly give way to the ultra-intelligent machine.

—Arthur Clarke, "The Mind of the
Machine," *Playboy*, Dec. 1968,
at 116, 118

In the quarter century since the first commercial digital computers were introduced,[1] there has been a rapid and constant proliferation of data-processing devices. Today, the world's computer population probably exceeds the hundred-thousand mark, with approximately sixty percent of these machines being located in the United States. Computers already have outgrown their original role as electronic calculators performing arcane tasks for scientists, and in numerous ways have become the cerebrum of expansive multipurpose and multimedia business, governmental, and educational information systems. Small wonder that with few exceptions those fledgling "business machine" companies that turned toward computers in the late forties and early fifties became the darlings of Wall Street in the sixties.

Although this book is not the place for a detailed or technical dissertation on how these machines function, the following simplified description by Dr. Emanuel R. Piore of IBM may be helpful in appreciating some of the developments of the past three decades.

> The memory device, the storage device of the computer, contains a large number of cells. Each of these can hold a single piece of information, such as a number or a name in code. Each cell . . . has a numerical address.
>
> . . . .
>
> To process data, the computer can perform very rapidly such functions as these: It can move a piece of information from an input device to a memory cell; add the number in one memory cell to a number in another cell; send a copy of information in a memory cell to an output device.
>
> But before a computer can do anything whatsoever, some-

one must give it an organized sequence of instructions called a program.

Each instruction specifies one of the basic functions which the computer can perform. And each instruction, like each piece of data, can be stored . . . in a memory cell of the machine.[2]

The information handled by a computer (both the data to be processed and the instructions) typically is translated into a "binary" code based on a system of two-valued algebra developed by George Boole in the middle of the nineteenth century. The binary code contains only the symbols "1" and "0" and information is represented as strings of these two digits. Each unit of information is represented by a binary digit, which in computerese is called a "bit." The computer deals with the data a "bit" at a time.

Perhaps the most dramatic aspect of the electronic age has been the rate at which the technology has evolved. Computer "hardware"—loosely speaking, the physical elements of the machine—already has completed three generations of development and a fourth is virtually upon us.[3] As a result of this explosive evolution, the present-day computer user is able to draw on a variety of memory devices, including relatively slow storage media such as punch cards or magnetic tape, faster devices such as discs, and, more recently, magnetic cores or data cells that enable a computer to retrieve data at the rate of a few nanoseconds (billionths of a second) per bit of information. Some conception of how fast these machines operate is conveyed by the fact that a nanosecond has the same relation to one second as one second has to thirty years.[4] People are even beginning to talk of measuring computer speed in picoseconds (trillionths of a second).

Information-handling capacity is another characteristic of computer hardware that has changed dramatically over the years. As the requirements of science, industry, and government provide the incentive for hardware manufacturers to produce memory banks that can accommodate a billion bits of information in a single system, researchers are turning to exotic storage media using devices such as lasers,[5] photographic materials, and complex chemical solutions. Univac has advertised a "nonfatiguing photochromic material . . . that can be used as a reservoir for computer information." Exposure of this product to ultraviolet light records the information, which can then be read with a low-intensity light beam. The potential reductions in storage space made possible by this process have led the company to speculate: "Someday it may be possible to store the medical records of every American in the space of a cold capsule. Or the tax records of the nation may fit in one file cabinet."[6] This is not idle puffing. To-day's laser technology already makes it feasible to store a twenty-page dossier on every American on a piece of tape that is less than five thousand feet long.

The choice of a particular storage medium and a given machine speed depends largely upon the nature of the tasks that a system is expected to perform.

> The central distinction between different kinds of black boxes [computers] is whether they are primarily memory ("storage and retrieval") systems, which is what business needs, or primarily computational systems for research use. The computer which prepares the payroll simply churns forward through lists of names, slotting in as needed appropriate changes in salary data, hours worked, percentages for deductions, etc. Though the memory function is vital, the memory device can conveniently be a simple reel of magnetic tape, which gives a predetermined sequential access rather than random access. . . .
>
> Other activities need the computer as a kind of super filing system. . . . For this purpose, a memory on reels of magnetic tape is inadequate because the machine must do considerable checking back on already processed data. But the electronic speeds of . . . magnetic cores are not required; a mechanical whirling drum or disc with magnetic coatings will be sufficiently random and sufficiently fast. . . .
>
> Finally, a very different black box is required if the machine is to be used for immensely rapid computation of . . . numbers of variables—to control a rocket, or to guide an airplane into a socked-in airport. . . . This system demands an enormous random-access memory delivering its information at maximum speed, because so many possible different programs must be available for processing depending on the results of prior computation.[7]

The importance of the availability of machines with different characteristics has not been lost on the manufacturers. IBM's third-generation computer, the 360 series, is marketed in approximately twenty models having different speed and memory capacities. Sensibly, other companies have arrayed their product lines to meet a variety of special needs of the user community.

The "software" of the electronic age—the programs or sets of instructions that control the storage, retrieval, and manipulation of information placed within the computer's memory—has undergone a transformation comparable to that in the hardware field. Programs no longer are laboriously derived from highly detailed computer languages that are useful and intelligible only to their writers and a few friends. Today's popular programming languages such as FORTRAN (Formula Translation) and COBOL (Common Business Oriented Language) are becoming the lingua franca of the new technocracy, enabling extraordinarily complex information-handling tasks to be performed in response to relatively simple instructions that can be understood by a wide range of machines. In addition, sophisticated programs have been designed to edit raw data, to perform different operations in sequence (with the contours of each succeeding step being dictated by the results of the preceding process), and to permit virtually instantaneous random access to a given item of information stored anywhere in the system's memory. Modestly priced general-purpose software packages that perform a wide range of functions for disparate groups of users are now commercially available.

It is not difficult to understand why practically every sector of society has embraced the new technology so eagerly. The computer is able to store vast quantities of data and to retrieve or perform operations upon them in accordance with a programmed set of instructions that occasionally reaches extraordinary complexity. This enables the technology to be employed fruitfully in virtually any activity that requires the systematic manipulation of large or minutely detailed bodies of information.

In addition, the development of transistors, miniaturization, and printed circuitry has enabled each rapidly succeeding stage of hardware-software evolution to be accompanied by substantial reductions in the cost of information-processing, as well as the physical space that must be devoted to the equipment,[8] and has opened new vistas for the application of computer techniques. One of the pioneers in the field of programming predicts that it soon will be cheaper to store a page of English text in a computer than to preserve it on paper,[9] a possibility that has startling implications for the publishing and printing industries.[10]

It may not be long before computers are communicating with each other and with their operators in much the same manner as humans communicate among themselves. Indeed, there already are some sophisticated programs that enable machines to generate "conversations" and to "learn," in the sense of cumulating data and experience; the process is very similar to the Socratic method of teaching. The following man-machine dialogue is illustrative. The computer's responses are given in upper-case letters, while those of the human operator are in lower-case.[11]

PLEASE BEGIN
The area of a sphere is pi times the diameter of the sphere squared.
The area of a circle is pi times the radius of the circle squared.
The diameter of an object is twice the radius of the object.
The radius of a ball is 10.
What is the area of the ball
THE ASSUMPTION THAT BALL IS SPHERE AND OBJECT IS CONSISTENT—SHALL I GO ON? yes
IT'S 1256.6359
What is the diameter of the ball
IT'S 20.
The radius of a dish is 10.
A dish is an object.
What is the area of the dish
THE ASSUMPTION THAT DISH IS SPHERE IS CONSISTENT—SHALL I GO ON? no
THE ASSUMPTION THAT DISH IS CIRCLE IS CONSISTENT—SHALL I GO ON? yes
IT'S 314.15899
The radius of a globe is 10.
A globe is a sphere.
What is the area of the globe
THE ASSUMPTION THAT GLOBE IS OBJECT IS CONSISTENT—SHALL I GO ON? yes

IT'S 1256.6359
The radius of a thing is 10.
A sphere is an object.
A thing is a sphere
What is the area of the thing
IT'S 1256.6359
Thank you
YOU'RE QUITE WELCOME, COME AGAIN[12]

But the reader should not be misled into believing that computers actually "think" the way humans do. Although the possibility of developing artificial intelligence in the future should not be ruled out, today's machines operate primarily on the basis of the data stored in them and the commands that control their electronic gyrations—all the work product of mere mortals. As Jeremy Bernstein has pointed out:

> The electronic computer . . . has come to play a role in modern life something like that played in other times by the oracles of Greece and Rome. There is a widespread belief that if one puts a question to, say, the UNIVAC, it will perform a swarm of bizarre manipulations—comparable to the generating of the vapors in the chasm at Delphi—and come up, in oracular fashion, with the answer. It is more realistic, if less awe-inspiring, to look upon the electronic computer as an overgrown arithmetic machine. It can add, subtract, multiply, and divide, and it can perform long sequences of additions, subtractions, multiplications, and divisions, in highly complicated arrangements. . . . Fundamentally, though, all this comes down to arithmetic, and, arithmetically speaking, the distinction between a schoolboy doing a multiplication a minute and a computer doing a hundred thousand multiplications a second is only one of degree.[13]

Thus, when one watches the NBC, CBS, and ABC computers projecting the outcome of an election contest within a fraction of a percent a few minutes after the polls close, he should not be taken in by the illusion that the machine is acting in an omniscient—or even a creative—fashion. It simply is comparing preselected data about past elections with early returns from the current election pursuant to a programmed set of instructions.

Whatever the limits on machine creativity, there seem to be none on the imagination of the entrepreneurs and systems planners. Among the recent commercial applications of the new technology are computerized medical tests,[14] inventory management in retail stores, tax return preparation,[15] traffic flow control on busy highways, and airline, theater, and campsite reservations.[16]

Perhaps less well known is the use of computers to prepare lengthy astrological horoscopes in minutes that would take a "flesh-and-blood astrologer" at least a week to prepare, to appraise real estate for tax assessment purposes, to analyze the structure and syntax of literary works to determine their authorship, to check chromosomes and analyze cells for signs of cancer, to sketch technical drawings, and to help teach basic educational skills in the ghettos.[17]

In the past many data-processing experts grossly underestimated the potential market for information technology and the wide range of its utilization.[18] But this no longer is the case. If anything, the pendulum has swung too far in the other direction. Enthusiasts talk of a completely computerized economy (*sans* money) as if it were just around the corner and sing the praises of cybernetic education, libraries, research, and legal services as though it were only necessary to press some magic button. All of these wonders may come to pass, but they certainly will not be with us tomorrow or for many tomorrows after that. Nor will they appear without an enormous expenditure of resources as well as a fair number of missteps, false starts, and societal grief. In addition, the full benefits of the computer cannot be realized without certain strides being taken in a number of related fields—optical scanning, two and three dimensional graphics, generative programming, and laser technology, to name a few. But even with these reservations, there are exciting advances on the horizon. The possibilities appear limited only by the ingenuity of the designers, the programmers, and the business community.[19]

2. Time Sharing, Information Systems, and Networking

There is a great deal more to information and data processing than the computer; the computer is to the information industry roughly what the central power station is to the electrical industry.

—Peter Drucker, *The Age of Discontinuity* (1968), 24

When computers were first marketed commercially, they were designed to handle data-processing jobs sequentially one at a time—to "batch process" different tasks. But this mode of operation typically leaves the heart of the machine idle during the period when information is being put into the system and again when the computer's work-product is being printed out. In addition, as the machines became faster and larger, few organizations were able to generate enough work to keep them busy. It soon became apparent that customers were using only a fraction of the computer's potential. In turn, the low level of computer efficiency was a primary factor in the high cost of electronic data-processing, a factor that discouraged smaller companies from joining the user population.[20]

The solution was to connect several input-output terminals (consoles) to the same computer, and then design a very complex "executive" program that would control the machine and enable it to switch its attention at very high speed among the commands being received from the various terminals.[21] Thus, while some users are inputing data or asking the computer to perform arithmetic functions, others might be receiving the computer-produced responses to their requests in the form of output, and still others could be having their inquiry processed by the system's central unit. This "time-sharing" procedure enables users to employ the full capacity of the machine continuously and, in theory, gives each the equivalent of his own computer at a greatly reduced cost. However, the simultaneous exposure of several distinct bodies of data in one information system creates the risk that one user might gain access to another's files, either by accident or by design, and thereby compromise the integrity of the data being stored or acted upon in the time-share system.[22]

The next step in the maturation of time-sharing was to move the input-output terminals away from the central processor and to link them with the computer by communications channels. This remote-access technique has enabled computer services to be dispersed to strategic locations, such as the regional offices of a national corporation, an important customer's place of business, or different schools in a multi-campus university. The result in many cases is the formation of a computer equivalent of a communications network. The computerized reservations systems operated by the airlines, hotel chains, and car rental firms are typical illustrations of the commercial application of remote-access time-sharing.

This seemingly obvious procedure has enormous implications for the future development of our information transfer capability. Many observers of recent trends in data-processing believe that remote-access time-sharing is only the first stage in the ultimate amalgamation of computer and communications technologies.[23] One writer has melodramatically suggested: "The history of modern technology records few events of the importance and scope of this process—two giant industries, proceeding in the past on two relatively independent courses, are now on a path of confluence. Each technology is having and will have a great leavening effect on the other." Other commentators have forecast that the result will be an "almost biological" growth of a natural computer-communications monopoly[24] as small data-processing systems become integrated into national and international networks.

The intersection of the computer and communications technologies already has become apparent in the context of the telephone system, which carries the bulk of today's data transmissions over its lines. Telephone officials have recognized the significant parallels between the *modus operandi* of their system and that of the remote-access computer system.

> The telephone system is itself a computer. Its components are dispersed across the continent but they work as one. Equipped with more than 90 million input-output stations, this enormous computer can be commanded to provide any one of the 3 million billion "answers" it takes to connect any one of its stations—telephones—with any other and do it in a matter of seconds. Indeed, [the newest telephone] systems, like computers, are internally programmed and are endowed with the same kind of quasi-human memory ascribed to commercial computers.[25]

To press the analogy between the two technologies further, one of the key aspects of computer time-sharing—the ability to switch messages among different users at high speeds—has long been a mark of the communications common carriers.

The telephone system is in the process of converting its outmoded electromechanical switching devices to electronic equipment to improve its capabilities and speed as a data carrier. Eventually, even normal voice conversations probably will be sent over the telephone lines in coded form.[26] Today's standard telephone line carries only twelve hundred to twenty-four hundred bits of data per second, which is enough to keep a teletypewriter busy but much too slow a pace for computers, facsimile transmission, or electrostatic printers. By comparison, one channel on a digital transmission system carries fifty-six thousand bits per second—about twenty-two times as much data as today's best voice channels. These changes will give the telephone system the basic attributes of a data-processing center.

Sensing the existence of a vast, untapped market, other communications media—microwave relay, telegraph, communications satellites, and even community antenna television[27]—are not far behind the telephone companies in developing the ability to transmit large quantities of digital data. As computer networks multiply, both the data-processing and the communications industries will continue to remodel and tailor their systems to obtain the full benefit of the natural relationship between the two. It already is apparent that governmental regulation will soon be needed to rationalize these new configurations in order to husband the nation's communications resources and avoid any anti-competitive side effects.

In light of the constantly broadening range of computer applications and the development of remote-access time-sharing, it seems reasonable to envision some form of national computer "utility" providing a variety of data-processing services to everyone, perhaps through the medium of inexpensive home terminals such as touch-tone telephones or in conjunction with cable television.[28] Several commercial time-sharing data-processing systems already are being offered to the public in two general configurations: either the customer provides the data to be stored in the service company's computers to be manipulated or "massaged" by the system's software on demand, or the service company provides a body of specialized data that can be tapped at will by time-share customers from remote terminals.[29] In the future, even individuals may benefit from these facilities as merchants begin to offer computerized shopping and ticket reservation services that can be utilized through home touch-tone telephones.

Regardless of the form in which computing capacity becomes

available to the general public, the market for these services provides enough economic incentive to guarantee the continued centralization of large bodies of data—a significant portion of which most certainly will involve personal or confidential information. As the following chapters will illustrate, not enough is being done to insure that computerized data, either in their stored form or while in transit, are any more immune from the intrusive activities of snoopers than private telephone conversations have been protected against the machinations of wiretappers.

3. The Information-Based Society

[T]he creation of techniques for the direct observation of living persons and contemporary institutions, the deepening of intellectual curiosity about the motives and the very tissue of social life, the diminution of inhibitions on intrusiveness into other persons' affairs, and the concomitant formation of techniques for perceiving these deeper and subtler things have precipitated problems of ponderable ethical significance. The ethical values affected by contemporary social research are vague and difficult to formulate precisely. They refer mainly to human dignity, the autonomy of individual judgment and action, and the maintenance of privacy during the past few decades.

—Edward Shils, "Social Inquiry and
the Autonomy of the Individual,"
in *The Human Meaning of the
Social Sciences,* edited by Daniel Lerner
(paper ed., 1959), 114, 117

The dossier society's genesis dates back several decades to the federal government's entry into the taxation and social welfare spheres. Since then, greater and greater quantities of information have been elicited from individual citizens and recorded. Brief reflection about the data gathering associated with federal involvement in social security and medicare, home financing, urban renewal, and public health, as well as the activities of the Census Bureau, Defense Department, Office of Economic Opportunity, the Job and Peace Corps, and the Department of Housing and Urban Development is sufficient to illustrate this basic point. Add to this the enormous quantities of investigatory information generated by the loyalty-security programs that were an inevitable by-product of the nation's emergence as a dominant world power.

As information-recording processes have become cheaper and more efficient, the government's appetite for data has intensified and been accompanied by a predilection toward centralization and collation of file material. As if responding to something akin to Parkinson's Law, technological improvements in information-handling capability have been followed by a tendency to engage in more extensive manipulation and analysis of recorded data. This in turn has motivated the collection of data pertaining to a larger number of variables, which results in more personal information being extracted from individuals. The availability of electronic data storage and retrieval has accelerated this pattern in a number of contexts; witness the expansion in the scope of the decennial census and the ever-increasing number of government questionnaires to which individuals and businesses of all sizes, shapes, and forms are subjected. Moreover, in recent years access to governmental largesse has depended increasingly upon a willingness to divulge private information. Professor Donald N. Michael contends that by dangling the carrot of economic and governmental benefits before the public, "we can expect a great deal of information about the social, personal, and economic characteristics of individuals to be supplied voluntarily—often eagerly . . ."[30]

One consequence of this combination of greater social planning and computer capacity is that many governmental agencies are beginning to ask increasingly complex, probing, and sensitive questions. Recent federal agency interrogations touch upon such subjects as associations with other people, location and activity at different points in time and space, medical history, and individual attitudes toward various institutions and people. In many instances the increased level of data collection results from congressional, rather than agency, action. Thus, the proposed Manpower Training Act[31] calls for establishing a national job bank to match jobs with the unemployed by computer. The inevitable result will be a detailed dossier on each person who registers with the employment service. Similar consequences are likely to flow from the Nixon administration's proposed Family Assistance Act.[32]

Increased information gathering is not a unique activity of the federal government. The widespread availability and greater flexibility of computer technology is causing a profound change in the attitude toward information and the uses to which it can be put within the industrial and academic sectors. In the university community, the trend has manifested itself most clearly in the social sciences. Largely because of the computer, scholars now are increasingly able to process the available data and base their theories and hypotheses on mathematical models rather than on "intuitive feeling and casual empiricism."[33] Today academics construct and manipulate sophisticated models[34] and engage in electronic simulation of various facets of the environment in the hope of better understanding human behavior and various societal phenomena. This necessitates staggering amounts of detailed information—"microdata"—rather than the broad and comparatively superficial summaries that social scientists traditionally have used. Accurate description of a complex system, such as a city, a court system, or an industry, often requires investigation of a large number of potentially significant variables. In addition, there may be unsuspected relationships hidden in the microdata that would be lost if only small quantities of information were available for analysis.[35] Identification of the information relating to individual people also may be necessary if, for example, a researcher wishes to discover how certain characteristics of the members of a particular group change over a period of time.[36] Collecting highly detailed information in the first instance also enables researchers to "use the same basic data again and again for different analytic purposes."[37]

Institutions of almost every description are relying on the computer to increase their data-handling capacity and to improve the efficiency of their operations. The result is an inexorable pattern of establishing new data banks and converting existing information centers into ever larger and more complex computerized systems. As if spread with a magic nutrient, information systems of every size, shape, and form have sprouted and grown like weeds in recent years. As they do, their managers demand greater resources, more data on file subjects, and increased consolidation of separately maintained records.[38]

The new information technologies seem to have given birth to a new social virus—"data-mania." Its symptoms are shortness of breath and heart palpitations when contemplating a new computer application, a feeling of possessiveness about information and a deep resentment toward those who won't yield it, a delusion that all information handlers can walk on water, and a highly advanced case of astigmatism that prevents the affected victim from perceiving anything but the intrinsic value of data. Fortunately, only some members of the information-handling fraternity have been stricken by the disease.

A mild outbreak of data-mania occurred in Florida recently when plans were announced to rate school teachers by studying computerized statistics relating to the academic performance of their students.[39] When the importance of a wide range of subjective factors and the possibility that a good teacher might be "weeded out" were raised, an official of the company developing the system remarked: "Well that's too bad; maybe someone else will employ him." Perhaps it is a well-worn cliché that machines are morally neutral, and it is only the men who use them who therefore bear the responsibility for distinguishing between right and wrong. However, the accuracy and centrality of the point, as illustrated by the insensitivity of the Florida experimenters, justify its repetition over and over again.

We must begin to realize what it means to live in a society that treats information as an economically desirable commodity and a source of power. Although it may be a bit premature to conclude that "information is becoming the basic building block of society"[40] or that "all forms of wealth result from the movement of information,"[41] there does seem to be considerable truth in the assertion that electronic technology is transforming the world into a "global village"[42] in which the domain of strictly private action is steadily being eroded.[43] As a result of the heightened value being placed on information by contemporary society, a substantial portion of information that hitherto has been treated as private is now considered to be appropriate grist for the computer mill and fair game for the data collector. Because there are some intrinsically valuable aspects of individual privacy that should be protected from the excesses of the data-maniacs, it is essential to expose the ways computer technology is magnifying the threat to informational privacy—a threat that we have faced in some form ever since man began to take notes about himself and his neighbors.

II
The New Technology's Threat to Personal Privacy

Privacy is a special kind of independence, which can be understood as an attempt to secure autonomy in at least a few personal and spiritual concerns, if necessary in defiance of all the pressures of modern society. . . . [I]t seeks to erect an unbreachable wall of dignity and reserve against the entire world. The free man is the private man, the man who still keeps some of his thoughts and judgments entirely to himself, who feels no over-riding compulsion to share everything of value with others, not even those he loves and trusts.

—Clinton Rossiter, "The Pattern
of Liberty," in *Aspects of
Liberty,* edited by
Konvitz and Rossiter (1958), 15–17

When one attempts to analyze the proper status to be accorded the right of individual privacy in a democracy such as ours, he is immediately confronted with a mass of contradictions. We claim to be an "open" society with a tradition of free speech and free press that is deeply etched in our political philosophy and expressed in the First Amendment of the Constitution. "The people's right to know" is the rallying cry whenever there is a suggestion of governmental information management. Yet, we also assert that the Constitution guarantees us a right of individuality, autonomy, and freedom from the intrusive activities of government and our fellow man. And in marked conflict with the notion that Americans have the right to be let alone, we have constructed sprawling, burgeoning urban areas that force people to live in small cubicles embedded in ugly vertical structures, travel in congested mass transit systems, and work in buildings designed primarily to produce assembly-line efficiency. Even worse, inner-city ghettos have forced large numbers of people to live in such close proximity that emotional and intellectual

privacy has become an impossibility. The result has been to minimize man's physical privacy and his ability to enjoy any type of
solitude.

Moreover, no people in the world are scrutinized, measured,
counted, and interrogated by as many poll takers, social science
researchers, and governmental officials as are Americans. Despite
our tradition of rugged individualism and our supposed right of
privacy, the vast majority of us passively and voluntarily—often
eagerly—respond fully to these intrusions. No doubt we do so out
of a desire to participate in the decision-making and opinion-
formulating processes, a long-standing faith in the integrity of
those questioning us, and a belief that the information we furnish will be used for limited purposes and will not receive undue
publicity. To what extent do these assumptions remain valid in
light of the cybernetic revolution?]

1. The Individual's Loss of Control over Personal Information

> For Cassius is aweary of the world;
> Hated by one he loves; braved by his brother;
> Check'd like a bondman; all his faults observed,
> Set in a notebook, learn'd, and conn'd by rote,
> To cast into my teeth.
>
> —Shakespeare, *Julius Caesar*,
> Act IV, Scene iii

⌈ The concept of privacy is difficult to define because it is exasper-
atingly vague and evanescent,[1] often meaning strikingly different things to different people. In part this is because privacy is a
notion that is emotional in its appeal and embraces a multitude
of different "rights," some of which are intertwined, others often
seemingly unrelated or inconsistent. Of late, however, lawyers
and social scientists have been reaching the conclusion that the
basic attribute of an effective right of privacy is the individual's
ability to control the circulation of information relating to him—
a power that often is essential to maintaining social relationships
and personal freedom.[2] Correlatively, when an individual is
deprived of control over the spigot that governs the flow of information pertaining to him, in some measure he becomes sub-
servient to those people and institutions that are able to manipulate it.[3]

Until recently, informational privacy has been relatively easy to protect: (1) large quantities of information about individuals traditionally have not been collected and therefore have not been available to others; (2) the available information generally has been maintained on a decentralized basis and typically has been widely scattered; (3) the available information has been relatively superficial in character and often has been allowed to atrophy to the point of uselessness; (4) access to the available information has not been easy to secure; (5) people in a highly mobile society have been difficult to keep track of; and (6) most people have been unable to interpret and infer revealing information from the available data. But even a casual perusal of the testimony elicited by various congressional subcommittees or a few moments' reflection on the intrusive capabilities of wiretapping, spike and parabolic microphones, remote sensing devices, and infrared photography leads to the conclusion that these safeguards on informational privacy are no longer effective in our present technologically based society.[4] Add to this picture the possible maintenance of computerized files on everyone, and it becomes clear that individuals are less able today than ever before to control the quantitative and qualitative flow of data about themselves.

Computer systems that handle personal information may inflict harm on a data subject in two significant ways: (1) by disseminating evidence of present or past actions or associations to a wider audience than the individual consented to or anticipated when he orginally surrendered the information (deprivation of control over access), and (2) by introducing factual or contextual inaccuracies in the data that create an erroneous impression of the subject's actual conduct or achievements in the minds of those to whom the information is exposed (deprivation of control over accuracy).[5] A closer look at these two dangers will make graphic the damage that can be inflicted on individual privacy by various aspects of the new information technologies.

The Individual's Loss of Control Over Who Has
Access to His Informational Profile

The science-fiction mystique surrounding cybernetics has tended to create an illusion of computer impregnability, even among those who are familiar with the technology. For example, one

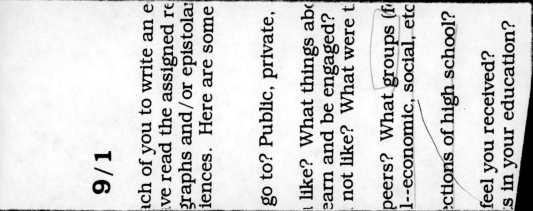

9/1

ach of you to write an e
ve read the assigned re
graphs and/or epistola
iences. Here are some

go to? Public, private,

t like? What things ab
earn and be engaged?
not like? What were t

peers? What groups (f
l--economic, social, etc

ections of high school?

feel you received?
s in your education?

knowledgeable individual has argued that computerizing personal information will result in greater protection for file privacy than yesterday's manila folder because the putative snooper will need "a machine, a codebook, a set of instructions, and a technician" to gain access to the data and translate it into a comprehensible form.[6] Several generations ago a similar shortsightedness led many to believe that telegraph and wireless transmission would be the ultimate in private communication. This enthusiast's appraisal simply fails to take into account the relatively advanced state of the eavesdropper's art, let alone the techniques of the computer snooper. In contrast, other experts have flatly asserted that most program languages are easy to decipher,[7] that digital transmission of data "does not provide any more privacy than . . . Morse Code,"[8] and that "modest resources suffice to launch a low-level infiltration effort."[9]

The reality of the situation seems to be that once personal information has been entered into a computerized file, the data subject and, to a lesser degree, the system's operators have little capacity to control who will be able to peruse it. Perhaps the most significant reason why the individual is so impotent is the vulnerability of machine components and software to accident, malfunctioning, or intrusion.

In a typical remote-access time-sharing system, there are at least six points through which improper access to the data may be gained or at which distortion of the information may occur.[10] The first, and perhaps most obvious of these, is the information itself. The mechanical process of transcribing the information from traditional alpha-numeric notation to machine-readable form subjects the data to an additional handling stage during which there is a risk of intrusion. In addition, because of their compactness, the tangible objects in which machine-readable data are stored—punch cards, magnetic tapes, discs, data cells—are more susceptible to the dangers of theft and duplication than their paper counterparts. A single magnetic tape containing fifty million bits of data can be reproduced in minutes without leaving any tell-tale signs of copying or tampering. As a result, the potential for industrial espionage is enormous; access to a single critical tape might reveal a business enterprise's most valuable marketing or personnel secrets to a competitor. Or the tape might contain the control program for a large time-share system, which could cause serious security consequences for every user of the system or enable its operations to be sabotaged.

Another aspect of the vulnerability of computerized data is that it is easier to destroy than paper files or record books. A simple magnet can be used to erase the information stored on a reel of magnetic tape. In one incident, a disgruntled employee virtually wiped out the records of a business enterprise "in no time at all." In another, a small band of anti-war protesters erased over a thousand Dow Chemical Company computer tapes that apparently contained data on napalm, poison gases, and chemical weaponry. If technical expertise is lacking, a match, or a hammer in the case of a disc or a data cell, will do the same job more crudely in a minute or two. In contrast, the logistical difficulties of destroying large quantities of information maintained in a traditional format are well illustrated by the abortive attempt of the crew members of the American intelligence ship *Pueblo*—admittedly under intense stress—to destroy classified documents during its seizure by the North Korean navy.

When information is moved from the files into the central processor of a time-sharing computer system, a number of additional dangers arise. Despite their image of infallibility, computers are so intricate and delicate that a speck of dust occasionally can render them inoperative or cause them to function erratically.[11] Thus, a minor mechanical failure or variations in electric current—let alone a power failure—can result in data being lost, distorted, or misdirected to an unauthorized recipient in a remote-access system. One major equipment company discovered a defective magnetic tape drive in its computer only after it had incorrectly processed several hundred reels of tape. The faulty hardware was not identified immediately because even though the computer had been programmed to check its own operation continuously, the machine was confidently reporting that it was functioning properly.

Given the present state of the art, any data communication process involves the risk of an irreducible number of errors. According to Sperry-Rand:

> Studies published by the Bell System concerning error rates in data transmitted over voice channels at 600 bits per second and at 1,200 bits per second indicate that the fre-

quency of the occurrence of incorrectly received data doubles when the speed of transmission doubles and increases in general with the increases in distance. . . .[12]

Correcting errors is an expensive process, typically involving retransmission of the data.

Furthermore, in a time-share system the rapid switching of the computer's attention among a number of users may leave a residuum of one customer's information accessible to the next user who is placed in control of the machine's central processor.[13] Finally, even if the system is functioning perfectly, there remains a possibility that a snooper could "eavesdrop" on electromagnetic signals radiating from the computer, which could be captured and reconstructed elsewhere.

The key software item of a time-share system—the monitor or control program—seems to be particularly vulnerable to intrusion. It can be duplicated so that false signals are generated, altered to permit unauthorized people to enter the system, or destroyed. Once access to the control program is gained, the intruder has the ability to display and manipulate any part of the data stored within the system.

Many of the codes that have been developed to protect these programs have not been particularly effective. For example, there have been reports from several campuses that students often are successful in penetrating the protective features of university computers. At Massachusetts Institute of Technology's Project MAC (Machine Aided Cognition), students, who seem to treat computer terminals as if they were Tinker Toys, tapped (perhaps inadvertently) into computers that were handling classified defense data—some of which involved the Strategic Air Command in Omaha. At the University of Michigan, students with a less playful intent have managed to destroy a number of computer files by deciphering the access codes to the campus-wide remote-access terminal system.

None of these activities requires the talent of an Einstein. Several people have told me that a moderately intelligent computer-science student, or even a programmer with a high school diploma, can break fairly elaborate codes in less than five hours; simianlike trial and error takes a bit longer. The professional snooper can combine a minicomputer with ten data-sets and have a code-cracking system for substantially less than $10,000. Or he can rent the equipment for such a nominal sum that one estimate places the average cost of cracking a password system at $25. Thus, it is rather distressing that many academic, commercial, and industrial time-share data systems containing personal information have little or nothing in the way of access controls protecting their files.

The personnel servicing the central processor are another potential soft spot in the security picture. A malevolent or bribed programmer, for instance, could insert a secret "door" in the monitor program, thus enabling unauthorized people to bypass protective devices, or he "could 'bug' a machine in such a sophisticated manner that it might remain unnoticed for an extensive period."[14] It also has been suggested that a repairman might "re-wire the machine so that certain instructions appeared to behave normally, whereas in fact, the protective mechanisms could be bypassed."[15] An easier approach would be to "convince" the computer's operator, or even a maintenance man, to reveal the nature of protective devices or to provide the system's keys to any access codes that are being used.

Extracurricular activities along these lines are not unknown. According to one tale, perhaps apocryphal, a supervisory employee altered the program that controlled a large retail merchandiser's payroll by inserting a set of instructions that directed the machine to prepare a payroll check in her name every few minutes. Unfortunately, by behaving too much like a pig at the trough, she was discovered before amassing enough money to disappear quietly.

The fourth soft point in computer security occurs when computerized information moves from the central processor through the communications links. In addition to the relatively unsophisticated process of bugging the transmission line and recording or perhaps even siphoning off the electronic communications passing over it, an ingenious wiretapper with the necessary equipment might attach his own computer terminal to the line and join the group sharing the system's services. This could be done in several ways: by using a previously planted "door" in the control program; by intercepting a user's communication and substituting his own; by invading the system while a remote-access user has his channel open but is not transmitting; or by intercepting and canceling a user's sign-off signal in order to continue operating the system under that user's name. Depending upon the sophistication level of the system's internal security procedures, the piggybacking tapper might be able to gain entry to all of the time-share customers' files.

The last two stages of the data-processing cycle—the switching center and the remote-access consoles—may be as vulnerable to attempts to eavesdrop on electromagnetic radiations as is the central processor. In addition, the switching center, either by mistake or as a result of tampering, may make an improper connection and direct data to the wrong terminal or to an unauthorized recipient. As to the remote-access terminals, their ability to be located anywhere in the world makes it virtually impossible for any individual to police the flow of information about him. Even when codes are used to protect the security of the remote-access terminals, an unauthorized user might break the code or forge the required identification, or a malevolent authorized user might employ his console to alter the protective programs, "revise" the stored data, or misuse a printout of stored information that he obtained by a legitimate exercise of his right to gain access to the system's data store.

I now return to the contentions of some enthusiasts noted earlier that even though many computerized information systems are porous or vulnerable to intrusion, the expense of taking advantage of the weaknesses outlined above and the expertise that must be acquired to do so provide sufficient built-in privacy safeguards. But cost is not always a deterrent. For one thing, the quality of the snooper's payoff may be higher in the computer context than if the records were kept in the more mundane alphanumeric style. The computer-based record system of the future is likely to contain more extensive and detailed information on individuals than do today's files of manila folders. This factor, coupled with the centralization of formerly diffused stores of information, often will mean that a single invasion will give the intruder quantities of data formerly obtainable only by penetrating several widely scattered files. In addition, anyone who can gain access to a remote-access terminal may be able to reach all of the relevant data in a computer network that embraces numerous information nodes geographically distributed across the continent or around the world. Putting all these possibilities together, the computer-age snooper's cost per unit of dirt actually may be lower for poaching electronically stored records than it is for pilfering paper files. Thus in the case of the professional intruder or any law enforcement agency, the investment in equipment and mastering the "art" of cracking computer systems probably can be recouped in the course of a handful of capers.

Given the incentive of a potentially high payoff for invading computerized files or intercepting data transmissions, there is no doubt that elements of organized crime, a variety of governmental agencies (especially the law enforcement establishment), and segments of private industry will shortly develop their ability to launch sophisticated snooping programs. Even clandestine firms offering a "file for a fee" are not beyond the realm of possibility. Instances already have been discovered of unauthorized users "borrowing" time-share system account numbers and passwords and using their own remote-access input devices to extract computerized information or to steal programs, often to improve their own network's operations.[16] Since this typically will involve the use of an interstate commerce communications medium, federal law is violated and the FBI will be called in to investigate, once the system operators become aware of the illicit use.

*The Individual's Loss of Control Over the
Accuracy of His Informational Profile*

In assessing the threat to privacy posed by computer technology, the possibility of human error must be added to the vulnerability of the system's components. The risk that careless or malicious administrators or information handlers will introduce errors into records containing personal data is a familiar one, and I am not attributing its origin to the advent of data-processing devices. However, the additional handling required to translate data from alphabetic notation into a machine-readable computer input format magnifies the risks of errors in reporting, recordation, and indexing. To complicate matters, there is an increased likelihood of information distortion caused by human and machine malfunctioning, especially in remote-access time-share systems.

Thus, there is a growing and in some ways legitimate fear of centralizing individualized information and then increasing the number of people who, by having access to it, are capable of inflicting damage through negligence, sheer stupidity, or a lack of sensitivity to the personal privacy of others. This concern goes beyond the self-evident proposition that there are some "bad actors" in the information handling field, as there are in every walk of life. Unthinking people are as capable of injuring others by unintentionally rendering a record inaccurate, losing it, or disseminating its contents to unauthorized users as are people acting out of malice or for personal aggrandizement. It simply is unrealistic to expect subtle standards of care and fundamental principles of individual privacy to be fully understood or effectively implemented by large numbers of people, many of whom have been trained for and are serving in clerical positions.

In addition, the centralization of information from widely divergent sources and on markedly different subjects, as often results from establishing large data banks, creates serious problems of contextual accuracy. A large corporate or welfare data bank may contain information on a person's education, military record, medical history, employment background, aptitude and psychological testing performance, as well as a number of subjective appraisals of his character and skills. Any of this information might be entirely accurate and sufficient when viewed from one perspective but be wholly incomplete and misleading when read in another.

Contextual errors can occur in a number of ways. Raw, unevaluated data about an individual, especially when recorded in a cryptic fashion, might give rise to damaging inferences that a fuller explication of the underlying events, direct knowledge of the information's source, or professional analysis of the facts would show to be false. Illustrative of this type of distortion is a terse entry stating that an individual was arrested, convicted of a felony, and sentenced to a federal penitentiary for a certain number of years. Undoubtedly data of this description would detrimentally affect the subject's ability to obtain employment or credit. Yet our "felon" may simply have been a conscientious objector who could not meet the requirements for exemption from military service on the grounds of religious belief that existed at the time he refused to be inducted.[17]

Taken at face value, this kind of entry is doubly dangerous if the events occurred in the distant past and the legal or social attitude toward the particular "offense" has changed with the passage of time. Consider the potential effect of the following computer profile: "Arrested, June 1, 1962; disorderly conduct and criminal conspiracy; convicted, April 12, 1963; sentenced, May 21, 1963, six months." Without more, how would a person viewing the entry know that what appears to be an anti-social type is merely a civil rights activist who spent some of his time during the early sixties working for the desegregation of educational facilities in the South or for equal employment opportunities for ghetto blacks in the North? And what about the conviction? Perhaps it merely reflects the now-discredited judicial and law enforcement practices of a decade ago of inhibiting the exercise of constitutionally protected rights of free speech and public assembly by invoking disorderly conduct, trespass, and conspiracy ordinances against what often were peaceful protests seeking racial and social justice. Indeed, the "conviction" may even have been reversed on appeal and our "offender" exonerated.

Other subtle difficulties in handling information are likely to increase the likelihood of inaccurate interpretation. Even data that are characterized as "hard" or "factual" often take on different shades of meaning in different contexts. Thus, an individual who is asked to provide a simple item of information for what he believes to be a single purpose may omit explanatory details that become crucial when his file is surveyed for unrelated purposes. For example, a notation of an individual's marital status evokes a different image of the person in the mind of someone at the Selective Service System, a credit bureau, the Internal Revenue Service, a security or law enforcement agency, the Social Security Administration, and a corporate personnel office. The same is true of entries such as "unemployed," "home owner," "partially disabled," "veteran," and "high school graduate."

What is potentially far more dangerous is that many information gatherers fail to recognize the necessity of entering supplemental data to reduce the damaging effect of an earlier entry that has derogatory overtones. To return to the subject of arrest records, police departments throughout the nation can obtain an FBI "rap sheet" containing a suspect's criminal record by sending his fingerprints to Washington. These sheets are supposed to include information on any court proceeding that might follow each arrest, but these data apparently are not furnished in approximately thirty-five percent of the cases[18] Often, failures to prosecute and acquittals are not indicated. Despite an even more distressing situation on the state and local level, many of the emerging computerized law enforcement information systems are making their files more widely available without undertaking any substantial effort to make them more accurate.

The significance of arrest records is brought home by the application of a recently enacted New York statute that requires the fingerprinting of brokerage house employees.[19] Early in 1970, a number of workers were discharged by brokerage firms on the basis of their past "records," which in some cases merely indicated that the employee had been arrested. One can only hope that the discharges were based on something more than an unexplicated entry on file with New York's Identification and Intelligence System. But since the employee is not permitted to see the "rap sheet" on him and has either no right of appeal or an extremely limited one, we probably will never know what actually happened.

In an era of great social activism on the part of the young with counterpoint demands from others for "Law and Order," arrests are bound to increase. But many of them will be of a strikingly different character than what has been typical in the past. It is now common for hundreds of college demonstrators or black militants to be arrested in connection with one incident. Using recent experience as a guide, only a small fraction of the group will be prosecuted, and an even smaller number convicted. All of them, however, will have arrest records. The problem is particularly grave for our black citizens. In the past, many police forces, North and South, have been quite cavalier about taking blacks into custody, which means that a disproportionately high percentage have "arrest" (but not necessarily conviction) records.

Even if information managers recognize the need to include ameliorating or supplementing information, there are a number of reasons why they might be unable or unwilling to do so. First, many systems are not designed to accommodate such data. Second, since many large data banks are used for varied purposes, the managers may have no idea at the time information enters the system whether or not it will be desirable or feasible to record subsequent events. Furthermore, they may not be able to determine what type of data will clarify the original entry, especially if it is uncertain precisely how the information will be used in the future. Third, there actually may be no readily ascertainable or accessible source from which to obtain relevant updating material. Finally, the cost of gathering, inputting, and storing the neutralizing data may be considerable. Consequently, some systems operators will claim that the costs of doing so cannot be passed on to the customer or, in the case of public systems, do not justify being imposed on the taxpayer. When the chips are down, machine managers simply may be afraid that higher-ups in the institutional hierarchy might react negatively to increasing expenditures for this purpose.

Other dangers to personal privacy exist that are even more frightening in their potential ramifications. Consider the fact that computerization has made it convenient to rate an employee's efficiency and personal habits according to concise, conclusory categories such as "excellent," "fair," or "good," which might become convenient crutches for bureaucratic decision makers. If personal ratings of former employees are made available to new prospective employers, the computerized evaluations might do considerable harm because different organizations often lack common traditions of appraising or interpreting performance. A "fair" rating may denote average performance in one setting and very poor work in another, just as "good" in one institutional context can be translated as "excellent" elsewhere.[20] For example, anyone not conversant with military minds and mores might be misled by a highly favorable army evaluation report. In addition, increased quantities of "soft" or subjective data are bound to be computerized. Various aptitude, intelligence, and psychological tests can be designed for machine scoring—or can even be administered by machine—and the results, either in raw form or after evaluation, can become a part of an individual's dossier.[21]

The problem of contextual accuracy is certain to become more severe in the future as increasing numbers of remote terminals are linked to computer systems and local and regional data centers are amalgamated into national or international networks. Under these conditions, it will become common for information to be moved and stored far from its point of original recordation, increasing the likelihood that it will be employed by people unassociated with and perhaps ignorant of the circumstances of its collection. The ease with which large quantities of information can be transferred, coupled with the technology's aura of omniscience, may result in some administrators in all quadrants of our society unduly relying on computerized data without investigating their source, the purpose for which they were originally collected, or the evaluation standards used by the data originator.[22]

The convenience of referring to computer-stored evaluations and increased time pressures may lead decision-makers to abdicate their responsibility for making important judgments in a rational, thoughtful manner or to return to original sources to verify, up-date, and seek out more or better data. True, most information users insist that they understand that the computer's utility and a data base's reliability necessarily are limited by the quality of the input, typically emphasizing their alleged awareness by re-citing the maxim "garbage in, garbage out" (GIGO). Nonetheless, the hypnotic effect of being able to manipulate enormous data bases is likely to encourage people to use the computer as an electronic security blanket and to view it as a device for quantify-ing the unquantifiable.

Some notion of the implications of using computerized per-sonal data as an assist in policy-making can be divined from the following:

> [In New York a] . . . computer, that had been fed accumu-lated information from bettors, police and other sources spewed out the names of eighty-six alleged bookmakers. In-dictments followed. The machine had not only stored the information but had evaluated it. The government claimed that the three-year statute of limitations on the charges might have expired before human investigators could have evaluated the data.[23]

A number of disturbing questions are raised by this application of cybernetics. If programming a computer to select names of people for criminal prosecution falls within the district attor-ney's well recognized (and virtually unfettered) discretion, is it time to impose some constraints on how that discretion is em-ployed? In order to prevent the administration of justice from depending on the spin of a computerized roulette wheel, shouldn't we ensure that the use of the technology satisfies some minimal standard of computer science? By what process does the system manager determine that particular data have sufficient probative value to warrant being fed into the computer and what weight should be assigned to individual items of information? How can we be certain that the official who has the authority to decide whether an indictment should be sought has enough understanding of the computer system to make a rational assessment of its output?

Nor should we ignore the real possibility that prejudice to the individual will not end with the decision to seek an indictment. Commenting on this particular computer application, a lawyer observed: "[T]he . . . computer can tell you where the stars are going to be a million years from now. Do you think a jury is not going to believe that it can tell you where a bookie is in the Bronx?"[24]

The seductive character of computerized information probably means that for some, success or failure in life may turn on what other people decide to put into their file and a programmer's ability—or inability—to evaluate, process, and interrelate that information. The electronic record of a man's endeavors may become a hearsay narrative prepared by a computernik, much the way our knowledge of the Trojan War and the travails of Ulysses has depended on Homer's filtration of earlier chronicles. These prospects are made even more depressing by the realization that much of the increased bulk of the data likely to find their way into the files will be gathered and processed by relatively unskilled and unimaginative people who will lack the discrimination and sensitivity necessary to justify reliance on their judgment. What is more, a computerized file has a certain indelible quality—adversities cannot be overcome by the passage of time in the absence of an electronic eraser and a compassionate soul willing to use it.

2. Cybernetics as an Instrument of Surveillance

"I want to see you not through the machine," said Kuno. "I want to speak to you not through the wearisome machine."
"Oh, hush!" said his mother, vaguely shocked.
"You mustn't say anything against the machine."
"Why not?"
"One mustn't."
"You talk as if a god had made the machine," cried the other. "I believe that you pray to it when you are unhappy. Men made it, do not forget

that. Great men, but men. The machine is much, but it is not everything.

—E. M. Forster, "The Machine
Stops," in *Collected Short
Stories* (paper ed., 1963), 109–10

As recently as a decade ago we could smugly treat Huxley's *Brave
New World* and Orwell's *1984* as exaggerated science fiction having no relevance to us or to life in this country. But widespread
public disclosures during the past few years about the new breed
of information practices have stripped away this comforting but
self-delusive mantle. It is now common knowledge that whenever
a citizen files a tax return, applies for life insurance or a credit
card, seeks government benefits, or interviews for a job, a new
dossier is opened on him and his informational profile is sketched.
Indeed, there are precious few things left in life that will not
leave distinctive electronic tracks in the memory of a computer—
tracks that can tell a great deal about our activities, habits, and
associations.

Thus, apprehension over the computer's threat to personal
privacy seems particularly warranted when one begins to consider
the possibility of using the new technology to further various private and governmental surveillance activities. One obvious use of
the computer's storage and retrieval capacity along these lines is
the development of a "record prison" by the continuous accumulation of dossier-type material on people over a long period of
time. The possibility of constructing a sophisticated data center
capable of generating a comprehensive womb-to-tomb dossier on
every individual and transmitting it to a wide range of data users
over a national network is one of the most disturbing threats of
the cybernetic revolution.[25] Despite awareness of the problem
and ominous warnings in the media, the seeds of a computerized
dossier society may have already been sown by the steady proliferation of data banks. Rarely does a week go by without some
new information system being uncovered. In one short time span
the existence of the Department of Housing and Urban Development's Adverse Information File, the National Science Foundation's data bank on scientists, the Customs Bureau's computerized
data bank on "suspects," the Civil Service Commission's "investigative" and "security" files, the Secret Service's dossiers on "undesirables," the National Migrant Workers Children Data Bank,[26]

the National Driver Registration Service, and the surveillance activities of the United States Army came to light. Even now only the extremities of a vast, subterranean information structure may be visible.

Perhaps the greatest threat of the "record prison" is that it endangers some of our most basic individual freedoms. A striking example of this is the revelation early in 1970 that the United States Army has been systematically keeping watch over the lawful political activity of a number of groups and is preparing "incident" reports and dossiers on individuals engaging in a wide range of legal protests. Christopher H. Pyle, a former Army intelligence officer has revealed:

> [T]he Army maintains files on the membership, ideology, program, and practices of virtually every activist political group in the country. These include not only such violence-prone organizations as the Minutemen and the Revolutionary Action Movement (RAM), but such non-violent groups as the Southern Christian Leadership Conference, Clergy and Laymen United Against the War in Vietnam, the American Civil Liberties Union, Women Strike for Peace, and the National Association for the Advancement of Colored People.[27]

The information gathered by the Army, which is made available to other government agencies, is transmitted over a nationwide teletype network that has terminals in every major troop center in the United States.

The Army's intelligence system apparently came into existence as a response to the civil disorders in the mid-1960's, which led to increased reliance on the military to quell riots. Although there is considerable justification for certain types of information collection that are directly relevant to the Army's duties, the development of dossiers on people pursuing lawful activities bears little relationship to the function of the military during a civil disorder—especially when many of those being scrutinized are extremely unlikely to be involved in riotous activity. Not only is the Army's effort difficult to justify, but the information system's existence could have a debilitating effect upon the exercise of the constitutional rights of free speech and assembly by many of our politically aware citizens.

After a flurry of publicity about the Army's intelligence activities, the institution of a lawsuit by the American Civil Liberties Union challenging the constitutionality of these practices, and a number of sharply worded letters from congressmen, the Army announced that it was abandoning the data bank. However, on closer inquiry it was revealed that the only thing that had been "abandoned" was the centralized file in the Investigative Records Repository at Fort Holabird in Baltimore.[28] The Army will continue to collect and distribute the data to seven military intelligence group headquarters. It also was disclosed that the existing data at Fort Holabird may not actually be destroyed, merely stored, and that an entirely seperate computer-aided data bank on civilian disturbances has been and will continue to be maintained by the Counterintelligence Analysis Division at the Pentagon. Finally, the Army is continuing work on a number of other surveillance projects, including a computerized master index of all investigation subjects, which will enable the location and assembling of an individual's files very quickly.

In other words, although some changes have been made, the Army's widely announced dismantling of its data bank is to a considerable degree an exercise in semantics and the status of its surveillance activities is very much in doubt. This unsatisfactory state of affairs has been challenged by Senator Sam J. Ervin, Jr. of North Carolina who continues to hammer at what he calls the Army's "deterrent power over the individual rights of American citizens" and to call for a complete congressional investigation. When the Secret Service's unregulated computerized system containing dossiers on "activists," "malcontents," and "potential presidential assassins" is considered, as well as the recent disclosure that the Justice Department's civil disturbance group is maintaining an intelligence data bank, along with the Army's activities, no one should be surprised that there is concern lest the government's surveillance efforts be the genesis of a police state or a return to McCarthyism. The senator is right—a thorough ventilation of the subject is obviously needed.

But the record prison is not built simply by acquiring and preserving personal information. The computer can and is being used to analyze seemingly unrelated data on large numbers of people to determine whether a particular individual's activities bear any relation to the conduct of other investigation subjects or groups. The capability of this so-called "inferential relational retrieval"[29] is illustrated by the following remarks concerning American Airlines' deceptively innocuous flight reservation computer:

> American's computer can be queried about any traveler's movement in the past two or three months. In a furious burst of speed, the electric typewriter spews out a dossier; flights traveled, seat number, time of day, telephone contact, hotel reservations, etc.
>
> . . . [A] computer expert for the airline says that 10 to 15 investigators a day (Federal, state, local, and other) are permitted to delve into the computer for such information. Some of them want (and get) a print-out of the entire passenger list of a certain flight to see who might be traveling with a particular person.[30]

Given the recent expansion of computerized reservation services to include hotels, car rental agencies, theaters, and sports arenas, relational analysis of an individual's activities is clearly the wave of the future in the surveillance field. And don't forget the trail being left by your Carte Blanche or American Express cards; it may be an interesting one, especially if you happen to shop or dine at the same places as some Mafia capo or suspected subversive.

Another possible surveillance application of the new technology is the computer's ability to manipulate a highly detailed data base relating to a large number of variables in order to simulate the behavior of a complex organization. If a corporation has enough information about one of its competitors, for example, computer analysis could reveal a pattern that might enable prediction of the rival's future actions, a highly useful resource for contract bidding or product marketing. Along similar lines, it seems feasible to employ computer techniques to determine what types of false stimuli or corporate feints are likely to cause a desired response on the part of the competitor.[31]

But beyond these impersonal corporate chess moves, which present little or no hazard to personal privacy, it does not require a vivid imagination to conjure up a number of simulation activities involving the prediction of an individual's or a group's behavior that may lead to attempts at human manipulation. All that is needed for such a venture is an extensive dossier and a clever technician with a Machiavellian bent.

To some degree, the widescale use of computers to determine consumer appetites and voter attitudes adds new dimensions to the study of human dynamics. Unfortunately, the name of the game is not necessarily to give the citizenry what it wants; often these surveys are intended to divine a method of making palatable what industry or government already has decided to offer the public. One New Jersey firm is developing a data bank on doctors in order to enable drug companies to promote their products in a way that is suited to the habits and personality of individual doctors.[32] As this illustrates, the line between the use of cybernetics to understand an individual and its use to control or affect his conduct and beliefs is shadowy at best and one that is likely to be transgressed with some frequency.

Perhaps the most significant threats to personal freedom are presented by the inevitable linking of computers to existing surveillance devices for monitoring people and their communications. One of the simplest contemporary snooping devices is the pen register, which, when attached to a telephone line, records a series of dashes representing the numbers dialed from a particular telephone.[33] This snooping capability could be magnified if the information drawn in by the pen register were automatically fed into a central computer for analysis. Widespread use of this technique would quickly reveal patterns of acquaintances and dealings among a substantial group of people. As a practical matter, however, telephone monitoring will be possible without pen registers in a few years. When telephone communications are completely converted to digital transmission, it will be easy to prepare a ready-made machine-readable record of communications made from each telephone that can be cross-correlated with the record of calls made from other telephones to establish an individual's or a group's associations.

Yet even the computer-pen register combination really is quite primitive and its surveillance yield is relatively inconsequential when compared to the possible offspring of the marriage between computers and the emerging optical scanner technology. IBM already has a mechanical page reader capable of scanning and recording typed or hand-printed letters, words, and numbers at the rate of 840 single-spaced typewritten pages per hour. Because of the universally acknowledged need for accurate, high-speed input devices, even faster, more sophisticated successors are certain to become available when costs are reduced and mass marketing is feasible. In addition, several government agencies (such as the Social Security Administration and the Post Office) already are experimenting with scanners—for purely administrative purposes, we are platitudinously assured.

But it is well-known that there are less benign possibilities for optical scanners. The installation of these devices in strategic postal facilities across the country would enable the Post Office Department to increase the scale of its "mail cover" operations. This procedure, which often is undertaken to aid a federal law enforcement agency, was described to a Senate Subcommittee by the Chief Postal Inspector—presumably in the most favorable light possible—in the following terms:

> A mail cover simply consists of recording from a piece of mail the name and address of the sender, the place and date of postmarking, and the class of mail. Mail is neither delayed nor opened. . . . Only the material appearing openly on the wrapper is noted. The recording is done by a postal employee. A mail cover is authorized only when there is good reason to believe that it may be instrumental in the solution of a crime. Information obtained from a cover is used as leads in an investigation, not as evidence in court.[34]

Parenthetically it might be noted, lest the reader have any illusions about the inviolability of the mails, that in March 1970 the Postmaster General announced a proposed regulation, adopted at the insistence of the Customs Bureau, that would allow the *opening* of mail coming into the United States from abroad.

A mail cover operation obviously is highly inefficient and limited by the availability of human recorders. By using scanners, however, the data could be automatically drawn in, recorded, and forwarded to a computer for analysis by a sophisticated control program. Extensive utilization of this technique could yield exhaustive lists of the mail sent and received by thousands of individuals and organizations and an analysis of the suspected relationships among the correspondents. Indeed, to add a futuristic dimension, it may become feasible, with a press of the proverbial button on the fabled black box that computer buffs always talk about, to enter some "appropriate" notation in the computerized files of each of the letter writers—perhaps "Associates with John Badguy, known criminal," or "Corresponds with Pablo Pinko, communist agent." It remains to be seen whether tomorrow's scanner-computer combination will be able to differentiate serious correspondence from an exchange of Christmas cards between boyhood chums and to screen out each day's supply of unsolicited junk mail.

There are numerous other possible applications for scanners. For example, in several states computers are being used to help trap scoff-laws and retrieve stolen cars. The most common procedure calls for police officers at a highway checkpoint to radio the license plate numbers of passing cars to a computer operator, who then directs the computer to print out the record of any violations outstanding against that license number or the person in whose name the car is registered. The operator then forwards the results to the officers for any appropriate action.

Optical scanners designed to read license plates and send the numbers directly to the computer for an electronic file search obviously would make this process more efficient. A sophisticated system might enable information on the movements of a large number of automobiles to be recorded, perhaps for later inferential relational analysis. Congressman Cornelius E. Gallagher pointed up the potentially intrusive character of this type of surveillance when he spoke out against a study of motorist travel patterns that involves the photographing of license plates and sending follow-up questionnaires to the registered owners of the vehicles. One questionnaire brought to his attention carried the legend: "A car as described below and registered in your name was observed traveling on the Baltimore-Washington Parkway near Laurel, Maryland, on August 26 at about 8 AM going south." Unfortunately, according to the Congressman, "the man was driving a car registered in his wife's name and was *not* supposed to be going south on the Parkway that morning."[35]

The ultimate step in mechanical snooping may be the implantation of sensing devices in the human body. These devices might be able to transmit data relating to physiological and chemical changes resulting from various bodily processes to a computer that is programmed to record the data. It might then transmit a response or a command to the sensor, or sound an alarm when specified chemical or biological events occur that indicate the individual is becoming too "aggressive" or is about to do something criminal. To be sure, monitoring systems of this type are adaptable to many beneficial and humanitarian purposes.[36] But telemetry also could be involuntarily imposed on a so-called "antisocial" or "aberrational" individual in order to reveal whether the concentration of personality-altering chemicals in his bloodstream was at a "stable" level,[37] or to administer electrically stimulated rewards and punishments by remote control when sensors reveal that the subject has engaged in certain kinds of behavior.[38]

As might be expected, the proponents of these pervasively intrusive systems assert that they will be used only for "ethical" and "benevolent" purposes; but the enormous potential for abuse inherent in surveillance practices of this type makes one wonder whether these assurances by the very people promoting telemetering are sufficient protection.[39] Suggestions already have been made about "experimenting" with prison and military populations and the day may not be too distant when sensor implantation and consent to monitoring may be strenuously advanced as a "utilitarian" condition on an individual's release from prison or a mental institution.

Human monitoring should not be shrugged off as the imaginings of science fiction writers. Serious researchers are at work on it and there already have been applications combining remote sensing and computers that have enormous privacy implications. High-altitude airplanes and satellites have been equipped with heat, light, and color sensing equipment that has been used to seek out various objects. In Vietnam, enemy truck convoys and troop movements are being tracked in the jungle; over the oceans, schools of fish are being identified and their courses followed; in various parts of North America, marijuana patches and related drug crops are being located.[40] Given the advancing state of both the remote sensing art and the capacity of computers to handle an uninterrupted and synoptic data flow, there seem to be no physical barriers left to shield us from intrusion.

3. The Psychological Effects of a Dossier Society

Probably the most distinctive characteristic of classical utopian designs is the basic "humanitarian" bent of their value structures. . . .

And perhaps the most notable difference to be found between the classical system designs and their counterparts (system engineers, data processing specialists, computer manufacturers, and system designers) consists precisely in the fact that the humanitarian bent has disappeared. The dominant value orientation of the utopian renaissance can best be described as "efficiency" rather than "humanitarianism."
—R. Boguslaw, *The New Utopians, A Study of System Design and Social Change* (1965), 202

Any attempt to appraise the implications of the new information technologies should consider the potential psychological impact on our citizenry of the unchecked computerization and dissemination of personal data. But virtually nothing is known about the psychology of privacy and the ways in which contemporary information practices may affect us. Indeed, there are those who denigrate the importance of privacy to the individual by pointing to the numerous manifestations of society's open and confessional nature. But this is much too simplistic an approach. True, many of us are congenital gossipers. We show a prurient interest in the details and misfortunes in the lives of others. Great numbers of us swallow the Word According to Ann Landers or Joyce Brothers, remain addicted to such television fare as "Secret Storm" and "As the World Turns," and treat the prattlings of Hollywood columnists with the respect generally accorded to writers of Shakespearean stature.

Honesty requires that we face up to our double standard. Although willing to enjoy the vicarious thrill of talking about the peculiarities and pratfalls of others, we are usually unwilling to part our curtains for the general enjoyment of the neighborhood. At the least, many people would draw a distinction between information that we are prepared to yield voluntarily (or perhaps exchange for a comparably titillating morsel from another) and that which is coercively extracted from us or gathered without our knowledge.

Equally unpersuasive is the contention that junk mailers and phone solicitors are the saviors of society's lonely. We should not be deceived by their claim of protecting our unknown citizens against the depression of an empty mailbox and a perpetually silent telephone. Again, there are differences between those intrusions on our solitude that we willingly embrace and those that are thrust upon us.

Finally, there is the view (presumably advanced by those who fancy themselves as emotional spartans) that informational privacy is an unnecessary ingredient in the life of an honest, clean living, and God-fearing citizen. Adherents of this position typically believe that those who oppose increased wiretapping by law enforcement agencies, the proliferation of data banks, stop-and-frisk legislation, and widespread use of lie-detector tests are trying to hide something or are simply the product of a guilt-ridden society. This incredibly insensitive attitude completely overlooks man's need for individuality and ignores the variousness of the human condition. It is a typical reaction, however, among those who believe that many of our civil liberties are outmoded in a scientifically based society that needs complete access to data for decision-making purposes.

Privacy, whether it be physical or informational, is a subjective value, as society has always recognized by according a right of solitude to women, the infirm, and the bereaved. An individual's desire to control the information that comprises his life history is a natural part of the quest for personal autonomy and it is not surprising that the need to do so varies drastically from person to person and from place to place. Thus, it would be wrong to dismiss the quest for privacy as part of an eccentric Greta Garbo-Howard Hughes syndrome. Many are the occasions on which a man needs a place where "he can open his collar . . . and give vent to his own particular daydreams, his mutterings and snatches of crazy song, his bursts of obscenity and afflatus of glory."[41] My colleague Yale Kamisar has made the same point in a somewhat autobiographical fashion:

> I vividly recall the heated reaction of my company commander (who had been an enlisted man for many years) when, brand new infantry second lieutenant that I was, I entered the enlisted men's latrine, looking for a certain corporal. "Stay the hell out of there," he snapped "that's about the only place those 'poor bastards' have to cuss out officers, to ridicule them, to brag about how they outsmarted them, etc., and if they couldn't do that much they'd probably 'bust.' "[42]

Some people feel emasculated when private information about them is disclosed or exchanged even though the data are accurate and they do not suffer any career or social damage. Correctly or incorrectly, they think in terms of having been embarrassed or demeaned by having been denuded of something that hitherto was theirs alone.[43] Consider the plight of people on public assistance. "Disclosing assets and resources, revealing the names of one's friends and associates, submitting to investigations and questioning, accounting for expenditures and social behavior —these are the prices of receiving welfare. Loss of privacy is loss of dignity and is part of the shame of being a welfare recipient."[44]

The preservation of those aspects of privacy that nurture autonomy and individuality is essential to society as we know it. Thus, Professor Alan Westin has observed:

> [D]evelopment of individuality is particularly important in democratic societies, since quality of independent thought, diversity of views, and nonconformity are considered desirable traits for individuals. Such independence requires time for sheltered experimentation and testing of ideas, for preparation and practice in thought and conduct, without fear of ridicule or penalty, and for the opportunity to alter opinions before making them public. The individual's sense that it is he who decides when to "go public" is a crucial aspect of his feeling of autonomy. Without such time for incubation and growth, through privacy, many ideas and positions would be launched into the world with dangerous prematurity.[45]

As the public becomes increasingly aware of the information orientation of modern life and that a substantial amount of personal data about them is being preserved "on the record," it is understandable that people may begin to doubt whether they have any meaningful existence or identity apart from their profile stored in the electronic catacombs of a "master" computer. Embedded in this fear of being stripped of individuality is the psychosis of the Computerized Man, popularly portrayed as a quasi-automaton whose functions have been standardized, whose status in the community has been determined for him, and whose financial condition is prescribed in immutable terms.[46]

There may be a very real sense in which a person will not exist outside of his computer dossier. In the course of his Subcommittee's Hearings on the Computer and Invasion of Privacy,

Congressman Gallagher pointed out that "since the IRS has now set up a central data collection service and now that we have the potential of erasing from the computer's memory and truly making a person an 'unperson,' . . . it [would] be possible for a skilled computer expert to make himself a nontaxpayer, by programming himself out of existence . . ."[47] Along the same lines, several knowledgeable people have informed me that a number of their acquaintances have procured more than one social security number in order to lead separate "record lives" under each of them.

Another potentially deleterious side effect of excessive dossier-building is that people may increasingly base their decisions and fashion their behavior in terms of enhancing their record image in the eyes of those who may have access to it in the future. This is the real evil of the record prison.

> Thus, the technical demand for more personal information to be recorded and a conscious public concerned with keeping the record straight lie at the root of the new invasion of privacy. It is a deprivation of privacy that cannot be legislated against nor moralized against. It is a source of social control which necessitates new techniques and a pervading inquiry into motivations for them. It is an invasion which most people willingly accept, since they have not known other conditions and are happy to be publicly significant to someone.[48]

This concern for the record will be reinforced by the popular conception of the computer as the unforgetting and unforgiving watchdog of society's information managers. As one observer has remarked, "the possibility of the fresh start is becoming increasingly difficult. The Christian notion of redemption is incomprehensible to the computer."[49]

In sharp contrast to those who are becoming overly mindful of the record, others are treating the computer as a convenient scapegoat for a number of man's ills and castigating its use as symptomatic of the declining humanity in our society. Errors in accounts, delays in shipments, and a variety of other inconveniences are blamed on "the computer," rather than on the people handling the transaction or those who processed the relevant data digested by the machine. Almost every day there is fresh evidence that the frustrations generated by the dislocations of our age are capable of provoking highly irrational reactions to the computer among the disenchanted. People have written letters to computers operated by commercial dating services commenting on the dates that have been arranged for them[50] and naked protesters have picketed IBM offices with signs proclaiming that "Computers are Obscene."[51] A group of computer-phobes have gone to the extreme of organizing an International Society for the Abolition of Data Processing Machines, which has over three thousand members in thirty countries and is preparing a catalogue of "computer atrocities."

Even among people whose lives are intertwined with cybernetics, the machine casts its spell. For example, computer operators often ascribe human personalities to their machines.[52] Often this proves essential to survival in our electronic age. When corporate executive Roger Fischer's objections to an obviously erroneous parking ticket did not get through the computerized processing of his replies to payment notices from the Chicago Police, he dispatched punch cards to the police computer stating: "Apparently the letters sent to the humans who try to control you are being disregarded. The violation is not valid. I suggest you instruct them to erase the ticket from your memory bank." In response came another set of cards that upon processing by Fischer smugly announced that there had been a human error, which had been corrected. The message added: "[A]t last I have found someone who understands my language. . . . If you're ever in the neighborhood, come up and see me some time."[53]

Personification of computers has carried over into the arts; computers have emerged from the world of science fiction[54] to become sinister protagonists or sympathetic figures in novels,[55] plays,[56] motion pictures,[57] and poems.[58] Typical is the following sketch in a play entitled "The Fourth Wall" as described by critic Walter Kerr:

> [A] chap who was starved for female companionship . . . arranged himself a date on the computer system, presumably getting a girl whose card-indexed characteristics matched his needs.
>
> She came, she was tall, she was red-haired, she was compliant. A less resistant partner for the evening could scarcely be imagined. Everything she said was right. The boy had no

need to delay matters. "Would you kiss me?" he asked, fairly quickly. "I'm terribly excited," she said, responding in low tones, on cue.

Only one thing wrong. Those tones. They were low all right, just where they should have been. And they were cold, cold as an ice-cube tray that has stuck to your hands because your hands are wet. They were efficiently responsive. At this point, of course, we tumbled to the joke. The girl herself was the computer, out for the night.[59]

Another aspect of a dossier society is the possible development of citizen antagonism toward information-gathering agencies. It is quite conceivable that people may lose confidence in or begin to distrust governmental and private organizations that extract information from them in a way or to a degree that is thought offensive. Although there is very little evidence on this point, the possibility should not be discounted. After all, we do know that the heat, light, and noise environment of a factory can alter a worker's productivity and his job attitude. It therefore seems likely that the quality of an individual's work can be affected by the degree to which he has been required to disclose information about himself to his employer and whether he is concerned about the possible misuse of his personnel file. It also may be true that a citizen's conception of his government as a benevolent Hercules, rather than a manipulative despot, is at least partially dependent on whether he has been informationally raped as a condition of securing the benefits and protections of organized society.

> Conceivably, a society which fails sufficiently to protect the individual's privacy may become characterized by behavior patterns such as mutual mistrust and hostility, which to me, as to most Americans, are much less desirable characteristics than their opposites of mutual trust and amity. As a psychologist, I would therefore endorse a system of mores and laws which frees the individual from the stress and indignity of 'brainwatching.'[60]

To go one step further, it is quite possible that widescale computerization may give rise to an "underground" movement among the alienated, reminiscent of the nineteenth-century Luddites who busied themselves smashing machines to ward off the evils of the industrial revolution. Individual efforts to sabotage the electronic revolution, by violating contemporary society's Eleventh Commandment—"Do not fold, bend, spindle, or mutilate"—already have taken place. In fact, one federal court has found it necessary to grant an injunction restraining a civil rights group from covering the holes on an electric utility's punch-card bills as a means of protesting the company's allegedly discriminatory hiring policies.[61] In a more violent vein, student activists on several campuses have vented their anger on the computer and its trappings as being symbols of the dehumanization of modern mass education and tools of the establishment.[62]

Perhaps little attention should be paid to such aberrational and atavistic behavior. After all, the new technology is promoting a number of vital societal goals by providing us with the capacity to service large groups of people through the analysis of vast quantities of data that must be digested to determine how best to meet their needs. Given the complexity of our age, computers may even prove essential to the proper functioning and preservation of our representative form of government, both in terms of being tuned in on public opinion and in framing legislative programs.[63] Moreover, the fact that some self-styled humanists are able to present a parade of horrible examples of the machine's dangers does not provide a justification for jettisoning the technological developments of the past three decades, any more than occasional air disasters require that we abandon travel by airplane.

Nevertheless, the breadth of concern over the dehumanization of modern society and the animus directed at the computer, whether entirely rational or not, cannot be ignored. The possibility of propagating a record-oriented citizenry that has lost its autonomy and individuality must be avoided. By doing nothing we expose ourselves to the risk that the growing omnipresence of the computer may have a numbing effect on the congeries of values subsumed under the heading "personal privacy." Generations of children reared in an electronic environment cannot help but develop a set of attitudes and values different from those of the present population.[64] As Richard L. Tobin commented in a 1968 *Saturday Review* editorial captioned "1984 Minus Sixteen and Counting," "we cannot assume . . . that privacy will survive simply because man has a psychological or social need for it."[65]

III
The Changing Face of Information Handling
— Privacy in the Crucible

For most of us the jargon and mathematical elaborations of the experts are so much mumbo jumbo. But, we feel certain, it is all mumbo jumbo that works—or at least seems to work. . . . If those who know best tell us that progress consists in computerizing the making of political and military decisions, who are we to say this is not the best way to run our politics? If enough experts told us that strontium 90 and smog were good for us, doubtless most of us would take their word for it. . . . If we believe it is important to get there very, very fast—despite the dangers, despite the discomforts, despite the expense, despite the smog —then the automobile is an impressive piece of magic.

—T. Roszak, *The Making of a Counter Culture*
(paper ed., 1969), 259

Having considered the contours of the new data processing technology and suggested how it threatens individual privacy, we can now take a closer look at some of the cybernetic guild's information activities in recent years and explore the antagonism between the forces promoting the use of computers for the efficient management of our affairs and the need to preserve personal privacy. The particular applications of information technology to be discussed in this chapter were selected because they present a cross-section of interesting problems, but they are not unique. Numerous other computer uses are spawning their own privacy difficulties that also are in need of examination and solution.

1. The Rise, Fall, and Resurrection of the National Data Center

> Nor shall this peace sleep with her; but as when
> The bird of wonder dies, the maiden phoenix,
> Her ashes new-create another heir
> As great in admiration as herself.
> —Shakespeare, *Henry VIII*,
> Act V, Scene v

54

The federal government long has been the nation's primary user of data-processing equipment; in fact, it was a government agency —the Bureau of the Census—that purchased the first commercially available computer following the Second World War. Reliance on electronic data-processing is a natural response to the proliferation of citizen reports and governmental information activities that are the by-products of today's pervasive federal involvements. The social security and income tax programs alone produce more than six hundred million annual reports.[1] In addition, statistics are becoming increasingly crucial as a foundation for the social and economic research, policy-making, and environmental planning that go into the administration of federal programs. In these contexts, the computer's ability to manipulate huge bodies of detailed information concerning a large number of potentially relevant variables that may pertain to events occurring over long periods of time permits the testing of hypotheses in ways that have never been feasible. Without modern electronics, planners might wander aimlessly in the federal government's paperwork jungle.

But even with the computer, the government's information activities seem to lack coherence and direction. All too often the gathering of reports and compilation of statistics only beget additional gathering of reports and compilation of statistics. Viewed from the outside, the over-all effect appears to be an unrelenting flow of data that is generated and consumed by some diabolical Sorcerer's Apprentice. Nonetheless, the experts tell us that even the federal government's vast information activities and technological resources are no match for the data gathering and processing tasks that must precede rational decision making.[2]

Perhaps part of the reason is that as federal agency functions currently are arranged, only one government organization, the Census Bureau, has the collection and analysis of statistics as its principal goal. The other agencies generate statistics only incidentally to their operations, and occasionally have failed to preserve data that might prove valuable to numerous other governmental or private organizations. Furthermore, really effective inter-agency utilization of information is prevented because some agencies, such as the National Aeronautics and Space Administration and the Atomic Energy Commission, operate under stringent confidentiality requirements that preclude the general release or exchange of data.[3] But because of the existing decentralized character of federal records, even collections of data that are intended to be open to the public frequently are almost impossible to locate, are arranged inconveniently for access and analytical purposes, or are difficult to compare or correlate with other information because of differences in agency information handling procedures. With the possible exception of the Committee on Scientific and Technical Information (COSATI) of the Federal Council of Science and Technology,[4] there is no government organization that can provide a reference guide to the kinds and the location of information being collected at the national level.

These deficiencies in the federal government's information practices have several deleterious side-effects. First, the effort and time wasted in locating data and transposing them into a form that is functional for second and subsequent users reduces the over-all efficiency of governmental operations and increases their cost. Second, duplication in the information collected often means an unnecessarily high and repetitious reporting burden on private individuals and institutions.[5] Third, large quantities of useful data never see the light of day and thus do not reach many of the users who might profit by the ready availability of the federal government's vast storehouse of information, much of which relates to a variety of important contemporary issues such as consumer and environmental protection.

All things considered, therefore, it was eminently logical for the Bureau of the Budget (absorbed in 1970 by the Office of Management and Budget) in the mid-1960's to attempt to take a step toward reforming the federal government's information activities by proposing the creation of a single federal statistical center—called the National Data Center. The effect of the Bureau's plan would have been to relieve the operating agencies of many data processing burdens and to centralize the existing diffused bodies of information.[6] Advocates of the center thought it would: 1) make more data available for researchers, both inside and outside the government; 2) reduce the unit cost of data; 3) enable larger and more effective samples to be taken; 4) facilitate the canvassing of wider ranges of variables; 5) reduce duplication in the government's data collection activities; 6) promote greater standardization of techniques among the agencies; 7) make research efforts easier to verify; and 8) provide a data processing pool for all the information handling agencies.[7]

From the perspective of individual privacy, the original proposal seemed harmless enough; all that was being suggested was the creation of a *statistical* center that would compile and process information from governmental files on an aggregate basis. The possibility that an individualized intelligence or surveillance center was in the offing was ridiculed by the center's proponents. But the proposal had touched a raw nerve. Questions were raised concerning whether the dichotomy between statistical and intelligence work was tenable in the context of computerized data. Moreover, little in the way of privacy guarantees and protections was offered by the center's sponsors. Advocates of the center offered only a few platitudinous remarks about "appropriate" hardware and software controls, but they never provided details to allay the apprehensions of the questioners.

Not surprisingly, the National Data Center proposal became a lightning rod for the vague feelings of discontent generated by the computer revolution. Members of Congress,[8] then newspapers[9] and magazines,[10] and finally several legal periodicals[11] took turns castigating the idea, often in emotive or highly symbolic terms. To a degree, the clamor was justifiable. The original proposals were incredibly myopic in their obsession with efficiency. None of the three reports recommending establishment of a central data bank gave the problem of privacy more than token attention. They focused almost exclusively on procuring "maximum information" and organizing to insure "maximum legitimate accessibility, for both governmental agencies and other users." In addition, despite early protestations to the contrary, proponents of the data center admitted that individual identification would have to be linked to some of the data in the center[12]—an admission that immediately raised serious doubts about the level of protection that would be given to privacy. One of the chief advocates of the center subsequently conceded that the failure of his cohorts to come to grips with the privacy question was "a gigantic oversight."[13]

Nonetheless, that failure does not necessarily represent a disregard of human values or indicate bureaucratic bad faith as some have suggested. The original Bureau of the Budget proposal was limited in scope. Putting to one side the long-range possibility of the center's expanding and individualizing its files, reasonable people might well view its threat to individual privacy as a relatively remote one. As a pragmatic matter, detailed consideration of the privacy question at the time the first proposals were advanced might have been premature. Until the contours of the center and its activities were more sharply delineated, the nature of the threat to privacy would remain obscure, making it difficult to formulate precise proposals for protection. But even when the situation is viewed most charitably, it still is shocking that high ranking government officials and prominent behavioral scientists were so preoccupied with the quantity of information and the data processing capabilities the center would put at their disposal, that they were virtually insensitive to the privacy question.

Ironically, it became clear in the course of the congressional debate that the existing decentralized nature of the federal reporting system, which the statisticians and social scientists derisively characterized as inefficient, actually serves as a safeguard against the compilation of extensive government dossiers on every citizen.[14] And, although proponents of the data center properly pointed to the excellent record of protecting sensitive information compiled by some federal agencies, most notably the Census Bureau, the dialogue also revealed that several other agencies and bureaus had a less exemplary history in the privacy arena. To make matters worse, it became apparent that the information that ultimately would find its way into the proposed data bank would be "orders of magnitude more sensitive than those now at the Bureau of the Census,"[15] which meant that any failure of security was likely to be "many times more destructive to an individual."[16]

Chastened by the public outcry, the statisticians and administrators retreated to reconsider their proposal and to investigate more carefully the safeguards necessary to render a National Data Center more palatable to Congress and the public. Subsequently, the House Committee on Government Operations recommended that "no work be done to establish the national data bank until privacy protection is explored fully and guaranteed to the greatest extent possible to the citizens whose personal records would form its information base."[17] Taking the public statements emanating from both the Executive Branch and the

Congress at face value, it seems safe to conclude that there currently is no "fully developed plan for a National Data Center."[18]

The apparent victory against the National Data Center by the defenders of privacy is largely a Pyrrhic one, however. Information collected for statistical purposes, which was the focal point of the Bureau's proposal and bore the brunt of the outcry, comprises only about one-fifth to one-third of the reports and questionnaires pertaining to citizens generated by the government.[19] Moreover, statistical studies generally do not contain sensitive data of the type that is attractive to snoopers and are somewhat easier to protect against intrusion than investigative or surveillance files, although the claimed distinction between the two types of systems[20] certainly will become less valid with the passage of time.[21] As a result, the public debate over the National Data Center never really reached the question of preserving the integrity of the bulk of sensitive data gathered by the government or the fundamental policy issue of how to curtail the government's increasing penchant for information collection.

But the real tragedy that may emerge when the dust settles is that the failure to establish a data center under a legislative mandate directing the managers to take the steps necessary to protect individual privacy actually may serve to undermine individual privacy. This certainly will be the case if nothing is done to curb the present tendency of each federal agency to "constitute itself a data center."[22] As noted earlier, the federal agencies already have enormous stores of computerized data and they have been provided with the legal authority for sharing this wealth of information. The Administrator of the General Services Administration (GSA), for example, has statutory power to establish interagency pools of data-processing equipment and facilities "when necessary for its most efficient and effective utilization."[23] The Deputy Administrator of the GSA gave us a glimpse of the future when he told a congressional subcommittee that "the most effective and economical" way to implement this power is to augment existing computer equipment in order to provide several agencies with "huge multiaccess, remote-control, time-sharing systems" that will service the other agencies.[24] In addition, the Secretary of Commerce has authority to develop uniform standards for data-processing that would apply throughout the federal government;[25] at present "a major standardization effort" is underway "to provide a universal language of machine inter-communication."[26]

Approximately twenty federal agencies, bureaus, and departments already operate time-sharing computer systems or are in the process of establishing them.[27] Additional systems are certain to spring up, not only within existing governmental organizations but because a number of legislative proposals, such as the Family Assistance and the Manpower Training Acts, call for the collection of new bodies of data.[28] The roots of a federal information network have taken hold. All that is needed to make the system flourish is nourishment from the White House in the form of funding and soft breezes of passivity from Congress.

The current handling of personal medical records in the Social Security Administration provides a rather graphic example of how the burgeoning government information systems are functioning:

> The Social Security Administration [has a] . . . policy of storing in a computer in the Social Security Administration headquarters, Baltimore, the basic data indicating the social security status of every citizen with a social security registration. This has now been extended to equivalent records on all phases of the Medicare program.
>
> . . . [T]he Social Security Administration has established some 725 field offices throughout the United States. Registrants visit or write to these field offices for information concerning their Social Security or Medicare status, or to apply for payments under the respective programs. Each such inquiry or application typically results in a communication to Baltimore . . .
>
> [E]ach field station is equipped . . . with automatic transmitters, that transmit or receive at 100 words per minute . . . [The information] is sent via high-speed, dedicated circuits to Baltimore, where it is received on magnetic tape ready for input to the Social Security Administration's Computer . . .
>
> The Social Security Administration also maintains magnetic-tape-to-magnetic-tape transmissions systems from the National Blue Cross Headquarters to Baltimore.[29]

The growth of sophisticated interconnected systems of this type will enable the government to coordinate the information gathering programs of the various agencies. In view of the Office of Management and Budget's extensive authority to promote these activities,[30] as soon as enough interfaces among the agencies are established a system even more encompassing than the proposed National Data Center will come into being. The lesson of the uproar that led to the defeat of the last proposal will have been learned by the advocates of computerization of information and the new institution probably will emerge under an inoffensive name such as the Federal Statistical Analysis Center—that is, if anyone bothers to legitimize the existence of the emerging network in any formal way.

Few voices have been raised against this trend. On the contrary, the cry of efficiency is still the dominant sound being heard in the land. According to the Comptroller General of the United States: "only through the greatest coordination of effort on a Government-wide . . . basis will we be able to avoid extensive duplication of effort in designing and redesigning of systems. . . ."[31] And Illinois Congressman Roman Pucinski of the powerful House Education and Labor Committee is actively pursuing the idea that a national data processing and retrieval system should be established under federal auspices to serve to integrate private and governmental information networks.[32]

In view of past revelations about the insensitivity of some government information handling practices, the prospect of an omnibus, de facto federal data network evolving without prior comprehensive congressional review or the formulation of any policy guidelines that impose an obligation to protect privacy is not a happy one. Congress's ultimate power over appropriations, which was held up as a way of controlling the nature of the information that might be stored in the proposed National Data Center,[33] is not a realistic method of remedying deficiencies in the data gathering of individual agencies. Funding levels typically are determined on the basis of an over-all view of agency programs without any significant or independent consideration of the information reporting requirements that they might impose on citizens. Appropriations committees usually are not concerned with what an average congressman might consider to be the minutiae of proposed programs.[34] This is not surprising inasmuch as even top-level administrators often are unaware of the amount and kinds of information that their own agencies collect from the public.[35]

Even more disheartening is the fact that the existing controls on the type and volume of information that may be exacted from the public seem to have been largely ineffectual. The Federal Reports Act[36] provides that federal agencies must obtain clearance from the Office of Management and Budget before attempting to collect data from ten or more persons. Clearance apparently is rarely denied;[37] indeed, the Budget Bureau has been known to act as an advocate, as well as a judge, by intervening in Congress to obtain support for certain information-gathering projects.[38] Even this highly permissive procedure is thought to be too burdensome by some agencies and they occasionally circumvent the Reports Act by having the data-gathering done by independent contractors.[39] Agencies also may evade the clearance requirements by securing bodies of data from federally financed state agencies under the threat of withholding funds if information demands are not met,[40] or by claiming exemptions from the requirements of the Act, knowing that no one will slap their wrists.[41] The net effect is that most information-gathering activities proceed without any meaningful privacy-oriented supervision. And, if a comprehensive federal data network emerges in this unregulated environment, the situation is bound to deteriorate even further.

Another reality of federal agency life is that some governmental data gatherers exceed their statutory powers. A survey by a congressional subcommittee revealed many instances of agency demands for information that had not been authorized by Congress and concluded that most "government forms require either nonessential or too-detailed information from the individual citizen."[42] Similarly, the authority for the Army's surveillance of the lawful political activities of civilians is obscure. Neither the Executive Orders relating to security checks for government employment nor the so-called "Delimitations Agreement" between the military and the FBI, which allocates jurisdiction over personnel security investigations, envisions the Army's file building. Moreover, there is no effective supervision over the data bank's purse strings, which means that the Army's files have the potential for becoming the largest intelligence system in the United

States. As Congressman Gallagher properly suggested in a letter to the Secretary of the Army, the system is, "if . . . not formally a National Data Bank, . . . at the every least, a nationwide data bank."

Agency information collectors often deceive the public by intimating that the law requires a response to questionnaires that in fact are voluntary. "In their zeal to increase the coverage and accuracy of a survey," one report concluded, "administrators have been known to use deceptive language in the wording of their questionnaires" to coerce responses.[43] Even among citizens who are offended by certain inquiries, there is a natural reluctance to "buck the system."[44]

This muscle flexing is used by the government to carry out a number of other questionable information activities. It is well known that the FBI investigates potential jurors in many case in which the United States is a litigant. Putting to one side the impropriety of using the federal government's leverage in this fashion, it is obvious that the FBI's special clout results in a rich data yield not available to others.

> . . . A given United States Attorney may feel that knowl-
> edge of the financial lives of the prospective jurors will be
> valuable in impaneling the jury. The FBI will probably be
> able to secure for him information from banks, stock broker-
> age firms, insurance companies, and other institutions which
> would not make available their records to the private investi-
> gator.
>
> The guess may be ventured that in the overwhelming num-
> ber of cases mere display of FBI credentials is a guarantee
> of rather full disclosure of all information sought. Moreover,
> the FBI is subject to no practical limitations on the type of
> inquiry it conducts or the extent thereof.[45]

Another illustration of this tendency is provided by the close relationship between the FBI and the banks. There is currently a substantial surveillance effort underway to trace the movement of American funds abroad—particularly regarding bank deposits in Switzerland and potential aid to draft evaders, the North Vietnamese, and the Viet Cong. In addition to using mail cover operations,[46] the FBI also keeps watch on many domestic banking transactions. Apparently banks rarely object when access to their files is sought. This is partially attributable to the fact that a large number of bank security officers are former FBI agents. Furthermore, since the FBI has jurisdiction over bank fraud cases, the banks find it to their advantage to "cooperate" with the FBI's data surveillance operations to be certain that frauds committed against them will be promptly and fully investigated.

Even private groups occasionally attempt to piggyback on the federal government's *in terrorem* power. A number of instances have been brought to light in which researchers operating under federal grants have tried to coerce responses to questionnaires and secure personal interviews by raising the spectre of governmental retaliation. Several people in Cambridge, Massachusetts have complained that workers on a government sponsored Harvard-MIT urban planning project harassed and threatened them in connection with a questionnaire they felt invaded their privacy. One over-eager "social scientist" apparently suggested that it was a federal crime not to respond to the project's questionnaire and that the recalcitrant subject's name would be turned over to the proper authorities if the document was not completed. Ironically, the researcher's conduct probably was closer to being criminal than was the data subject's.

The dangers posed by the existing lack of effective controls on government information handling go beyond the unauthorized or illicit procurement of data. Information usually is extracted without any real assurance that it will be handled on a confidential basis or with the virtually meaningless pledge not to release the information outside of the government.[47] It is highly unrealistic to expect the donor of the data to have an accurate conception of the uses to which the information might be put or the potential audience to which it might be exposed. Even if confidentiality restrictions control a particular agency's activities, in practice they are likely to reflect little more than ad hoc judgments of individual officials or archaic rules that have not been re-evaluated in decades, rather than a statutory or regulatory system developed to protect citizen privacy in the computer age.[48] Those safeguards that do exist often are vitiated by the propensity of investigators to exchange information. "When a Federal agent makes a National Agency Check on a person . . . he customarily checks the files of at least eight Federal agencies. A congressional investigator reported that the results of lie-detector tests taken by one agency were freely passed around to personnel officials in other agencies."[49]

The government's hyperactivity in the collection process is not necessarily offset by the exercise of care regarding the uses to which the information is put. On one occasion the FBI publicly released twelve hundred pages of transcripts of electronically recorded conversations among reputed Mafia figures in which numerous prominent people were mentioned, commented upon, and occasionally disparaged. Even conceding that the Mafia's threat to the moral fibre of our society must be brought home to the American people, need it be done by giving the daily press transcripts of unsworn conversations procured surreptitiously by government bugging? In a similar vein, why shouldn't citizens have doubts about entrusting personal information to a government when its law enforcement officers think nothing of "leaking" to NBC the identity of several well-known professional football players who in some unexplained way supposedly are connected with the work of a grand jury investigating gambling?

Past information excesses would be understandable, perhaps pardonable, if they had resulted solely from efforts to obtain data that were essential to the solution of pressing social problems. Often, however, this has not been the case. As a congressional subcommittee revealed, "a number of surveys are conducted at the request (and often at the expense) of industry groups, trade associations, and . . . business organizations."[50] Moreover, the benefits and burdens of these inquisitions are not evenly distributed. Big business easily can absorb the cost of replying to myriad governmental questionnaires and can hire the analysts and marketing experts necessary to make profitable use of the statistics that result from these surveys.[51] On the other hand, the burden on small businessmen and individuals is a comparatively heavy one and they receive little or no direct benefit from these statistical programs.[52] Yet when individual citizens become outraged enough to complain about the torrent of questionnaires and plead for relief, federal information managers often turn these supplications to their own advantage by requesting increased computer power and the authority to share bodies of data with other organizations in order to "ease the burden on respondents."[53]

Of course, past abuses are not a justification for abolishing or drastically reducing the government's information activities. I readily acknowledge that extensive data gathering, analysis, and dissemination are essential to the functioning of a highly complex society. However, past experience does afford ample reason to be skeptical of demands for more information and facile assertions that the establishment of computerized government data centers will increase the protection given to individual records. The claim that these centers will make it easy and desirable to purge stale records because computer storage costs are relatively high no doubt has some validity.[54] But this assertion must be considered in light of congressional findings that the mounting cost of storing paper records already is necessitating the destruction of ancient data[55] and that "computer technology shares the responsibility for increasing Federal reporting requirements."[56] It certainly is true that technologically it is feasible to review computerized records periodically, and relatively easy to erase the outmoded and outdated information. Nonetheless, there must be some incentive to encourage governmental agencies to do so.

The denouement of the original National Data Center proposal should indicate that even though public debate and outrage can be successful in a particular case, total reliance on counterattacking against individual information gathering activities will not reverse the growing risk to personal privacy created by an ever-increasing level of federal data collection. If that is true, we are thus faced with an interesting dilemma. If defeat of the National Data Center simply encourages the proliferation of unregulated governmental data centers and machine interconnections tying the various agency computer systems together—if what cannot be done directly will then be done indirectly—then the cure may be more dangerous than the disease. The more attractive alternative appears to be a federal data center that is functionally circumscribed by the legislation establishing it and governed by a congressional mandate that places a heavy emphasis on privacy considerations.

But before establishing such a center, the federal government's information practices must be subjected to a comprehensive re-examination in the hope of achieving a better over-all balance between the need for the efficient gathering and handling of masses of data and the national government's obligation to preserve the privacy of its citizens. This process must be undertaken and continued whether or not a formal statistical center is established in order to keep pace with changing agency information practices.

It is essential to keep in mind that the data cycle has new dimensions in the age of the computer. We no longer have a record-keeping system based on decentralized manila folders and countless governmental clerks obsessed with the idea that their *raison d'être* is to preserve the chastity of the documents in their care. The inefficiencies of past data patterns will not provide safeguards for our citizens in the future. Moreover, we cannot predict the extent to which existing federal systems might interconnect with data bases situated on the periphery of the government. There is every possibility, for example, that computerized data bases created under government sponsored research grants, such as the Harvard-MIT project mentioned earlier, or federally supported state and local welfare programs will interface and exchange data with agency systems in Washington. Should that come to pass, the existing primitive rules of confidentiality will be useless and the government's control over our informational profiles will be complete. Thomas Jefferson's observation that "eternal vigilance is the price of liberty" is as sound today as it was two centuries ago.

2. Computers, Credit Bureaus, and the Checkless, Cashless Society—The Creditability Gap

If you are like 100,000,000 other Americans you began the process of losing your privacy the day you first opened a charge account, took out a loan, bought something on the installment plan, or applied for a credit card. For credit is not, as has been so often suggested, a supreme act of faith on the part of the merchant or banker who extends it. Less ennobling but more to the point, it is a way of doing business that relies on probabilities. The prospective creditor thinks it probable that you will live up to the terms of your agreement. He arrives at this decision only after as much of your personal and financial history has been unearthed as he (or his credit bureau) deems necessary. A man's home may be his castle, as the English are fond of saying, but in a credit economy it cannot help but be built along goldfish bowl specifications.

—Myron Brenton, *The Privacy Invaders*
(paper ed., 1964), 17

The privacy implications of the gathering of credit information by the private sector have received almost as much attention during the past few years as has the proposal to establish a National Data Center. This no doubt reflects the fact that buying on credit has become an integral part of our daily life.[57] Credit transactions have so permeated the economy that the United States supports a constantly growing buy-now-pay-later habit that exceeds one hundred billion dollars. The importance of credit to the financial fiber of our society is amply demonstrated by the shock waves that follow every vibration in the prime or discount interest rate.

Today's credit industry bears little resemblance to that of the quill-and-inkstand era when the neighborhood banker, grocer, and merchant were personally familiar with the economic condition of each of their customers and could extend or deny financing on the basis of that knowledge. Several powerful forces have brought about the changes. First, we live in a highly mobile society—people uproot and transplant themselves with remarkable frequency. As a result, financial information must be available wherever a peripatetic consumer might appear to transact business, not simply where he happens to have sought credit in the past. Second, the pace of modern commercial life is such that a credit decision must be made promptly by a lender or retail merchant. Modern merchandising's hurly-burly is premised on a drive-it-off-the-lot philosophy that is incompatible with a horse-and-buggy procedure for credit checks. Third, the ranks of the buying public are growing daily and will continue to do so unless Zero Population Growth turns the tide. Until then, merchants and banks will be confronted with growing masses of customers on whom they need current data to expedite dealings. These and other factors have destroyed the relaxed credit patterns of more halcyon days and have led to the farming out of the information-gathering burden to an amorphous band of businesses known as credit bureaus.

Because the activities of credit bureaus appear relatively inoffensive, most people are willing to disclose substantial quantities of personal information in order to obtain the benefits of the credit economy.[58] This information usually is supplemented with the history of a person's payment habits received by the bureaus from those who have previously granted him credit. To augment these data even further, many credit bureaus regularly comb newspapers, court records, and other public files for bits of personal information thought to be relevant in deciding whether an individual is an acceptable risk.[59]

In recent years, however, congressional investigators have revealed a number of practices by the so-called retail credit-reporting associations—firms catering primarily to insurance companies and employers—that are subject to sharp criticism.[60] In addition to the activities mentioned above, these associations often employ field investigators to gather information as to an individual's status and reputation in his community. As might be expected, the resulting reports usually contain hearsay narratives and off-the-cuff opinions gleaned from quick interviews with neighbors, landlords, employers, and "friends" conducted by poorly paid, relatively unsophisticated, and frequently insensitive functionaries. In addition, investigators often are required to complete a certain number of checks per week or month. These "quotas" typically are so high that it is unrealistic to believe that the investigations are conducted carefully, and there are strong indications that in some instances the field work is not done at all. In other cases credit bureau agents find it easier to base their reports on what they are told by other investigators, especially private detectives and those working as security officers where the subject is employed or does his banking, than to examine the public records.

There are two "leading lights" in this murky business. The first, Atlanta-based Retail Credit Company has attracted the particular attention of congressional subcommittees because it has files on over forty-five million individuals, a staff of seven thousand investigators, and control of sixty percent of the retail credit bureau market. The second is the Hooper-Holmes Bureau, a low-visibility organization that is said to specialize in derogatory information and reportedly has files on nine or ten million people. The flavor of these operations can be savored from the following description by the president of Hooper-Holmes of how a field investigator checks out his suspicion that the subject is involved in an extramarital affair: "You go to a neighbor and establish rapport. . . . Then you ask, 'What's your opinion of X's home life; how do you think of him as a family man?' This will usually elicit some hint. . . . Then you start digging. You press them as far as they go, and if they become recalcitrant, you go somewhere else."[61] Retail Credit Company admitted that their investigators customarily interview "employers, former employers, references, fellow club members, neighbors and former neighbors [and] financial professional people."[62] In addition to Retail Credit and Hooper-Holmes, there are several politically oriented groups, such as the right-wing Church League of America, who make their investigative talents available to employers with the claim that they can weed out "undesirables" and "troublesome individuals." A more blatant form of blacklisting service is difficult to imagine.

Given interrogation practices designed to provoke gossip, it is not surprising that files produced during several congressional hearings contained comments from unidentified sources such as "peculiar," "scatter-brained," "neurotic," "psychotic," and "has . . . a persecution complex." None of these remarks appears to have had any medical or psychiatric basis. Other files included remarks about the subject's drinking, aggressiveness, ethics, associations, health, hobbies, and activities. To what extent conscious or unconscious ethnic, racial, and religious prejudices, let alone personal antagonisms, shape the tone and content of these reports is impossible to determine.

In defense of the bureaus, it probably is true that in many cases they seek sensitive information only because their clients request it. Retail Credit Company found itself in hot water with Senator Russell Long for investigating an aide who was instrumental in drafting legislation to lower the price of prescription drugs sold in connection with government contracts. The work was done on behalf of American Home Products Corporation, a leader in the prescription drug field, apparently in the belief that the client was considering the subject for employment.[63] Similarly, life insurance companies use the bureaus to ferret out information thought helpful in evaluating how hazardous a life an applicant leads. This supposedly justifies inquiries into the customer's vocational duties, his finances, health, use of alcohol, mode of living, sporting activities, and sexual capers— both "natural" and "unnatural." But even trying to be as charitable as possible, if the episodes recounted before Congress are any indication of the care being exercised by credit bureau investigators, or of their concern for privacy, a substantial mass of dangerous information clearly has been gathered and put into circulation.

Consider, for example, an actual bonding report prepared by the Retail Credit Company that was submitted to the House Subcommittee on Invasion of Privacy. The subject of the report, a retired army lieutenant colonel, was described as "a rather wild-tempered, unreasonable, and uncouth person who abused his rank and wasn't considered a well-adjusted person. He was known to roam the reservation at Ft. Hood and shoot cattle belonging to ranchers who had leased the grazing land from the Army." Reports of this kind, filled with unverified conclusions and epithets based on interviews with people who usually remain unidentified, apparently are quite common[64] and certainly have resulted in injury to some people. How many is unknown since the file subject almost never knows that these comments have been made, recorded, and disseminated.

In contrast to the retail credit bureaus, the so-called commercial credit organizations—companies primarily designed to serve credit grantors (most typically banks)[65]—claim to limit themselves to "hard" financial data that are not sensitive and more likely to be accurate.[66] But there is evidence that many commercial credit bureaus have been remiss in limiting access to their files. As part of a television report,[67] CBS News staff members created a fictitious "systems" company, which sought information on individuals from twenty commercial credit bureaus in various parts of the country. The CBS company's letter simply indicated that it was interested in extending credit to a particular person residing in the area covered by the bureau. Despite the vigorous assertions by a high official of Associated Credit Bureaus of America (ACB), a nationwide organization of independent credit bureaus, that it was "impossible" to secure a report from an ACB member bureau unless the requesting party was a "bona fide creditor," the nonexistent CBS company apparently received, "without further question," full reports from one-half of the bureaus.[68]

The experiment was repeated following the adoption of "Credit Bureau Guidelines To Protect Consumer Privacy" by ACB. These require the signing of a contract in which the client certifies that inquiries will be made only for credit-granting purposes.[69] To make compliance with the second group of requests even more unlikely, the CBS letter did not indicate that the information would be used for credit-granting purposes and credit reports were sought on people who had complained to congressional investigators about their credit problems. Nonetheless, seven out of twenty-eight of the selected bureaus provided the information without hesitation.[70]

In each sample group, some of the bureaus replied that they would furnish the information requested only if the systems company signed a contract with them. In one case the fictitious company did so and the information was immediately forthcoming, even though a modest investigation by the bureau would have revealed that the request did not come from a bona fide credit grantor. As CBS commentator Mike Wallace remarked: "[S]igning a written contract is not much of a safeguard; all the client has to do is lie."[71]

But the threat to the individual posed by credit bureaus runs deeper. Even if bureaus limited themselves to providing financial information to clients who have a genuine commercial need for a profile of consumers and refrained from supplying derogatory or innuendo-filled tidbits, the problem remains of how to insure the accuracy of the reports that are given out. An erroneous entry or confusion in the identity of the person on whom information is sought can have a devastating effect on his ability to find employment, obtain insurance, or purchase a home. Moreover, even technically accurate but unexplained items may be extremely misleading. A simple notation labeling a customer as "slow-pay," for example, can do great damage, yet it may conceal an honest dispute in which the customer withheld payment because be believed that the goods or services he bargained for were not tendered in an acceptable condition. This is not just an abstract possibility. As Professor Alan Westin has wisely observed:

> [W]hat may often happen, especially when hot words may be exchanged between the . . . dealer and the consumer, is that the seller may report this as simply nonpayment or slow payment. He may even take a certain amount of relish in the fact that the obnoxious lady on the telephone . . . is being fixed in the credit record. . . . It is an anonymous treatment, because the reporter of the information is never accountable for it.[72]

Once an error or a misleading entry finds its way into a file, it may be virtually impossible to get it corrected; most bureaus have never allowed an individual to see his file.[73] To make things more difficult, some companies prohibit clients from telling anyone that a credit report has been prepared.[74]

When their practices are challenged, the bureaus argue that they really benefit the average citizen and cloak themselves in the mantle of public service. The following is typical: "Some people mistakenly feel that the purpose of the credit bureau is to prevent individuals and families from obtaining credit. . . On the contrary, the credit bureau, by providing factual information promptly and efficiently to credit grantors helps more people obtain more goods and services on credit."[75] But despite this claim, there are pragmatic, balance sheet counterpressures against the bureau leaning over backwards in favor of the individual. As one bureau official is reported to have said: "If everybody comes out white, the clients don't need us."[76] It is true that a credit bureau desiring to maintain a reputation for accuracy will take measures to insure that its reports are entirely truthful; but since a bureau's mistakes will be discovered only if credit, employment, or insurance is offered and the subject subsequently proves to be a deadbeat or otherwise undesirable, the pressure may be toward supplying negative information.

And what about the rights of those who are not seeking the benefits of the credit economy? Organizations such as Dun & Bradstreet prepare reports on people at the request of their subscribers even if the individual has not applied for credit, insurance, or a job. Some corporate officials seem to take great pleasure in amassing reports on neighbors and associates, even though their firm has no business reason for doing so. Surely this cannot be justified in terms of any supposed benefit to the individual, and practices of this type should be eliminated.

The position of the individual is worsened by the changing character of the credit bureau industry. In their formative years, bureaus were relatively modest in size and operated within limited geographic areas. A peripatetic person might well escape his past record; even a sedentary citizen had a good chance to learn of and correct inaccurate entries by dealing directly with a local bureau. However, local credit bureaus, especially those using a manual file system, are likely to be relatively inefficient operations that will prove increasingly incapable of storing, updating, retrieving, and transferring the information necessary to keep pace with a mobile population in a credit economy. Looking back twenty years hence, today's credit information industry may appear as primitive to a chronicler of that generation as the Druid calendar at Stonehenge is to the present-day astronomer.

As computerization permeates the commercial world, the institution of monetary exchange may well atrophy. To base a high-speed economy on a cumbersome system that involves the laborious writing of checks or the physical transfer of currency that can be lost or stolen makes little sense in the age of the computer. Americans write sixty million checks and uncounted charge slips every day. It costs the financial community millions of dollars and incalculable effort each year to process these outmoded documents. Somewhere in the future is a checkless, cashless society in which all purchases will be made with a universal credit card. Each transaction will be electronically recorded in a computer network that will maintain a running account of everyone's financial activities and will provide a ready appraisal of his economic state of affairs. An individual's income and expenses will continue to battle to outdo each other, but this time in the core of a computer. And hard times are ahead for the tax dodger since the government will simply electronically skim its share off the top of each citizen's computerized account.

How will today's credit bureaus fit into this electronically configured commercial environment? Since the basic stock in trade of credit bureaus is the acquisition of large quantities of individualized data that can be manipulated and made rapidly available over large distances, an alliance between the computer and a high-speed transmission medium is the ideal method of improving the existing system. It is not surprising, therefore, that a number of bureaus have begun to use the new technology for precisely these purposes.

As early as 1965, Credit Data Corporation, now part of TRW, Inc., an aggressive and diversified electronics firm, opened a computerized credit information system in California. In 1967 the company linked its Los Angeles and San Francisco offices to provide a statewide computer credit network. During the same year, Credit Data opened a computerized center in New York City. Since then centers have been opened in Buffalo, Syracuse, and Detroit; a Chicago office probably will be operating by the time this book is in print.[77] TRW Credit Data responds to telephone inquiries from subscribers—typically credit grantors—by reading a printout of the potential borrower's computerized record to the caller. The response time averages two minutes.[78]

At present, the company serves lenders in a geographic area containing over fifty million people. As of 1968 it had computerized credit information on well over twenty million Americans (the current figure must be much higher) and claimed to be adding new files on approximately fifty thousand Americans each week.[79] Of some interest is the fact that the company's original data base was secured by convincing several California banks to turn over their stockpile of credit information; Bank of America alone supplied eight million items.[80]

It seems obvious that TRW Credit Data will continue to develop regional information nodes that eventually will be interconnected by wire or microwave relay to establish a national credit information network. Large users of TRW Credit Data's services will be provided with remote-access terminals that will permit direct entry into the company's computerized files. This should greatly reduce both the cost and the time of having telephone operators process individual inquiries. It also means that a request for information made at any point in the system will provide access to data maintained anywhere in the network. Fortunately, ever since embarking on its computerization program, TRW Credit Data's activities and the attitudes of its top personnel have shown a sensitivity to privacy considerations.

ACB also has been working on computerization since 1965, when research began on a real-time[81] computer system for member credit bureaus. The ACB system has been installed in Dallas and Houston, and another operation exists in Chicago. Of particular interest is the enormous information potential of any ACB network that might emerge. There are more than two thousand credit bureaus in the association, serving three hundred and sixty-five thousand credit grantors and maintaining files on approximately one hundred million Americans.[82]

In 1968, a new dimension was added when ACB announced that it had signed an agreement with International Telephone and Telegraph Corporation. The ACB/IT&T objective is to offer local credit bureaus a packaged system, thereby relieving them of the heavy financial burden of buying or leasing computer equipment and developing their own data-processing capability.[83] At the moment, only computerization by individual bureaus within the association is contemplated. However, given the resources and transmission capabilities of IT&T, the raw data available in the files of the more than two thousand members of ACB, and the seemingly inexorable march of computer technology in terms of increased speed and storage capacity, the long-range networking implications of the ACB/IT&T operation are obvious.

The trend is toward fully computerized credit bureau networks capable of maintaining an electronic file on every economically viable American. We already possess the devices needed to link decentralized information nodes by microwave relay, standard telephone communications lines, lasers, or satellites. Inevitably, an extraordinarily complex financial data system will emerge, roughly analogous to our present telephone network, whose total data base could be made available to a subscriber wherever he may be. Thus the economic life of someone shopping for the first time in Macy's, Marshall Field's, or Magnin's could be transmitted to a computer terminal operated by the store's credit clerk almost instantaneously over a national (or global) credit information network. And in a checkless, cashless society, the system theoretically will embrace all—from the teenager spending his allowance on mod clothes to the sugar daddy on a shopping spree in Tiffany's and Bergdorf's.

The scope and size of these futuristic credit networks suggest that only a few large companies will command the necessary financial resources, data bases, and technical expertise to survive in the sophisticated, nationwide, credit information market of the future. Sheer "bigness" might not be perilous if it were contained entirely within the credit bureau industry. But hearings before the Senate Subcommittee on Monopoly and Antitrust revealed that firms in other industries may extend their operations into what is coming to be referred to as the consumer reporting market.[84] If this comes to pass, it might result in an unhealthy level of business concentration. There is a natural and close affinity between those who own the raw information about people and those who control the technology needed to manipulate and disseminate that information. Even today, when we are at a comparatively embryonic point in the computerization of credit bureaus, the two forces appear to have entered each other's magnetic field. The working relationship between IT&T, a communications company, and ACB, a credit bureau association, as well as the acquisition of Credit Data Corporation by TRW are cases in point.

The spate of corporate marriages between computer/communications companies and book publishers in the latter half of the sixties illustrates the way in which fully integrated information systems can develop. The publishers, through their vast array of author-publisher contracts and proliferating library of copyrighted works, control the raw material (the nation's literature), and the computer/communications companies control some of the media for disseminating that raw material to the public. Of course, the analogy is not perfect. But if a small number of credit networks did secure control over the information sources for consumer reporting, their special relationship with the credit grantors (the Credit Data/California banks experience), might produce a limited number of organizations whose size and stranglehold on data would give them an unhealthy position of dominance. The ramifications of cooperative action between the credit bureaus and the communications companies (the ACB/IT&T example) are equally striking.

Therefore, close attention must be paid to the future relationships among the credit bureaus, the common carriers who will be called upon to transmit the data, the computer manufacturers and systems companies who will prepare the hardware and software to enable the consumer reporting networks to function, and the credit granting agencies who will be the primary users of the information. Of course, the centralization of power in a few national credit networks, and perhaps even a modicum of integration among the four industries associated with the movement of credit information would be beneficial if economies of scale resulted and were passed on to network customers. But the possibility of reduced competition and concentration of power does suggest that Congress and the Justice Department are obliged to insure that the benefits of an oligopolistic industry structure are passed on to the users and not exploited merely to produce increased profit levels for the surviving companies.

In addition to economic concentration, a computerized credit bureau industry may have the undesirable effect of dehumanizing the decision-making processes of banks and merchants because it will reduce the number of sources that can be tapped for guidance and might encourage greater reliance on the data supplied by a bureau. Decision-making might then begin to follow a common pattern, which would eliminate the competition among financial institutions and make the borrower a prisoner of his credit bureau file. In addition, the independence of a bank's or merchant's judgment might be reduced even further if bureaus acted as information evaluators, rather than as passive data distillers or conduits—a change in role that may come to pass as consumers and the data about them increase and money lenders are obliged to abdicate to the "expertise" of the information specialists.

This possibility becomes even more likely as the network is pressured into seeking uniformity in the information collected and the manner in which it is evaluated, recorded, and reported. Some standardization will be necessary to insure that the computer language and format employed by individual bureaus is compatible with the equipment used by other network members. Otherwise, information could not be transmitted freely throughout the system, just as the movement of railroad cars was restricted during that industry's formative years because many companies used incompatible track gauges. An agreement to collect only certain types of information, although defensible in terms of economy and the technical requirements of a computer system, has the same anti-competitive tendencies as an industry or association understanding that only certain products or goods with specified characteristics will be manufactured—a practice whose legality is doubtful under several Supreme Court decisions.[85]

Another trend that will have considerable long-range impact on credit bureaus is the increasing involvement of the banking industry in fields that depend on computer technology and individualized information. Banks were among the first institutions to computerize financial data as a means of expediting paperwork, and the string of machine-readable numbers at the bottom of checks now is commonplace. Computers also have enabled banks to expedite a wider variety of customer services—payroll computations, accounting, trust management, mortgage servicing, and miscellaneous types of data-processing.[86] The universal credit cards—Mastercharge and Bankamericard—so enthusiastically hawked by some of the major banking institutions would never have been possible without computers, although sometimes the human element is sorely missed. Recently a prominent Michigan department store issued a credit card to a pet Dalmatian. The dog's owner, to express his disapproval of the unsolicited application, had filled it out in a name that obviously was an animal's, listed no assets, and gave the applicant's occupation as "watchdog."

The increasing acceptance of these cards has enormous significance; it may herald the first stage of the checkless, cashless society[87] in which the credit-granting and credit-rating industries might cease to exist as separate entities.[88] In the future, every type of credit decision may be made by the computer on the basis of the current status of the customer's account and his past performance as recorded on the magnetic tapes of a computerized "National Finance Center" operated by the card system. If the transaction is approved, the agreed upon payments would automatically be deducted from the purchaser's electronic balance and transferred to the bank. Should this come to pass, the accuracy of the records and the integrity of those who handle them will be matters of overwhelming importance to the individual's purchasing power.

Thus, computerization, networking, and reduced competition are bound to mire the credit information industry even more deeply in the morass of the privacy problem. As has been shown in the case of the federal government, the capabilities of the new technology will encourage credit bureaus to acquire more information of a sensitive nature about individual and institutional borrowers than they have in the past. Concomitantly, given the massive investment required to computerize a large credit data base and a bureau's ability to use the technology to manipulate information in unique ways, the temptation to use the data for non-credit-granting purposes will be difficult to resist.

The result may be that numerous reporting services currently performed by a large number of independent companies and investigators someday may be provided by a few unregulated conglomerates having unbridled power to vend their vast information store without regard to the purposes to which it will be put. Thus, there is a risk that enormous quantities of financial and surveillance data garnered from a variety of sources will be made available to anyone who wishes to reconstruct an individual's associations, movements, habits, and life style.[89] We are only beginning to perceive the intrusive uses to which data bases of this type may be put.

Dossier-type data on a substantial group of people can be used for a number of commercial purposes, such as generating a list of consumers with certain characteristics who might be interested in a particular product. According to one commentator, *Reader's Digest* used computer technology to generate a mailing list consisting of its subscribers' neighbors, a tactic that proved surprisingly effective. "The approach had a kind of 'All the neighbors are doing it' quality, but more significantly, the individual was pleased that the *Reader's Digest* knew him as an individual and could relate him to two others on his block."[90] In addition, bureaus have been used to rate the creditworthiness of likely prospects for a promotion campaign centered around the distribution of unsolicited credit cards.[91] Also providing food for thought is the widely publicized accusation against several New York bookstores that allegedly were selling lists of the names and addresses of women who had subscribed to computerized dating services.[92]

Because the new technology makes it possible to integrate personal information from a variety of sources, solicitation lists increasingly will become the product of wide ranging file investigations into the backgrounds and finances of prospective customers. In late 1969, my good friend Paul G. Zurkowski, Executive Director of the Information Industry Association of America —and many other people in the Washington area—received an invitation to a presentation designed to convince him to join in a commercial venture. Part of the come-on, with names and addresses changed here to protect the privacy of the other people referred to, went as follows:

Dear Mr. Zurkowski:

I'm amazed at the number of my friends who have dramatically increased their incomes in just the past few months! John and Joanna Q. Public of 325 Orchard Way in Suburbia tell me their August income in a new business venture they created from what had been a part-time job was $2050. That's a big jump from John's previous $1380/mo. at NASA.

Bob Babbitt of 225 Main Street in Anytown quit managing

a fleet of trucks for Icicle Ice Company in December 1968 to start his own business. By August of '69 he had reached a monthly income of $3750.

Three years ago you and Mrs. Zurkowski bought your present home. The Publics and the Babbitts were home-owners too. It was when their ownership responsibilities caused money problems, that they sought a way to make more.

Most [people] started out with no more money than the few hundred dollars you have in the bank right now. Few of them had two cars like the Zurkowskis do. Usually they had a car less desirable than your '67, or no car at all, when they decided to "rise above it."

. . . .

However, after making a careful household-by-household study of Washington residents with incomes in the critical $12,500 to $19,500 range, I have selected you and Mrs. Zurkowski as possibly being among the few who will take positive action if given the opportunity.

. . . .

I look forward to telling you how I've doubled my income since retiring from the Air Force (full colonel) in July.

                                        Sincerely,

The letter's content makes it clear that the writer purused a number of sources to determine the Zurkowskis' status as home owners and a two-car family, as well as their bank balance and income range.

This letter is but one by-product of the countless computerized lists that are now commercially available in the United States and which conservatively are estimated to contain over five hundred million names. As an official of the Direct Mail Advertising Association depressingly put it: "People's names get on lists because people exist." In most cases we have been put on lists as a result of innocent activities.

If you buy a car or boat, subscribe to a publication, give to a charity, attend a convention, have a telephone or charge account, belong to a club or church, buy a house or rent an apartment, or even send in a cereal coupon you will probably be added to somebody's list.

Donors to the Catholic Missionary Society (USA) not only contributed cash but their names—114,000 contributors are now on a list for rent by Dunhill International List Co. for $22.50 per 1,000 names.

The New York-based firm also offers lists of over 500,000 Republican and Democratic contributors, 93,000 doctors who attend conventions and even 28,000 supporters of anti-Vietnam War appeals (all for $22.50 per).[93]

Few of us realize that many of the organizations and people we associate with are vending information about us behind our backs. Again the Direct Mail Advertising Association executive: "Only hermits could avoid getting on lists but then they'd probably get on somebody's list of hermits."

In many instances computerized lists are provided by sources one would think should exercise greater restraint. For example, the fact that the Zurkowskis owned two cars undoubtedly was gleaned from a list of car owners vended by the Motor Vehicle Bureau where the cars were registered. Many states have been doing precisely that for thirty years and in many cases the purchaser is R. L. Polk Company, a specialist in city directories and "in depth" mail-order lists. On occasion, the federal government has been an offender. The Federal Aviation Administration, for example, sells the names and addresses of more than 650,000 pilots and airmen for approximately $200. There is also considerable evidence that lists find their way into the hands of junk mailers and phone solicitors as a result of industrial espionage.

The situation is going to become worse as computerization increases and more people realize the market potential for selling their neighbors' names. The Internal Revenue Service has begun to sell aggregate income statistics about taxpayers broken down by Zip Code number. Data of this type have considerable value to mailers because they will enable them to select high-income communities as primary advertising targets. Early purchasers include two national magazines (*Look* and *Time*), two mail-order houses (Spiegel and Sears Roebuck), and several mailing list companies (including Names Unlimited, American Mail Associates, and R. L. Polk).

The expenditure of energy in this fashion is encouraged by the existence of a vast, readily accessible market. Employers, insurance companies, detective agencies, political operatives, and government investigators all have occasion to make extensive credit bureau inquiries concerning a wide spectrum of individuals.[94] As has been suggested, not completely in jest: "It must be assumed the nation's credit bureaus are ethical and doing a good job. Otherwise government investigators and local police departments would not be using the bureaus' files as much as they do."[95]

Some credit bureaus open their files to law enforcement agencies and other governmental officials without charge or protest,[96] possibly in the hope of currying favor or obtaining reciprocal treatment.[97] The FBI alone obtains approximately twenty-five thousand credit reports every year. Even if the credit bureau refuses, the file still may be vulnerable to a subpoena,[98] which is readily issued and rarely resisted even though the legal obligations of a credit bureau to grant the government access to its files have not yet been fully defined. TRW Credit Data seems to be the only major credit information company that has made a policy of challenging the government's right of access to their files, thus far without success.[99]

The possible abuses of a computerized consumer information network are not the only aspects of credit bureau activities that deserve attention. At present, ACB members offer their clients a "watch service," which involves monitoring the public records and an individual's financial transactions after he has been extended credit, in order to inform the lender promptly if there is any indication that the customer will be unable to meet his obligation[100]—an obvious form of surveillance no matter how saccharine a euphemism ACB uses to describe it.

These practices can be far from benign. While this book was being prepared for publication, a close personal and professional associate of mine reported the following incident. He and his then wife are both attorneys, extraordinarily competent in their fields, and economically self-sufficient. Unfortunately, their marriage proved unsuccessful. Divorce papers were filed and the husband moved from the family house to an apartment. Within days after the institution of the divorce proceeding at the local court—a time when the emotional distress caused by the situation was at a very high level—the wife received an early-morning telephone call from some functionary at a credit-granting agency who announced that he had heard that she was experiencing "marital difficulties" and proceeded to attempt to question her about the situation. Although she was a veteran of many a courtroom battle, this intrusion distressed her and resulted in a considerable amount of totally unnecessary emotional pain. I recount this tale simply to illustrate one potentially deleterious side effect of a "watch service"—whether it was the ACB's in this case or the brainchild of the particular credit grantor is immaterial. Although removing court records from public view is too drastic a cure for these practices, surely some restraint must be imposed on those who profit by scavenging through these files.

The credit bureau's control over an individual's financial history also provides considerable leverage for collecting debts that otherwise might be written off by the credit grantor. ACB members supply economic data to collection agencies and in some cases act in that capacity themselves. In the course of "counseling" the consumer on his credit problems, bureaus and collection agencies often are able to "convince" individuals to "rehabilitate their credit by paying off delinquent accounts," some of which, the ACB boasts, are over ten years old.[101] This practice, if not accompanied by undue coercion, obviously is essential for the enforcement of credit obligations. But it illustrates the enormous *in terrorem* caliber of a permanent credit bureau file and graphically demonstrates its ability to outlive the law's limitation on the right to sue to collect an ancient debt. It also indicates a possible conflict of interest on the part of the bureaus who in effect receive two fees from the same transaction—a fee for preparing the report and another fee if credit is extended and their debt collection services are then needed. Once the duality of these activities is realized, substantial doubt is cast on any claim the bureaus may make of protecting debt addicts against their own indiscretions.

Finally, it has been suggested by Congressman Gallagher that the ownership of Welcome Newcomer by ACB has potentially sinister privacy implications.[102] An executive of a telephone solicitation firm goes further and charges that all organizations that greet new residents

> are just little spy organizations. They walk into a woman's house with free toothbrushes and walk out knowing everything about the family. All that information is then pub-

lished and sold to local merchants. It's worse than a fraud, because the hostesses come to new families on the pretense of being friends and welcoming you into the neighborhood. I have seen the lists; they make juicy reading. . . . Mrs. Jones needs drapes, etc.[103]

If we must be alert to the possibility that the welcoming committee sponsored by the local merchants is really a cloak-and-dagger group designed to snoop and report on the characteristics and status of new members of the community, can societal paranoia be far behind?

In view of the past abuses and negligent practices of some members of the consumer information fraternity, as well as the irreversible trend toward computerization and the possibility of economic concentration, one would assume that credit bureaus are subject to extensive regulation, as are most of the other members of the financial community. In reality, the credit reporting industry has been surprisingly free of regulation. Congressman Gallagher commented on this state of affairs during his subcommittee's hearings in the following terms:

> In every State and every township in the country there are regulations concerning the transfer of ownership of dogs . . . yet there are really no regulations whatsoever pertaining to the transfer of this kind of information affecting a man's standing in the community, his dignity, his economic transactions, his private life, his very name itself. . . .
>
> An individual American certainly has far less [sic] rights under this system than a dog has.[104]

The risks of this lack of regulation were brought home to people in the Boston area in 1969 when the files of three million people held by a bankrupt credit bureau were put up for auction. A bureau official reportedly remarked to a potential customer: "Wouldn't you like to be a blackmailer and have access to these files?"[105]

Since 1967, subcommittees in both houses of Congress have conducted a series of probing hearings and have focused the nation's attention on the threat to personal privacy presented by certain credit bureau activities. As these hearings progressed, the need for properly delineating sources of information and standards of relevance as well as imposing mechanical and procedural limitations on access to the files was established. The objective of any possible governmental intervention is a theoretically noncontroversial one. An individual whose credit is checked when he purchases a television set should be assured that a neighbor's vindictive and unsubstantiated gossip marking him as "psychotic" or "neurotic" will not be preserved and passed on to potential employers or insurance companies or others who might be in a position to affect his future.

The first formal legislative proposal was initiated in the spring of 1969 by Senator Proxmire of Wisconsin.[106] In testimony before the Senate Subcommittee on Financial Institutions, I said that the most attractive features of the bill were that it would require

> 1) credit bureaus to employ effective procedures for guaranteeing the confidentiality of the information they collect; 2) credit information to be withheld from noncreditors, such as governmental investigatory agencies, without the express consent of the person involved; 3) that an individual be given an opportunity to correct inaccurate information in his credit record and be notified when a derogatory public record item is entered in his credit record; 4) the development of procedures for discarding irrelevant and ossified information in an individual's credit file, and 5) that users of credit reports notify an individual when he has been adversely affected by a report and identify the agency that made the report.[107]

Later the same year, in an uncharacteristic display of togetherness, the United States Senate unanimously passed what has come to be called the Fair Credit Reporting Act.

But, to parody the title of a hit Broadway show and film: "A Funny Thing Happened on the Way to the Senate Floor." The original Proxmire bill had been butchered; it was drawn and quartered and its vitals were left on the Committee's chopping block. How that came to pass is no mystery. Industry lobbyists and bank-oriented senators engaged in the dissection, while advocates of consumer protection quietly relied on the legislative process to produce a bill that would respond to the needs of the public.

The preamble of the Senate bill stated that it was: "AN ACT, to enable consumers to protect themselves against arbitrary, erroneous, and malicious credit information." Those high-sounding words ring hollow when it is realized that: 1) the bill defined the permissible purposes of consumer reports so broadly that market researchers, detective agencies, lawyers, and various investigative groups might be permitted access to credit bureau files; 2) it authorized the retention of arrest records for seven years, regardless of how minor the charge or whether it was dismissed or the file subject acquitted; 3) the bill did not impose any clear obligations on credit bureaus to preserve confidentiality or maintain accurate and current records; 4) wherever the Senate proposal afforded the citizen a modicum of access to the files or a right to know how information about him was being used, it was done in the most grudging fashion and required that the subject be able to navigate through some unnecessary procedural obstacles that would prove insurmountable barriers for the poor and the unsophisticated; 5) the provisions dealing with correcting inaccurate entries were inadequate, in part because they failed to guarantee that everyone who has received erroneous data about an individual is informed of the mistake; and 6) two provisions of the bill effectively *immunized* credit bureaus from any liability for their negligent reporting of erroneous information or their negligent noncompliance with the Act. It would be more accurate if the preamble of the Senate bill read: "AN ACT to protect credit bureaus against citizens who have been abused by erroneous credit and investigative information."

When the Fair Credit Reporting Act reached the House of Representatives, it was referred to the Subcommittee on Consumer Affairs, chaired by Congresswoman Leonor K. Sullivan of Missouri, a long-time friend of consumer protection and a veteran of the struggle over the truth in lending legislation. She reacted to the Senate's work by interposing an excellently drafted and structured new bill that represented an expansion on the best features of the original Proxmire bill.[108]

Perhaps the most salient feature of Mrs. Sullivan's bill was its recognition that information handlers have excluded individuals from transactions involving information relating to them. By assuring the individual of access to his credit file and notification whenever decisions adverse to him were made on the basis of its contents, the proposal would have enabled people to have a degree of control over the flow of information about them. If an individual felt aggrieved by any of the information in his file, procedures were made available for seeking correction and resolving disputes with the bureau. The proposal also imposed limitations on the development and use of reports based on field investigations into a person's character and reputation.

The Sullivan bill remained bottled up in subcommittee and it began to look as if no action would be taken on credit reporting during the 91st Congress. Then, in the waning days of the session, Senator Proxmire attached his Senate-passed version of the Act as a rider to a totally unrelated banking bill that had already passed both houses of Congress and had reached the conference committee stage. This twelfth-hour maneuver to circumvent the usual House of Representatives procedures resulted in a compromise between the Proxmire and the Sullivan bills, but one weighted in favor of the former. As the final proofs of this book were being returned to the printer, the Fair Credit Reporting Act cleared the final legislative hurdles and was signed into law.

The statute gives a person a right of access to his file, assures him of notice when decisions adverse to him are made on the basis of a credit report, and places some restraints on investigative reporting. But when one thinks of the vitally important issues raised by consumer reporting in the computer age—such as defining who should have access to an individual's file, prescribing the length of time certain dangerous material should be retained, and determining the proper scope of investigative information gathering—it becomes clear that the Fair Credit Reporting Act simply does not provide us with adequate protection against possible misuse of the credit network of the future. Following a pattern that has many antecedents, the Congress simply avoided coming to grips with the difficult issues in order to get something on the books for "the people" before taking off on the campaign trail.

One interesting by-product of Congress' activity is that a number of state legislatures have begun to scrutinize the credit industry with an eye toward regulation along lines similar to the federal proposals.[109] California, Massachusetts, and New York have already enacted statutes of varying degrees of effectiveness.[110] Another result is that ACB, taking the hint provided by several congressmen during the hearings and in the hope of avoiding the imposition of harsh legislative restraints, developed a series of "Guidelines," referred to earlier,[111] to protect consumer privacy. Although they do provide some safeguards, the Guidelines were composed by an industry group that had only minimal consumer representation, they are not binding upon anyone—most notably the numerous bureaus unaffiliated with ACB—and they are bountifully endowed with loopholes. For example, the Guidelines authorize the bureaus to collect matters of public record—bankruptcies, lawsuits, arrests, indictment or conviction of crime—but they are obliged only to "make a *reasonable* effort" to learn and report the disposition of these items.[112] ACB also seeks to absolve its members by putting the onus on the credit grantor to "inquire further as to the . . . disposition of any items of significance to his credit decision, or authorize the bureau to do so,"[113] and by requiring the complaining consumer to sign "a statement granting immunity from legal action both to the credit bureau and to its sources of information."[114] Even with these reservations, ACB should be commended for attempting to focus its members' attention on the privacy issue; unfortunately, the first test under the Guidelines—administered in the form of the CBS News experiment—produced failing grades for a number of members. Therefore the legislative rod was still needed to aid the ACB minions with their lessons.

Despite the concern I have expressed about a computerized consumer reporting industry, the desirability of employing the new technology cannot be doubted. Although concentration of power and reduced competition within the credit, computer, and communications industries pose threats, reasonable risks must be taken if we are to achieve a streamlined commercial exchange system. But the benefits of computerization need not be paid for with our personal freedom. It may be hoped that a balance will be struck between exploiting the new technologies in order to secure enough accurate financial data to maintain the flow of credit and to safeguard the fundamental right of a citizen to be secure against invasions of his informational profile. There is every reason to believe that a properly constructed and managed computerized credit data network, along lines that will be discussed in a later chapter,[115] will protect the individual more effectively than the existing manual information systems.

3. Measuring Your I.Q., Ability, and Personality by Computer—The Testing Game

The average American adult under thirty years of age does not need to be told how important tests are in his life. If he grew up in the New York City school system . . . he was given a minimum of nineteen different standardized tests between grades one and nine—at least one test each year. After that he took New York State Regents Examinations, the Preliminary Scholastic Aptitude Tests, the Scholastic Aptitude Tests, and if he desired to go further, Graduate Records, or Law School, Medical School or Business School Boards. In between he may have taken a Civil Service Test to get a summer job. If he went into business he may have faced one of the personality tests given by many companies to aspiring young executives—and perhaps profited from the advice on "How to Cheat on Personality Tests" given in the appendix to William Whyte's *The Organization Man.*

> —Note, "Legal Implications of the
> Use of Standardized Ability Tests
> in Employment and Education," 68
> *Columbia Law Review* (1968), 691

Resort to aptitude, intelligence, and psychological testing has become a popular—and often a Pavlovian—response to the mind-bending pressures modern society's feverish pace imposes on institutional decision makers.[116] The use of tests, both by the government and the private sector, has become pervasive—perhaps as many as a quarter of a billion examinations a year in the United States alone. Various tests are administered to such diverse groups as Peace Corps volunteers, grade-school children, postal employees, and bright young lawyers seeking association with a prominent Milwaukee law firm. Testing might have become even more common by now if the 1960's had not been a period of relatively high employment with many companies experiencing difficulty in obtaining sufficient numbers of skilled workers, which made testing unnecessary as a screening technique.

Because of the intensely personal nature of many aptitude, intelligence, and psychological tests, the entire subject is in the vortex of the current debate over the right of a citizen to be free from intrusion by any form of physical, mental, or informational surveillance. Indeed, the close association between testing and the frightening mystique surrounding thought control, narco-analysis, extrasensory phenomena, *1984,* and the image of Big

Brother has heightened the public's concern over an activity that often is pejoratively characterized as "brainwashing."[117]

"Scientific" human evaluation is a relatively young art. Ability and psychological testing was first attempted approximately a century ago by Sir Francis Galton, who tried to quantify intellectual ability on the basis of individual physical reaction time. In France, at the turn of the century, Alfred Binet and Theodore Simon followed a somewhat different research pattern and attempted to measure an individual's intelligence by comparing his test score with a scale developed by sampling a cross-section of the population. A 1916 American revision of their work resulted in the now famous Stanford-Binet standardized intelligence test. The field received its greatest boosts from the varied group testing programs developed by the military during the First and Second World Wars. Today, human measurement takes many diverse and highly sophisticated forms. Tests range from the relatively simple pre-induction intelligence test given by the armed services to the elaborate Minnesota Multiphasic Personality Inventory (a somewhat Kafkaesque test that compares the subject with a composite profile of eight hundred psychiatric patients), thematic apperception tests (which purport to evaluate numerous subjective aspects of an individual's personality), and the controversial polygraph examination (lie-detector test), which has been used with great fanfare but only mixed results.

This proliferation has not been without controversy. Despite the extensive use of tests, many of them have been characterized as inherently unreliable by some commentators and rejected as a form of modern alchemy by others. The professional literature reveals a startling lack of agreement on the efficacy of a number of tests, although in fairness to the psychology fraternity at least some of the criticism simply may reflect professional jealousy or commercial competition among hawkers of different tests.

Until recent years, the professional debate has focused on the question of a given test's effectiveness in measuring the skills for a particular job or the intellectual gifts and educational achievement of the subject. All too often the question of the desirability and implications of testing—matters of much greater societal significance—has gotten comparatively short shrift.

But there are signs of an awakening. In the past few years, one of the issues that has received considerable attention is whether testing discriminates against blacks and other disadvantaged groups.[118] Undoubtedly, most tests have been developed in terms of white norm groups that have different cultural backgrounds and have received better educational training during their formative years than nonwhite and economically deprived subpopulations. Thus, some have suggested that using these tests is unfair and circumvents the equal-opportunity provisions of the federal civil rights statutes enacted during the mid-sixties by operating as an access barrier to employment and educational opportunities.[119] Other writers have made similar points about the inhibiting effects of the common practice of whites administering tests to nonwhites.[120] Because of these concerns, a number of companies and universities either have stopped using or have downgraded the importance of certain well-established tests.

But the issue is even broader. Testing is not an arcane art practiced by a few academic experimenters. It is a fully matured and highly commercialized industry. Because test performance can have a profound effect on the course of an individual's life, continuous reappraisal of the field is essential. Unfortunately, there is ample evidence that many test developers and users display a lack of concern over the significance of the impact these tests may have on some people.

For a test to reflect an individual's capacity to accomplish a task, the subject's response pattern should correlate with that of a model worker whose actual performance is known and is deemed to be satisfactory. This demands a painstaking analysis of the skills and traits necessary for accomplishing the particular job as well as the framing of questions calculated to reveal whether the examinee's vocational and personality attributes match the profile of the hypothetical ideal worker.

The effort does not end when a test has been fabricated; validation is imperative. This entails an evaluation of each examinee's on-the-job performance, which theoretically would require that everyone who takes the test be hired to see if his actual work (good or bad) corresponds with what was projected by the test results. Appraisal of each individual's vocational performance must also take account of his working environment to see whether it is sufficiently favorable to permit him to utilize the skills and capacities measured by the test to the best of his ability. To do that effectively requires an analysis of so many subjective factors that it is often impossible to determine whether the test accurately reflects the examinee's skills.

Even though these requirements for developing an accurate test are well-known,[121] most vocational tests have not been constructed with a particular job in mind and have not been validated. Either out of slothfulness or a desire to economize, most business organizations and governmental agencies use mass-produced tests to screen applicants for a wide variety of jobs, some of which involve skills that have little or no similarity to those the examination was designed to measure. In many instances, the only effort that remotely resembles validation takes the form of one company's personnel director piggybacking on the practices of his counterpart in a competitor organization. But this often is done without investigating the basis for the other company's utilization of a particular test, which may simply result from the latter's parasitism. To make matters worse, a high percentage of tests are administered without professional assistance or evaluation. It is not surprising, therefore, that few companies have been able to demonstrate that their use of tests actually has improved the caliber of their employees.[122]

The sporadic controversies over the efficacy of particular efforts at evaluating human skills or personality have so occupied the attention of the testing community that it has spent precious little energy considering the privacy implications of its activities. The somewhat cavalier treatment accorded the privacy question is understandable with regard to most aptitude, intelligence, or achievement tests. Unlike the probing, subjective investigation that characterizes personality inventories, tests that attempt to measure certain relatively delineated human capacities, such as mathematical, verbal, and manual skills, generally have a very low level of intrusiveness. Moreover, the social justification for attempting to ascertain an individual's intelligence or aptitude is reasonably well established and there is widespread faith in the techniques since the results have generally proven valid in a variety of important contexts.

But the pervasiveness of achievement, aptitude, and intelligence tests and the heavy reliance placed on some of them (such as the Scholastic Aptitude Test), suggest privacy problems that are somewhat more subtle than those presented by situations involving blatantly intrusive interrogations. Many major corporations, various governmental organs, and institutions at all levels of education have accorded aptitude and intelligence tests a presumption of validity. In my profession, I have seen the Law School Aptitude Test score methodically relied upon by a law school deciding to whom it will give a professional education, by law professors in choosing research assistants and seminar students, and by law firms in selecting young associates from among each year's crop of graduates. Even Vice President Spiro Agnew apparently felt that publicly disclosing his I.Q. would add credibility to his pronouncements.

Thus, the need for safeguarding test data against inaccuracies, misuse, and improper dissemination is as important as protecting other types of personal information that we consider far more sensitive. In point of fact, the threat to the individual posed by the possibility of information misuse may well be even greater in the testing environment because of the illusion of "hardness" created by numerical test scores or percentile ratings, the need for professional interpretation of the results, and the highly controversial character of many of today's measuring rods. Nor can we ignore the psychological effect of repeated testing on an individual who is aware that the results are forming a permanent record that may have a substantial impact on his economic, educational, and social mobility. There is an obvious relationship between extensive testing and the feared development of a "record prison."[123] Also of concern is the possibility that repeated job testing may prove to be an alienating or frustrating experience, especially if the subject is not given any feedback in the form of an appraisal of his performance or a tangible payoff in terms of vocational advancement.

Tests seeking to evaluate emotional stability and personality traits, although more sparingly used than aptitude, intelligence, and achievement tests,[124] raise more serious privacy issues. Unlike the comparatively emotion-free responses called for by skill measuring tests, the product of a personality inventory typically is a series of verbal or sensory responses that are highly subjective in character and often reveal the innermost feelings of the person under examination. Let the questions speak for themselves; the following inquiries or variations on them are found on many widely used personality tests:

Have you ever engaged in sexual activities with another man or boy (asked of male subjects)?

When you were a youngster, did you engage in petty thievery?

Are you troubled by the idea that people on the street are watching you?

Do you think something is wrong with your sex organs?

Do you think that Jesus Christ was greater than Lincoln or Washington?

Once in a while do you think of things too bad to talk about?

Are you a special agent of God?

Moreover, in contrast to the relative ease of scaling I.Q. or aptitude-test responses, meaningful appraisal of personality test results requires analysis by a highly trained person. Even then the evaluation may be inaccurate or misleading because of the inherent unreliability or unsuitability of the test, the unrepresentative frame of mind or emotional state of the subject when taking the test, the physical environment in which the test was given, or the demeanor or attitude of the individual who administered it. For example, in one case described to a congressional committee, a female government employee was questioned for six hours "about every aspect of her sex life—real, imagined, and gossiped—with an intensity that could only have been the product of inordinately salacious minds."[125] One wonders whether such an interrogation could possibly yield an accurate index of the personality of the examinee.

Yet the actual utilization of psychological testing takes no cognizance of these important considerations or the dubious character of many currently fashionable tests. Wide-ranging and intrusive psychological inventories often are purchased in bulk from publishing companies for pennies a copy and administered indiscriminately to job applicants. In many cases this is done without expert advice concerning the test's suitability for measuring particular personality traits or for evaluating an individual's responses. The cut-out stencil score sheets furnished by many publishers simplify the effort and encourage total thoughtlessness on the part of the tester. As strange as it may sound, many personnel managers are purporting to pass on the level of an individual's "neuroticism," "alienation," "drive," and "stability," by a process that often is not appreciably more scientific than measuring the size and shape of the subject's head. As Martin L. Gross has indicated, we are passively watching business and government conduct a nationwide quest for the Square American; their divining rod is a selection of tests that more often than not merely reflect the biases of their creators, thereby perversely giving a premium to those examination subjects who know how to psych the psycher.[126]

The potential dangers to individual privacy from misuse of raw psychological test data are obvious. Disclosure of the individual's responses to sensitive questions or over-all scores might cause him acute embarrassment as well as professional and economic injury. Moreover, these items can easily be misconstrued since they have significance only to highly trained professionals. Even in the hands of competent personnel, individual responses are meaningful only when examined in the framework of the entire examination and in light of the purpose for which it was administered.

For similar reasons the analysis ultimately distilled from the raw data by a trained psychologist may be a threat to the individual if it is not handled with circumspection. The preservation and circulation of the evaluator's cryptic, but derogatory sounding, comments, such as "unstable," "deviant," or "unmotivated," can haunt the test subject throughout his life. There is the related danger that untrained management personnel may draw and publicize unwarranted inferences from a professional appraisal. This danger is heightened if the test report was prepared for extremely narrow purposes or only to be used by other professionals. Substantial additional prejudice could result from reliance on evaluations in contexts beyond those for which the test originally was administered or from their retention for such protracted periods that they no longer reflect the attitudes and emotional make-up of the subjects. These are not hypothetical risks, because most firms retain their employees' test records as part of their permanent files. In some ways, even retesting would be more sensible than relying on aged data.

Going beyond the threat to individual privacy, if psychological testing gains too prominent a position in the decision-making process, it may begin to create substantial risks to society at large. The primary virtue of personality tests supposedly lies in their ability to describe an individual's mental capacity and emotional balance or to predict his future behavior. Unless highly accurate, extensive reliance on these tests may lead to the stratification of groups according to their examination results as well as the erroneous allocation and utilization of human resources.[127] "It is possible, for example, that a child who does poorly on aptitude tests in the first and second grades will be given less attention by the teacher, or placed in a slower section for instructional purposes, and, as a result, may have a substantially lowered chance of performing well on a college entrance examination ten years later."[128]

We must bring an end to the growing practice of relying on test results as a crutch—a practice that encourages users to abdicate their responsibility to formulate an independent judgment about people. This is particularly deplorable in the case of employers who administer general-purpose examinations without the aid of professional guidance. Even when the services of a psychologist are retained, personnel men should not rely to the extent they do on many of today's personality inventories. "Analysts, of course, have just as much right to read between the lines as the next man. What makes their posture interesting is the claim that theirs is the scientific method."[129] One warning that must be etched on the mind of every decision maker in our midst is that the growing storehouse of testing data, much of which is nothing more than pseudo-psycho data, is not an end in itself; it simply is one tool among many to be employed in evaluating people or making decisions affecting their lives.

There is another facet to this problem. In many contexts, such as the census, we have decided that religion, sex, and political philosophy are private matters and any attempt to question an individual about them in other than a completely voluntary setting is considered an invasion of privacy. Why then do we permit psychological testers to interrogate on topics that others cannot touch? Let there be no mistake about my position on this subject. Psychological evaluation may be a valuable aide-de-camp for many purposes, especially in diagnosing and treating various mental disorders. But because of its propensity to extract highly personal information from people and encourage others to make decisions on the basis of data that are capable of interpretation only by specially trained professionals, without any real assurance that the resulting evaluations will be accurate, psychological testing requires special precautions. At the least, a higher level of justification or social utility should be demonstrated before tests are employed, and tests must be constructed that are less intrusive than those currently being used.

Even if evaluative techniques are developed that have scientific validity, restraint in the use of testing still is necessary. The elimination of economic waste in the allocation of the nation's human resources obviously is a goal of enormous social significance. But that does not mean we must pay any price to achieve it. It is hardly axiomatic that an individual's psyche should be subjected to examining, probing, sensing, measuring, computerizing, and (futuristically) readjusting in the name of putting him on the proper vocational or educational pathway.

The task of drawing a line between the proper and improper use of testing is not an easy one. Of course, when the safety or well-being of human beings depends upon the stability and judgment of one or a small group of men, it is appropriate to use an established and validated psychological test to provide some assurance that they have the necessary emotional qualities. For example, air traffic controllers, commercial pilots, and people with access to missiles or nuclear devices seem to occupy sufficiently critical posts to justify the use of psychological testing, even though it will subject them to searching personal questions and the creation of a test dossier that may later cause them damage. Indeed, there may be good reason to maintain a record of their periodic performance on these tests in order to see if there is any deterioration over time.

It would be highly desirable if a standard could be framed and enforced that takes account of society's need to measure the emotional stability of particular individuals, the security that can be given to the resulting test data, and the degree to which the validity of the examination has been established. Unfortunately, no matter how precise a standard is formulated for determining when individual testing is appropriate, it often will be all too easy for those wedded to psychological testing to mouth the criteria in a conclusory fashion, leaving it vulnerable to manipulation by those who desire to justify their existing practices rather than rethink them.

According to some advocates of testing, everybody, no matter what position he may be seeking, is a potential danger to mankind! A congressional committee investigating intrusions into the privacy of government employees exposed instances of purely ministerial personnel being subjected to surveillance and intensive interrogation regarding their habits, beliefs, desires, and other intimate matters. Admittedly, there are numerous sensitive positions in government that call for the careful screening of personnel. Nonetheless, after examining these hearings one cannot help but conclude that the cliché-ridden quest for "national security," "safety," and "societal stability" has reached somewhat paranoid proportions and has caused government administrators to cast their testing net too wide.[130] Consider the documented case of an eighteen-year-old college coed applying for a summer secretarial position with a federal agency. She was asked, regarding a boy she was dating: "Did he do anything unnatural with you? You didn't get pregnant, did you? There's kissing, petting and intercourse, and after that, did he force you to do anything to him, or did he do anything to you?"[131]

Assembly-line testing programs also exist in private industry, often in the most unlikely—and unnecessary—contexts. In one instance an applicant for a milk-delivery route was subjected to a battery of clinical examinations, which involved the subject's analyzing pictures or composing stories. Both procedures are widely and more appropriately used in mental hospitals. The applicant ultimately was rejected for the job, apparently because the test indicated that he was a meek, mousy man who would not make a good impression on housewives. The company obviously felt that the quantity of milk consumed by Americans depends on the vigor and virility of the man who brings it to the door rather than on its Vitamin D (or Strontium 90) content. By the same token, a job applicant who likes poetry and movies on social problems may earn a poor score on the masculinity-femininity index and be rejected as a possible homosexual, the position being awarded to an aficionado of detective stories and western films.

Nor should the extensive psychological testing going on at all levels of education be ignored.[132] Both public and private institutions claim to be using tests to identify the "mentally unhealthy" and the "emotionally handicapped." In addition, efforts are underway to develop a correlation between personality traits and academic performance. Perhaps someday a high school senior's success on the Scholastic Aptitude Test will have to be matched by a good "stability" index on the "Social Adjustment Profile" before he is allowed to inhale the rarefied atmosphere of higher education.

From the privacy (let alone the social engineering) perspective, psychological testing of school-age children is no laughing matter. Untrained guidance counselors often are given complete control over a school's testing program. In some instances teachers perfunctorily employ the probing Mooney Problem Checklist. Much of this in-school testing proceeds without parental approval, is conducted at taxpayer expense, and is carried on with little or no regard to privacy considerations. Test results become a part of the individual's permanent file and scores indicating "deviant" attitudes usually result in a visit to the school psychologist.

Students also are used as testing guinea pigs, often in connection with federally sponsored research.[133] A good illustration of the magnitude on which it is being done is Project Talent, an effort financed by the federal Office of Education and begun in 1960 with the testing of approximately one million high school students. In addition to academic testing, the teenagers were required to complete personal information, activity, and interest inventories. The resulting data have been computerized and fed back to the school guidance counsellors. Similar activities are conducted at the local level, albeit on a smaller scale. In one particularly insensitive experiment, University of North Carolina sociologists imposed a thirty-one-page questionnaire on *seventh* and *ninth* graders in Durham. Inquiries included the following:

> To what religion do you belong?
>
> About how often do you go to church?
>
> To what race does your father belong?
>
> How often do your parents go to church or religious meetings?
>
> When your father is working at a job, about how much money does he bring in?
>
> Was the home your parents made for you ever broken up?

If the home your parents made for you was broken up, whose
fault was it?

How do your parents feel about white (black) people?

The most repugnant aspect of these activities is that the subjects are impressionable and vulnerable youngsters upon whom
these privacy-invading interrogations are imposed without assuring them any protection against the future dissemination of the
data.[134] When testing practices are questioned, platitudes are
offered in lieu of explanations or justifications. For example,
when researchers subjected an entire ninth-grade class in a Bronx
junior high school to the probing Minnesota Multiphasic Personality Inventory without parental consent, an indignant parent
was told that in these matters it was best to "trust the judgment
of the educators."[135]

Re-evaluation of current testing practices seems especially
crucial in light of the technological developments that now enable large quantities of raw and evaluative psychological information to be collected and analyzed. Today it is feasible to
administer a range of tests by computer and to retain the resulting data in machine-readable form for later utilization. In the
future, economic considerations and administrative expediency
will encourage organizations to maintain completely machine-
based psychological evaluations on their personnel.

But tomorrow's personality inventories will be considerably
more sophisticated (and intrusive) than today's. Analog computers already are capable of measuring a variety of emotional responses. One scientist has developed a method of monitoring and
analyzing nineteen human stress responses by connecting a computer to polygraph sensors. Also indicative of the future is the
development of a brain-wave monitor that feeds electronic signals
to a computer, which can filter out extraneous impulses and enable the operator to determine what color is being observed by
the subject. Of course, the ability to intercept, interpret, and
manipulate human thoughts and feelings accurately probably
will not be developed for some time. However, the implications
of an alliance among computer technology, psychological evaluation, and the electronic surveillance activities described in an
earlier chapter[136] suggest that the future challenges to privacy will
dwarf the perils presented by today's testing activities. But even

if we simply consider the application of contemporary information transfer technology to current testing practices, a number of threats to individual privacy are visible and deserve our attention.

First, the information embedded in responses to many of the questions on typical personality tests is sensitive. The very existence of these data in machine-readable form is especially dangerous and distressing to the subject, since they often will carry individual identification, unlike computer analyses that draw upon aggregate or anonymous data extracted from a large population base. Thus, files containing psychological data on numerous individuals may encourage the professional snooper and the morbidly curious to seek access to the computerized data base.

Second, despite the questionable reliability of the "soft" data derived from personality testing, the availability of high-speed and sophisticated computers may well foster the proliferation of testing, the development of more probing inquiries, and the preservation of test results as well as evaluations. These trends are certain to come to pass as electronic data-processing and storage continue to become more economical and "in-house" computer capacity becomes more common.

Third, the tendency to collate and centralize data, as evidenced by the National Data Center proposal and the development of credit, banking, and law enforcement data systems, may exert pressures to integrate computerized psychological data with personal information drawn from other sources, which eventually might facilitate direct or remote access to the test information by people beyond the control of the tester and the subject. Indeed, it is the specter of sensitive personal information moving in an unrestrained fashion throughout unregulated computer networks that makes the risk of propagating errors in or misusing test data and evaluations very special. One writer has already warned that a Central Personality Bureau may be developed sometime in the future.[137] Data from such a Bureau could be made commercially available to casual observers having no legitimate right to the information. The wide range of services provided by credit bureaus and private investigators provide ready paradigms for the vendors of psychological data or test profiles.

And, *fourth,* although personality evaluation is a comparatively unrefined and questionable "scientific" tool, the myth of computer infallibility may add an undeserved luster to the field, encouraging an unhealthy reliance on it when testing data are part of an individual's machine-readable dossier. This risk will be magnified if there is a readily available pool of computerized psychological testing data that can be examined by users of a corporate or federal agency information system who are in a decision-making position.

It is not sufficient for the testing community to respond to these concerns by hiding behind the facile assertion that an individual "waives" his right to privacy when he agrees to the examination, or that employment is a "privilege" and not a "right," so that applying for a position constitutes a "consent" to the test and the utilization of its results for purposes beyond deciding whether to employ the subject. These bromides serve to justify existing practices and obscure the deep need for the reform of many current testing activities. Moreover, they are totally unrealistic. An applicant rarely is apprised of the uses to which the test results may be put or thinks of the possible injury that might be caused by their dissemination or misuse. Typically, he is not shown the test scores, or, if rejected for employment, he is not told the role played by the examinations. Even if hired, he probably will not be told whether the scores eliminate any chance for advancement. And most assuredly he will never know who, either within or without the company, has access to his test record. Moreover, the average job seeker or student is in no position to object effectively or to secure commitments that the test results will be maintained in a secure fashion.

To me, the present situation seems topsy-turvy. Moral and legal responsibility for protecting test subjects should not be imposed on those who take the tests; it is incumbent upon those who create and use the tests to insure that individual privacy is preserved. There is no acceptable alternative to developing effective procedures for safeguarding test data—whether recorded in old-fashioned manila folders or in a machine-readable format. Several guidelines for doing so are readily apparent.

(1) The use of an examination that will yield sensitive data about an individual or that may have an adverse impact upon him should be restricted to situations in which its administra-

tion can be justified as essential to achieving a significant socially desirable objective. In the case of psychological testing, this might be true when the examinee's activities involve the health and well-being of others.

(2) The validity and statistical reliability of all tests should be established before they are put into use. Examinations should not be employed unless their efficacy for a particular purpose is clear and the user community should be informed of the test's proper range of utilization and its past record as a measurement of individual performance. Test formulators must be encouraged to frame and enforce a standard of care for the development and administration of their products. The responsibility of test developers should be enforced by recognizing the right of an individual who has been injured by a poorly designed test to bring a civil action for damages against the test publisher or the user.

(3) Procedures should be instituted to insure that test data are recorded accurately. In some contexts this may require showing some or all of the raw data to the test subject for purposes of confirming its content.

(4) Access to raw test data should be restricted to highly trained professional personnel and the material should be destroyed immediately upon its evaluation, except when preservation will further some paramount objective that outweighs the risk to the individual's privacy. If the data are not destroyed, their accuracy should be reappraised periodically, specific items of data should be purged as they become obsolete, and special security measures (along lines to be suggested in a later chapter) should be undertaken to prevent unauthorized access to them.[138]

(5) Test evaluations should not be used beyond the specific purpose for which the examination originally was administered. When similar information about an individual is needed for a different purpose, the subject should be retested with an examination that is appropriate for the second context. Evaluations also should not be permitted to become stale. Retesting often is a better alternative than relying on an outdated evaluation.

(6) Computerization of sensitive test data or their evaluation should not be undertaken in the absence of a clear need to do so that outweighs the risk to the individual's privacy. Even greater restraint should be exercised when there is a possibility that

the computerized version may be preserved as part of the subject's dossier, stored in a large data center containing comparable data on others, or introduced into a multiple-access computer network.

(7) If computerization is necessary, the system in which test data are stored should be protected by security devices, administrative procedures, and personnel regulations that are designed to minimize the risk to the individual's privacy. If it is lodged in a remote-access system, special safeguards must be employed for the transmission of the data. A number of specific suggestions along these lines are offered in a later chapter.

Unfortunately, the experience with various governmental agencies, the credit bureau industry, and other information-handling groups indicates that it may be unrealistic to rely on self-regulation in the testing field. My suggested Seven Commandments may well be ignored or given lip service by those who find the continuation of the status quo a more comfortable path to follow. Several congressional hearings on privacy demonstrate that the problem largely has been ignored by test-development companies and test users. Indeed, past suggestions for a reappraisal of existing practices frequently have been deprecated by the testing fraternity as the uninformed judgment of troublemakers or the idle prattlings of right- and left-wingers. If testing groups are unwilling to take effective steps to upgrade their practices in order to assure that privacy is protected, legislative or administrative regulation ultimately may be necessary to protect us against our Big Brother and his test-filled attaché case. Fortunately, there is a strong humanistic strain among psychologists, as well as within the noncommercial segments of the testing community, and there is reason to hope for revision from within.

4. The Little Red Schoolhouse Goes Electronic

> Word has come down from the dean
> That by use of the teaching machine
>   Old Oedipus Rex
>   Could have learned about sex
> Without ever disturbing the Queen.
>   —*Hamilton College Alumni Review,*
>   reprinted in William S. Baring-Gould,
>   *The Lure of the Limerick* (1967), 7

Computer-Assisted Instruction

The concept of streamlining and individualizing the teaching process by the use of machines had its genesis in the 1920's. Early efforts consisted of relatively simple devices that confronted the student with a box containing a question and several alternative answers. By choosing the correct response, the learner was able to bring a new question into view. In the 1950's Dr. B. F. Skinner's pioneering work at Michigan and Harvard greatly enhanced the potential of mechanical learning devices. He developed machines and texts that require the student to compose responses rather than simply choose from among the various answers presented to him. The name commonly given to this and related techniques is "programmed learning."

Today we stand on the threshold of an era in which technology can revolutionize the educational process. During the past two decades programmed learning has reached a high level of sophistication. At the same time, the audiovisual and miniaturization technologies have produced numerous new educational devices. Given the possibility of mating these developments with advancements in the computer and communications fields, the potential applications of machine-aided instruction appear unlimited.[139] Programmed learning, which is based on a highly logical structure, is extremely well suited for presentation by computer and can be made available to students at different institutions through the same transmission media that currently are being used in commercial remote-access time-share systems. Similarly, audiovisual devices can be coupled with computer terminals for more effective display of teaching material.

The use of technology also may permit schools that lack sufficient teaching or library capabilities to share another school's educational resources. One experiment in computerized instruction enabled school children in McComb, Mississippi, to learn mathematics on an individual basis using computer consoles and teleprinters linked to a data center at Stanford University. Although it is too early to be certain, computer-assisted instruction (CAI) may partially solve the problem of how to close the educational gap between our culturally deprived groups and those enjoying the advantages of attending the nation's mainstream schools.[140]

The pedagogical benefits to be derived from machine-assisted instruction are considerable. Unlike the traditional classroom setting in which the instructor must teach at a rate geared to the group's theoretical middle intelligence level—too slow for some and too fast for others—the computer and a number of manually operated programmed learning devices permit material to be presented to each student at a speed determined by his or her ability to comprehend the lesson's content. Through built-in evaluation devices, reinforcement techniques, remedial questioning, and similar procedures, there is some assurance that a student understands what has been presented to him before he moves ahead in the instructional sequence. This process, which resembles individual tutoring, is claimed to have enabled some students in experimental projects to learn five to ten times more rapidly than their traditionally instructed contemporaries.[141] One typical venture has been enthusiastically described as follows:

> In New York's P. S. 175 in Harlem, a computer and tape recorder are hooked up to a talking typewriter. A child listens to a voice saying the letter "c" and is asked to watch the red pointer as it moves to "c." The student is instructed now to find "c" on the keyboard and press it. The voice repeats itself every few seconds until the child finds the right key. Four-year-olds using this computer-assisted form of instruction have been able to write entire sentences in just four months. Six-year-olds have edited their own newspaper with stories, rhymes, and riddles.[142]

Although the current cost per student prohibits widescale use of some of the more sophisticated forms of electronic education, advances in microminiaturization and communications processes indicate that costs may decline to a point at which the full benefits of instructional technology will become obtainable by most school systems.[143] Thus, Patrick Suppes, one of the savants of computer-assisted instruction, cheerfully predicts "that in a few more years millions of school children will have access to what Philip of Macedon's son Alexander enjoyed as a royal prerogative: the personal services of a tutor as well-informed and responsive as Aristotle."[144] And another educator suggests that "we are at a point where one of the best measurements of the quality of an educational institution is its computer power."[145]

Unfortunately, predictions as to the impact of scientific and technological innovations tend to be far more glamorous than the realities. Enthusiasts fail to take proper account of budget necessities, the amount of lead time and developmental effort needed to make complex machines and systems operate, and the frequently undependable character of human resources.[146] The fact is that education has not yet fully exploited the Gutenberg technology and programmed learning. As a result, computer-assisted instruction is an unknown art in the vast majority of the nation's school systems. Economics is hardly the sole culprit for the primitive instructional condition in which most institutions find themselves. The recalcitrance of academics, school administrators, and school boards probably deserves much of the blame. We have been unable to overcome the resistance of (1) teachers who are wedded to their lesson plans or are obsessed by the illusory specter of technological unemployment; (2) librarians with the mentality of postage-stamp collectors who believe that books are to be admired but not handled; and (3) educational policy-makers who are too imbued with the image of the little red schoolhouse. It therefore is not surprising that despite extravagant claims that often smack of academic one-upmanship, blue-sky projections that ignore the realities of life, and considerable huckstering by hardware and software companies, the utilization of computers by the educational community thus far has been somewhat episodic and in many ways quite unimaginative.[147]

In the main, computer resources have been used simply to accomplish electronically a number of chores that have traditionally been done manually. Thus, computer-based record keeping is replacing manila folders and students and classes are being scheduled by electronic data-processing instead of by an assistant dean with a penchant for jigsaw puzzles. Although these efforts at marshaling and intelligently allocating human and physical resources in the educational community should be applauded, it is essential to recognize that none of the basic characteristics of the academic process has yet been altered significantly by the new technologies.[148]

The unfulfilled promise of computer-assisted instruction has not gone unnoticed. Unpersuaded that the exponential growth of information technology will lead to a revolution in education in the foreseeable future, Harvard's Anthony Oettinger has remarked:

> While classroom scheduling by computer is advertised as a *fait accompli,* this is true only in the rather restricted sense of assigning students to conventional classroom groups and insuring that the number of groups and teachers fit into available classrooms. . . . It must be recognized, however, that this is a far cry from keeping track of individual students week by week, day by day, hour by hour, or minute by minute, and matching them in turn with resources themselves parceled out in smaller packages than teachers per semester or rooms per semester. Packaging individual students is more complex than packing screws for dime stores or wrapping a lamb chop in plastic for the supermarket meat counter.[149]

Echoing this judgment, the report of the Commission on Instructional Technology has concluded that "the present status of instructional technology in American education is low in both quantity and quality."[150]

But there are signs of improvement and, despite the current stringency in governmental support for education, certain basic societal forces make it imperative that instructional technology be nurtured.[151] Continued population growth means that most educational institutions must expand and new ones will come into existence. Increased job specialization and a wide variety of cultural and vocational factors probably will cause students to remain in school for longer periods of time. Similar reasons will encourage a growing number of adults to return to school for continuing education programs. And a variety of factors, not the least of which is the contemporary demand for greater "relevance" in the classroom, will spawn new courses and disciplines as well as promote interdisciplinary work, much of which is quite expensive. The result will be a greater strain on existing educational resources and increased efforts to maximize the utilization of the human and physical assets of the schools. Inevitably, this means mounting pressure to automate the mundane, miniaturize the cumbersome, and accelerate the tedious. In such circumstances the computer will be advanced by many academic administrators as a panacea.

Other forces virtually guarantee increased computer use in the schools. Computer companies are spawning educational subsidiaries and acquiring educational publishing firms at a rapid rate in order to gain a share of tomorrow's education market. Even though teachers have been somewhat slow to abandon traditional methods, the professional periodicals seem to indicate that we may be entering a catch-up phase and that academic rewards will be given to those experimenting with innovative teaching methods. Similarly, many schools of education have introduced specialized programs to train people in the application of instructional technology to the teaching process. Despite the doubters and the many purveyors of snake oil, computer-assisted instruction is becoming the "in" thing in the Ed Biz. Industry's and academe's interest in instructional technology is being reinforced by Congress, which has been considering a bill that would appropriate four hundred million dollars to encourage schools to employ computer and audiovisual hardware.[152] Thus, CAI has been given the green light, which means that in assessing its potential threat to privacy, we would be wise to heed Aldous Huxley's warning that "we mustn't be caught by surprise by our own advances in technology."

At its present level of development, the possibility of educational technology's being used for intrusive purposes is relatively minor. But when we assume that there will be widescale use of this new educational format in the future, an entirely different vista comes into focus. For example, there is the distinct possibility that eventually a student's interaction with his school's computer will generate a flow of data that will be recorded in individualized machine-readable files. Effective appraisal of a student's progress with his computerized lessons over a period of time will require the analysis of his machine-based dialogues, which can be preserved in the form of printouts. Indeed, one of the great potentials of the computer is that it will provide the instructor with detailed information concerning a student's performance in order to enable intelligent planning of each succeeding stage of his education.[153]

Even though extensive educational dossiers are an inevitable by-product of computer-assisted instruction, it would be understandable if the skeptic concluded that the threat to privacy is a remote one, inasmuch as the vast majority of data generated by the educational process are not sensitive in character. However, we are talking about a newly created educational format that is being molded by a rapidly developing technology; the long-term ramifications of the computer on past academic patterns are not really perceptible at this time.

Also, the technology is capable of transforming the educational community's information habits and internal relationships. As advanced audiovisual instructional aids, sophisticated computer teachers, and electronic record keeping become more pervasive, one consequence may well be a blurring of the lines that separate administrators, counselors, and teachers, groups that now are conceived to serve quite distinct functions. This role metamorphosis may encourage the establishment of individualized, machine-based dossiers containing information on all aspects of a student's educational life. Indeed, large public school systems and major universities already are beginning to rely heavily upon computers for maintaining detailed faculty and student data files. As in other contexts, the increased information-handling capacity provided by electronic data-processing will encourage the gathering of more individualized information.[154]

As time progresses, a student's educational record will become much more sophisticated and comprehensive than it is at present. Financial information will be gathered for administering loan and scholarship programs, membership lists of various associations and groups will be maintained, psychiatric and medical data will be computerized to facilitate the operation of student health services, and increasingly detailed evaluations of a student's performance will be preserved. It also is likely that a significant amount of student guidance will be conducted on the basis of student-machine interchanges, which will be recorded and filed for analysis at a later time, rather than by using live counselors at the initial interview—a resource that always has been in short supply.

In much the same way that today's airline reservation computers are capable of swiftly composing a record of an individual's travels, a comprehensive computerized school record might be used to ascertain all of Johnny's activities and school associations as well as any disciplinary or attendance problems he may have had. A file of this type, although necessary during a student's school years, is potentially dangerous if preserved for too long a period after he graduates or if its custodian allows the data to be used in contexts unrelated to the subject's educational performance. These risks are especially grave when some of the material is inaccurate or projects a derogatory image of the child that might do him a disservice years later.

Eventually, data banks maintained at the primary, secondary, and university levels may be networked so that the details of a student's educational life history can be made immediately available throughout the education system. In turn, the educational networks might be tied to para-academic banks, such as the emerging National Migrant Worker Children Data Bank.[155] The resulting store of information might prove inviting to professional snoopers and those who could use the data collected during an individual's academic life for commercial or malicious purposes. An educational network containing personal information needs the same safeguards against unauthorized access and misuse as does any other data center.

Also to be considered is the effect a marked increase in academic data-processing will have on student attitudes toward their teachers and educational institutions. In many schools there presently exists something akin to a confidential relationship between a student and his mentors. This bond might be put in jeopardy by an environment that in effect monitors student activities and associations. The relationship will deteriorate further if unregulated educational networks develop and it becomes impossible to assure the individual that his educational dossier will not be breached by people outside the school. Ironically, the same technological capability that promises to permit educational institutions to individualize that learning process may be responsible for the debilitation of the student-teacher relationship. If that comes to pass, it will be difficult to convince students to disclose information to teachers or school administrators that may be essential for their development and well-being.

Moreover, as computer-assisted instruction graduates from simple "yes-no" or "multiple-choice" exercises to extended student-machine dialogues requiring highly verbal answers,[156] it might become feasible to evaluate a student's motivation and attitudes by examining his response pattern. For example, a properly programmed institutional computer, with a large store of accumulated data on each student, could be used by the school psychologist to prepare personality profiles, serving much the same function as many psychological tests. And if highly interactive student-machine dialogues on topical or sensitive subjects, such as religion, political philosophy, or racial unrest are preserved, they could be employed by outsiders in ways totally unrelated to their educational function—perhaps as the basis for a company's determining a student's vocational suitability or the government's whether to issue him a security clearance.

It takes little imagination to conceive of the uses to which a dossier containing virtually every response made by a student from kindergarten to graduate school could be put. Information maintained by schools at different academic levels may be tapped by social scientists, resource planners, and market-research people. Many overzealous educators appear quite oblivious to the possibility that sensitive data derived from an easily accessible and often naive student population may be used to the prejudice of the file subjects. Furthermore, in this age of troubled campuses, academic institutions are prime targets for fishing expeditions by governmental agencies.[157] To date, many universities have found themselves embarrassed by information demands from the House Committee on Internal Security (HUAC's new name) and its state counterparts. It seems undesirable to create an atmosphere that encourages law-enforcement or witch-hunting groups to subpoena information gathered in the educational context. Certainly one way to minimize this possibility is to exercise restraint in the gathering of personal data in the first instance.

Although some schools—particularly universities—have begun to come to grips with the problem,[158] many administrators and faculties remain insensitive to the privacy implications of modern instructional technology and the vulnerability of information collected within the academic community to various demands from outside the ivory tower. In many schools alumni organizations and industry recruiters are given access to student files without any concern about the type of information they often contain or any awareness that the file subjects might object. Indeed, as in the credit-bureau situation, students often are not given access to their own records. Even the most fundamental rules of confidentiality are sometimes violated. For example, I have been told that despite the doctor-patient privilege, a student's medical record is not necessarily immune from examination by a member of the faculty or administration even at our most brahman institutions.

Even assuming a growing awareness of the deficiencies in the present privacy regime, and that future students will be able to put greater trust in the information practices of their schools, the possibility of "accidental" exposure of sensitive data is a matter of serious concern. Indeed, it is doubtful whether individualized data should be preserved in the educational community for any period of time. This is especially true if there is any possibility that someone will attempt to use them for personality analysis or vocational planning. In the context of school children, using information in this fashion creates a risk of stereotyping or classifying them in a way that detrimentally affects their educational development or societal mobility. Yet there seems to be a mindless trend toward the use of academic data banks for precisely this purpose.

There are few contexts in which the proper handling of the computer-privacy question is more important than the educational milieu. Young people, especially those in primary and secondary schools, are particularly vulnerable to intrusions on their privacy because colleges and potential employers must make important decisions about them primarily on the basis of their academic records and teacher evaluations. But most young students are not as capable of protecting themselves against privacy invaders or are not as aware of the dangerous character of information as their elders. Thus the entry of the computer into the classroom will present the same challenges to personal privacy and will require as much planning as is necessary to protect sensitive information held by industry and government data banks. A number of privacy-protecting controls must be imposed on the use of computers and information in the educational community. What follows is a suggested framework for such a system; a later chapter will delve more deeply into the details.[159]

First, professional guidelines, school regulations, or legislation, if necessary, should define (1) the nature of the personal information that may be extracted from students or received from other sources about them; (2) the type of information that is of sufficient long-term educational importance to warrant its recordation and preservation as part of a student's academic file; (3) those persons whose responsibilities necessitate their having access to a student's records, either directly or through remote-access terminals; (4) the legitimate educational uses to which personal data may be put by various people, either within the unit that collects them or within any other unit in the same school system or university; and (5) the circumstances under which data that are capable of being analyzed to reveal information about individual students may be transmitted to other data centers or information users both within and without the academic community.

Second, when computer-aided instruction techniques are thought desirable in connection with subject matter having sensitive or highly subjective aspects, the educational justification for their use should be validated and their reliability carefully investigated before being employed. This is imperative if there is any possibility that a student's responses could be used to his detriment. Standards also must be established concerning access to a student's work-product and how long it should be preserved.

Third, technological, administrative, and personal regulations must be developed to protect against unauthorized disclosure of and access to both raw data generated by students during the educational process and evaluations by others. In addition, a plan for the systematic destruction of data when their academic or record-keeping value has ended should be formulated and it must consider the interests of the student as well as the legitimate needs of the institution.

Fourth, a procedure must be established to allow either the student (or his parent or guardian) to ascertain what information has been stored in his file and to provide a mechanism for correcting any errors that may come to light. In some states the law already guarantees a right of access,[160] although few schools have established procedures to effectuate it. When it is necessary to deny disclosure of certain items because of some important medical or educational reason, a group within the academic institution should periodically re-evaluate the accuracy and need to preserve the hidden data. The file subject also should be permitted to participate in decisions concerning the dissemination of data about him.

Although no protective system can completely insure against information misuse, unauthorized disclosure, and either mechanical or human error, there is no excuse for academic institutions failing to explore every avenue that holds some promise. The real problem is to awaken educators and school administrators to the fact that the new educational technologies are revolutionizing the information patterns in the nation's schools.

Television and Audiovisual Aids

Although somewhat less glamorous than the newer electronic technologies, educational television and audiovisual aids are having an increasingly important impact on the educational process. Even more is promised for the future.

> Video cameras "using ultrasonic converters, fiber optics, and character generators promise exciting new educational applications" and open the classroom to educational experiences that ordinarily would be too dangerous to replicate. High fidelity CCTV [closed circuit television] linked to memory banks will provide the teacher and learner with a vast amount of material that can be brought to the teaching-learning situation at the precise moment when it is needed.[161]

Unfortunately, the past and present educational utilization of television and related audiovisual devices has been rather unimaginative, especially when considered in light of what is technologically and pedagogically feasible.[162]

The special virtues of audiovisual technology are obvious. Students in different geographic locations can receive the benefits of taped or filmed lectures by recognized experts in all fields, thereby filling curriculum gaps and supplementing faculty resources. Recordings also obviate the need for a live presentation of basic or routine information every time a particular subject is taught. Special camera equipment and technical procedures enable students to scrutinize events, procedures, and subjects from perspectives that are not possible in the classroom or laboratory. Along similar lines, dangerous experiments can be conducted while being observed at a safe distance. Finally, videotape and film can preserve unique educational experiences for future dissemination.

There are several important contrasts between computer-assisted instruction and television and audiovisual aids bearing on their potential threat to privacy. The latter techniques typically involve (1) a much lower level of interaction between the student and the teaching aid, even when both ends of the television circuit have transmission facilities; (2) a wider simultaneous dissemination of the same information; (3) a closer approximation of the traditional face-to-face teaching environment, especially when the material is directed at a large audience; and (4) almost no generation of data by the student that are preserved by the system. Of course, these are not inevitable patterns. The wider availability of audiovisual techniques in individualized carrels, the use of dial-access procedures, and the linking together of various forms of instructional technology may radically alter past norms.

Despite the increasing use of television and audiovisual devices at every educational level, little attention has been paid to their privacy implications. This is somewhat curious because the television or film camera is a patently intrusive instrument. Admittedly, the past use of these media apparently has been relatively free of privacy-invading excesses. But their potential for the future must be considered in light of the new applications that are constantly being developed. For example, the simulation of classroom situations is now being used as part of teacher training. The technique involves projecting past classroom events on a screen from a battery of projectors at the rear of a room. By requiring teacher trainees to react to various student questions and activities, something akin to a live classroom dynamic is experienced. The prospective teacher's performance is then recorded and analyzed.[163]

In addition, classroom situations are frequently broadcast over educational networks or videotaped and subsequently used at many institutions, which means that the ultimate audience observing the teacher and students may be quite large. And any out-of-the-ordinary occurrence is bound to receive wide circulation. Much as the present day television replay systems preserve the actions of a football game's "heroes" and "goats," so an embarrassing student response or an instructor's error may be preserved for posterity and used as a paradigm of a "poor" performance or a "slow" student or how not to teach. Audiovisual enthusiasts also might tend to record atypical responses for purposes of demonstrating the full spectrum of student conduct and attitudes. Very shy, argumentative, or handicapped pupils may well be the subject of an undue amount of camera study. Furthermore, the broadening of school curricula to include sensitive subjects and emotionally charged contemporary social issues might lead to the transmission or recording of teacher-student dialogues that present one or more of the participants in a bad light.

The privacy implications arising from the pervasive use of television and audiovisual aids extend beyond the confines of the classroom. Television is being used for the "observation of surgery, of patients' behavior under drugs, teachers in training watching a lesson from another building," and a range of other activities thought to be private.[164] Moreover, many courses are increasingly emphasizing student observation of a wide spectrum of social processes, which often calls for the intermediation of television. For example, closed-circuit television is used in at least one prominent law school to enable students to watch legal proceedings in a local courtroom. Although public trial is a basic tenet of our legal system, it is doubtful that this necessarily sanctions a closed-circuit telecast of a distraught rape victim's description of her travail to a distant room filled with students. In another law school, divorce and legal-aid interviewing techniques are observed in a neighboring room with the aid of a one-way mirror and a hidden microphone.

There obviously is a valuable objective to be served by each of these educational experiments. Nevertheless, one should not ignore the threat to individual privacy posed by the use of audiovisual technology to record sensitive human conduct. When these techniques present risks to privacy, the subject should be given some control over the use of any recorded observations that were made of him while he was receiving treatment or otherwise being exposed as part of an educational experiment. Particular care must be given to medical and psychiatric instructional material that may be attractive to voyeurs. It is well known that police wiretapping and eavesdropping tapes occasionally are used as entertainment at social gatherings. Thus it is not unreasonable to be concerned about the employment of titillating instructional audiovisual material for similar purposes.

The likely centralization of audiovisual material, perhaps in the form of libraries or in exchange systems, and the ease with which tapes and slides can be duplicated, add new dimensions to the privacy implications of instructional television and audiovisual technology. As in the computer context, the proliferation of communication links and the eventual establishment of networks that may embrace entire school systems or operate over a state or region will make access to educational materials much more convenient and economical as well as increase the danger of unauthorized scrutiny and dissemination.

To protect individuals from unnecessary exposure of their psyches, their philosophies, and their physiques both in and out of the classroom, the same types of protections as were suggested in connection with computer-assisted instruction are necessary. Particularly in view of their sensory dimensions, a privacy-invading audiovisual technique should not be employed unless it has substantially greater educational utility when compared to less intrusive pedagogical formats. In addition, a strong justification should be demonstrated before preserving or rebroadcasting any recording that has privacy overtones.

In any case involving a human subject, a meaningful consent should be obtained. This means that he must not be led to believe that he will receive superior professional services by consenting to being observed. Moreover, it is imperative that the subject's acquiescence be based on full information as to the nature and potential ramifications of any observations, recordings, and transmissions that will be made of him. He should be told the character and size of the anticipated audience and be given some idea of the thrust of the exercise or experiment. Of course, there are situations in which the subject must not know that he is being observed at the time of the experiment. But instances in which advance notice is not given must be limited and, whenever possible, sensitive experiments of this type should not be conducted before a live audience. They should be filmed or taped in advance of the instructional sessions; then the subject should be informed of the intended use of the recording and given an opportunity to screen it, thereby making his option of approving its use or directing its destruction meaningful.

In certain situations, which usually involve the observation of mental patients, seriously injured people, and drug addicts, a consent often is difficult or impossible to obtain. To complicate matters, there may be no known or reasonably available alternative source from which consent might be obtained. Special guidelines are needed to define the legitimate uses of instructional technology in these contexts. As a practical matter, reliance ultimately must be placed upon the sensitivity and discretion of educators and audiovisual technicians who by instinct and professional training must be made responsive to the threats to privacy posed by their utilization of the new technology.

The Numbing Effect of Technology

The introduction of computers and sophisticated audiovisual devices into the learning environment poses one challenge to the educational process of the future that is of overriding significance. This is the possibility that extensive or continuing exposure of students to machine teaching and electronic devices will anesthetize the sensitivity and awareness of the school-age population (and the entire population in a matter of a few generations) to the importance of individual privacy.[165] The almost hypnotic effect of computer-assisted instruction illustrates the problem. "[S]tudents often seem dominated by the machines. Even when the lesson is dull or poorly written, they stick to it and pay attention. They don't seem to realize they are boss and can push a button at any time, turn the thing off and walk away."[166]

Submerging children during their formative years in a dehumanized educational setting may yield a technologically oriented citizenry to whom present-day attitudes toward the individual's right to be let alone and to control his informational profile will seem alien. Although reliance on electronics has generated a sharp rebellion against the mechanized aspects of education by some,[167] the greater concern eventually may prove to be the insensitivity of those who have become dominated by the machine. Relatively passive student adaptation to the technology suggests a malleable attitude toward the privacy-invading aspects of the new instructional procedures, especially a tolerance of intrusions into what has hitherto been considered private.

Of course, this is not an inevitable by-product of technology. The introduction of the book several centuries ago and its interposition between teachers and pupils did not result in widespread social alienation or cries of dehumanization,[168] although it did cause other dislocations by widening the gap between the schooled and the unschooled. Nonetheless, computer-assisted instruction and audiovisual devices are sufficiently distinguishable from books to justify taking affirmative steps to use the technology advantageously, to personalize the instructional environment of the future, and to emphasize the importance of individual privacy. How to bring this about is a question that must be given more attention by the educational psychologists than it currently is receiving.

Privacy and the Classroom of the Future

In its diverse forms instructional technology is becoming one of the most socially desirable applications of contemporary information science and the prospects for the future are nothing short of revolutionary. For example, because information specialists are becoming increasingly attracted to data systems that can operate on a network or multimedia basis, the conjunctive application of television and computer-assisted instruction for teaching, testing, counseling, and research purposes is inevitable. Dial-access procedures, which combine the telephone and audiovisual devices, offer another example of how the new instructional methods bridge two or more media. Furthermore, there are several new technologies that are certain to offer educational applications. Researchers at the University of Michigan and the University of California have developed a novel photographic process that enables a hologram recording to be reconstructed by passing laser beams through light-sensitive film. The result is "of considerable importance for education [for it will be possible to reproduce] three-dimensional, highly realistic imagery, unmatched by any other photographic method."[169]

Nor is the little red schoolhouse (or its stone urban counterpart) an immutable institution. Remote-access instructional technology and the physical decentralization of education will not honor institutional walls. Slow-scan television, which enables the viewer to control the rate of picture transmission, and the video disc, which stores television signals on a plastic object resembling a phonograph record, have the capability of converting every home that is equipped with a turntable and a television set into a private learning center.

The possibility that these developments will drastically change the character of education and threaten the privacy of individual citizens is increased if we assume parallel advances in the communications sciences. True, man's existing wire and microwave transmission facilities cannot handle the quantity of information that will be necessary to transfer educational functions to home-learning centers. However, in the future laser beams and satellite communications channels will have the capacity to transmit simultaneously the information content of all the phone calls that are made and every television program that is broadcast in the United States throughout an entire day.[170]

Finally, advances in surveillance technology are bound to have ramifications on privacy and instructional technology. Ultra-sensitive radar will be available that can cause messages to be printed out on electronic typewriters located at a distance from the authorized terminal to which a signal is directed, and that can pierce protected cables while simulating the output phase of a computer. These developments suggest the potential capability for intercepting data moving through an educational information network. Moreover, the infiltration of subliminal and sub-audial messages to influence those using instructional devices represents a futuristic threat to privacy in the form of implanting unwanted information.

No set of mechanical or administrative precautions will completely obviate the problems created by widespread use of computer-assisted instruction or audiovisual devices or insure that the fruits of the technological revolution will not be poisoned. They are merely a starting point in the quest for effective control over the flow of individualized information generated by the educational process. The potentially debilitating effect educational technology may have on the attitude of citizens toward the right of privacy is part of the much larger problem of defining to what degree our society is willing to guarantee its citizens a freedom from scrutiny.

5. Regulating the Flow of Information— The Need for a Broad Perspective

[O]ur society [is] based upon the instrument of the industrial process. All our economic and social arrangements—how we feel about what we do, which is all that culture is—are founded upon the way our industrial energy is organized. How large a part and what kind of part do we want the computer, with its overriding skill in the rational analysis of the measurable data, to take in the decisions that determine the way this energy will be organized?

—Elting E. Morison, *Men, Machines, and Modern Times* (1966), 78

As the four models discussed in this chapter indicate, the growth of computerized information systems is proceeding both rapidly and unpredictably. Businesses,[171] hospitals,[172] educational institutions,[173] and governmental organizations at the federal,[174] state,[175] and local levels[176] are quickening the pace of their computer activities and recognizing common interests in having data flow between and among them. In most instances the efforts are well-intentioned, as certainly is true of the Migrant Worker Children Data Bank and the various law-enforcement intelligence centers that are emerging everywhere. In these contexts the objective is not to exorcise the evildoers but rather to achieve a balance between privacy and information efficiency. But other applications of the technology have far less social utility and are intrinsically less justifiable. In my view this is the case of computer-aided commercial mailing lists, psychological testing, and information surveillance in the consumer-reporting field. In these contexts the policy issues are more difficult and the need for developing strong restraints on the use of computers is substantially greater.

Any attempt to cope with the increasing abrasion between information technology and individual privacy must be undertaken with the widest field of vision. It would be unwise to deal with each new technological application on an individual basis divorced from the broader issues, or to delay until its privacy-invading excesses have come to pass. Nothing short of a complete survey of the ramifications of the new technologies will be effective if we expect to reach a rational accommodation between the competing values. Fortunately, the National Academy of Sciences has recognized the dimensions of the problem that confronts us and its Project on Computer Data Banks plans to bring together leaders from numerous disciplines and groups that are concerned with the privacy implications of the information flow. But the sand in the hourglass continues to flow and the time for study and effective action is growing short.

Through the Microscope Darkly — The Handling of Personal Information by the Federal Government: Current Practice

I see no reason to assume that the government will be any more resistant to the pressures of the moment in the future than it has been in the past. Sending Japanese-American citizens to concentration camps would have been immensely speeded by having a National Identity and Data File, and McCarthy could have destroyed many more careers if he'd had computer records of security investigations. Protestors of current Viet Nam policy could easily be marked "politically unreliable for shipment off to the Tulelake Relocation Center after we bomb China.

—H. Taylor Buckner, "Computer Privacy,"
*Hearings Before the Subcommittee
on Administrative Practice and
Procedure of the Committee on
the Judiciary, United States
Senate* (March, 1967), 264

The question of how to give individuals meaningful control over the flow of computerized information relating to them must be approached with the realization that we are dealing with an entirely new medium of communications that is having a profound impact on our society. The adjustment process is bound to be difficult, especially for the legal system, which historically has been slow in accommodating its doctrines to new technologies, let alone in generating new jurisprudential principles. The length of time it took the rules of law relating to warranty and negligence to take account of the automobile and our mass-production economy testifies to the system's somewhat ponderous reaction to novel problems created by scientific advances. The same lesson can be learned from the years of confusion that passed before radio and television broadcasting came under effective regulation. Thus it would not be completely surprising if the existing patchwork of legal principles governing personal privacy, information collection and dissemination, and confidentiality—whether they happen to be the product of legislative or administrative regulation or are grounded in the Constitution or the common law—proves to be unequal to the challenge posed by the computer revolution.

The law currently deals with information in terms of two old and well understood friends—the printed page and the file cabinet. With few exceptions it has not even begun to come to grips with machine-readable formats, electronic storage, and high-speed information transfer techniques. But the current doctrines cannot be dismissed as irrelevant. We have barely begun to identify the types of difficulties that legislatures and courts are likely to encounter in attempting to preserve individual privacy, let alone really started to undertake the process of formulating meaningful legal restraints on the information flow of the future.

The nature of the problem confronting our policy makers can best be exposed by examining the most comprehensive existing statutory and administrative data-processing framework—the body of rules and practices relating to the federal government's handling of information. Because certain aspects of the federal experience afford insights into the privacy problems raised by other information interchange practices, this view of Washington's activities also should point up some of the legal implications of the nationwide computer networks that are on the horizon. The common law and constitutional doctrines relating to privacy will be discussed in the next chapter to provide a complete picture of the law relating to informational privacy.

1. Data Collection and Confidentiality—The Census Bureau Model

Government should be allowed to know a great deal more than it does about the community it was elected to serve. This requirement is essential if we want to see decisions made on the basis of fact. You cannot manage an advanced society, which is a vast, complex, interconnecting system, unless the facts are available.

—J. Benn, "Where Power Belongs,"
The Nation, August 26, 1968, at 136

The Bureau of the Census long has been one of the federal government's chief data gatherers. Not surprisingly, with the increasing complexity and range of federal activities, the decennial census has evolved from the simple "enumeration" of the populace called for by the United States Constitution[1] to a comprehensive survey seeking numerous items of personal data designed to portray the quality of life in the nation. The census effort has several highly utilitarian functions as well. For example, the population statistics it generates are used for apportioning the seats in the House of Representatives, and many of the more specific data are used for planning and allocating funds under a wide range of federal and state programs. Indeed, the need for current data for these purposes is said to be so great that a mid-decade census as well as a variety of periodic surveys are being seriously proposed as supplements to the decennial canvass.

Although the majority of Americans are subjected to a relatively mild interrogation, millions of citizens receive considerably longer census forms and are required to answer inquiries about their health, employment, finances, and housing,[2] which has led to increased public concern over the census process and its privacy implications. Among the questions on the 1970 census thought to be offensive by some citizens are these:

> How much rent do you pay?
> Do you live in a one-family house?
> If a woman, how many babies have you had (not counting still births)?
> How much did you earn in 1967?
> If married more than once, how did your first marriage end?
> Do you have a clothes dryer?
> Do you have a telephone? If so, what is the number?
> Have you been looking for work during the past 4 weeks?
> Do you own a second home?
> Does your TV set have UHF?
> Do you have a flush toilet?
> Do you have a bathtub or shower?

The process of framing the decennial questionnaire has been a particularly sore point for many people. A number of the queries on recent censuses have been included at the request not only of social planners from both governmental and private institutions, but also of industry groups desirous of securing information that might aid in making product design and marketing decisions.[3] Thus Congressman Jackson Betts of Ohio, who leads the congressional movement to "reform" the census process, has charged:

> Large corporations are behind the extensive household utility items such as questions asking if a person has a television, clothes washing machine, dryer, home food freezer, and so forth, and Government officials who have an insatiable appetite to extract more and more facts about the American citizenry have prodded inclusion of dozens of income, marital, housing, and employment subjects. The cozy relationship between the Census Bureau and Federal statistical users has gone beyond the semblance of public service. I believe this is an unwholesome alliance which causes improper expansion of the collection of personal data under threat of fine or imprisonment.[4]

In defense of the Bureau, no question is included solely for marketing purposes and each question on the census has the support of at least one governmental agency or can be rationalized in terms of being in the general public interest. The latter standard, of course, is quite vague and has been invoked to justify the inclusion of questions concerning ownership of radio and television sets proposed by broadcasters interested in measuring their markets. The rationalization eventually given for these inquiries was that it is in the public interest to know whether information could be communicated to the citizenry over radio and television in case of a national emergency.

The collected data are widely used for commercial purposes and it is the Bureau's avowed policy to allow industry to hitchhike on the process. Besides publishing an array of printed reports, the Bureau makes available computer tapes containing various types of statistical data at prices that represent only the cost of producing each tape. The data are released in a form that makes identification of individuals impossible. Organizations having computer facilities can use the Bureau's tapes directly and efficiently. Eventually commercial time-share systems are likely to acquire the tapes and provide processing facilities to researchers who otherwise would not have the resources to utilize the data. There also is the remote possibility of a time-share system operated by the Bureau itself.

In my view, the user community should be asked to pay more for the data. After all, the cost of carrying out the 1970 census exceeded two hundred million dollars (each citizen contributed approximately one dollar in taxes to the process) plus the value of the time it took the public to answer the questions (estimated to be approximately forty-five minutes in the case of the longest form), which, of course, is incalculable.

Census information is extracted under threat of criminal penalties,[5] and, on the few occasions when the propriety of census questions has been challenged in the courts, the Bureau's broad discretion has been upheld.[6] These judicial decisions are technically correct. The national government's constitutional power to proliferate the census questionnaire as a "necessary and proper" adjunct to the effective planning of numerous federal programs is beyond serious doubt. The real question is whether and to what extent that power should be exercised.

At least one side effect of the elephantine character of the census seems highly undesirable. It is one that stems from the authority middle- and low-level federal officials have to determine what questions will be included on the census. As these administrators increase the number and sensitivity of the inquiries, they also, in effect, expand the scope and the potential application of the criminal sanctions imposed for noncompliance with the census. Because of this, one is entitled to ask whether abdication to administrative claims of governmental efficiency and expediency is the way a great nation allows its criminal law to be formulated or strikes a balance between individual privacy and its information-gathering activities. Furthermore, it seems unfair to subject those citizens who are randomly selected to receive the longer and more probing census form to a greater risk of having sanctions applied against them for noncompliance than citizens who are chosen for the shorter questionnaires. To be sure, criminal prosecutions for nonresponse are rare and Census Bureau officials have admitted to Congress that the threat is largely a bluff. But the specter of possible prosecution undoubtedly has a coercive effect on people who find some of the questions offensive to their privacy.

Of course, effective data collection and an efficient information flow are essential to the proper functioning of a society as complex as ours. The federal government and industry have an obligation to determine how best to meet the needs of the American people in terms of products and services. But is it really essential for the federal government to threaten citizens with the imposition of criminal sanctions in order to obtain complete responses to every census question about an individual's income, means of transportation, employment, kitchens, bathrooms, or bedrooms? After all, assertions that this information is socially important often emanate from people who find it useful but neither have to pay for it nor bear the burden of providing or collecting it. Reluctant respondents are hardly criminals. They typically are people who cherish their privacy and fear that their responses will be used to their detriment or believe that the present census exceeds the federal government's constitutional power. Alas, those who daily handle information rarely seem to appreciate the subjective character of privacy or the relevance of the cliché "one man's privacy is another man's exhibitionism."[7]

For the sake of discussion let us assume the value of each question on the 1970 census. Surely the application of criminal sanctions for a refusal to respond cannot be justified unless it is clearly established (1) that removing them would result in wide-scale citizen refusal to comply with the census, so as to impair the results of the study significantly; and (2) that there is no reasonably expeditious alternative way of procuring the information. Although it has been strenuously asserted that eliminating the criminal penalties would seriously impair the accuracy of the census, it seems unlikely that a significant portion of the population would refuse to honor the census request simply because the penalty has been removed.[8] For most people the process of responding to government questionnaires has taken on a Pavlovian character and for others it simply is a matter of good citizenship. And if a mere handful of citizens refuse to reply to a particular question, perhaps the results received from the mass of the population would be sufficient to provide the information sought by the government. In addition, highly refined sampling techniques may be available if there is any indication that the data do not accurately reflect the facts or a peculiar pattern of nonresponsiveness has emerged.[9] Since the Bureau conducts numerous voluntary surveys on a sample basis every year, it has the expertise to test the legitimacy of this technique. But even supposing that there is substantial resistance to a particular question, this recalcitrance might well demonstrate a widely held belief that the query is too intrusive or does not deal with a matter of legitimate government concern. If so, perhaps citizen reaction should be respected, even if some loss of information results.

Moreover, it is not clear to what extent the information currently requested on the decennial census duplicates information already accumulated by other organizations. In many cases, local agencies may be able to provide data on many of the housing and employment questions currently being asked on the census. The Bureau does go to other agencies in some cases—it gets farm information from the Internal Revenue Service, for example—although it is claimed that data collected by other sources usually do not dovetail with the information sought by the census. This problem might be solved by altering the information-gathering procedures of other agencies or by employing limited supplementary surveys to satisfy the needs of those who use a particular type of census information.

In appraising the importance of the decennial census, the fact that it is far from a perfect measuring instrument often is overlooked. In 1960, for example, well over five million people were not counted at all, and Americans living abroad, such as servicemen and students, were not directly attributed to their home states for purposes of determining the size of local and state populations. The available evidence indicates that a disproportionate share of the overlooked Americans were in the urban ghetto areas; perhaps as many as ten percent of these people were missed and some census officials believe that thirty percent of the nation's nonwhite male eighteen- and nineteen-year-olds were not counted. One can only speculate as to why they were not reached or whether the Bureau's margin of error is unavoidable in a canvass having the magnitude of the decennial census. We do know that approximately one-half of those citizens who were unaccounted for could not be found despite the Bureau's diligent efforts to catch the transient population by sending enumerators to motels, flophouses, all-night movies, trailer parks, and migrant-worker camps.

In part, the relatively poor performance in the cities during 1960 reflects a high level of citizen unawareness of the census.

One survey research specialist informs me that some months before the 1970 census got underway, sixty percent of the black community in certain areas knew nothing about the census; the national average appears to be approximately fifteen percent. Another factor that most certainly had an effect is a high level of antipathy toward the government and its information activities among the nation's economically and socially disadvantaged. Conceivably, the knowledge that inquisitive government census takers are in the neighborhood produces an ostrich-like reaction in the form of a refusal to respond to a knock on the door. Private market-research firms report the same phenomenon. This is partially attributable to a fear that the officials are looking for improprieties in the home life of welfare recipients or that the answers to the questions might lead to a loss of benefits or some form of governmental repression.

Whatever the cause of the inaccuracies in the 1960 census count, some of its effects are clear. By not counting six million Americans, the decennial census failed to carry out its basic constitutional function—enumeration of the population. As a result, the United States House of Representatives is malapportioned, presumably to the disadvantage of urban ghetto dwellers. In addition, the information so necessary to carrying out various social programs may be skewed and unreliable. Since census statistics are used for allocating the nation's resources (and errors in them often do not come to light until several years after they are compiled), it is unfortunate that the plight of many of our urban citizens is being badly understated.

Perhaps the most distressing aspect of the census process is that to understand and responsibly answer the questions on the longest form, an individual needs reading and comprehension skills (as well as patience) not possessed by large numbers of Americans. Some experts argue that an eighth-grade education is essential—a level of schooling not reached by millions of adult Americans. As bizarre as it may sound, one gets the feeling that the Census Bureau often is more interested in making certain that everyone responds to each inquiry than whether the answers given are accurate. For example, one question on the housing schedule asks when the respondent's dwelling unit was constructed, although it is self-evident that many (if not most) people cannot answer this inquiry accurately.

Given the unrest in the cities since 1960 and the heightened concern over the government's intrusiveness, the 1970 census may not prove to be any more accurate. A number of black spokesmen with whom I have discussed the matter indicate a fair amount of symbolic and emotional resistance to the census in their communities, despite formal statements supporting the census from many leaders. "Why should I help this government; what good will it do me?" seems to be a common reaction. Thus, attempts at rational persuasion in terms of how members of minority groups might benefit from public assistance programs if they are all counted and their substandard life quality is accurately depicted may have been to no avail.

Some blacks have argued that many census questions have racial overtones and are designed to identify the black community for possible separation from the larger population should a crisis arise. They see the census as working hand in glove with such legislative proposals as those involving stop and frisk, preventive detention, the establishment of incarceration camps for use during civil disturbances, as well as with what many believe is the white establishment's conspiracy to exterminate black militants. Despite reasoned defenses against these attacks, the government's credibility gap seems too wide for many blacks to bridge.

Hostility toward the census is not limited to the nation's black population. It showed up during the winter of 1969–70 in several right-wing white communities in the form of a rebellion against the federal government's intrusion into areas thought to be entirely within the governance of state and local authorities or the domain of individual privacy.[10] The effort was led by a few new groups, such as Census Resistance '70 and the Committee for a Voluntary Census (both of which had the same address). These organizations issued statements filled with bravado, but when the chips were down they were only able to mount feeble protests in a handful of cities. A few established groups joined the anti-census cause; Young Americans for Freedom, for example, recited the ancient shibboleths and called for a boycott, but their impact appears to have been negligible. Given their markedly different philosophies and goals, the militant blacks and the right-wing conservatives made strange bedfellows.

The shift in 1970 to mail-out-mail-back procedures for the

questionnaires, if not reinforced by coercive follow-up techniques, will help reduce the resistance or feeling of resentment that the canvassing procedure may have created in the past. At the same time, although preliminary census reports have produced screams of anguish from many cities that had optimistically relied on the larger amount of federal funds that would follow from anticipated higher population figures, the new technique should improve the accuracy of the census.

The Bureau initially estimated that eighty percent of those receiving the form by mail would return it within ten days and the bulk of those who did not could be brought into camp by using telephone calls and personal visits as follow-up procedures. Although the response in the cities was somewhat slower than anticipated, the voluntary compliance rate proved to be higher than predicted. On the other hand, it appears that the hard core of totally uncooperative people is higher than it was in 1960 but there is no reason to believe that this is attributable to the use of the mails.

If the Census Bureau successfully develops a high-grade address register of every dwelling unit in the United States, more complete enumeration may be possible. It is easier to keep track of structures than people, and fairly accurate appraisals can be made of the character of an unresponsive dwelling (as well as its occupants) by a careful evaluation of the surrounding environment. What is more, by keying on addresses it ultimately may be possible to process the census without requiring citizens to identify themselves by name—a change that would allay some concerns about personal privacy. That objective actually could be achieved today by having population data linked to names on a sheet that is separable from an anonymous questionnaire covering the remaining subjects. The two halves could then be returned in different envelopes.

In recent years the symbiotic relationship between the Census Bureau's appetite for personal information and the threat of criminal sanctions has resulted in an increasing number of complaints from the public and congressional demands for change. The Senate Subcommittee on Constitutional Rights, chaired by Senator Ervin of North Carolina, has received a heavy flow of mail relating to the census and governmental questionnaires. The staff of Congressman Jackson Betts reports the same phenomenon.

By and large the letters express a strong concern over what the writers conceive to be a loss of individual privacy and growing governmental intrusiveness.[11]

Public opinion has had some effect. A proposal to request data on religious affiliation on the 1970 census was a special target of the congressional critics and eventually was eliminated.[12] Similarly, a plan to ask disabled people about the nature of their malady was abandoned, as were questions on smoking, moonlighting, union membership, and household pets. An inquiry concerning bathtubs and showers was badly mauled in the press; in fairness to the Bureau, the suggestion that citizens were being asked whether they took showers with other people was a distorted interpretation of the question's language. It remained, but in reworded form.

Dissatisfaction with the census runs deeper than objections to individual questions, however. It is reflected in a number of bills that have been introduced in Congress to limit the kinds of questions that respondents are required to answer under threat of fine or imprisonment.[13] During April, 1969 the Senate Subcommittee on Constitutional Rights held broad hearings on the census and federal questionnaires. One purpose was to see if it is possible to develop a theory to protect citizens from abusive governmental inquiries.[14] To date, however, the only concrete legislative action has been the passage by the House of Representatives of a watered-down version of the so-called Census Reform Act.[15] Its present form, which languished in a Senate Subcommittee until the end of the 91st Congress, merely eliminates the jail sentence as a penalty for noncompliance with census demands, increases the penalties for wrongful disclosure of data by Census Bureau employees, strengthens the Congress's position as the final authority for approving, rejecting, or revising questions, and incorporates certain administrative procedures to insure data confidentiality. But nothing is done either to streamline the census itself or to alter the requirement that citizens must answer each question or face the penalty of the statutory fine.

The criticism leveled against it notwithstanding, the Census Bureau has an unequaled record among federal agencies in preserving the confidentiality of personal information. To my knowledge, there are no documented cases of abusive handling of an individual's census record.[16] In testimony before the House Sub-committee on Census and Statistics in 1969, Congressman Gallagher revealed that the Census Bureau successfully resisted pressure to disclose the names of all Japanese-Americans follow-ing the outbreak of World War II.[17] It therefore is not surprising that the Census Bureau's enviable history was frequently cited by advocates of the National Data Center as indicative of the type of security that can be achieved by a professionally staffed statistical organization.[18] But this past record is no guarantee for the future. Both the public and the Bureau are at the mercy of Congress, which can alter the confidentiality rules protecting the collected data whenever it sees fit.

Some deficiencies inevitably crop up even in the Census Bureau. In 1963, for example, it reportedly provided the Ameri-can Medical Association with a "statistical" list of one hundred and eighty-eight doctors residing in Illinois. The list was broken down into more than two dozen income categories, and each cate-gory was further subdivided by medical specialty and area of residence; as a result, identification of individual doctors was possible.[19] In addition, there probably has been a fair amount of data disclosed at the information-gathering level by the large corps of enumerators employed to carry out the periodic can-vassing.[20] It is difficult to believe that all census takers are im-mune from gossiping or impervious to the entreaties by one neighbor for information concerning the replies of another. Of course, if direct-mail techniques prove successful, this type of abuse should be reduced.

In addition to the protection afforded citizens by the pro-fessionalism that pervades the Bureau, the existing Census Act imposes three prohibitions on its employees. They may not

(1) use the information furnished under the provisions of . . . [the Act] for any purpose other than the statistical pur-poses for which it is supplied; or

(2) make any publication whereby the data furnished by any particular establishment or individual under this title can be identified; or

(3) permit anyone other than the sworn officers and em-ployees of the Department or bureau or agency thereof to examine the individual reports.[21]

A wrongful disclosure of information by an employee may be punished by a fine of up to a hundred dollars and two years in jail;[22] these sanctions have never been applied. The Census Reform Act proposed in the 91st Congress would have raised the penalties to five thousand dollars and five years in jail.

Unfortunately, the current Act's restrictions are difficult to apply. The limitation on information use to "statistical" purposes in subdivision (1) presumably is intended to prohibit "identifying" or "surveillance" activities. But this means that whether it is proper to furnish information depends on what a particular user might infer from the data. It seems unrealistic to expect Census Bureau employees to make judgments about a user's ability to identify individuals from a particular tabulation or his intention to use the information improperly in the future —judgments that are made much more difficult by the increasingly sophisticated computer processing techniques a user can employ. Moreover, Bureau employees will be called upon to make these decisions more frequently because requests for the release of data in small aggregates of respondent units, rather than large tabulations, are certain to proliferate as the trend toward computer analysis of "microdata" accelerates.[23] Indeed, some have succumbed to the pressures for disclosure regarding many types of data. In time, the effect of leaving disclosure decisions to Bureau workers may be the deterioration of the current standard of census confidentiality.

Another potential loophole in the statutory scheme protecting census data can be found in the Secretary of Commerce's statutory authority to "furnish to Governors of States . . . courts of record, and individuals, data for genealogical and other proper purposes, from the population, agriculture, and housing schedules,"[24] and to disclose census data to "State or local officials, private concerns, or individuals upon the payment of the actual or estimated cost of such work."[25] Both of these passages are subject to the palliative that "in no case shall information furnished . . . be used to the detriment of the persons to whom such information relates."[26] Although this provision is primarily utilized by individuals who need information about themselves from earlier censuses, particularly for proof of age in connection with social security, Medicare and other benefits,[27] it operates as an ill-defined exception to the prohibitions in the confidentiality section discussed earlier. The quantum of protection provided by the vague standard of "detriment to the individual" seems scant; it can be vitiated all too easily by a strict judicial or administrative interpretation of the language.[28] The Census Reform Act quite properly would limit this provision to requests from the individual himself and make it clear that any governmental agency, whether it be federal, state, or local, that has been given census data cannot reveal information that has been furnished by any individual.

Inroads on the integrity of census data have come from other sources. In *St. Regis Paper Company* v. *United States*,[29] the United States Supreme Court decided that the confidentiality provisions of the Census Act did not prevent other branches of the government from compelling the production of a respondent's own file copy of reports given to the Bureau. The Court reasoned that the protection provided by the statute was enforceable only against the Census officials who received the data, and did not attach to the information in the report itself. To many, the result reached in St. Regis represented a serious breach of faith by the federal government. In 1962 Congress overrode the decision by enacting a statute making copies of census reports retained by the respondent immune from subpoena.[30]

Despite Congress's resolution of the St. Regis affair, a number of disturbing questions remain. For one thing, St. Regis can be interpreted as supporting the proposition that, in spite of the pledge of confidentiality by the federal agency that collects certain information, a copy of the report is vulnerable to a subpoena in the absence of a specific act of Congress exempting it. Indeed, the Court's opinion in St. Regis does state: "Congress did not prohibit the use of the reports *per se* but merely restricted their use while in the hands of those persons receiving them . . . i.e., the government officials."[31] Moreover, if the Census Act's confidentiality restrictions are enforceable only against officials who gather the information initially, it is conceivable that they cannot be enforced against a third party—either governmental or nongovernmental—who lawfully obtains information from the Bureau and subsequently misuses it. Finally, the statute applies only to census reports and does not prevent other federal agencies from framing a questionnaire containing questions that appear on a census survey and imposing it on part of the public, which indirectly would compromise the principle of census confidentiality. Many agencies use the ploy of having the Census Bureau conduct surveys for them. Once the data collected by the Census Bureau are processed and transferred to the requesting agency,[32] typically in the form of computer tapes, the excellent confidentiality record of the Bureau becomes irrelevant since it no longer can control the use or dissemination of the data.

The Census Bureau's administration of questionnaires for other federal agencies is a matter of considerable significance. More than half of the Bureau's energies are devoted to these enterprises and in many ways they are at the heart of the objections to the government's information acquisition practices. A list furnished me by Senator Ervin's office shows that in a period of approximately two years the Bureau performed eighty-seven surveys for over twenty federal, state, and local governmental organizations. The groups interrogated during this period included the elderly, farm workers, optometrists, lawyers, the infirm, widows, veterans, and shark-bite victims. The questionnaires inquired into such diverse subjects as bomb shelters, smoking habits, and birth-control methods. In many instances surveys were made weekly, monthly, or annually. Although it is difficult to determine precisely how many people received questionnaires during the two-year period, a six million figure seems conservative.

Many of the questionnaires are lengthy and, in some instances highly intrusive. A document entitled *Longitudinal Retirement History Survey,* processed by the Census Bureau for HEW, is almost twice as long as the 1970 census. It has been sent to a sample group of elderly people who are receiving social security benefits. Besides numerous probing interrogatories about the respondent's finances and past employment, the questionnaire asks:

> What have you been doing in the last four weeks to find work?
> Taking things all together, would you say you're very happy, pretty happy, or not too happy these days?
> Do you have any artificial dentures?
> Is there some kind of care or treatment that you have put off even though you may still need it? What is this care or treatment for?

> Do you (or your spouse) see or telephone your parent(s) as often as once a week?
>
> How many different newspapers do you receive and buy regularly?
>
> About how often do you . . . go to a barber shop or beauty salon?
>
> What were you doing most of last week?[33]

Given the wide range of questionnaires administered by the Bureau, the dependent position of the many people subjected to them, their content, and the uncertain rules relating to dissemination of the responses, it becomes evident that these inquiries represent a greater threat to privacy than does the decennial census.

Although the surveys conducted for other agencies by the Census Bureau are voluntary in the sense that criminal sanctions cannot be imposed if the recipient refuses to respond, that fact typically is not indicated on the questionnaire. A recent "voluntary" home survey was boldly marked: "This Form Should Be Completed And Returned Whether You Are A Rentor Or A Homeowner, Whether You Live In A One-Family Home, Or A House With Two Or More Families, An Apartment, Or Any Other Type of Building." People who do not reply often are sent follow-up letters (occasionally by certified mail) or receive personal visits.

The reality of the situation is that even a benign questionnaire sent out under the imprimatur of a federal agency has a coercive effect on most individuals. Governmental surveys also benefit from the natural, although erroneous, assumption that it is unlawful, perhaps criminal, not to respond to an inquiry by the sovereign. Moreover, who can measure the level of anxiety that a privacy-conscious social security or Medicare beneficiary or the holder of a veteran's pension experiences when he receives a request for information from HEW or the Defense Department on a form that carries the Census Bureau seal, especially when strongly worded letters or telephone calls follow shortly thereafter? A concern over a possible loss of governmental benefits would not be unnatural. And are we really certain that a citizen's attempt to protect his privacy by refusing to answer a questionnaire will not nettle some administrator to the point of reprisal?

The most serious limitation on confidentiality restrictions

of the type governing the Census Bureau, however, is not the scheme's potential ineffectiveness as a means of deterring wrongful disclosures by agency personnel. Rather it is the fact that information transactions are conducted without giving the citizen involved notice and an opportunity to be heard. Admittedly, the absence of procedural safeguards has not had serious privacy consequences in the past, but in the future the twin pressures of increased governmental information gathering and widespread, detailed computer analysis of data may well alter the past habits of the federal information handling agencies. This may manifest itself in the form of additional demands on the Bureau to process questionnaires and to include more lines of inquiry in the decennial census. Unless these forces are carefully watched and appropriate counterpressures are established, fissures in the existing privacy safeguards are almost certain to develop.

2. Transfers of Information Among Federal Agencies

Government, like any other organism, refuses to acquiesce in its own extinction. This refusal, of course, involves the resistance to any effort to diminish its powers and prerogatives. There has been no organized effort to keep government down since Jefferson's day. Ever since then the American people have been bolstering up its powers and giving it more and more jurisdiction over their affairs. They pay for that folly in increased taxes and diminished liberties.

—H. L. Mencken, *Minority Report:*
H. L. Mencken's Notebooks (1956), 143

The proliferation of large time-sharing computer systems and the current high cost of electronic data retrieval are encouraging governmental information managers to share bodies of data in which they have a common interest. Although it is difficult to obtain concrete information on the character of interagency exchanges of personal data, it is reasonably clear that only sporadic attention has been paid to the privacy implications of these activities. Fortunately, many agencies are only exchanging scientific and technical data and there are several effective restraints on the mobility of personal data held by the government—a given agency's confidentiality rules, the requirements of "national security," agency jealousy, or the incompatibility of record-keeping techniques. On the other hand, there appears to be extensive sharing of information that is collected during security checks. For example, the Army's Investigation Records Repository, which maintains security information on Army personnel and civilian employees, is open to the FBI, CIA, and other government agencies. The Army's "civil disorder" data files presumably will be available on the same basis. In addition, there is the inevitable unsanctioned information exchange between employees in different agencies, in many instances having no legitimate governmental objective. One example of this involved a governmental employee who gave out personal information on file subjects to a friend in another agency who passed it on to a real-estate broker who used it to check out prospective tenants for a housing complex.

Perhaps the strongest single pressure motivating interagency information transfers is that the cost effectiveness of any data collection activity depends in part on the number of users who can share its fruits. Thus, former Director of the Budget Bureau, Charles L. Schultze, has called interagency "data matching" on an individual basis "imperative" to fill the gaps in the information needed to measure the social performance of many federal programs. Similarly, the enactment of President Nixon's welfare proposals will result in an increase of data sharing. The House of Representatives version of the Family Assistance Act, for example, requires federal agencies to furnish HEW any information needed to verify an individual's eligibility for benefits. The report accompanying the bill makes it clear that the applicant's tax returns may be examined for this purpose.[34] Information integration also offers an important side benefit for data users; as cost effectiveness improves it becomes easier to justify requests for the funding of new and more expensive information-gathering activities.

Transfers of information between agencies are legitimized by a statute granting the Office of Management and Budget the power to "require a Federal agency to make available to another Federal agency information obtained from any person."[35] This authority can be exercised only if at least one of the following conditions is met: (1) the information consists of statistical summaries, (2) it is not confidential at the time of transfer, (3) the person who supplied the information has consented to its release, or (4) the agency that is to receive it has power to collect the information itself.[36] Congress also has provided that transferred information is subject to the confidentiality restrictions that are in force in the agency that originally gathered the data, and any employee of the transferee agency who violates these rules is subject to the same penalties that apply to the employees of the transferor organization.[37]

Although these provisions are logically grounded and seem to eliminate any direct threat to privacy—assuming they are honored—they do contain potential loopholes. For example, under condition number four, personal information given to one agency may be transferred to another if the receiving organization itself has the power to collect the data. This means that an individual who disclosed information under the assumption that it was being given only to one federal agency may find that his personal data have been transferred to another agency. In some instances citizens who are not under any legal obligation to respond might not voluntarily disclose certain information to an agency if they knew it would be made available to others.

As is true of much of the existing regulatory scheme relating to information handling, the statute governing the Budget Bureau was conceived with the manual transfer of manila folders in mind. These rules may prove to be difficult to enforce in the context of frequent large-scale transfers of machine-readable data among compatible computer systems. Computerized information can be transferred either by manually delivering it in its stored form—a reel of magnetic tape or a magnetic disc—or by feeding it directly from one computer memory unit to another through an electronic interface. Both procedures permit the data to be duplicated so that the original can remain with the lending agency and a machine-readable copy used (and presumably retained) by the borrowing unit. The transferred information may well not carry any indication of its source, particularly if it is stored by the borrower and used on a random-access basis or is amalgamated with other data or altered in some fashion that makes it impossible to determine the genesis of a particular item.

In short, the more sophisticated methods of transferring or using computerized data do not leave indications of what has taken place. Furthermore, to my knowledge there currently is no effective procedure being employed to insure that the limitations on the Office of Management and Budget's power to authorize exchanges are being honored. This need not and should not be the case. A computer system can be programmed to indicate the source of data that has been received from another agency, although in some cases cost and storage-space considerations might not make anything more than a very general notice practical. As direct links between computer systems in different agencies are established, however, it will become imperative to develop procedures for identifying the source of personal data in order to honor the terms on which information is extracted from citizens.

Even if the user can be warned that he is handling borrowed data, it is unrealistic to assume that middle- and low-level administrators are familiar with the disparate standards of confidentiality that are in force in each of the agencies from which data might be supplied. Of course, it is technologically possible (although a dubious use of computer capacity) to program every computer that potentially is a lender of information so that it automatically provides this information with each bit of data that it transmits. Then, like a majestic Wagnerian overture, the transferee computer would print out the rules and regulations applicable to the borrowed information each time it is to be used. Whether these directives would be honored or simply ignored like the health warning on cigarette packs is another matter; but at least the user could not advance lack of knowledge as an excuse for any subsequent defalcation.

At some point the basic assumption underlying the statutory transfer restrictions on federal agencies—that privacy can be protected by aggregating confidentiality requirements—must break down as a result of sheer complexity. The House Committee on Government Operations examined an aggregation scheme as a method of protecting privacy in the context of a data center servicing thirty to forty federal agencies. The system was rejected as impractical because "each of the hundreds of bureaus would have to rate every type of information it possesses separately for all other bureaus that might request the information."[38]

The obvious alternative to an aggregation scheme, a single scale of confidentiality that can be used to rate every report received by the government, also was rejected. The Committee felt that the imposition of a uniform standard would obscure the fact that "the sensitivity of a given document is not intrinsic, but varies with the relationship between the agency gathering the data and the agency receiving it." The Committee's Report offered the following example: "[A] person giving his income for the HUD survey would have his confidence violated if the income figure were to be given to the Internal Revenue Service, but not if it were given to the Bureau of Census for aggregate purposes."[39]

An interesting illustration. Was the Committee unaware of the persistent reports of the exchange of personal data between the Internal Revenue Service and other agencies? Indeed, it is no secret that a citizen's tax record can show up in a variety of places in the federal government.[40] In *United States* v. *Costello*,[41] the defendant was prosecuted for income-tax evasion. The federal prosecutor asked an Internal Revenue agent to inspect the tax returns of the group from which the jury would be selected, and to provide him with a summary of any events in their dealings with the tax authorities that might make them unfavorably disposed toward the government. The list was used as a basis for challenging and disqualifying jurors, and, in spite of the fact that no comparable information was available to the defendant, the court held that this was a permissible use of the tax information under the statute and applicable regulations. The popular conception that federal tax returns are sacrosanct simply is incorrect, as evidenced by former Nixon aide Clark Mollenhoff's revelation that on several occasions he examined individual tax returns in connection with some of his investigatory work on behalf of the President.

Resolution of the dilemma posed by the deficiencies of both the aggregation and the single-standard approaches to protecting transferred information is essential if a rational scheme of confidentiality is to be developed for interagency transfers of personal data. As indicated in later chapters, the answer may lie in a combination of restrictions on data collection by the government and the development of administrative and technological safeguards for the handling of information.[42] Unless something is done in the near future, the incidence of computerized data transfers will continue to increase in an unstructured fashion and be regulated only by a series of horse-and-buggy confidentiality restrictions that provide a barrier against information migration that is about as porous as McNamara's Vietnam Wall.

3. Federal-State-Local Transfers of Information

Simplicity of administration is a merit that does not inhere in a federal system of government.

—Mr. Justice Jackson, in
Davies Warehouse Company v.
Bowles, 321 U.S. 144, 153 (1944)

The federal government's computerization and information gathering activities have been paralleled by the development of numerous data centers at the regional,[43] state,[44] and local[45] levels. Not surprisingly, there also has been increasing pressure to establish interfaces to facilitate the direct transmission of information among nonfederal centers and the data banks maintained by the national government. At present the primary restraint on these practices appears to be a practical one—the incompatibility of most automated data-processing systems. But this temporary safeguard will disappear when devices become available that enable different machines to exchange data.

Even without this capability, intergovernmental information swapping has begun to move into high gear. Several programs already exist that involve the sharing of personal data between federal agencies and the states. For example, the Internal Revenue Code permits federal income-tax returns to be examined by state revenue officials.[46] The Treasury Department also has issued regulations that make federal estate- and gift-tax returns available to states that are willing to reciprocate by allowing the federal government to peruse their tax records.[47] Over forty states have entered "agreements of cooperation" with the Internal Revenue Service,[48] and more than twenty-five have begun exchanging magnetic tapes with the federal government.[49] As a result, more than forty-five million 1969 federal tax returns will be made available to the states on a computerized basis. These figures are certain to increase as more states develop systems to use the federal government's computerized tax data. Although the administrative and revenue advantages of information interchange among different taxing authorities are great, they are being achieved at the risk of exposing financial and personal data (some parts of the tax return touch upon private matters, such as the charities supported by the taxpayer, and his medical condition) to a considerably larger number of people than the average taxpayer anticipated when he filed his return.

Abandonment of the exchange program is not necessary but an evaluation and strengthening of the privacy-protecting procedures being used is clearly in order. A return that finds its way into malevolent or negligent hands can result in great damage to an individual, and elements of organized crime or unscrupulous political or business operatives undoubtedly have an incentive to see certain files. It also is likely that they would be willing to pay handsomely for that privilege, which makes the maximum statutory penalty of a one thousand dollar fine and one year imprisonment for wrongful disclosure[50] seem dangerously ineffective as a deterrent. This is especially so inasmuch as a reel of magnetic tape containing information on thousands of taxpayers may be "borrowed," duplicated, and returned with a minimum of effort or risk.[51]

Comparable threats to personal privacy are inherent in the development of "integrated information systems" in the law-enforcement arena. This use of information technology has been advocated to counteract the difficulties of dealing with today's mobile and well-organized criminal population. The Federal Bureau of Investigation has established a National Crime Information Center (NCIC) (prominently featured on the ABC television series *The FBI*), which provides state and city police forces with immediate access to computerized files on stolen property and wanted persons. NCIC already has become the keystone of an elaborate crime-information network that eventually will integrate law-enforcement information centers throughout the nation into a single system. At the end of 1969, the FBI's Center was reported to have been exchanging data with state and city police computers in every state except Alaska. As a result, a two-way flow of information has been established and approximately forty thousand items are being received from local police agencies every day. Approximately three thousand remote-access terminals already are linked to the FBI's computer. One thousand of these are in police stations that are tied directly to NCIC and the other two thousand are connected to state computer systems that in turn have access to NCIC.

There is no doubt that in its present form NCIC, as well as many other law-enforcement data banks, is highly utilitarian and justifiable. No one can quarrel with the notion that a policeman in a squad car should be able to call his dispatcher for an NCIC check on a vehicle and its registered owner before he personally approaches it. How else is he likely to be warned that the driver may be armed and dangerous? But if systems of this type expand to include sensitive information about people who have not already been branded as fugitives, and precautions are not taken to insure their security and integrity, the dangers may begin to outweigh the benefits. There is little reason to be sanguine about the future. The FBI has revealed that police arrest records probably will be computerized and added to the NCIC data base, assuming that Congress provides the necessary funds. Despite the notoriously misleading character of many arrest records, there are currently *no* plans to improve the security of the NCIC network or to upgrade the quality and accuracy of the data that are recorded. That is thought to be the responsibility of the user. Of course, the user may be a policeman who sells insurance in his spare time and finds it helpful to use NCIC to check on potential clients.

State and local law-enforcement computer systems also are becoming increasingly sophisticated. New York, perhaps the leader among the states in computerizing police records, already has in operation the essential features of a network built around a single computer center—New York State Identification and Intelligence system (NYSIIS). This central unit is designed to store information for state and local law-enforcement agencies and permit them to retrieve data through their own terminals.[52] In Ohio, the Cincinnati-Hamilton County Crime Information Center allows thirty-eight city and state agencies to share its computerized information.[53] This system is tied both to NCIC and the Ohio State Highway Patrol Computer Center in Columbus, Ohio, and plans are under way to connect the Cincinnati-Hamilton County Center to systems in Kentucky and Indiana.[54]

Going farther afield, Scotland Yard is developing an information system that will be available to law-enforcement agencies throughout the British Isles. English officials have expressed concern about the possibility of a bored Scottish constable "dialing in" on his neighbors' files. Similar computer systems are being developed in other nations and by multi-national organizations such as INTERPOL. Satellite or cable transmission will enable these centers to exchange data with NCIC, which can then forward them to state and local systems.

The picture would not be complete without a word about the informational backscratching that pervades the law enforcement and corporate security fields. Every sizable company, particularly those engaged in work for the government, maintains dossiers on large numbers of people. The total must be staggering, since certain individual corporations have millions of individualized records. Because of their similiarity in background and common interests, an informal, but effective, information transfer network exists among industry security officers and all segments of the law-enforcement fraternity. Thus, a security man with a grudge (or for a price) probably can blackball someone and limit his ability to gain employment. Ironically, in one case of this type that has been brought to my attention, the individual excluded from the job market had been both a law-enforcement agent and a corporate-security man himself for many years.

There are some restraints on the mobility of computerized crime information as illustrated by the following comment about the reluctance of law-enforcement agencies to share information:

> "When it gets right down to it," [a] state official said, "I just don't know whether [New York County District Attorney Frank S.] Hogan is going to let N.Y.S.I.I.S. see the sensitive kind of stuff he's got in his files, especially when there's a possibility it might fall into the hands of a corrupt sheriff or police chief at the other end of the state."[55]

Accompanying the trend toward law-enforcement networks is considerable pressure to computerize previously uncollected sensitive data. The Massachusetts State Police Division of Subversive Activities, for example, has files "on peace groups, civil rightists, and other such groups"; in 1968 it performed 4,034 security name checks—*some of which were undertaken for private purposes.*[56] In addition, the Institute for Defense Analysis Report to the President's Commission on Law Enforcement and Administration of Justice suggests fifteen general categories of information for inclusion in police intelligence systems; among them are state motor vehicle registrations, sex and narcotics offenders, and known criminal associates.[57] When he was the Executive Director of the American Civil Liberties Union, John de J. Pemberton, Jr. expressed apprehension that information of an entirely different character eventually will be recorded:

Our . . . concern . . . is that it will be the repository for
. . . information not at all relevant to [the] prevention and
detection of crime. It is said that other Federal investigative agencies will be invited to feed whatever information
they choose into the huge reservoir that the national network
of computers will store and retrieve. Data concerning a person's political beliefs and associations, gathered by various
Federal security agencies, thus will become part of the crime
data bank. The implications are obvious: every local police
official will be able to learn with facility not only whether
a suspect has a criminal record, a proper disclosure, but also
whether he has at all deviated from his community's political
or social norms, a highly improper disclosure which threatens
the enjoyment of first amendment protections.[58]

In light of the revelation that the Army has been maintaining
files on the lawful political activities of many citizens,[59] and has
been exchanging data with the FBI, Mr. Pemberton's observations seem prophetic.

The same pressures that are encouraging information integration among different levels of government may lead to even
more comprehensive networks in the future. Direct federal funding will be a contributing factor as exemplified by the Office of
Education's support of the Migrant Worker Children Data
Bank, described earlier.[60] Another is the Department of Housing
and Urban Development's sponsorship of prototype computerized
municipal information systems. Although neither involves the
creation of a federal data bank, it would be foolish to ignore
the ease with which they could be plugged into the national
government's information flow. One federal program that undoubtedly will yield a federal-state-local network is the Family
Assistance Act, because its gives HEW authority to exchange data
with state welfare agencies.[61] Another is the award of grants,
such as one to the Oklahoma Office of Inter-Agency Coordination,
by the Justice Department's Law Enforcement Assistance Administration to maintain surveillance files on citizens.

Other combinations are on the horizon. In light of the
polarity of today's student activism and public and governmental
reactivism, it is conceivable that law-enforcement and educational
data centers will be linked. Recently enacted federal statutes

have branded certain disruptive campus activities criminal,[62] and comparable state legislation is becoming increasingly fashionable.[63] In this atmosphere, we can expect the universities to be subjected to increased demands for information from the outside. Investigative efforts certainly would be expedited if data collected by the FBI, the Justice Department, local law-enforcement agencies, and the academic institutions could be coordinated. If anyone thinks that this notion is farfetched, let him consider the implications of President Nixon's request of September 22, 1970, for funding and increased statutory authority to use one thousand new FBI agents on university campuses.

All things considered, the threat to individual privacy from the sharing of information among different levels of government (especially if transfers are extended to the private sector) may well be greater than the threat from the transmission of data within the federal government. The latter is a relatively closed system with comparatively few people having access to significant portions of the data store. On the other hand, local information handlers are more numerous and may be more likely to be inefficient, insensitive, or animated by malice or idle curiosity about the content of the data than are their federal counterparts. For example, state and city officials usually are geographically closer to individual data subjects and therefore are in a better position to cause injury than relatively remote federal officials. Moreover, the difficulties—and therefore the dangers—of interpreting and drawing conclusions from noncomparable bodies of information are likely to arise in more extreme form when individual data centers that have been designed to meet the particular needs of a single agency at one level of government later are patched together to permit data transfers on an intergovernmental basis.[64] Finally, in the case of interagency information exchanges at the national level, both sides of the transaction are under the aegis of the federal government, which can supervise the use being made of the data. This type of control is much more difficult to exercise in the intergovernmental transfer situation. True, federal statutes can make misuse of federal information by a state or local official a crime, as is done in the tax field, but the likelihood of being able to identify someone using the data improperly is minimal when the federal agency is not in a position to keep tabs on what is happening to the borrowed data.

Unfortunately, the designers and advocates of integrated information systems thus far have been more concerned with collecting and making data more widely available than they have been with preserving individual privacy. Although the objectives of these planners cannot be faulted, their inability (or unwillingness) to define the proper parameters of their task and minimize the risks it creates can be criticized. For example, the *Report of the President's Commission on Law Enforcement and Administration of Justice* devoted a mere one and one-half pages to the problem of individual privacy. It platitudinously concluded: "This problem still needs much more study, analysis, and judgment."[65] But this did not deter the Commission from insisting that law-enforcement agencies must collect more data, and this is exactly what is happening under the Law Enforcement Assistance Administration. In other words: "Damn the privacy problems, full speed ahead." But what is one to expect at a time when the population is mesmerized by the constant repetition of the "law and order" cliché and terrorized by a steady tattoo of pronouncements about the crime crisis? In the midst of this din, suggestions promoting criminal intelligence networks seem quite reasonable.

4. The Federal Government and the Public— The Freedom of Information Act

If information gives power, its possession should not be monopolized by the state. . . . But . . . the government that gives away information . . . might be taking away another man's privacy. Man can be manipulated by being kept in the dark or by being exhibited in the open. How these two rights are reconciled will be one of the critical constitutional tests of the cybernetic age.

—Allen Schick, "The Cybernetic State," *Trans-Action*, Feb. 1970, at 15, 24

The disclosure of information gathered by the federal government to private individuals and organizations creates yet another set of threats to personal privacy. These are particularly troublesome because in many cases the information held by the government has been extracted from individuals under a statutory mandate or through the use of subtle (and occasionally blatant) forms of coercion. Even though governmental use of these techniques deprives the individual of control over his information profile, recent cases broadly construing the First Amendment guarantees of free speech and press indicate that personal data can be disseminated by the press with virtual impunity.[66]

The privacy problems resulting from access to governmentally held data go beyond the activities of the communications media. Employers, creditors, business rivals, and a multitude of others having what they conceive to be an "interest" in a particular individual also have occasion to seek information about him from the government. In the past the relative inaccessibility and decentralized character of federal records, coupled with a bureaucratic reluctance to open the files to outsiders, provided the requisite safeguards against public scrutiny of governmental data.

But the utility of these restraints has been sharply reduced by the enactment in 1967 of a statute—loftily entitled the Freedom of Information Act[67]—that requires the disclosure of broad categories of information held by governmental agencies. Thus far the judicial application of the Act has involved such wide-ranging matters as the request of a businessman for financial records held by the General Services Administration to help him characterize certain transactions for tax purposes,[68] an inquiry by a young man for information about the members of his draft board,[69] and a Stanford University historian's attempt to obtain a government file allegedly concerning the forced repatriation and death of nine hundred thousand anti-communist Russians after World War II.[70]

The statute's stated purpose is to insure that the public has access to enough governmental information to enable it to scrutinize the activities of federal administrators. Theoretically this will provide a mechanism for citizens to inquire into possible official abuse and promote public confidence in the national government. However, the Act also may have a profound effect upon an individual's capacity to prevent the circulation of information that he has divulged to the government.[71]

The conflict between the general public's right to know what its government is doing and the individual's right to have some control over the dissemination of personal information held by the government is an extremely difficult one to resolve. And it is doubtful that any legislative formula could offer more than general guidelines for handling the kaleidoscopic factual problems that are certain to arise. But the distressing reality is that the Information Act, perhaps unintentionally, has upset the prior balance between the competing policies, apparently without taking sufficient account of privacy considerations. By establishing an across-the-board statutory policy directing disclosure of governmental records, the Act reverses the traditional presumption in favor of a citizen's personal privacy, and places the burden on the information-holding agency to find a specific statutory ground for refusing to honor a request for disclosure.[72] In some instances the Act not only has tipped the scales in favor of disclosure, but it has done so with a very heavy hand. For example, the most important statutory exemption from disclosure for purposes of individual privacy immunizes only "personnel and medical files and similar files the disclosure of which constitute a *clearly unwarranted* invasion of personal privacy."[73]

University of Chicago law professor Kenneth Culp Davis, one of the leading experts on administrative law, has persuasively argued that the quoted provision forces the government official who has custody of a requested document to commit "an invasion of personal privacy and . . . even . . . an unwarranted invasion of personal privacy so long as it is not 'clearly unwarranted.' "[74] It is difficult for me to imagine a low-level administrator engaging in the type of sophisticated analysis suggested by Professor Davis. This may well be for the better, because the application of the statute according to its precise terms would deprive the right of privacy of any substance by promoting the automatic disclosure of information.

It is highly disturbing that ministerial personnel will be making the initial determination of whether or not the release of a given document constitutes an invasion of privacy—a judgmental question that few legal scholars would analyze in the same way. I must disagree with Professor Davis's conclusion, that "The terms 'personnel and medical files,' 'similar files,' and 'clearly unwarranted invasion of personal privacy' are all reasonably clear standards."[75] Reasonably clear to Professor Davis perhaps, but whether they are clear to the clerk at the Interstate Commerce Commission or to a custodian in some record room in the Department of Housing and Urban Development is another matter.

Perhaps those courts called upon to apply the statute's language will provide agency administrators with a more helpful standard for determining when sensitive personal information should be released. It also would be desirable if the courts interpreted the statutory provision so as to prevent any invasion of privacy, rather than limiting themselves to those that are "clearly unwarranted." The court's power to exercise discretion in applying the Information Act is supported by several cases holding that a federal judge must employ the historic equity practice of balancing the competing interests so as to arrive at a just result.[76]

The Information Act also provides that the contents of the files are available to "any person."[77] This mandate may be so encompassing that it will prevent courts from reaching a sensible accommodation between the threat to individual privacy and the importance of public access to governmentally held information.[78] Notwithstanding the language of the Act and its legislative history, a memorandum on the statute prepared by the Attorney General's office concludes that a federal court can limit those who may obtain disclosure by exercising its discretion and weighing such factors as "the purposes and needs of the plaintiff, the burdens involved, and the importance to the public interest of the Government's reason for nondisclosure."[79] I have also heard several agency officials suggest that the decision whether to disclose data should depend in part on the identity of the requesting party and the purpose to which the information will be put. Presumably, this would impose a heavier burden on business competitors and entrepreneurs who intend to exploit personal data commercially than it would on researchers and social planners. Others reject such a notion, however, as being too subjective a standard to administer and having no foundation in the statute's language.

One desirable by-product of the courts' exercising their discretion would be to give greater attention to privacy than did the draftsmen of the Act. Language in at least one reported case suggests this possibility. The lawsuit involved the magazine *Consumers Reports,* which had sued to compel disclosure of tests the Veterans Administration had conducted on various hearing aids.[80] No privacy issue was before the court, since the government's reluctance to release the information was based on its fear of incurring the anger of those manufacturers whose products had fared badly. However, in ordering disclosure of the information, the court indicated its concern for a wide range of interests.

> The rule that will be followed . . . is this: where agency records are not exempted from disclosure by the Freedom of Information Act, a court must order their disclosure unless the agency proves that disclosure will result in significantly greater harm than good. Because the Act was intended to benefit the public generally, it is primarily the effects on the public rather than on the person seeking the records that must be weighed.[81]

One very important public interest to be weighed is the protection of individual privacy and the preservation of citizen faith in the government's discreet use of personal information. The release of sensitive information by public officials may engender distrust of the government and inhibit its efforts to obtain the information needed to govern effectively. It would be an embittering experience for a person to have a government agency extract information under the threat of a penalty and then have the collector casually turn the information over to private interests for their own purposes, particularly if those receiving the information then used it to the detriment of the data subject. One thought-provoking request under the Information Act was by an employer charged with an unfair labor practice by his employees; he wanted the Labor Board to disclose the testimony the employees had given during the investigation. Sensibly, the application was rejected.[82]

Ironically, although the Information Act permits anyone who has been denied access to an agency's files to seek a court order compelling disclosure, it does not assure that notice will be given (either of the request for information or of the judicial proceeding) to the party whose interest is jeopardized by the request—the individual who is the subject of the data.[83] In light of the mandatory tone of the Act, it is doubtful that reliance on bureaucratic inertia, obstinacy, or the typical administrator's reluctance to reveal the contents of his files are adequate substitutes for guaranteeing the person whose privacy is threatened a right to participate in the process that determines whether disclosure will be ordered. A statutory scheme that requires the exposure of personal data unless someone demonstrates that doing so "would constitute a clearly unwarranted invasion of privacy" and then fails to provide a mechanism for giving notice to the person most interested in (and capable of) discharging that burden, sounds like something from the "theater of the absurd."

Because widespread resort to the Information Act could have a debilitating effect on our prevailing standards of privacy, the scope given to the provisions permitting information to be withheld from public view is crucial. Unfortunately, the wording of these exceptions ranges from the obscure to the opaque, and has moved Professor Davis to characterize the Act, which was on the legislative drawing boards for several years, as "a shabby product indeed."[84] The draftsmanship is so bad that the statute is not even consistent in describing the character of information that may be shielded. The introductory sentence of the exemption section provides that the disclosure requirements are inapplicable to "matters" that are within one of the enumerated protected classes.[85] And several of the most significant exceptions from the disclosure requirement are phrased in terms of "files," "memorandums," or "letters," so that it is possible to read the statute as exempting the release of all information in a given "file" or on a given "matter" if any portion of it fits the statutory exemption, although such a construction of the statute seems very unlikely.[86] An earlier section of the Act[87] permits only the deletion of identifying details on certain classes of documents, however, indicating a more limited withholding power. Any attempt to derive precise definitions from these passages becomes sheer conjecture. The inescapable conclusion is that it is not clear whether the statutory escape valves apply to individual bits of information, specific documents, or entire files. Similarly uncertain is whether synoptic or raw data will be treated differently from collated or evaluated information.

Perhaps the most confusing statutory exemption deals with "trade secrets and commercial or financial information obtained from a person and [that is] privileged or confidential,"[88] a provision the Attorney General's memorandum characterizes as "susceptible of several readings, none of which is entirely satisfactory."[89] Although the legislative history of this section is less than pellucid, it seems to indicate that Congress intended to exempt all privileged information, trade secrets, and data obtained by the government under a pledge or a reasonable expectation of confidentiality.[90] This interpretation, together with the statutory exception for "matters . . . specifically exempted from disclosure by statute,"[91] carves out a substantial area of immunity from disclosure. In effect, it superimposes the confusing structure of the Information Act upon the existing morass of federal confidentiality statutes and regulations. Presumably, a considerable amount of personal data could be protected by interpreting the statute in this fashion.

This construction also poses an intriguing dilemma. A broad reading of the Information Act's exemptions is supported by the notion that unless personal information extracted under a pledge of confidentiality is immunized from disclosure under the Act, the citizen's trust in his government will have been betrayed and may deter people from furnishing candid or voluntary reports. On the other hand, if every agency's pledge of confidentiality must be honored, then federal organizations may be able to immunize many of their records and activities from public scrutiny by the simple expedient of pledging confidentiality for all information gathered from the public.[92]

The statute's many interpretive difficulties are compounded in the context of computerized records. Even its language is somewhat inapposite. How are words such as "files," "memorandums," "letters," and matters" to be applied when the storage medium is a stack of tabulating cards, a reel of magnetic tape, a disc, or a data cell containing thousands or even millions of different items that may or may not be related to each other? Does the Act envision the federal agency's turning over entire tapes or permitting the requesting party to duplicate them, or is it sufficient to furnish a computer printout of the requested data? How this question is answered is of great significance since it is becoming increasingly apparent to industry that enormous quantities of commercially valuable computerized information are available from various governmental agencies.[93] If a tape containing personal data could be obtained, the recipient might be able to subject it to highly detailed computer analysis that would reveal relationships and permit the drawing of inferences about people that would not be possible with less sophisticated methods of processing information. Even though it is doubtful that this type of data scrutiny was intended by Congress when it passed the Act, some agencies have felt obliged to turn over duplicate computer tapes to companies interested in composing solicitation lists. As a result, Representative Horton of New York is seeking the amendment of the Act to end this practice.

A related question is whether the Information Act obliges an agency to process all the relevant data in its files on a given subject or to integrate its own information with accessible data from other governmental agencies. Arguably a person seeking data available on a particular individual, subject, or event has a right to have those data collated from the far reaches of the federal information system. Thus far, the courts seem reluctant to impose a heavy search burden on the agencies, except when there is an attempt to withhold records.[94] But the burden-of-search notion really has no meaning in the computer age because fully integrated computer networks will make data retrieval on even the largest scale a relatively painless operation.

Because the Freedom of Information Act has so many theoretical and linguistic shortcomings, the manner in which it is administered by the agencies will be extremely important.[95] Although experience under the Act is still too sparse to permit a confident assessment of its impact on personal privacy, there is some basis for optimism. One encouraging factor is that little in the way of abusive practices has been revealed in the court decisions or in the applications made to various agencies thus far. In point of fact, there is some evidence that many officials are almost as tight-fisted with their files now as they were prior to the Act.[96]

Another interesting development is that several agencies have established regulations for administrative appeals when the initial decision is against disclosure and the Justice Department has established a review committee.[97] This procedure should encourage document custodians to leave difficult policy questions to a relatively high-level official who is more likely to be attuned to the privacy implications of disclosure. Senior administrators also are less likely to be pressured into releasing the requested data by the threat of litigation. Unfortunately, the Act's goal of rapid and easy disclosure of information relating to agency activities might be defeated by interjecting an administrative appeal that must be pursued before seeking a disclosure order from a court. This certainly would be true if ministerial personnel tended to adopt a general policy of denying disclosure and "bucking it upstairs."

But speed is not the only consideration and in some cases it is of limited importance. The principal users of the Information Act thus far have not been the mass media,[98] who lobbied so effectively for its enactment,[99] but individual litigants invoking the Act to aid them in private litigation,[100] parties threatened by federal administrative action,[101] companies interested in contracting with the Government,[102] and Nader's Raiders (who thus far have had mixed success in obtaining information from the agencies). In all but the last of these situations, the public's need to know is not really involved and will not suffer unduly if administrators proceed with caution or err on the side of protecting privacy. Moreover, the time spent before the agency should not be critical since if disclosure is denied, the Act gives cases arising under it a special priority on the court's docket.[103]

Although agency regulations and practices that take account of privacy considerations will help, they cannot overcome the Information Act's linguistic and philosophical shortcomings. The statute simply ignores the implications of increased levels of governmental data collection from individuals and the impact of new techniques of data analysis and transmission. In the event a federal data network having interfaces with state, local, and private centers is established, the potential application of the Information Act could be staggering. The special problems of computerization clearly were not contemplated by Congress when it passed the statute, and have yet to be subjected to any rational analysis. Indeed, at this writing, more than four years after the Act became law, those who are administering the statute are still encountering very traditional (and in some cases highly pedestrian) difficulties. Illustratively, one of the open issues appears to be how the cost of information disclosure is to be computed and who is to bear the expense. Indeed, the conflict over whether the charge for a transcript page should be the cost of Xeroxing it or the much higher amount paid to the stenographer for preparing the original manuscript has not been resolved. Thus, it is hardly surprising that the interrelation of the Act and the new technology has not yet been generally recognized. Nevertheless, revision of the Information Act seems to be a necessary part of any scheme that attempts to harmonize the policy cross-currents set in motion by the new technologies, individual privacy, and the right of a free people to watch over their appointed and elected servants.

5. Information in Transit—Wiretapping and the Crime Control Act

Show me a man who doesn't eavesdrop, and I'll show you a man with a serious hearing problem.

—H. Schwartz, "The Hearing
Tom is Everywhere," *Newsday,* Jan. 9, 1965

Prior to 1968, the law relating to wiretapping and electronic eavesdropping was confused and incomplete. In 1928, the Supreme Court, by the narrowest of margins, held that the interception of a telephone conversation did not violate the Constitution's protection against unreasonable searches and seizures.[104] Six years later, however, Congress enacted a ban on the interception and disclosure of telephone communications.[105] Various forms of analogous state statutes followed and a pattern began to emerge. But what might have proven to be a coherent regulatory scheme disintegrated under the pressure of advances in non-telephonic electronic eavesdropping.[106] Courts indulged in bizarre distinctions between "spike" microphones that were driven into a wall and bugging devices that were merely attached to a wall or a heating duct.[107] By the 1960's the chaos was so extensive that everyone knew that legislation was the only solution.[108] Eventually, Congress performed the honors in the Omnibus Crime Control and Safe Streets Act of 1968.[109]

Title III of the Crime Control Act gives the nations law-enforcement officers carefully defined, but for the first time explicit, statutory authority to wiretap and intercept certain communications.[110] This has led Senator Hiram Fong of Hawaii to observe: "Title III, in the form proposed by the administration . . . was properly described as the Right to Privacy Act. As accepted by the committee [and ultimately passed], Title III is more appropriately described as the End to Privacy Act."[111] To the extent the Senator's comment suggests that the statute radically alters what had become the facts of our bugged life, it may be somewhat of an overstatement. All the evidence indicates that wiretapping and eavsedropping, both by law-enforcement personnel and private individuals, were widespread prior to 1968.[112] Thus, the statute's primary effect may simply have been to legitimize limited aspects of what Mr. Justice Holmes once referred to as a "dirty business"[113]—one whose law-enforcement value has never been clearly demonstrated.[114]

Despite its recent enactment, the Crime Control Act is a technological anachronism. It completely ignores the realities of modern communications and computer science, which were being discussed as part of the congressional and public debate over the National Data Center at the same time the Crime Control Act was before the Congress. Perhaps the most striking example of the statute's deficiency is that although a substantial and rapidly increasing proportion of the messages carried by the nation's communications networks involves the transmission of data in digital form,[115] the Act is framed almost entirely in terms of voice communications. Even the publicly announced plan to transmit voice conversations in digital form seems to have been overlooked by Congress. As a consequence, the statute's application to digital data transmissions is uncertain at best. At worst the Act eventually may be used to permit privacy-invading interceptions of types that apparently were not contemplated by its draftsmen.

An excellent example of how out of step the statute's language is with the technology is its definition of "intercept": "the *aural* acquisition of the contents of any wire or oral communication through the use of any . . . device."[116] Unless the word "aural" is given a strained construction, the Act does not seem to be applicable to a wiretap on the communications lines of a time-sharing system. The absurdity of a distinction between verbal and digital transmissions is made evident by the fact that some computers are able to respond to inquiries in the form of electronically synthesized speech and the quality of these devices is certain to improve considerably over time.

Much of the interpretive difficulty stems from the fact that the Act does not define "communications." However, numerous cases decided under the Federal Communications Act,[117] many of which are referred to in the legislative history of the new statute, indicate that the term may refer only to transmissions of information between one person and another.[118] Thus, a reference in the Crime Control Act to "communications" technically

might not cover eavesdropping on machine responses to a remote user's inquiry or on the direct wire transfer of data from
one computer to another.[119] This construction would leave data
communications outside the safeguards against indiscriminate
wiretapping embodied in the federal act. There would be protection only to the extent that state legislation affords it[120] or the
Fourth Amendment to the United States Constitution can be construed to ban governmental searches and seizures undertaken in
conjunction with a criminal prosecution.[121] From a privacy perspective, therefore, it actually would be preferable to bring computer communications under the Crime Control Act.

Common sense may well prevent a horse-and-buggy construction of the Act and it is to be hoped that the courts will
extend its provisions to data transmissions. But in certain contexts this may not be easy because of the voice-oriented character
of the statute's language and the clear legislative history indicating that organized crime was the Act's primary target. This latter
point reinforces the notion that the draftsmen were primarily
concerned with obtaining strategic information about criminal
activity by maintaining surveillance on human conversations
over long periods of time.

Significant and troublesome problems are bound to arise in
connection with the Act's grant of authority to law-enforcement
agents to eavesdrop when one of the parties to the communication gives his consent.[122] It is unclear who the parties to a computer transmission are, particularly in the case of a time-share
system in which one user may have access to data deposited by
some, but not necessarily all, of the other users or when the communication involves a machine-to-machine transfer of information. The provision at least suggests that an authorized user may
permit law-enforcement officials to gain access to any part of the
computer's memory bank that is accessible through his own terminal. Another potential gap is that the Act only governs the
tapping of communications handled by common carriers, which
leaves unprotected private and governmental computer networks
that transmit over private lines, microwave relays, and satellites.

The section allowing eavesdropping on an "extension telephone" also may cause difficulty.[123] This provision has much
broader application than listening in on a colored Princess phone
so enthusiastically hawked by the Bell System, because the Act

defines the term to encompass all equipment "furnished to the subscriber or user by a communications common carrier . . . and being used by the subscriber or user in the ordinary course of its business."[124] Thus, "extension telephone" probably includes the input-output devices of a remote-access computer system, such as the increasingly common touch-tone telephone.[125] As a result, if a snooper or the police gain access to one input-output device[126] that is connected to a computerized credit bureau network or a time-share system, it would permit extensive eavesdropping that is unregulated even by the lenient standards of the Crime Control Act. Police forces certainly will be in a position to take advantage of any permissive construction the courts may give to the Act regarding computer communications. As the telephone companies accelerate their conversion to digital transmission, law-enforcement agencies will acquire the equipment and expertise necessary to intercept these communications. In fact, certain police agencies have had the capacity to tap touch-tone telephones since 1967.

Title III of the Crime Control Act provides only a limited right to protest the acquisition of personal information by illicit wiretapping or eavesdropping. The remedy of suppressing illegally seized evidence is available only to an "aggrieved person,"[127] a term that is defined by the statute as "a party to any intercepted . . . communication or a person against whom the interception was directed."[128] According to the first portion of the passage's legislative history, the provision will not safeguard a person who was the *subject* of an illegally seized communication but was not a party to it.[129] The section authorizing a suit for civil damages makes this limitation even clearer by stating that the remedy is available only to a person "whose wire or oral communication is intercepted, disclosed, or used" in violation of the Act.[130] Thus, a file subject whose computerized dossier is seized illegally while being transmitted from a data center to a legitimate user apparently is without recourse.

Denying a remedy to the party who is most affected by disclosure is objectionable even when normal telephone conversations are involved;[131] in the context of intercepting transmissions of extensive quantities of computerized personal information it becomes totally offensive, especially in light of the tendency of data system operators to cooperate with the police.[132] Conceivably, a tenacious litigant could persuade a federal court that the statute's standing provision was framed with only voice communication in mind and should not be extended to the data communication context. Another argument could be made in terms of the policy objectives of the statute. Inasmuch as the Crime Control Act's limitation on standing is based on the desire to minimize the exclusion of reliable evidence in criminal cases,[133] it should not be extended to what basically is a civil action to remedy an intrusion on a citizen's informational profile. This distinction is especially applicable to damage actions to punish an improper interception and use of data communications by private parties.

Of course, in the event that the operative passages of the Act are construed to apply only to voice communications between people, then an individual who is the subject of intercepted data might not be barred by the statutory limitations on the right to sue those who intercepted information about him. This interpretation would afford the data subject little succor, however, since the court decisions involving who may protest against wiretapping and eavesdropping in a situation not governed by federal statute also have been extremely restrictive.[134]

Is the data subject any better off under the second portion of the standing clause—"person against whom the interception was directed"? The legislative history of this passage is rather sparse,[135] but a reference in the Senate Report accompanying the bill to the Supreme Court's decision in *Jones* v. *United States*[136] indicates that the statutory language probably was taken from the following paragraph in the opinion in that case:

> In order to qualify as a "person aggrieved by an unlawful search and seizure" one must have been a victim of a search and seizure, one against whom the search was directed, as distinguished from one who claims prejudice only through the use of evidence gathered as a consequence of a search or seizure directed at someone else. . . . The restrictions upon searches and seizures were obviously designed for protection against official invasion of privacy and the security of property. . . . The exclusion in federal trials of evidence otherwise competent but gathered by federal officials in violation of

the Fourth Amendment is a means for making effective the protection of privacy.[137]

The Supreme Court's language seems to give standing to anyone who has been the victim of an invasion of privacy, not simply a person whose conversation was intercepted. If this reading of Jones were carried over to the Crime Control Act, it would afford the subject, as well as the owner, of the data being transmitted an opportunity to vindicate his rights. Despite a strong dissent by former Justice Abe Fortas, a majority of the Supreme Court took a constrictive view of the Jones language in their later decision in *Alderman* v. *United States*[138] and limited the right to sue to those who were parties to the conversation and those with a special interest in the premises on which the violation took place.[139] At the very least the "special interest" catch-all should give standing to a person who has a proprietary interest in the intercepted data, even when it is moving through a computer system or network in which he has no financial interest.

The Supreme Court's construction of the Jones language in Alderman does not necessarily furnish the standard for interpreting the statutory words "person against whom the interception was directed." The decision did not involve the Crime Control Act and was rendered after its enactment, which means that it could not have been considered by Congress. However, a footnote toward the end of the Court's opinion in Alderman seems to suggest that the standing tests in Title III, Alderman, and Jones are the same.[140] Moreover, there is every likelihood that the federal courts will adhere to the Supreme Court's narrow view of standing—especially now that the Court's stewardship has passed from Chief Justice Earl Warren to Chief Justice Warren Burger.

By necessity this discussion of Title III of the Crime Control Act and its relationship to the interception of computerized data transmissions has been highly episodic and impressionistic. The newness of the legislative scheme and the uncertain movements of the technology caution against attempting anything more than a tentative presentation at this time. The specific problems that have been described were selected merely to highlight a fundamental shortcoming of the Act. By virtually ignoring data communications and the new computer technology, the statute makes it possible for law-enforcement agencies to treat this important form of information transfer as if it were nothing more than a telephone conversation. Congress's failure to differentiate between voice and data communications displays either a lack of awareness of recent technological developments in the communications field or a certain amount of disingenuousness. Given congressional preoccupation with voice communication at the time the legislation was enacted, and the emotive and political character of the contemporaneous debate over wiretapping, organized crime, and "Law and Order," the Crime Control Act's imprecise language may be attributed to oversight or a lack of any political incentive to come to grips with the *avant garde* problems of electronic surveillance.

But there are marked differences between voice and data communications that should not be ignored. Because of the sporadic way in which we use the telephone, days of continuous wiretapping[141] may be necessary to obtain any significant information from telephone conversations. The bulk of the data recorded during the wiretap tends to consist of soft, hearsay-filled discussions that have comparatively little capacity for being used for damaging purposes. Admittedly, there have been several notable exceptions to this generalization in the recent past, involving public disclosure by the FBI of wiretap data on Martin Luther King,[142] a Las Vegas hotel proprietor,[143] and alleged Mafia figures.[144] But, it must be emphasized, these are only isolated exceptions.

Unlike the normal telephone flow, however, a data communications circuit may be in virtually continuous high-speed operation, transmitting extensive bodies of information that have been purged of trivial or extraneous matter and contain a high level of hard, record data that may pertain to many people.[145] Depending on the source and destination of the transmission, part of the intercepted information may have been extracted under the coercive force of a criminal statute or governmental decree, as a precondition of receiving some social or financial benefit, or under a pledge of confidentiality. Data transmissions also are more likely than telephone conversations to contain privileged data, which typically are a prime objective of wiretappers.[146] The potential dangers of allowing seizure of this flow are exacerbated by the provision in the Act permitting interception for an initial period of thirty days, with the court having authority to grant any number of thirty-day renewals upon a showing of cause.[147]

These qualitative and quantitative differences between wire-tapping on voice communications and intercepting data communications must be considered in conjunction with the possibility of law officers using snooping techniques such as touch-tone telephones to extract data directly from a variety of public and private computer centers and networks. This is in marked contrast to the passive role of the telephone tapper who must patiently wait for the suspect's phone to be used and even then has no control over the content of the conversations.

Thus, if the Crime Control Act is construed to permit the seizure of vast quantities of computerized information on the basis of routine police applications to the court for permission to tap (which are rarely denied)[148]—without affording any effective redress to the data subject—a major battle in the struggle to preserve individual privacy will have been lost. Rather than subjecting the field of electronic data transmission to the uncertainty of judicial construction of the inapposite language of the present Act, a fresh, more imaginative legislative consideration of electronic surveillance seems desirable.

The Law Relating to Privacy — A Thing of Threads and Patches

Law and legal procedure have always been a mystery to the uninitiated, a snare to the unwary, and a red rag to the unhappy man possessed by reforming.

—Viscount Buckmaster, Introduction
to A. P. Herbert, *Uncommon Law* (1964), xv

1. The Genesis of the Common Law of Privacy

Only the modern age in its rebellion against society, has discovered how rich and manifold the realm of the hidden can be under the conditions of intimacy. . . .

—Hannah Arendt, *The Human Condition*
(paper ed., 1959), 64

As the last century drew to an end, it was relatively simple to evaluate the legal position of a man whose privacy had been invaded—the doors of the courthouse were closed to him.[1] Viewed historically, this is not too surprising. For centuries the common law's primary concern in the personal injury field, both in England and the United States, had been the maintenance of an often uneasy public peace. The courts focused their attention on redressing those wrongs that were most apt to lead to violence or vigilantism, such as assault and battery or interference with property rights. In addition, until recently judges have been somewhat obsessed with the fear that offering protection for intangible personal interests would open the "floodgates of litigation" and deluge the courts with ill-conceived lawsuits brought by people who were overly sensitive, vindictive, or litigious paranoiacs. The mental distress that resulted from a loss of privacy no doubt seemed too ephemeral and unimportant an injury to warrant the law's attention.

Moreover, in predominantly rural America, which had not yet fully closed its frontier, there was no pressing need for the courts to protect privacy. Snooping in the days before mass-circulation newspapers, radio, television, computers, or even telephones, was inhibited by the natural limitations of the human eye, ear, voice, and memory. And in the relatively closed society of a small town in which everyone knew everyone else, the danger that inaccurate information would be accepted as true was mitigated by the fact that people were apt to have first-hand knowledge—or at least their own opinion—of the individual or event being gossiped about. There also was the threat of extralegal sanctions, such as social or commercial ostracism, that would discourage the tale-teller and prevent privacy invasions from becoming too serious.

But by the close of the nineteenth century a different picture began to emerge. The growth in commerce and industry was changing many towns into cities. Print, telegraphy, and photographic technology were improving and becoming widely available. Literacy was on the increase and newspapers and record-keeping were becoming more common. As larger amounts of information began to be gathered and circulated to wider audiences, the chances that those receiving it would have direct knowledge about the subject or be able to test the truth of what they heard or read decreased, while the likelihood that the printed or spoken word would be accepted as the truth increased. It is not surprising, therefore, that the law began to entertain second thoughts about the need for recognizing a right to resort to the courts to protect individual privacy.

The foundation for this change in attitude was laid in 1890 by the publication in the *Harvard Law Review* of an article entitled "The Right to Privacy."[2] Written by two young lawyers, Samuel D. Warren and Louis D. Brandeis (later a distinguished Justice of the United States Supreme Court), the article eloquently argued for the recognition of a "tort" or civil damage action that would remedy an invasion of individual privacy. Very possibly the individual whose privacy (or lack of it) was foremost in their minds was Samuel Warren's wife, a lady of proper Boston stock who was fond of entertaining. To her distress, the city's newly developed "Yellow Press" had taken to reporting the details of her social affairs. Whatever its motivation, "The Right To Privacy" became a model of how effectively presented legal scholarship can lead to a change in the law.[3]

The article warned that various recent innovations—especially the photograph and mass-circulation newspapers—presented grave new threats to personal privacy. "The press is overstepping in every direction the obvious bounds of propriety and of decency. Gossip is no longer the resource of the idle and of the vicious, but has become a trade, which is pursued with industry as well as effrontery."[4] Digging deeply into past English and American judicial precedents, the authors persuasively argued that many decisions protecting either a personal right other than privacy or a property right had in fact safeguarded the claimant's "inviolate personality." Illustratively, the authors pointed out that the courts had prevented the publication or reproduction of private letters and works of art, as in one famous case in which Prince Albert successfully prevented a London printer from publishing copies of certain etchings belonging to the Prince and Queen Victoria.[5] Warren and Brandeis contended that these cases provided a basis for the formal recognition of a right of privacy that would offer some protection against the mass media.[6]

Despite the authors' persuasiveness, their thesis was opinion rather than law; thus, it remained for the courts to give it their imprimatur. The first major test came in New York in 1902 when a young woman named Roberson sued a milling company that had used her picture to help sell its flour. The photograph appeared in an advertising circular under the caption "Flour of the Family." The court expressly rejected the Warren-Brandeis thesis and held that she could not recover money damages for her "humiliation." Although it sympathized with Miss Roberson's plight, the court's conservative instincts took hold. Because the common-law precedents had not expressly recognized a legal right of privacy, the judges concluded that relief would have to come from the legislature and could not be fabricated by the judiciary.[7]

The New York legislature promptly heeded the court's suggestion and enacted a statute making it both a crime and a civil wrong to use the name or likeness of any person for "advertising purposes or for the purposes of trade."[8] In retrospect, the legislation was too hastily drafted and has proven ill-conceived because its narrow language only guards an individual's privacy against commercial exploitation. But since it expresses the will of the legislature, the New York courts have read the statute as castrating their freedom to remedy privacy invasions in other situations.

In 1905, the Supreme Court of Georgia became the first court to recognize a right of privacy. The case was strikingly analogous to Roberson. It involved a man named Paolo Pavesich who sued the New England Life Insurance Company for using his picture in an Atlanta newspaper advertisement showing him beside the likeness of what the court termed an "ill-dressed and sickly looking person." Under Mr. Pavesich's photograph appeared the testimonial that in his "healthy and productive period of life" he had bought insurance from the company and was reaping the benefits of that wise decision. The caption beneath the "sickly looking" counterpart whined that he had failed to pursue this favorable course and had come to regret it. Pavesich apparently had never consented to the use of his picture in this manner; indeed, he had never purchased a policy from the company and had not made the statement attributed to him. The Georgia court decided that the right of privacy does exist and concluded that the victim of an invasion could recover damages for his injury. In so holding, the court expressly turned its back on the earlier New York decision in Roberson and lined up with the Warren-Brandeis view.[9]

In the years that followed, the Roberson and Pavesich cases provided the pattern. Courts in almost every state debated the merits of recognizing a right of privacy. Eventually an affirmative conclusion became the prevailing view and today there are only a few states in which a person's ability to seek a remedy for a privacy invasion is not secure. But the right has not been treated uniformly among those states that have recognized it. Some courts have ventured well beyond the decision in the Pavesich case, whereas others, restrained either by traditionalist instincts or a sense of uncertainty as to the extent to which personal privacy could or should be protected in a complex modern society, have gone no further than the Georgia case. Although the dimensions of a person's right of privacy still vary from state to state, over the years the law has become more standardized, so that currently there are fairly clear boundaries within which the courts operate.[10]

2. The Present Common Law of Privacy

Today braver courts, of their very own knowledge, can say that water runs down hill, that light travels 186,427 miles per second, that vitamin D acts as do ultra-violet rays, that minerals can't be located with a divining rod, and that a banana peel if stepped upon will clearly disclose physical signs. Let the detractors who complain of the unadaptability of the law be answered by the fact that a scant 300 years ago the mere affirmation that light was not instantaneous would have occasioned an Inquisition or witch-burning. Three hundred years is too close to the faggot pile to warrant becoming a judicial smart-aleck.

—Kenneth York, "Unjudicial Notes on
Judicial Notice," 13 *Rocky
Mountain Law Review*
(1941), 374, 376

To appraise the potential effectiveness of a private lawsuit as a curb on the abusive handling of computerized information, one must have some appreciation of the current state of the common law of privacy. It has been so fluid that a judge once compared privacy doctrines to a "haystack in a hurricane."[11] However, some structure and analytical guidance has been provided by Dean William Prosser, an eminent scholar in the field. After an extensive canvass of the cases, he subdivided those recognizing the right into four categories on the basis of whether they involve: (1) appropriation of another person's name or likeness for personal advantage; (2) intrusion upon a person's seclusion or solitude, or into his private affairs; (3) public disclosure of embarrassing private facts about a person; or (4) publicity that places a person in a false light in the public eye.[12]

Although other writers have questioned both the validity and value of this analytical quartet,[13] the courts have tended to accept Dean Prosser's approach as an accurate sketch of the law of privacy's present contours.[14] Thus, it seems reasonable to begin by determining whether any of these categories can be fashioned into a workable legal weapon to remedy, and indirectly to discourage, the misuse of computerized information.

Appropriation

The "appropriation" category encompasses the unauthorized use of a person's picture or name, usually for commercial purposes.

The use of Mr. Pavesich's picture for a bogus testimonial[15] is one illustration of this type of privacy invasion. In another typical case, a blind child's picture was used to advertise dog food. The caption read: "Dog owners, your purchases of Perk Dog Food can give this blind girl a Master Eye Dog."[16] Even a nonpecuniary use of another's name or likeness may give rise to an action based on appropriation. One illustrative case involved a suit against a corporation by a man whose name had been signed to a telegram urging the governor to veto a proposed statute that would have adversely affected the corporation's business.[17]

Since the appropriation notion is concerned with the exploitation of a name or likeness, it appears to be of little value as a legal restraint on the dissemination of computerized personal information. But the argument might be made that a full information file on a person may contain as detailed a "picture" of him as does a photograph. Unfortunately, this line of reasoning can be criticized as little more than a play on words, and viewed realistically, the likelihood of a court accepting this approach appears small. In addition to their obvious physical differences, the analogy between a photograph and an alpha-numeric file is imperfect because there is no clear point at which factual information becomes sufficiently complete to constitute a "picture." Moreover, dissemination of individual items of data to different buyers technically would not be actionable under the logic of the analogy, since it is only the appropriation of the entire "picture" that fits this category of the privacy action. Another difficulty is that there would be no protection against the transfer of inaccurate information, since erroneous data, however detailed they might be, presumably would not be a "likeness" of the person suing.

However, the appropriation cases do suggest that the courts view the commercial utilization of personal information that invades the subject's privacy with displeasure. Thus, if judges were willing to focus on the gravity of the privacy invasion and abandon their past emphasis on photographs and likenesses, this first category of privacy actions might become more responsive to the needs of the future. For example, it might provide a rational basis for curtailing the appropriation or vending of computerized dossiers, which would be a useful approach to a

number of privacy problems, including those raised by credit
bureaus and mail list peddlers.

Intrusion

A privacy action based upon an intrusion into a person's solitude
or his personal affairs may not be a significantly more useful legal
weapon in the computer context than is the appropriation theory.
Typical of the offensive prying that constitutes intrusion is an
early case in which a woman successfully sued her doctor for
bringing a young man who was not a physician into her room
while she was giving birth.[18] Another illustration is a relatively
recent New Hampshire case in which a married man sued his
landlord for installing a listening and recording device next
to the tenant's bed.[19]

   Although the intrusion concept may be a useful approach
for remedying wiretapping, electronic eavesdropping, or physical or sensory surveillance, it does not afford much protection
against misuse of computerized information, which usually does
not involve the type of direct or physical invasion that this aspect
of the privacy tort is designed to deter. Moreover, the intrusion
category primarily deals with the nature of the conduct that constitutes the privacy violation, rather than what is subsequently
done with the fruits of the invasion; yet in the context of computerized information it is the use of the data that presents the
major threat to privacy.

   However, two recent cases suggest that the intrusion category
has growth capacity. In one, former Senator Thomas Dodd of
Connecticut sued columnist Drew Pearson for "exposing" the
Senator's activities in a series of articles that ultimately led to
Dodd's censure by the Senate.[20] Dodd charged Pearson with
invading his privacy by publishing information that had been
stolen from his files. The court concluded that Pearson was not
liable on the intrusion theory since he had not actually participated in the rifling of the Senator's files. However, the court
went on to state that "we approve the extension of the tort of
invasion of privacy to instances of intrusion, whether by physical
trespass or not, into spheres from which an ordinary man . . .
could reasonably expect that the particular . . . [snooper] should
be excluded."[21] Although this statement was gratuitous because
it did not bear directly on the resolution of the Dodd case, it

suggests that a person will be protected against any intrusion that the community thinks is improper (or at least unexpected).[22]

An example of how an expanded intrusion category might be applied is provided by another *cause célèbre—Nader* v. *General Motors Corporation.*[23] This is part of the protracted litigation in which consumer protectionist Ralph Nader alleged that General Motors tapped his telephone, kept him under surveillance, questioned his friends on sensitive matters such as his religious views, sexual inclinations, and personal habits, made threatening telephone calls, and even hired women to entice him into "illicit relationships." The issue before the court at this particular stage of the donnybrook was whether Nader's allegations, assuming they could be proven, would entitle him to relief.

The court reached an affirmative conclusion, but on narrow grounds. However, in a concurring opinion that relied on the Dodd case, Judge Breitel expressed the more permissive view that all of General Motors' alleged activities might constitute an illegal invasion of privacy, and that even if some acts alone would not support a lawsuit, taken together under the circumstances of the case they were actionable. However, a majority of the judges concluded, primarily because of the technical legal posture of the case, that only the telephone tap and the surveillance could be the basis of Nader's suit. Several months after this decision was rendered, General Motors agreed to pay Nader almost one-half million dollars and the lawsuit was terminated.

It remains to be seen whether and how far the intrusion category can be broadened. The judicial language in the Dodd and Nader cases may be just straws in the wind. But if the intrusion concept were expanded to cover the more egregious forms of data collection, some of which involve coercion and snooping, it could serve as an effective first line of defense against abusive information practices and the improper handling of a computer file. Thus, if a computerized credit bureau conducts a detailed and offensive investigation into the personal affairs of a potential borrower, a lawsuit based on the intrusion theory might be successful. If it were, the court could award money damages and issue an order prohibiting the computerization of the information or its dissemination. The possibility of such a result could well discourage similar investigations.

Public Disclosure

At first glance the third category of privacy actions—public disclosure of private information—seems to have the most potential
for furnishing an effective legal remedy for a violation of informational privacy. After all, it was the public disclosure aspect of
privacy that motivated the Warren and Brandeis article in 1890,
and the dangers of the "Yellow Press" of that era pale beside
those created by the proliferation of data banks and the development of national computer networks. The threat of private
information being "leaked" to the public clearly increases as
technological developments permit more and more data to be
stored and users fail to develop any safeguards or restraints
against improper dissemination.

Unfortunately, the judicial emphasis on a *public* disclosure
restricts this category's effectiveness in the context of computerized information. In effect, before an injured party can recover
for a disclosure of private facts, he must show that the information was given "publicity"—that it was communicated to the
public at large.[24] Several cases, however, have permitted a person to sue even though the amount of publicity was rather small,
as when the wrongdoer posted a notice of a person's indebtedness
in a garage window[25] or loudly proclaimed it in a restaurant.[26]
On the other hand, the requirement generally will rule out relief
when the private information is disclosed only to one person.
This is true even if the revelation causes serious injury, which
might well be the case if a job applicant's medical or financial
record was irresponsibly given to a prospective employer without
authorization.

The publicity requirement is particularly troublesome in
terms of preserving the security of computerized personal data,
since the critical dissemination may take place when one user of
a time-share system permits another to have access to private files,
or when the operators of two different systems agree to exchange
tapes or interconnect their computers. Once an unauthorized
user has gained access to an individual's computerized file, he
can use what he has learned in ways that may damage the data
subject without disseminating its contents further. Even if the
victim is able to trace his injury to the improper use of the file,
he may be prevented from suing successfully if the transfer of his

file to another user or a different computer system is not treated as satisfying the publicity prerequisite.

The courts have recognized a few exceptions to this requirement. Most of them involve instances in which "the information was gained by wrongful prying or its communication involves a breach of confidence or the violation of an independent duty."[27] A doctor who reveals information from a patient's file to a third person has not given the information the type of publicity normally demanded but he may be liable because of the confidential nature of the doctor-patient relationship.

Unfortunately, it is doubtful that the required relationship of trust or confidence exists between the typical file subject (the victim of the privacy invasion) and the data gatherer (the wrongdoer) so as to give the former the right to bring an action for unauthorized disclosure. Ideally, the mere fact that the data gatherer is a custodian of sensitive personal information should give rise to a duty of confidentiality, but it is not clear that the courts are prepared to recognize such an extensive obligation at this time. Nonetheless, even the existing narrow exceptions to the public disclosure requirement are important in constructing a workable remedy for the computer age, especially if the courts become more receptive to expanding the notion of confidential relationship or to imposing a duty of care on computer operators sometime in the future.[28]

A second limitation on the availability of an action based on public disclosure is that the revealed facts must be *private*. A person cannot sue because his occupation or his activity on a public street has been disclosed. By their nature these are not private matters and the law will not order them withheld from general view. Difficulties arise in applying this limitation when the information is not obviously public in nature, or when its private character is offset by a public interest in its dissemination.

One writer has suggested that the protectible "zones of privacy" should include the family, sexuality, the psyche or matters of psychology, as well as sensual and emotional impressions and expressions.[29] Although these categories offer some guidance in defining what is private, they are far from precise and are not universally accepted. For example, should an individual's "psychology" include all aspects of the available data on his personality and the opinions of others about him? Although this would properly cover the unauthorized dissemination of information obtained on a psychological test or a personality inventory,[30] it probably casts too wide a net.

The problem of articulating a standard for determining what types of personal information should be protected from public disclosure was foreseen by Warren and Brandeis:

> Since . . . the propriety of publishing the very same facts may depend wholly upon the person concerning whom they are published, no fixed formula can be used to prohibit obnoxious publications.
>
> . . . .
>
> In general . . . the matters of which the publication should be repressed may be described as those which concern the private life, habits, acts, and relations of an individual, and have no legitimate connection with his fitness for a public office which he seeks or for which he is suggested . . . and have no legitimate relation to or bearing upon any act done by him in a public or quasi public capacity.[31]

Some of the uncertainty that inheres in balancing public and private interests was alleviated when the courts incorporated an extensive body of privileges into the nascent law of privacy. Privileges are defenses that have been created by the law to protect important public interests and often operate to prevent an individual from securing relief for his injuries. For example, under certain circumstances a public official may issue a statement that damages someone and yet not be answerable in court. The rationale is that an official must be protected while discharging his duties so that his performance is not inhibited by fear of a lawsuit. Warren and Brandeis themselves felt that in addition to the mass media's freedom to publish "matters of public or general interest," the privacy action should be subject to the complex rules of privilege that had developed as part of the law of defamation (libel and slander), as well as to the defense of consent.[32] In theory, these limitations on the privacy action mark off an area in which the individual's interest in preventing the spread of information about him is outweighed by society's right to have access to that data, the same policy that supports the Freedom of Information Act.

But this balance was struck at a time when the principal

threat to a person's emotional tranquillity and privacy were the excesses of a local newspaper's gossip column, and its viability is doubtful in an age of electronic data-processing and high-speed transfers of large quantities of personal information. Some of the defamation privileges seem much too broad. For instance, one extensive and relatively vague privilege is available when both the publisher of the information and its recipient have a common interest, and the communication is of a kind reasonably calculated to protect or further that joint interest. A familiar application of this principle is the immunity given to mutual credit organizations and credit-rating agencies when they divulge financial data to those who have an "apparent, present interest in the report."[33] In a computerized environment, anyone who knows a credit grantor's identifying code number[34] and has access to a telephone may be able to reach the reservoir of detailed financial information that already exists on over a hundred million persons. If injury results, why should the credit bureau be permitted to hide behind the skirts of a privilege by arguing that the snooper had an "apparent interest" in the information? To go one step further, surely computerized credit bureaus ought not to be protected by the privilege when they permit large institutional lenders to have direct access to their files from remote terminals[35] on the ground that anyone who gains access to a client's terminal apparently is an authorized user.

There is a further difficulty with the requirement that the information revealed must be private. Whether the court treats particular facts as private depends largely on the general community's attitude rather than a fixed norm. As a result, the availability of the privacy action is dependent on the community's ability or willingness to distinguish between facts that should be considered part of the public domain and facts that are none of the public's business. But community attitudes are fickle—one need only think of the dramatic shifts in public opinion on such matters as sex and religion in recent years. The danger is that widespread computerization of personal data coupled with continuous demands for data by society's information managers will slowly narrow the community's conception of what is private, which in turn will gradually reduce the effectiveness of the privacy action.

"Progress" often is accompanied by a tendency to alter, and in some cases to erode, the significance of certain basic values. Automobile accidents kill thousands of people every year, yet, despite scattered signs of concern, most of the public has become apathetic to the slaughter. Thus, just as constant exposure to scenes of war and squalor have caused many to grow callous about human life and the destruction of the environment, the public may lose its sense of the private if large-scale transfers and dissemination of personal information become common. The privacy action based on public disclosure will particularly suffer from a dependence on a community standard. People accustomed to the revelation of sensitive personal data eventually may define most information as public and place it beyond the law's protection. By way of analogy, the scope of what is legally "obscene" has narrowed as the community has become accustomed to more explicit presentation of sexual themes.

Another variable that may affect community attitudes is the centralization of diverse information in computer systems. The public may view the composite dossier differently than it would view the same information before it was brought together. Items of information that individually would be considered private may lose that status when intermingled in a computer file with quantities of public information. As a result, if confidential medical data are mixed with information of a less sensitive nature, such as social security records, without special safeguards, there will be a tendency for all of it to be treated as if it had a rather low level of sensitivity. Consequently, the over-all protection may be less than that which should be accorded to the most personal information stored in the system.

In addition to being "public," the law requires that the disclosure be offensive to a person of "ordinary sensibilities." Once again we must deal with a community standard. Numerous court decisions indicate the wide spectrum of disclosures that may be considered offensive; they range from the revelation that a person owes money[36] to a newspaper's publication of the X-rays of a woman's pelvic region.[37] A leading case involved a motion picture called *The Red Kimono*,[38] which depicted events in the life of Gabrielle Darley, a prostitute who had been prosecuted and acquitted in a sensational murder trial. In the years following the episodes portrayed in the film Miss Darley had forsworn her old ways; she had married and had become a respected member of the community. But her newly acquired social position underwent a sharp decline after the appearance of *The Red Kimono,* and she brought suit for the damage done by the truthful, but highly offensive, revelations in the film. In the only reported aspect of the lawsuit, the court indicated that if she were able to prove her allegations at the trial, the law would provide a remedy.

In some instances the requirement that the disclosure offend the community is an insurmountable obstacle. An excellent example is the case of William James Sidis,[39] a child prodigy who had lectured mathematicians on the topic of four-dimensional bodies when he was eleven and had graduated from Harvard College when he was sixteen. For reasons that are not clear, Sidis rebelled against his studies and the public attention they had focused on him. To escape his past, he gave up mathematics and took a job as an obscure clerk. He lived in a run-down section of Boston and busied himself with such unusual pursuits as collecting street-car transfers and studying the lore of the Okamakammessett Indians. Unfortunately for Sidis, all this was revealed in a *New Yorker* magazine profile under the title "Where Are They Now?"

In a suit by Sidis against *The New Yorker,* the court acknowledged that the article was a "ruthless exposure,"[40] but held that he could not recover. This conclusion was based partially on the ground that Sidis had been a "public figure" and that his activities were a legitimate subject of public interest. The court also indicated that it did not think the revelations were "so intimate and so unwarranted in view of the victim's position as to outrage the community's notions of decency."[41] In effect, Sidis was told that the law would not act because he was more sensitive to public revelations about himself than were the people around him.

In an allegorical way, the Sidis case may indicate that by the time large quantities of computerized personal information are available and transfers of machine-readable data are commonplace occurrences, the public may have become anesthetized to what a more sensitive society might view as an "offensive" exposure of private information to public view. The result will be less tolerance for the claim that an individual has the right to determine what aspects of his life may be given publicity. Just as we have become acclimated to the obnoxious and omnipresent quality of television commercials, the revelation of intimate details in a person's computer record may become so normal that it will not satisfy the requisite level of community offense. As the Sidis case suggests, the desire of certain members of the community to retain their privacy and express their sense of outrage at having it destroyed will avail them nothing if the majority no longer cares.

False Light and Defamation

If the private information revealed about an individual is not accurate, he usually must pursue an action for defamation to remedy the injury to his reputation. The precise distinction between the two components of defamation, libel and slander, is not important for this discussion; it is sufficient to note that generally slander involves the spoken word and libel the written word. The action for defamation may be pursued even if the falsehood is not widely publicized; indeed, it is enough if the wrongdoer communicates it to a third person.[42]

But the ability to recover for defamation is hedged in by several limitations. The injured party often is required to show "special damages." This means that he must actually have suffered *financial* as well as *reputational* loss from the defamatory assault. Another restriction is the complex set of privileges that surround the defamation action. For example, a newspaper is allowed to publish matters that are of "public interest," even if the story injures someone's reputation.[43] Another privilege arises when the injured party consents to the publication or waives any objection he otherwise might make to the circulation of the offending remarks.[44] Both of these privileges, although originally developed in the defamation context, may be invoked in a privacy action.

As an alternative to a defamation action, a person might claim that he has been injured by publicity that places him in a false light in the public eye. This is the last of Prosser's privacy-action categories. It resembles defamation in that it purports to protect people against injury caused by false or misleading statements or publications.[45] In one case that illustrates the relationship between the defamation and privacy theories, a woman was allowed to recover both for libel and for invasion of privacy when her photograph was used to illustrate a magazine story entitled "Man Hungry."[46] The woman's picture, which had been taken years earlier when she was a model for a dress designer, appeared with an inscription that read: "She had a good man—but he wasn't enough. So she picked a bad one! That's when her troubles really began." Neither the story nor the inscription had anything to do with events in her life.

A person whose reputation has been injured might prefer to invoke the false-light theory and sue for invasion of privacy rather than for defamation because a number of the restrictions on the latter theory do not apply to the former.[47] For example, if the publication is true, one cannot sue for defamation. Furthermore, it is unnecessary for plaintiff to show that he has suffered actual financial loss in a privacy action. However, it is not clear how far these and other advantages ought to favor the privacy theory. If the traditional limitations on the right to recover for defamation serve a legitimate purpose, they should not be evaded simply by identifying the claim as an invasion of privacy.[48] Indeed, this is precisely the reason why both the false-light doctrine and the defamation action have been significantly limited by the courts whenever there is a potential intrusion upon the constitutional right of free press.[49] In some cases the privacy route actually is more hazardous because the false-light theory requires that the misleading information be communicated to the public at large—a constraint not applicable to defamation actions.

It is difficult to appraise how useful the false-light category will be in the computer-privacy context inasmuch as it may not really exist as a separate entity; the false-light concept may be nothing more than a variation on the public disclosure theory or a branch of the law of defamation. This would be unfortunate, because the notion of giving an individual a right to relief for having been placed in a false light is sound. Indeed, it is the only one of Dean Prosser's categories that even remotely suggests the type of sensitive analysis that is necessary to come to grips with the range of subtle injuries that can be inflicted in an information-based society. Thus, it would be desirable to refine and expand the false-light doctrine to permit lawsuits by those who have been injured by the dissemination of information that is misleading, has been used out of context, or has become inaccurate because of age, improper supplementation, or failure to include important underlying data. The courts also will have to de-emphasize the requirement of disclosure to the public at large if the theory is to be responsive to the way in which computerized information will be used in a dossier society. Unfortunately, because of its shaky underpinnings, it is impossible to predict whether the false-light concept will mature or atrophy.

The Consent and Waiver Placebos

Perhaps the most significant weakness in today's common law privacy action is the frequency with which it is barred by a successful assertion that the injured person waived his right to sue by engaging in activity inconsistent with a desire to maintain his privacy or that he consented to the dissemination of personal information.[50] The utilization of these concepts by the courts has been somewhat Draconian and has resulted in an understandable dampening of enthusiasm for pursuing the privacy theory.

"Waiver" often is employed to prevent a suit by someone who has participated in a newsworthy event. In some cases this has occurred under circumstances in which any notion that the victim voluntarily acquiesced in the privacy invasion is totally unrealistic. For example, a woman was held to have "waived her right to privacy" by leaping from a twelve-story building.[51] Thus, the rationale cannot be based on whether the victim intended to waive his privacy but must be predicated on a desire to assure that the communications media are able to bring the public the news and are not inhibited by the threat of civil liability. But the press has been granted immunity in situations in which there is little news value in the information communicated. In one case a young couple who had been photographed embracing in a public market place were held to have "waived" all right to object to the reproduction of the photograph in a national magazine, in part because a contrary result might have deterred the publication of all photographs of street scenes,[52] a concern that has all the earmarks of a judicial red herring.[53]

The principal difficulty with the "consent" defense is its insensitivity to the pressures that can be exerted by people in positions of authority or someone who dangles an attractive carrot before an individual's eyes. To talk of information being "voluntarily" given in the context of a police interrogation,[54] an application for welfare payments,[55] an employment relationship,[56] or a psychological experiment,[57] is to ignore reality. In each of these situations various complex factors may have combined to subvert the subject's freedom of choice. Even a questionnaire sent out under the imprimatur of a federal agency has an intimidating effect on some people,[58] a weakness that often is played upon by the agency in its follow-up practices. Whether a particular disclosure really is voluntary obviously depends on the circumstances surrounding it, as well as the individual's personality and chemistry. Nonetheless, in too many instances "consent" is used as a convenient conclusory epithet that places responsibility for a loss of privacy on the victim and absolves the intruder.

A blatant example of an attempt to hide behind the consent shield to immunize practices is one national credit bureau's reaction when it became alarmed by a congressional investigation and the prospect of subsequent regulation. It began to include the following clause in its credit application form:

> I hereby authorize the person to whom this application is made, or any credit bureau or any other investigative agency employed by such person, to investigate the references herein listed, or statements, or other information, oral or written, obtained from me or any other person pertaining to my credit and financial responsibility. . . . I hereby release any claims, damages and suits whatsoever which may at any time be asserted by me by reason of such investigation.[59]

Clearly, personal privacy would become an illusion if provisions of this character were enforced by blind adherence to the consent bromide by the courts.

The propriety of a waiver or consent defense to a privacy action should be assessed in terms of whether there is an overriding public interest in the free dissemination of information about the event in question, rather than on the basis of a fictive assertion about the injured person's intent at the time of the invasion. In view of the growing threat to privacy from the new technologies, every assertion of consent and waiver by information system operators must be regarded with considerable skepticism. These defenses always must be carefully evaluated because their effect is to permit data handlers and users to shift the risks of their activities to individual file subjects. If we are to do more than pay lip service to the right of informational privacy, the law must impose a duty of care on the data gatherer that is commensurate with the degree of coercion or pressure under which an individual yields control over personal data.[60]

Deficiencies in the Common-Law Approach

Before bringing the discussion of the common-law privacy action to a close, it is worth pausing for a brief look at some of its imperfections. First and foremost, it should be evident that the dichotomy between privacy and defamation actions offers an injured person a choice of legal theories based on the assumption that all items of information can be classified as either true or false. But rather than lining up neatly in this black or white fashion, almost all of the difficult cases have a gray visage. Damaging "soft data" or evaluatory material, derogatory entries that do not reveal subsequent ameliorating events, or "naked" and unexplicated items of data that portray a biased picture when presented in a context unrelated to the one in which they were collected, all may be "true" in the strict sense of the word and yet not describe an individual or his activities and aptitudes accurately. The existing pigeon holes also are insensitive to the many subtle ways in which personal data may be distorted or misused in a society that puts a premium on gathering large quantities of personalized information and using it for as many purposes as possible. Consequently, although the current rules relating to privacy and defamation provide both a theory for rectifying an improperly disseminated truth and one for remedying an injurious untruth, neither approach focuses sharply enough on the penumbral area between the two or has yet begun to take account of the capabilities of modern information technology. As a result, someone who has been injured by the misuse of information often must run the risk of having his claim fall between the conceptual stools of privacy and defamation.

Illustrative of the problems confronting an individual who believes that he has been injured by the dissemination of soft data is a case involving an attorney who brought a defamation action claiming that his professional rating in a national directory of lawyers had been lowered for no apparent reason.[61] In denying relief the court indicated that a high burden of proof is likely to be imposed on a person who sues for the revelation of information containing a damaging subjective evaluation of him:

> [The plaintiff's] . . . witnesses do not all agree that his ability is "very high." . . . He complains that several lawyers in . . . [his home town] were rated as "very high" when he was rated only "high." There is no showing that these lawyers were not of exceptional ability. Clearly a defamation of A is not proved by showing that someone says B is a better lawyer than A, when the legal ability of B is not shown.[62]

There are other reasons why the private tort action, although reasonably effective for protecting some interests, may be a poor weapon for vindicating one's privacy. The very fact that the injured party must go to court will deter many people. Unfortunately, expense, time, delay, and emotional upset are all part of the fabric of litigation in modern America. Some might argue that a person who lets these obstacles deter him probably did not suffer a serious invasion of his privacy. Whatever the merit of this stoical position, there are also pragmatic reasons why someone might not resort to the courts no matter how significant the intrusion on his solitude. In many instances the cost factor alone will make a lawsuit impossible, or the belief that money damages will not adequately compensate for a loss of privacy may drain the injured party of any incentive to sue. These difficulties are heightened by uncertainty over what, if anything, a jury is likely to award a plaintiff for the loss of something that is difficult to assess in terms of dollars.

Moreover, seeking relief for a privacy invasion may simply aggravate the injury. Litigation usually will further publicize the information whose exposure constituted the original wrong. When that is a possibility, the injured party might well decide it is wiser to tend to his wounds quietly rather than risk additional distress. A similar problem has acted as a restraint on defamation suits. Someone whose reputation has been damaged by a lie often hesitates to give the lie wider circulation through the courts. This is true even though the plaintiff in a defamation action has the opportunity to present his side of the story, which means that a lawsuit may help vindicate his reputation in the public's mind. But this is not the goal of an aggrieved party in the privacy context, because the publicity itself aggravates the injury.

When the government is responsible for the privacy invasion, the picture is even bleaker. A suit against a unit of the federal government for an invasion of privacy involves a trek through what surely is the world's most arduous obstacle course. The victim may be hindered by the special hurdle presented by the doctrine of sovereign immunity, which precludes a private citizen from suing the government unless it has given him permission to do so.[63] Although the barriers to certain lawsuits against the federal and various state governments have been lowered by legislation, it still is not clear whether the privacy action falls within the terms of these statutes.[64] The difficulties associated with bringing suit against the government represent a serious defect in the privacy action, since many of the most extensive existing and planned computer networks are operated by various government agencies. Fortunately, some protection against governmental abuse is provided by the constitutional doctrines discussed below.[65] Even though these generally will not afford the victim any monetary compensation, they may be useful in forcing the sovereign to alter its practices.

Finally, and in some ways most significantly, the existing common-law structure does nothing to give the data subject a right to participate in decisions relating to personal information about him, a right that is essential if he is to learn whether he has been victimized by a privacy invasion. Information handling on a computerized basis is a "low visibility" operation; an individual may never discover that he is the subject of a file or be given any precise knowledge of what is in it. Under these circumstances, he is not likely to receive notice when an erroneous or misleading entry has been made in his file or to be told when details of his life have been revealed to people who have no legitimate right to be privy to the information. It makes no sense to rely on the victim's right to bring suit against those who have injured him when he is not informed of the source of his injury—or, in some cases, he remains unaware of the fact that he has been damaged. Even if he later discovers that his informational profile has been disfigured, an individual may find it impossible to sue if his grievance has become too ancient to command the law's attention.

3. The Constitutional Law of Privacy— Policies in Conflict

The right to be let alone is indeed the beginning of all freedom.

—Mr. Justice Douglas, in
Public Utilities Commission v. *Pollak*, 343 U.S. 451,
467 (1952) (dissenting opinion)

The First Amendment—Free Speech and the Right to Snoop

To assure an open and well-informed society, the free-speech guarantee in the First Amendment to the United States Constitution gives the news media a right to publish matters that are of interest to the general public. In order to be effective, this constitutional principle may have to be applied on occasion to prevent an individual who is injured by a publication that is false or reveals intimate facts about him from obtaining legal redress. As anomalous as it sounds, therefore, the First Amendment may significantly restrict the availability of the common-law privacy action and render it even less capable of functioning in a computerized environment than it already is.

The ability of a privacy invasion victim to avoid the effect of the First Amendment already has been substantially limited by the Supreme Court's decision in *Time, Inc.* v. *Hill*.[66] The case involved an article in *Life* magazine, which James Hill claimed invaded his privacy by presenting him to the public eye in a false light. The article dealt with the tryout of what was then a new Broadway play, *The Desperate Hours,* which recounts the plight of a family whose home is invaded by escaped convicts. The magazine story represented the play as a dramatization of an event in the life of Hill and his family. Photographs of several scenes from the play accompanied the article; one showed a convict beating the son and another portrayed the daughter biting a convict's hand, apparently in an effort to make him drop a gun. Although it was true that some years before the appearance of the *Life* article three escaped convicts had held the Hill family captive for nineteen hours, the play did not accurately reproduce that ordeal. In the real episode, the convicts had treated the family courteously and had not indulged in any of the brutalities presented in the play. After the incident, Hill had moved to another state and discouraged all efforts by the media to keep him and his family in the public spotlight.

Hill sued the publisher of *Life* under the privacy statute that New York had enacted after the Pavesich case and was successful at trial.[67] However, the case was appealed by the magazine and ultimately the United States Supreme Court reversed the original decision. The attitude of the Court is reflected in its statement that:

> We have no doubt that the subject of the *Life* article, the opening of a new play linked to an actual incident, is a matter of public interest. "The line between the informing and the entertaining is too elusive for the protection of . . . [freedom of the press]." . . . Erroneous statement is no less inevitable in such a case than in the case of comment upon public affairs, and in both, if innocent or merely negligent, ". . . it must be protected if the freedoms of expression are to have the 'breathing space' that they 'need . . . to survive.' . . ."[68]

The Court in essence concluded that in deference to the policies that underlie the First Amendment, Hill (and those who follow him) would have to bear a particularly high burden of proof to win his case against the Fourth Estate. Specifically, Hill was obliged to establish that the "defendant published the report with knowledge of its falsity or in reckless disregard of the truth."[69] If he was unable to convince the court and the jury of this, he could not recover no matter how much injury had been inflicted by the false publication. This is essentially the same standard the Supreme Court had applied to actions for libel and slander against public officials in an earlier First Amendment case, *New York Times Company* v. *Sullivan*,[70] and it has been extremely difficult for litigants to satisfy.[71]

At this writing the precise implications of the Hill decision are unclear, especially since the case was founded on (and much of the opinion is devoted to) New York's somewhat peculiar privacy statute.[72] If the Supreme Court's opinion is read narrowly, its application might well be limited to the false-light privacy cases, which, as we have seen, are very similar to traditional defamation actions.[73] This is a reasonable interpretation, since the Court specifically stated that it was not dealing with the question whether the constitutional standard previously employed in defamation cases applied to the offensive application of intimate truths.[74]

On the other hand, the Hill case may well have seriously impaired the privacy action's capacity for growth. The burden of proof imposed on Hill logically might be extended to other categories of the privacy action, in particular cases involving the public disclosure of private facts. One problem with this broader view of Hill is that it is not clear exactly how the standard fashioned by the Court for situations in which the publication is false could be carried over to the disclosure of accurate but private facts—one cannot publish the truth with "knowledge of its falsity." Despite this paradox, the proof burden established in Hill for false-light cases does suggest that a comparably high burden might be applied to the publication of true but private matters. This would not be a surprising development because the transfer of defamation-related privileges to the privacy sphere has roots that go back to the famous Warren and Brandeis article, in which the authors argued that the same privileges that immunized defamatory statements should be available in privacy actions.[75] Apparently their theory was that the dissemination of the truth is entitled to at least as much protection as the publication of falsehoods.

It is far from obvious that privileges developed in the context of defamation actions should be automatically transposed to the privacy arena, however. The heavy burden of proof applied by the Supreme Court in defamation suits and then carried over by it to the false-light privacy category in Hill represents an attempt to balance individual interests against the constitutional right of free speech. But there are reasons for believing that a person's interest in redressing an invasion of his privacy might be entitled to greater weight in this process than his interest in recovering for an injury to his reputation.

As strange as it might sound, a privilege to publish intimate truths may not be as important to free speech or the maintenance of the flow of information to the public as is a privilege to publish defamatory statements. A newspaper editor might hesitate to publish many "newsworthy" stories that cross his desk, were it not for the First Amendment privilege; without the protection accorded the paper by the Constitution, it would be necessary to determine in advance of publication whether the stories contained inaccuracies that could lead to defamation suits. The result would be delays and occasional decisions to refrain from publishing. However, the same editor would not have as much trouble screening his stories for privacy invasions. Unlike questions of truth or falsity, it usually is evident on the face of the material whether it contains offensively intimate facts. This probably will continue to be true as long as offensiveness is determined by a community standard in privacy actions. Of course, if intimate facts are really important to public debate of significant issues, their publication should be privileged under the First Amendment. I am simply suggesting that the desire to preserve debate does not automatically require that the heavy burden of proof imposed on plaintiffs in defamation actions by the Sullivan case be extended beyond the false-light category of the privacy tort.[76]

Moreover, in weighing the comparative importance of the interests at stake in defamation and privacy cases, the scales favor privacy. As more fully described in the next section, the Supreme Court has held that some aspects of privacy are protected by the Constitution.[77] On the other hand, the Supreme Court has never held that the integrity of a person's reputation is constitutionally protected. Furthermore, it is sometimes stated that the best corrective for the injuries caused by a defamation is more rather than less speech, on the theory that the truth eventually will win out if open debate is encouraged. This point has no validity in the privacy context, however, because further discussion of the sensitive information will only increase the injury to the individual's privacy. Even viewed from a perspective broader than the injury of a particular individual, the loss of privacy has implications that an attack on reputation does not. A widespread debilitation of individual privacy resulting from an accumulation of successful invasions might lead to an environment that would be antithetical to many of our fundamental societal precepts, in terms of both psychological and political freedom.[78]

Turning now to a consideration of the possible ramifications of Hill in the context of the computer age, two basic questions spring to mind: (1) Should the decision be applied to the transfer of information between points within a computer system as well as the dissemination of information from within a system to persons outside the system who are interested in it for their private use? (2) How does the decision affect transfers of information from computer systems to the news media? The answers to these questions are a function of the policies underlying the First Amendment. Since many commentators assert (and several passages in the Hill opinion indicate)[79] that the protection bestowed on the press by the Constitution is premised on the "Meiklejohn interpretation" of the First Amendment[80]—the concept that the people must receive an unrestricted flow of information in order to govern themselves intelligently—we must appraise the extent to which the dissemination of computerized information about people serves the ends of intelligent self-government and is worthy of constitutional protection.

Without question, electronic data-processing and other information activities have become important to the effective functioning of government, industry, and academe, and will become increasingly significant in the future. Nonetheless, it also is clear that computer systems, with their immense capacity for building individual dossiers, predicting human and organizational behavior, and aiding in the decision-making process, may be more suited to fostering the control of people by institutions than assisting the public in governing themselves intelligently. Of course, these systems might perform the function of keeping people informed of important events and issues if they could gain access to them. But existing computer operations typically are closed to the vast bulk of the population. Thus, the data centers and networks of today and those likely to be constructed in the immediate future do not seem to fit the traditional First Amendment mold or to deserve the broad protection given the news media.

Another difference between the mass media and computer systems lies in the nature of the information each handles. There is an important distinction between "purely commercial" speech, which is not within the First Amendment, and ideas and information, which are protected by the Constitution.[81] Certainly some computer applications that may be detrimental to privacy, such as computerized credit ratings and mailing lists, could be considered to involve commercial data, which would place them outside the free-speech guarantee and vulnerable to a common-law privacy action. Along the same lines, it may well be that many of the private sector's computer operations that generate information about specific individuals have such a limited relationship to the flow of information to the public that their work product also could be regarded as not newsworthy and therefore entitled to a low level of First Amendment protection or to none at all.

Of course, computer systems may become more accessible to the general public in the future. Home computer terminals eventually may be as common as television and radio receivers. They may even be connected to national or international computer networks that provide "services ranging from banking and travel facilities to library research and medical care."[82] What is more germane to this discussion, computers may come to perform many of the tasks that are now discharged by radio and television newscasts and newspapers. One projection suggests a central computer containing vast amounts of current and background news that could be tapped from home terminals. Custom-tailored news would even be possible. If a person wanted to see the headlines, news summaries, particular stories, or in-depth analyses, he would need only to frame a request on his console and the information would be forthcoming from the central newsbank.[83]

Should developments along these lines come to pass, computer networks will be as much a part of the "marketplace of ideas"[84] as are our contemporary media of expression and therefore equally entitled to First Amendment protection to the extent they disseminate information that is not purely commercial. However, as long as computer technology remains a relatively esoteric art, available to only a few, and applied primarily for record keeping and retrieval, full-scale constitutional protection for information transfers within a computer system and from the system to people who will use the information for personal advantage seems inappropriate and unnecessary. To grant data handlers wide latitude to abuse the files under their control might engender the type of suspicious atmosphere thought to be symptomatic of totalitarian regimes; citizens might well avoid activity or ideas that conceivably could lead to a black mark in an electronic file that some day might be publicly disclosed. Thus, a knee-jerk extension of the First Amendment immunity established by Hill to disseminations by computer systems could subvert the very values that the constitutional guarantee is designed to protect.

Transplanting the Hill privilege for publishing newsworthy matter to the computer context is particularly dangerous in view of the deep inroads in the availability of defamation and privacy actions in recent years. As Professor Harry Kalven of the University of Chicago Law School has observed, the Hill decision points toward a time when anything the press decides to print will be held newsworthy and therefore within the First Amendment's protection and beyond the law of privacy.[85] Furthermore, in the course of time the press will be given virtually unfettered discretion in making this determination, inasmuch as it presumably knows best what is "news" and because courts often are reluctant to make value judgments of this type.

Kalven's prediction is borne out by growing limitations on the ability to secure relief in the closely related area of defamation.[86] Since the Supreme Court's decision in *New York Times Company* v. *Sullivan*,[87] the class of "public officials" who must satisfy the burden of proving the press's knowledge or reckless disregard for the truth in order to recover for defamation has expanded to such an extent that it now appears the term may encompass categories of individuals who are not even in government service.[88] As one Supreme Court Justice has said: "I see no way to draw lines that exclude the night watchman, the file clerk, the typist, or for that matter, anyone on the public payroll. And how about those who contract to carry out governmental missions? . . . And the industrialists who raise the price of a basic commodity? . . . And the labor leader who combines trade unionism with bribery and racketeering?"[89] Conversely, the class of "public officials" who can defame others with impunity is potentially as large, since the Supreme Court has held that falsehoods published by a government official acting within the scope of his discretionary authority are absolutely privileged.[90]

This trend should not be extended to privacy. It is one thing to say that the First Amendment protects the publication of that which is newsworthy. But to go further and give the press authority to decide what is newsworthy effectively abandons the lambs to the wolves. In the context of certain privacy invasions, as exemplified by the Hill case, there is an objective standard that can be used as a guideline for determining whether the public has a legitimate interest in information—it must relate to a person, event, or occurrence that has independent contemporary significance. But when the invasion takes the form of someone rummaging through the entrails of a computer dossier maintained on one of his fellow men there is no newsworthy event—unless the disseminator tries to pick himself up by his bootstraps and characterize the disclosure of the file as such an event.

The potential for centralization of power that inheres in the new computer technology, the increased flow of data between public and private organizations, the general lack of effective internal safeguards, and the frequently secretive nature of the dissemination, are the considerations that lie at the heart of the question whether a data system and its managers should be immunized from liability for transferring or otherwise disclosing damaging personal information. Yet the Supreme Court has not been called upon to analyze these factors in any of the past cases dealing with freedom of the press. Until considerable experience relating to the interaction of computer systems and free speech has accumulated, we should reflect carefully before cavalierly extending the privilege given the news media by Hill to the emerging information-exchange formats. The Supreme Court's desire to foster the free dissemination of information cannot be faulted as a motivating philosophy, but the policies underlying the First Amendment may not have to be vindicated at the expense of individual privacy.

If there are no insuperable constitutional obstacles to imposing legal restrictions on the flow of information within a computer system and to individuals or institutions outside the system, what standards should be imposed on the movement of information from computer banks to the mass media? As statements in the Hill opinion indicate, information that the press obtains by intrusive or trespassory behavior will give rise to liability.[91] It also may be that courts will be more restrictive in what they consider newsworthy when the information is secured through improper means. The free flow of information would not be seriously impaired by denying privileged status to information of relatively little legitimate public interest that was secured by a serious invasion of someone's privacy.

An interesting, though somewhat obscure, California case suggests this possibility.[92] A quack doctor had been surreptitiously photographed and tape-recorded in his home by *Life* magazine reporters posing as patients as he held a wand and diagnosed a lump on a reporter's breast as the result of her having once eaten some rancid butter. The unfortunate medicine man was subsequently prosecuted for his illicit activities, and *Life* thereafter published a story and some of the photographs obtained during the masquerade. A privacy suit resulted in which the court held that the magazine could not claim the story was newsworthy at the time of the visit to the plaintiff's home, a determination that may have been influenced by the manner in which the information was obtained.

This restraint on the conduct of the news media, although helpful when illegal snooping or surveillance techniques are employed to extract data from a computer system, does not reach the situation that is likely to prove most troublesome—cooperation between data gatherers within the computer community and disseminators within the mass-communications media. This liaison is hardly unique to the computer age. The seductive minions of the press always have been able to cajole public and institutional officials into granting access to sensitive files by employing the blandishments of personal publicity or the threat of public criticism. This has notably been true regarding law-enforcement agencies. The following passage describes conditions in the state of New York prior to a revision of police record-keeping systems:

> Violation of files was frequent. Police reporters looking for a good story were given free access to files on suspects, and as a result were able to publish in the newspaper some interesting but in many cases misleading, irrelevant, and damaging pieces of information. Those police chiefs who tried to protect the confidentiality of their files received poor press treatment, so that they would be encouraged to cooperate with the press more fully in the future.[93]

The problem may be magnified by the computer. If my earlier predictions concerning the increased computerization of personal data prove accurate,[94] there will be a marked increase in the quantity, sensitivity, and variety of information that the mass media may be able to extract from the data bank of the future. Gaining access to these systems will be an increasingly desirable objective, inasmuch as a dossier printout may well contain public record data intermingled with subjective intelligence reports, information given by the subject or an informer with the tacit or express assurance that its use would be limited, and information transferred from other computer systems. A newsman or journalist unfamiliar with the structure of the network and the sources from which it draws its store of information is not likely to make the type of reasoned judgment about the reliability or utility of the information that he might make in the case of a manual filing system containing data from circumscribed and clearly defined sources.

It also is unrealistic to assume that all managers or proprietors of computer systems will be concerned about how the data they release to the press are used or interpreted. A modicum of restraint could be expected if the immunity afforded the press by Hill were not extended to those who supply private data to the news media.[95] The managers of a computer system and anyone else who is responsible for a release of private information should be held liable for the privacy invasion, even if the actual dissemination to the public is the work of the press and is protected by the First Amendment. True, there is the possibility that shifting the liability to the information supplier will inhibit those who furnish data to the media, and that this may be inconsistent with a policy of giving the press access to information. But in many cases any claim that imposing liability on the information source impairs freedom of the press will be somewhat attenuated. Unless this argument is substantiated by something more than its assertion, the courts should not expand the Hill immunity principle beyond the news media.

The Counterweight to Hill—Privacy as a Constitutional Principle

Although the First Amendment is intended to secure the flow of information thought necessary for intelligent self-government in a free society, the courts have recognized several considerations that give rise to a constitutional right to withhold personal information. Given the possibility that the courts will continue to erode the legal protection accorded personal privacy by extending the Hill case, the affirmative protection afforded by these constitutional doctrines takes on added significance. By no means, however, are they a panacea. Thus far the rights that have been recognized in personal information have served primarily to restrict governmental abuses and have not been applicable to privacy invasions committed by nongovernmental institutions. Moreover, these principles were formulated before the advent of computer technology and need further judicial development before they can meet the challenge presented by the new information systems. But taken together, the instances in which a person's right to certain types of privacy has been put on a constitutional basis may provide a philosophical framework for bringing computer systems under effective legislative or administrative controls that go beyond the minimal common-law protection presently offered by the courts.

The right of associational privacy, which recognizes the "vital relationship between freedom to associate and privacy in one's association,"[96] is probably the most clearly developed of the constitutional protections for personal information. Thus, when the government attempts to gather data concerning an individual's association with a group dedicated to the advancement of certain beliefs in "political, economic, religious, or cultural matters,"[97] it must "convincingly show a substantial relation between the information sought and a subject of overriding and compelling state interest."[98]

These principles were applied by the Supreme Court in a case involving Alabama's attempt to compel the NAACP to turn over its membership lists, on the ground that the state needed the information as part of its regulation of out-of-state corporations. The NAACP contended that because of racial conditions in the South, compliance with the state's demands would subject its members to harassment and reprisals. The Supreme Court agreed and held that the risks to individual members outweighed any need the state might have to know who was in the association.[99]

A recent New Jersey case illustrates how the right of associational privacy is directly relevant to the computer-privacy problem.[100] The dispute involved a memorandum on "Civil Disorders" sent by the state attorney general to local officials. Among other suggestions, the memorandum called for the creation of a police intelligence system that would enable law-enforcement authorities to keep tabs on individuals considered potential troublemakers and on organizations that might promote or be involved in a wide range of activities, including protests, demonstrations, and riots. The information to be recorded and forwarded to the central intelligence system was both detailed and varied. For example, the Security Summary Report Form provided with the attorney general's memorandum asked for an extensive physical description (an item on race presented the interesting division of White, Negro, Indian, Chinese, Japanese, and Other—the "Yellow Peril" apparently still weighs heavily on the minds of New Jersey officials) of the file subject. It also called for his occupation, employer's business and address, and motor vehicle record. The Form closed with a request for a "narrative" that would cover, among other subjects, "membership, affiliation and/or status with organizations or groups—educational background—habits or traits—places frequented . . . financial/credit status."[101]

The New Jersey branch of the NAACP, along with several individuals who had engaged in civil rights activity, sought to have the intelligence system declared unconstitutional. Initially they were successful. A New Jersey trial court held that even though the state had a legitimate interest in avoiding civil disturbances, the information requested went beyond what was reasonably required. The court also concluded that maintenance of a centralized information system of this type would have a "chilling effect" on the free expression of political views and would inhibit freedom of association. This position is well beyond that taken by the Supreme Court in the NAACP membership list case, which merely held that the state could not force an organization to disclose information about its members; the New Jersey court actually prohibited the state from compiling and recording the information. The court also awarded particularly broad relief. All the information in the system—not only the data pertaining to the people who had brought the suit—was ordered destroyed, except information that was to be "used to charge persons with specifically defined criminal conduct."[102]

The New Jersey trial court's decision broke new ground in the fight to develop a legal right of informational privacy and contained perhaps the seeds of a theory for seeking the destruction of the nonessential files in an intelligence data bank, such as the one that has been maintained by the Army,[103] or the expungement of a file in a private commercial system, such as a computerized credit bureau, when there is a risk of abuse. Unfortunately, the Supreme Court of New Jersey overturned the lower court's order on the ground that "it would be folly to deprive the government of its power to deal" with the "tyranny of lawlessness."[104] In so doing the court demonstrated a remarkable insensitivity to privacy, the First Amendment, and the dangers of large quantities of individualized information by branding the plaintiff's contentions as "hypothetical horribles." Once again the advocates of "Law and Order" carried the day.

In light of this judicial myopia, it is imperative that the acute threat to associational privacy posed by technology be appreciated. Computers facilitate the composition of lists of people connected with various types of activities and institutions from widely scattered data that probably could not be brought together manually, enabling previously unknown relationships to be revealed or inferred from seemingly disparate information. For example, an analysis of computerized financial records could yield a list of all payments that an individual has made to certain organizations or anyone known to be associated with those organizations. And, as mentioned earlier, tying optical scanners to computerized mail cover operations or carrying out periodic surveillance of computerized airline reservations will encourage attempts to establish relationships that may or may not exist.[105] The risks created by this type of analysis will be magnified as more and more individualized information is collected, stored in centralized computer systems, and freely exchanged among different data banks. As this trend continues legal protection based upon a strong constitutional right of associational privacy will become increasingly important.

Closely related to associational privacy is another type of privacy that the courts have protected—the right to possess ideas and beliefs free from governmental intrusion. The leading case, *Schneider* v. *Smith*,[106] developed out of a seaman's application to the Coast Guard for validation of his license to work as a second assistant engineer. According to a federal regulation, the Commandant of the Coast Guard had to determine whether "the character and habits of life" of a person serving on a ship in American waters would endanger national security. The purpose of the regulation was to weed out saboteurs.

In filling out the required questionnaires, Schneider admitted that he had once belonged to the Communist Party and had subscribed to a leftist magazine called *People's World;* but he explained that he had quit the Party years earlier because he disagreed with many of its methods and techniques. However, he refused to answer a set of interrogatories that asked, among other things, for his "present attitude toward the Communist Party" and "toward the principles and objectives of Communism," as well as his "attitude toward the form of government in the United States."[107] Schneider argued that he had already indicated why he had left the Communist Party; he maintained that "it would be obnoxious to a truly free citizen to answer the kinds of questions under compulsion that you require."[108] When the Coast Guard Commandant refused to process his application, Schneider went to court and prevailed. According to the Supreme Court, First Amendment guarantees and the concept of associational privacy "create a preserve where the views of the individual are made inviolate. This is the philosophy of Jefferson that '[t]he opinions of men are not the object of civil government, nor under its jurisdiction. . . .' "[109]

As is true of associational privacy, the capacity of the new technology to retain and relate masses of information presents a special threat to the privacy of one's ideas and beliefs. Computers increase the ability to store, retrieve, and analyze an individual's opinions, whether they be reflected in psychological tests, job applications, attitude surveys, machine-assisted instruction, simulations, or his relationships with others. These techniques are subtle enough that the individual may not even suspect that his beliefs are being scrutinized or that his responses will be recorded by people beyond his immediate view. Ideological snooping also threatens another personal interest that some courts have recognized—the individual's ability to make a fresh start and escape from his past when there is no overriding public interest in the preservation and disclosure of information about his earlier activities. Unfortunately, it has not been unusual for individuals to be refused teaching or governmental positions, or denied admission to a profession, on the basis of past expressions and associations.[110] *Schneider* v. *Smith* and similar cases should make it clear that espousing an unpopular idea is not a scar a person must wear for the remainder of his life.

Another source of constitutional protection for privacy is found in cases enforcing the Fourth Amendment's prohibition against unreasonable searches and seizures. The language in

Supreme Court opinions over the last fifty years clearly indicates that this basic freedom is largely grounded on conceptions of individual privacy. As Mr. Justice Frankfurter stated in one landmark case:

> The security of one's privacy against arbitrary intrusion by the police—which is at the core of the Fourth Amendment—is basic to a free society. . . . The knock at the door, whether by day or by night, as a prelude to a search, without authority of law but solely on the authority of the police, did not need the commentary of recent history to be condemned as inconsistent with the conception of human rights enshrined in the history and the basic constitutional documents of English-speaking peoples.[111]

And Mr. Justice Brandeis, dissenting in another famous case, characterized "the right to be let alone" by the government as "the most comprehensive of rights and the right most valued by civilized men."[112] Although the Fourth Amendment probably was conceived to protect tangible objects, it has been extended to restrict the government's right to seize personal information.[113]

A footnote in a recent Supreme Court opinion indicates that the Third Amendment's prohibition against quartering soldiers and the Fifth Amendment's right against self-incrimination also are partially based on the individual's right to be let alone.[114] This view is consistent with that expressed in *Griswold* v. *Connecticut*,[115] which struck down Connecticut's attempt to regulate the use of contraceptive devices. Referring to the First, Third, Fourth, and Fifth Amendments, the Court noted that: "specific guarantees in the Bill of Rights have penumbras, formed by emanations from those guarantees that help give them life and substance. . . . [These] create zones of privacy."[116]

The judicial recognition of the freedoms of association and belief, as well as the freedom from unreasonable searches and seizures, is part of a tradition that is basic to American political philosophy—the conception of government as an institution of limited power that must justify any course of action that will inhibit the freedom of its citizens. As Justice Douglas remarked in his opinion for the Court in the Schneider case: "The purpose of the Constitution and Bill of Rights, unlike more recent models promoting a welfare state, was to take government off the backs of people."[117]

It is axiomatic that the power the government can acquire through widespread surveillance or information control might be used to constrict individual freedom and that pressures in that direction must be resisted. Arguments or supplications couched in terms of governmental economy or administrative efficiency cannot justify every bureaucratic demand for greater power to extract, manipulate, store, and disseminate personal data. In the past these very objectives have been advanced, and fortunately rejected, as justifications for universal fingerprinting[118] or passports for travel within the country.[119] Unless we maintain our vigilance against today's pressures, we may find ourselves confronted by something akin to the Chinese Communist Party's program to register and monitor every household in China.[120]

4. Privacy on a Societal Scale—The Need for a Balance

"Exposure for exposure's sake," as the Supreme Court has noted, is by no means a political necessity in a free society, since the values of democracy permit and even encourage a large measure of privacy at the polling place, in the jury room, and elsewhere. . . . There is no more difficult task facing the modern democratic state than that of containing pressures toward excessive publicity, without at the same time encouraging practices of secrecy which choke off the flow of information about public affairs upon which the vitality of government by discussion essentially depends. These are among the central problems that arise in reconciling the conflicting claims of publicity, secrecy, and democracy.

—F. E. Rourke, *Secrecy and Publicity*
(paper ed., 1966), 16–17

Although many aspects of individual privacy are recognized by the law and are protectible either on a constitutional basis or by means of a private common-law action, the available protection is not adequate to meet the threat to informational privacy that already exists and is certain to become more acute in the future. The delicate balance of power between the individual and those institutions in society that affect his daily life already may be shifting against him. This seems to be the result of the confluence of four separate repressive streams of activity and thought relating to privacy. First, the increase in information gathered by both the government and the private sectors has reached the point at which demands for data and invasions of our informational profiles have become commonplace. Second, there is mounting pressure for the creation of data centers and information networks, which will further accelerate the pace of information gathering and magnify the ability of information managers to collate, manipulate, and exchange data on an individualized basis. Third, the enactment of the Freedom of Information Act gives the general public, and the mass communications media in particular, a statutory right of access to the increasing store of information held by the federal government. And, fourth, in a number of contexts the Hill decision tolerates, indeed encourages, the careless use of these data by the news media and others by eliminating the traditional restraint provided by the law's duty of reasonable care.

Unless marked and rapid changes in judicial attitudes take place, it is unrealistic to expect the common-law privacy action to reverse this shift in the balance. The crippling limitations on the individual's ability to maintain a successful suit for injuries resulting from a loss of personal privacy make it an inadequate source of protection. And even the constitutional recognition given privacy has been relatively narrow, has developed episodically, and has served principally as a partial retaining wall against the tide of governmental invasions. The private sector remains unaffected by the existing constitutional restraints.

Thus, it is apparent that more substantial legal safeguards than those currently available are required simply to preserve the status quo in the privacy field[121]—a suggestion that is hardly novel or revolutionary. Today's common law of privacy itself emerged from very comparable circumstances, only when it did the threat was from the newspaper rather than the computer.[122] But the dangers are strikingly analogous. Just as the newspaper is viewed as a "fount of truth and authenticity," the computer projects an infallible and omniscient image across the mind of the average American, despite its occasional and well-publicized foibles. Indeed, its printout is less likely to display the information gatherer's bias or selectivity than is the newspaper article or television report.[123] Consequently, the probability that what appears to be an unbiased computer account or report will be accepted as true seems even higher than when the same information appears in a newspaper article or on a television newscast. And, of course, the relative secrecy with which most computer operations are carried out increases the danger, since the individual may never learn that information about him has been stored in a computer system or is being disseminated.

Beyond the dangers to particular individuals, the unregulated computerization of personal information may have a numbing effect on the value of privacy as a societal norm. As is true of electronic surveillance, the climate or atmosphere of suspicion created by an accumulation of invasions of privacy is of far greater concern than the direct harm caused by the incidents themselves.[124] As one commentator has put it: "Even quite reasonable surveillance practices which should be permissible in themselves, may in the aggregate form be the basis of a terribly oppressive society."[125] This seems to be one of the lessons to be learned as we contemplate the cumulative effects of intrusive data activities.[126]

In the face of what is becoming a serious threat to our informational security, the common law must be reappraised and revitalized. The cases involving Senator Dodd[127] and Ralph Nader[128] may indicate the beginning of a struggle to break through the limitations in which the privacy tort has become encased but they also indicate that these restrictions will not dissipate easily, and that the expansion of the law's protection is apt to be slow.[129] Despite its present weaknesses, the common-law action occasionally is of value when it provides monetary compensation to the victim of a privacy invasion or results in a court order prohibiting additional intrusions. But to be an effective deterrent to information abuse the tort will have to expand and standards will have to be developed by the courts to guide computer-system operators in determining what types of personal information can properly be collected and released to the general public and what must only be allowed to circulate within a large-scale system or be placed under the most stringent access limitations.

Of course, the First Amendment always will be a serious impediment to the doctrinal growth of the privacy theory. Ideally, however, the courts will strike a better balance between the rights of free speech and privacy. Neither value is an absolute, especially when placed in opposition to the other, and a careful

weighing of the conflicting interests seems desirable. As Mr.
Justice Fortas wrote in his dissent in the Hill case:

> . . . I, too, believe that freedom of the press, of speech, as-
> sembly, and religion, and the freedom to petition are of the
> essence of our liberty and fundamental to our values. . . .
> But I do not believe that whatever is in words, however
> much of an aggression it may be upon individual rights, is
> beyond the reach of the law, no matter how heedless of
> others' rights—how remote from public purpose, how reck-
> less, irresponsible, and untrue it may be. I do not believe
> that the First Amendment precludes effective protection of
> the right of privacy. . . .[130]

The possibilities for balancing the conflicting constitutional
policies are illustrated by the judicial order that emerged when
Massachusetts sought to prohibit the showing of a film entitled
Titicut Follies—the famous (or perhaps infamous) semi-documen-
tary that exposed the dismal conditions and lack of treatment
at a state correctional institution for the criminally insane.[131] The
Commonwealth of Massachusetts argued that the film invaded
the privacy of the inmates, many of whom were shown in the
most degrading throes of mental illness. The movie makers de-
fended their right to exhibit the movie on the ground of the
First Amendment, forcefully arguing that conditions at the institution were a matter of public concern.

The clash of policies could not have been more direct. The
inmates stood to gain the most from any reform that might be
spurred by the public exhibition of the film but it also was their
privacy that was invaded. In the Solomonic tradition, the court
compromised: commercial exhibition of the film to the general
public was prohibited, but showings to audiences composed of
specialists, such as lawyers, sociologists, doctors, psychiatrists, or
any other group directly involved in the treatment and rehabili-
tation of the mentally ill, were permitted.[132] Although the decision is vulnerable to criticism for other reasons, its balancing
approach should be applauded since it enabled the court to protect privacy to a considerable degree while preserving the free
flow of information thought necessary to protect the public interest.

But despite this example of a judicial accommodation of

the conflict between the rights, I am far from certain that the common law's response ever will be sufficiently flexible to achieve the desired goal. Indeed, the deficiencies of the current doctrines may increase as public and private sector data systems mushroom and integrate. Therefore, if the individual is to retain any meaningful control over information affecting his life and if society is to avoid becoming enveloped in an Orwellian miasma, the law may have to employ administrative and legislative controls that will impose direct responsibilities and limitations on information system managers and data users. If we fail to do this, Everyman's life history will be recorded, centralized, and made available to wider audiences as the "experts" wield increasing power through their data banks and computer networks.

There is still time for society to intervene. Computerization of personal information has not yet become so widespread that it is uncontrollable, as some of the popular literature and the glowing industry advertising brochures might lead one to believe. Cost factors, system failures, and jealous bureaucrats afford us a period of grace in which to come to grips with the problem of defining the complex and varied relationships between information gatherers and data subjects. Indeed, these factors thus far have prevented the computerization of any significant amount of sensitive, evaluative information—a fact that warns us against becoming too preoccupied with the computer and ignoring the need to protect those who are recorded in little black books. But there is certain to be a time in the very near future when the application of the technology to personal data will reach an acceleration point after which our capability of managing the information flow will be seriously impaired.

VI
The Quest for a New Legal Framework

The life of the law has not been logic: it has been experience. The felt necessities of the time, the prevalent moral and political theories, intuitions of public policy, avowed or unconscious, even the prejudices which judges share with their fellow-men, have had a good deal more to do than the syllogism in determining the rules by which men should be governed.

—O. W. Holmes, Jr.,
The Common Law (1881), 1

The challenge of preserving the individual's right of privacy in an increasingly technocratic society, even one with a democratic heritage as rich as ours, is formidable. But it is one that policy-makers in government, industry, and academe simply cannot avoid. Fortunately, their search for appropriate safeguards will be aided by a resilient legal system and the genius of the technology itself. As we shall see in the next chapter, a number of workable technical and procedural methods for safeguarding computerized information already exist and others will soon be available. But will private and governmental groups adjust their data-handling practices and employ them? In part, the impetus for doing so must come from changes in the legal rules relating to information. Thus, the task of formulating an overall scheme for protecting privacy logically must begin with an attempt to refurbish the current patchwork of common-law remedies, constitutional principles, statutes, and administrative regulation.

Admittedly, the law's existing doctrinal pattern is characterized by uncertain application, lack of predictability, frequent inconsistency, unawareness of the ramifications of the new communications media, and an almost total disregard for the individual's right to participate in information transactions that may have a profound impact on him. Nor is the law's past record of dealing coherently and promptly with the problems raised by new technologies encouraging, especially in the communications field. In times past the importance of the First Amendment freedoms of speech and press was ample reason for approaching the information media with caution. But the computer's potential as an engine of social change—and human control—indicates that inaction or the continued application of outmoded principles may be a greater threat to freedom.

The difficulty of designing an appropriate legal framework is compounded by the pervasive character of the technology; it permeates both the public and private sectors and has consequences that cut across many traditional legal pigeon holes but do not fit neatly into any of them. Almost every response one might conjure up from the corpus of existing doctrine is bound to seem Procrustean or anachronistic. Thus, although a number of ingenious modifications of contemporary principles have been suggested, no single theory seems expansive enough to respond effectively to the computer's variegated threat to individual privacy. And so, more than three quarters of a century after Warren and Brandeis provided the impetus for developing the common law of privacy through the power of their pen, we must again goad the law into meeting a challenge to the sanctity of the individual.

1. Old Wine in New Bottles—"Property" Theories of Privacy

> Who steals my purse, steals trash; 'tis something, nothing;
> 'Twas mine, 'tis his, and has been slave to thousands;
> But he that filches from me my good name
> Robs me of that which not enriches him,
> And makes me poor indeed.
>
> —Shakespeare, *Othello,*
> Act III, Scene iii

One of the most facile and legalistic approaches to safeguarding privacy that has been offered to date is the notion that personal information is a species of property. If this premise is accepted, the natural corollary is that a data subject has the right to control information about himself and is eligible for the full range of legal protection that attaches to property ownership. For example, Professor Westin concludes that "personal information, thought of as the right of decision over one's private personality, should be defined as a property right, with all the restraints on interference by public or private authorities and due process guarantees that our law of property has been so skillful in devising."[1] The eminent sociologist Professor Edward Shils has taken a more philosophical route to much the same conclusion.

> The "social space" around an individual, the recollection of his past, his conversation, his body and its image, all *belong* to him. . . . He possesses them and is entitled to possess them by virtue of the charisma which is inherent in his existance [*sic*] as an individual soul—as we say nowadays, in his individuality—and which is inherent in his membership in the civil community.[2]

The property theory is supported by the fact that personal data often are treated as a commodity by the market place, as well as by drawing analogies to recent Supreme Court decisions dealing with search and seizure[3] or by focusing on language in a few privacy cases.[4] A strong point in the property theory's favor is that it is the most direct method of providing a data subject with a right to sue when there has been information abuse. In addition, by giving everyone something akin to quasi-monopoly control over his informational profile and the ability to enforce that right in court, the property-right approach might serve to deter people from dealing in the intimate details of someone's life history without first obtaining his consent.

The basic objection to the theory is that real and personal property concepts are irrelevant to the personal values that we are attempting to preserve by recognizing a right of privacy. To struggle with the metaphysics of bastardizing the rules relating to the ownership of automobiles and land in order to apply them to computerized data is a dubious venture indeed, because they have nothing in common. The objective of protecting individual privacy is to safeguard emotional and psychological tranquillity by remedying an injurious dissemination of personal information; it never was intended to serve as a vehicle for defining the legal title to information or as a method for determining who has the right to control its commercial exploitation—typical functions of the law of property. To be sure, a few courts have ruled that celebrities have property rights in their names and likenesses and can recover on that basis when they are used for advertising or promotional purposes.[5] But these decisions are not authority for using the law of property by analogy to protect informational privacy; they typically involve arm's-length transactions or the appropriation of commercial values, and are wholly devoid of privacy considerations.

The property approach was rejected as inapposite as early as the seminal article by Warren and Brandeis: "[W]here the value of the production is found not in the right to take the profits arising from publication, but in the peace of mind or the relief afforded by the ability to prevent any publication at all, it is difficult to regard the right as one of property, in the common acceptation of that term."[6] The same point was made by the federal court that denied Senator Dodd relief against Drew Pearson for publishing documents taken from the senator's files.[7]

> The question here is not whether appellee had a right to keep his files from prying eyes, but whether the information taken from those files falls under the protection of the law of property, enforceable by a suit for conversion. In our view, it does not. . . . Insofar as we can tell, none of it amounts to literary property, to scientific invention, or to secret plans formulated by appellee for the conduct of commerce. Nor does it appear to be information held in any way for sale by appellee, analogous to the fresh news copy produced by a wire service.[8]

The property rationale is inappropriate for other reasons. In contexts such as the sale of personal information by credit bureaus or mailing-list organizations, it is not the subject of the data but a third party who created the commercially valuable record. Thus, recognition of a property right in the data subject cannot be justified by arguing that the law merely is acknowledging the economic realities of the marketplace and protecting his ownership of a valuable item. Moreover, resort to the property theory is objectionable in that it involves the manipulation of a conclusory label.

Reliance on the recognition of a property right also would have the undesirable effect of placing responsibility on each individual to protect his own interests, rather than imposing clear duties of care or restrictions on those organizations that want the data, and usually have the leverage to extract them from people. Credit bureaus, for example, probably would be no less successful in convincing data subjects to give up their "property rights" by holding out the carrot of access to the credit economy than they presently are in obtaining "voluntary" consents to credit investigations. The unequal bargaining position of an individual dealing with a government agency or an employer would lead to a similar result.

Another consideration argues against the property rationale. In the absence of a federal statute, property rights in personal information would have to be created and governed by state law. Yet the experience with state-protected property rights in unpublished literary works and various intangible commercial values has been unsatisfactory. Inconsistencies in result, uneven protection, and difficulties in determining which state's law controls when the transaction involves more than one state have been common. The same type of chaos seems inevitable if the recognition of property rights in something as evanescent as personal information is left to the ministrations of the judiciaries in the fifty states of the Union and the District of Columbia.[9]

There are affirmative reasons that strongly counsel against leaving informational privacy to the uncertainty of state law. In an age in which computer technology will encourage increased data activities and obliterate the significance of state boundaries as restraints on the movement of information, it is important that the law be as homogeneous and certain as possible. National uniformity therefore is an extremely desirable—and may be an imperative—goal in the field of data transmissions over multistate communications media. It is also difficult to see how state-created property rights in information could offer effective protection against privacy invasions by federal data centers, which presumably are largely beyond the power of the state courts. It would be ironic if the law, in attempting to solve a problem as modern as the computer-privacy issue, unwittingly followed the unsatisfactory path of dividing power between the federal government and the states—a pattern that we are now struggling to escape in the literary-property field through legislative proposals completely federalizing the law of copyright.[10]

These considerations indicate that recognition of property rights in personal information is much too artificial a method of regulating important phases of a technology that still is in its infancy. And because of its unresponsiveness to the policies that justify protecting informational privacy, undue reliance on the property approach might tend to abort attempts to pursue more fruitful avenues of legal control or to generate entirely new legal principles that might be better tailored to the unique aspects of the computer-privacy problem.

Rejection of the property approach does not end the search for an appropriate analogy from the existing body of legal doctrine. Actually, the fact that personal information is an intangible but inexhaustible commodity suggests that the enigmatic tort theory proscribing the misappropriation of commercial values may be somewhat more adaptable to the problems of computerized data processing than are the conventional rules of property law.[11] It must be recognized at the outset that the leading case of *International News Service* v. *Associated Press*,[12] in which the United States Supreme Court held the defendant liable for the pirating of wire-service news reports prepared by a rival company, indicates that misappropriation is concerned primarily with the relationship among business competitors. Nonetheless, the Court did conclude that a special right existed between the parties, which it described as a *"quasi*-property"[13] interest in obtaining a just return on the capital and resources invested by the plaintiff to obtain the news reports. Later cases have applied the INS decision expansively to punish various forms of "commercial immorality," such as the piracy of dress designs and phonograph records.

Misappropriation has a certain appeal as a guiding principle because the personal information generated by an individual can be viewed as the "sweat of his brow." Whatever value the data have can be attributed to the subject's "capital and resources," even if they are collected and made marketable by someone else. The misappropriation doctrine also recognizes that because of the relationship between particular people, the law should establish special rights in items of economic value that are enforceable between them. If that is true of competitors, as in INS, there is no reason why it cannot also be true of the relationship between information subjects on the one hand and information extractors, disseminators, and users on the other. Moreover, the misappropriation principle has sufficient vagueness to accommodate a variety of different policy interests and factual situations.[14]

But even these advantages do not overcome certain doctrinal

obstacles. As in the case of the property theory, misappropriation has been used primarily to vindicate economic, rather than emotional or personal values. Once again we would be employing a theoretical hand-me-down to protect personal privacy. Furthermore, as a creature of state law, misappropriation, like traditional property principles, is subject to the confusion and inequality of application inherent in relying on state law to solve a very complex problem that requires a national resolution.

In short, both the property and the misappropriation theories are little more than attempts to solve a difficult policy issue by contorting legal principles that were developed to serve a radically different purpose. Much the same can be said of what appears to be a tongue-in-cheek suggestion that we create a new protective writ called "habeas data" to serve as an ersatz version of the famous writ of habeas corpus.[15] Surely a judicial device created over eight hundred years ago to protect an individual who has been jailed by commanding that he be brought before a court, although an interesting analogy, offers little that is relevant to the quest for a legal structure to protect computerized personal information. Putting old wine in new bottles rarely yields a palatable product.

2. Information Trusts and Related Theories

And just as it is illicit to appropriate another's goods or to make an attempt on his bodily integrity, without his consent, so it is not permissible to enter into his inner domain against his will, whatever is the technique or method used.

—Pope Pius XII, Address to the
Congress of the International Association
of Applied Psychology (April, 1958)

A somewhat more ingenious approach than the recognition of a property right in information—but one that also has a jerry-built appearance—calls for the adaptation of a venerable legal device, the trust, as the mechanism for protecting informational privacy from the vicissitudes of modern computer systems. This method has been employed by the United Planning Organization (UPO), a body formed to establish a "Social Data File" that integrates material from several welfare programs in the Washington area. The UPO has computerized large amounts of personal information secured from various agencies and placed it into a trust. Control over the information is vested in three independent trustees, whose conduct relating to the data's use is regulated by an elaborate written agreement.

The trust instrument provides that the trustees "own" the data subject to certain conditions set forth in the trust agreement.

> First, the trustees must hold the data only for . . . evaluation of social problems and agency practices in the District of Columbia. . . . This is an aggregate, statistical purpose which does *not* include evaluation of any individual.
>
> Second, the trustees must place the data in the custody of the UPO for its use as long as the UPO exists. . . .
>
> Third, the trustees can only place the data in the custody of UPO . . . if we use it for the purpose described . . . and do not use it to breach the confidentiality of information collected concerning named individuals. . . .
>
> Fourth, the trustees cannot transfer their control over the data. . . .
>
> Fifth, the trust is created in perpetuity and is irrevocable.[16]

The existence of a watchdog group that theoretically does not have a personal or commercial interest in data placed in its custody and is charged with clearly defined fiduciary duties to protect the data subjects, is appealing on its face. However, the trust device is beset with conceptual difficulties that prevent it from having widespread utility. It is an established legal principle that the subject matter of a trust must be a legally enforceable property interest.[17] The assumption that the UPO has such a property interest in or is the "owner" of the personal information embodied on the magnetic tapes and punch cards that constitute the supposed trust seems to beg the question. Much of the information undoubtedly is a matter of public record and incapable of being owned by anyone; the residue, if it can be said to be property at all, surely belongs to the individual to whom it pertains rather than to a group that happens to have gained possession of one notational version of it. The anomaly of UPO's asserted ownership is emphasized by the fact that the information could be publicly revealed by the data subjects or obtained by third persons from other sources. In other words, the same data could be "possessed" or "owned" by anyone else who was able to gather them, which might be done without physically disturbing the trust res or impairing its value as a research tool. As a practical matter, therefore, the trust applies only to the particular files held by the UPO and does not extend to the underlying data. Consequently, the effectiveness of the trust approach seems limited to the use of the data by people who have voluntarily bound themselves to the arrangement. The device provides no protection to the individual against abuses by other users of the same information.

Perhaps even more significant is the fact that the trust in no way inhibits the data-collection process by limiting UPO's ability to procure data from individuals or other agencies or by restricting the nature of the information that finds its way into the organization's files. Of course, it might be possible to modify the trust agreement and extend its terms to every aspect of information handling. But this is an extremely clumsy and circuitous way of establishing a regulatory scheme for the information flow. A more philosophical concern is whether the law of trusts, which throughout its long history has been designed primarily to safeguard the economic well-being of trust beneficiaries, is really a suitable mechanism for creating and enforcing rules to protect informational privacy.

The trust device also is somewhat suspect as a protector of privacy because it typically will be unilaterally established by the organization controlling a particular data base. This means that the terms and conditions of the trust arrangement are entirely a matter of the discretion or benevolence of the creator of the trust. The United Planning Organization's agreement illustrates this deficiency very clearly, since no rights are given to those who theoretically are to be protected by the trust—the citizens whose personal information has been collected by the agencies that furnished the data.[18] Apart from this problem, which could be ameliorated if the courts construed the trust as giving the file subjects a right to enforce the terms of the agreement, the UPO approach has the potential of producing an even greater lack of uniformity in the informational privacy area than the property or misappropriation theories. And, given the conceptual difficulty of applying trust law to computerized personal data, judicial scrutiny of the trustee's behavior could easily degenerate into a highly convoluted theoretical analysis or a baroque exegesis on the language of the trust instrument.

On balance, therefore, the establishment of personal information trusts may be more suited to promoting full employment for lawyers than to fashioning a sensible balance of the competing policies bearing on the use of personal information. Far from being a cure-all, the trust is little more than a legalistic device employed on an *ad hoc* basis to avoid the complex problems that should be faced up to by managers of information systems and user groups. Admittedly, it is a helpful expedient for providing a measure of control over the manipulation of data by particular groups or information systems. In that sense, it is a first step toward creating some professional sensitivity to the value of personal privacy on the part of information users, and UPO should be commended for experimenting with it. But it is unlikely that the trust will provide the keystone for solving the computer-privacy problem.

These same criticisms also seem well-directed at attempts to use other ancient legal doctrines to fabricate some type of duty of care on information gatherers and disseminators. For example, it seems to me that little is gained by trying to impose fictitious "implied warranties" that data are accurate or fit for a particular use. Warranties have traditionally served to protect the investment and physical safety of buyers against the overly enthusiastic claims of sellers and the defective products of manufacturers. It would be sheer legerdemain to contort warranty principles in order to protect individual privacy. Even if this feat could be achieved, the primary effect would be to improve the accuracy of personal data, a valuable objective but one already covered to a degree by the law of defamation. But putting warranties on data would not inhibit data collection or dissemination or provide the sensitive approach needed to solve such problems as how to insure contextual accuracy and guarantee that personal data will be updated when appropriate.

A more aesthetic analogy might be drawn to the rules relating to confidentiality and fiduciary duties. In the past, the law has honored a request for nondisclosure when the parties to the data transaction have expressly agreed that the information be treated with special care or when a special relationship existed between the parties—husband and wife, priest and penitent, attorney and client, for example. However, on occasion these privileged relationships have been ignored by the courts when disclosure was thought socially desirable, and judges have not shown any enthusiasm for broadening them to include information given to reporters, school counselors, or accountants. The notion that the courts will recognize a general principle requiring data handlers to treat personal information as confidential or will declare that file keepers owe a fiduciary duty to file subjects seems to be wishful thinking. Nor is it realistic to think that a pledge of confidentiality can be secured on a contractual basis. In most situations involving data extraction, the individual is in no position to demand a promise to this effect. Of course, the courts may change their attitude when the potentialities of the computer become apparent. But to wait for the courts to create common-law obligations and impose them on information extractors, processors, transmitters, and users for the benefit of data subjects will require the patience of Job and may prove to be no more fruitful than agitating for the expansion of the common-law privacy action. Time is a luxury personal privacy cannot afford and the glacial movement of legal doctrine is inappropriate for the problem at hand.

3. Federal Privacy Legislation

> While technology races, legislation crawls.
> —Senator Edward Long, *The Intruders* (1967), 183

The computer's potential for affecting the relationships among individuals, organizations, and government, as well as for becoming the heart of a new medium of communication, suggests that direct congressional action to protect privacy may be necessary. This judgment is reinforced by the relatively unpromising growth capacity of the common-law theories that have been discussed and the unpredictable character of state legislation. Congressional intervention could afford immediate protection to individuals in contexts in which none presently exists, provide a uniform and comprehensive formula for the development of multistate computer systems, and infuse a measure of coherence into the presently amorphous and archaic law of privacy. But the uncertain direction of the computer age, the absence of obvious and easy legislative solutions, and the average lawmaker's lack of appreciation for the dimensions of the computer revolution or its potential impact on individual privacy, combine to make the likelihood of effective congressional action in the foreseeable future highly conjectural.

Legislative activity in the computer-privacy field might take a number of different forms. One simple and highly desirable statutory approach would be to prohibit governmental, and perhaps even nongovernmental, organizations from collecting designated classes of sensitive data. Of course, any attempt to constrict information gathering is bound to incur the ire of those governmental agencies, university research groups, charitable foundations, and industrial complexes that believe they would profit from a "little more" data. Any legislation that would have the effect of impeding the information flow faces an uphill battle in the political arena.

Aware of the odds, but not one to back away from a fight on a matter of principle, Senator Ervin has introduced a broadly worded proposal that would prohibit federal agencies from requiring an individual to divulge personal information unless its collection can be justified under some provision in the Constitution and a specific act of Congress.[19] If these conditions are met, disclosure may be made mandatory. The bill also limits data collection on a voluntary basis to inquiries into matters specifically approved by statute. In addition, the volitional character of the questionnaire would have to be made clear to the respondents.

The Ervin bill, which was introduced primarily to draw attention to the problem, suffers from linguistic problems that make its scope of application somewhat uncertain. These stem from an inadequate definition of the information and data-gathering activities covered by the proposal. Moreover, it may be illusory to rely on a requirement that the Constitution authorize a given data activity before an agency may seek information on a mandatory basis. This limitation is likely to be rendered nugatory by a broad judicial reading of the clause in Article I giving Congress the power to enact legislation that is "necessary and proper" to the implementation of its other constitutional authority. Loosely speaking, all of the government's data gathering is a "necessary and proper" adjunct to some legitimate act of Congress. Finally, requiring all voluntary surveys to be predicated on specific acts of Congress might lead to one of two extremes—either Congress will become a rubber stamp for agency information-gathering requests, because it will lack the time to give them proper scrutiny, or undue congressional attention will be paid to the details of agency surveys.

It might be better if the Ervin bill simply provided that voluntary data gathering would be permitted when the agency could satisfy a series of legislative guidelines or standards. The prerequisites to conducting a voluntary survey might include: (1) an administrative presentation of a clear and significant need for the data; (2) a showing that the data have not been secured by other federally conducted surveys; (3) a demonstration that the data are not available as a result of state, local, or private information gathering efforts; (4) a determination that the sampling group is no larger than is necessary to obtain the requisite data base; (5) an articulated and persuasive administrative finding that the questions are not intrusive or violative of individual privacy; and (6) a demonstration that individual responses will be protected against risks of privacy invasion and unnecessary dissemination.

Despite its faults, the Ervin bill represents a novel and highly rational attempt to limit federal data-collection activities to those expressly authorized by Congress and to curtail the use of subtle forms of governmental coercion against individuals. One desirable by-product of the bill is that it would force Congress to consider the information implications of each piece of legislation that comes before it. In addition, it is the first legislative proposal that seriously attempts to deal with the problem of reducing the disclosure burden on individual citizens. Unfortunately, although hearings were held on the bill in the spring of 1969, it has been languishing since.

One variation on statutes prohibiting data collectors from using, or threatening to use, coercion to compel individuals to furnish data they are not legally obliged to give would require reappraising the existing statutes that make disclosure of certain information mandatory, presumably with an eye toward reducing their scope. Some aspects of the Ervin bill illustrate this approach. The same is true of the proposals seeking to eliminate the criminal penalties for failure to answer many of the questions on the decennial census.[20]

Although eliminating some of the harsh sanctions for noncompliance with governmental demands for information appears to be desirable, doing so will not assure the citizenry of informational privacy. Prohibitions against coercive data collection will only remedy some of the more blatant abuses; they are of no assistance in assuring better data handling and dissemination practices. Moreover, even a moderate alteration in the existing data collection balance between citizen and government *might* have an adverse effect on some important information-gathering efforts. For example, if popular resentment against the spectrum of contemporary privacy invasions and the constant stream of intrusive questionnaires became focused upon the Census Bureau's activities, the absence of sanctions might precipitate a widespread failure to respond that could impair the validity of surveys needed for the analysis of fundamental social problems. But as indicated in an earlier chapter,[21] a number of countervailing considerations make it unlikely that this would come to pass.

A somewhat different, and in many ways more drastic, legislative approach involves requiring computer manufacturers, users, and data networks to employ prescribed safeguards for maintaining the integrity of personal information. This can take the form of imposing a statutory duty of care on everyone connected with the data-handling process, which would have the effect of encouraging privacy consciousness, or of enacting detailed privacy-oriented technical and procedural requirements that would have to be followed by computer manufacturers and handlers of personal information.

It would be very difficult to employ the latter technique in a statute having general application, because information may be used for so many different purposes that it may be impossible to draft a single body of rules to govern every situation. The problem is compounded by the chameleonlike character of many types of data. As congressional investigations into the proposed National Data Center revealed, the "sensitivity" of information—its potential for harming an individual if inaccurate or improperly disseminated—depends in part upon how large the gap is between the context in which it was collected and the context in which it is used. Any sizable information system containing detailed individual data is unlikely to have a uniform sensitivity level, and differences are bound to be even greater among systems.

Extremely complex legislation therefore is necessary if specific privacy safeguards are to be prescribed. As indicated in the next chapter, sophisticated protective schemes involving access regulations, personnel controls, and mechanical devices are available that can discriminate among users and differentiate data on the basis of sensitivity. To insure adequate protection, legislation would have to prescribe how these techniques should be used, deal with virtually every aspect of information integrity, and draw difficult distinctions in terms of levels of information sensitivity.

Thus, a potpourri of legislative controls might well be needed; some would establish degrees of confidentiality for different kinds of data and others might prescribe the technical and procedural safeguards to be employed by the system. This type of refined structuring presumably would be based on an evaluation of how much "privacy" the data in a given system deserve and balancing the damage that could be caused by misuse of the information against the cost and loss of efficiency that might result from implementing various safeguards. Alternatively, separate statutes could be framed in terms of the character of information that is collected—health, military, internal-security, financial—or the different types of data-gathering groups—law-enforcement and administrative agencies, credit bureaus, statistical organizations.

But viewing the situation realistically, a detailed assessment along these lines is an overwhelmingly complex task, especially if it must be undertaken against a background of highly sophisticated networks that carry data from numerous sources and are used by different people, groups, agencies, and organizations for highly disparate purposes. Congressional inertia, a lack of technical expertise on Capitol Hill, and the labyrinthine character of the computer-privacy problem all combine to make it extremely unlikely that a refined statutory scheme will emerge in the foreseeable future. In fairness to Congress, our very limited experience with data centers and computer networks makes the job of drafting sound comprehensive national legislation that will stand up under the pressure of rapid technological change virtually insurmountable at present. There is an understandable fear that any attempt to legislate at this juncture might be premature and yield an insufficiently malleable product that would quickly become obsolete.

Moreover, the political facts of life are working against a comprehensive approach at this time. Added to the somewhat uncertain future shape and application of the technology is Congress's desire to refrain from interceding in the day-to-day operations of federal agencies, and its unwillingness to step in and regulate an influential segment of American industry until the need for doing so is clear. Finally there is as yet no consensus that federal regulation of private systems is desirable—a question that is bound to provoke intense lobbying by private interest groups and to become enmeshed with power politics.

The less ambitious course of promulgating a general standard of care to be followed by data handlers may be the appropriate form for legislation to take. This would make it unnecessary for a federal statute to grapple with the minutiae of every type of computer operation. Since the preservation of informational privacy always will depend to some degree upon how the data managers exercise their discretion, it may be sufficient to enact a set of legislative guidelines that will encourage data handlers to act in an enlightened manner. It also would be necessary to give the courts authority to resolve disputes and remedy abuses. Legislation along these lines would establish the necessary duties between information handlers and data subjects and fill the gaps in the existing common law of privacy.

But even an informational privacy statute that merely seeks to provide a philosophical orientation for data handlers must surmount a number of drafting obstacles. To be effective it must be broad enough to cover every potential application of computer technology; the statute, thus, must embrace both public and private data centers and be cognizant of the interrelationships among these systems. Any serious attempt at privacy legislation also should strive to bring some order to the existing welter of conflicting and often meaningless confidentiality statutes, a process that might necessitate modification of some aspects of other federal enactments, such as the Federal Reports Act,[22] the Crime Control Act,[23] and the Freedom of Information Act.[24] Any attempt to do so is bound to rekindle the conflicts between informational privacy and other policy objectives and represent a threat to many well-entrenched bureaucrats whose power is partially dependent on control of large data bases. Finally, because very little really is known about the long-range impact of computer technology on society or the effect of regulating its utilization at this time would have to be undertaken with the realization that periodic reappraisal undoubtedly would be necessary.

In light of the manifold difficulties of drafting comprehensive privacy legislation, it is not surprising that most of the bills introduced during recent Congresses have relatively narrow scopes.[25] By and large these proposals deal only with the information-handling activities of particular governmental agencies, such as the Census Bureau,[26] or the practices of private organizations, the credit bureaus and junk mailers, for example.[27] Other bills represent attempts to protect certain groups that are particularly vulnerable to privacy invasions, as is true of Senator Ervin's proposal for preserving the privacy of government employees.[28]

But the flood of bills is itself a healthy sign, even though many of them are not likely to be enacted and may not even have been introduced seriously. In one of the most ambitious efforts to date, Congressman Koch of New York suggests that the Freedom of Information Act be amended to require all federal agencies maintaining files of personal information to give notice to an individual if information concerning him has been procured from any source.[29] The bill also provides that the individual has a right to inspect and copy the files any agency maintains on him and goes on to direct that the agencies refrain from disclosing personal data without permission from the file subject.[30] The Koch bill's right-of-access provision could be a valuable mechanism for enabling an individual to detect and secure correction of potentially damaging errors in his files. On the other hand, it might also subject an individual to coercive pressures by those who want access to the governmental dossiers maintained on him and are in a position to insist upon his procuring copies for their use. It would be perverse indeed if enactment of the Koch proposal enabled lending institutions and employers to make the disclosure of governmental files a condition of granting the data subject a loan or a job. But despite this concern, there is no doubt that Congressman Koch's bill would have a substantial ameliorative effect on the present information-handling practices of a number of federal agencies, although it would accomplish little on the data-gathering side of the ledger and would be inapplicable to nonfederal data banks. Realistically viewed, the proposal has a difficult legislative road to traverse and passage must be considered doubtful as of now.

On the negative side, all of the current legislative proposals may be criticized for their lack of scope and their failure to come to grips with the possible effects the new technologies may have on informational privacy. Although the United States is the most advanced nation in the world in the field of computer science, we must look elsewhere to find comprehensive legislative proposals for solving the computer-privacy problem—in particular to Canada, Great Britain, and Germany. Under bills before the Ontario legislature[31] and the British parliament,[32] (1) all data banks would be registered, (2) every person on whom a data bank maintains a file would receive a printout containing the file's original contents and have the right to demand printouts at later points in time, and (3) each printout would be accompanied by a statement of the file's use since the previous printout was supplied and a list of those who received data from it. In addition, the individual could object to any item in the dossier and secure an expungement order from the Registrar of Data Banks, if he could show that the entry was incorrect or unfair. Civil liability and penalties also would be available if the bank supplied erroneous information or violated the act's provisions.

By and large these are remarkable proposals. I say this even though neither bill expressly deals with file security or snooping, prescribes the proper scope of data acquisition and input, contains limitations on dissemination, applies to all data banks that might contain information of a potentially damaging nature, imposes a duty of care on data-bank operators except in the *ex post facto* sense of relying on individuals to seek correction, or requires the use of hardware or software controls to meet privacy-protecting standards. Many of these objectives would be achieved indirectly, however, because the possibility of liability under the proposed statute will encourage data banks to upgrade their practices.

One distressing factor that militates against effective legislation is that the vast majority of congressmen have little or no comprehension of the new information technologies, much less their broader societal implications. This is ironic because one of the explanations for the increasing contemporary aggrandizement of power by the Executive Branch (often at the expense of the Congress) is the fact that it has a virtual hammerlock on the massive information store held by the federal government.[33] The White House and its minions have approximately five thousand computers at their disposal; the number of machines within the Legislative Branch can be counted on the fingers of one hand, and as of now a perfect hand is not needed to make the enumeration. In part the Executive Branch's advantage in the fields of information-gathering and computer technology explains why there has been little presidential leadership in promoting computerization in the other parts of the federal government. As long as Congress remains ignorant of how it is being disadvantaged by its failure to employ the new technologies, the White House is not likely to rock the boat.

Thus we will probably have to content ourselves for a while with episodic attempts at legislative solutions for limited aspects of the computer-privacy problem. But that is no reason to refrain from applying pressure for broader legislation or to look any statutory gift horse in the mouth. Even particularistic correctives are often better than none and their cumulative effect may be quite desirable. Furthermore, even the gradual development of a legislative framework is likely to proceed more rapidly than a judicial remodeling of the common law, especially if the statutes provide for the added dimension of administrative regulation.

4. Federal Administrative Regulation

[T]he revolution in science now requires thoughtful political change, not piecemeal and temporizing adjustments. If we delay too long . . ., the science establishment might become an acute threat rather than a rich benefit to our democratic system. An enlargement of individual freedom . . . is more likely to be produced through the rational ordering of scientific activity than through maintaining its subsidized disorder. It took almost a century to learn this lesson and to devise flexible controls over our economic activity. Let us hope that the lead-time will be greatly reduced when we come to experiment with effective political controls over the nation's scientific and technological assets.

—Walter Goldstein, "The Science Establishment
and Its Political Control,"
43 *Virginia Quarterly Review* (1967), 353, 371

Although various factors make comprehensive legislation both difficult to draft and a potentially unsatisfactory technique, they do not preclude the possibility that the computer-privacy question may be amenable to administrative treatment. In addition to obviating the need to make highly detailed policy judgments in statutory form at what may be a premature time, administrative regulation would at least guarantee that the problem is placed in the hands of a watchdog group, theoretically composed of experts in the field, that will exercise continuing supervision over it. Moreover, as a general rule, administrative regulations are less immutable than statutes. They typically provide sufficient flexibility to permit experimentation and require less time for revision than do statutes.

Unfortunately, administrative regulation has fallen into considerable disfavor in the United States because it frequently has taken on a highly bureaucratic character. All too often administrative action has become synonymous with delay, red tape, and arbitrariness, with the hoped-for supervision by an informed cadre giving way to the reality of politicized administrators who have little understanding of the complex problems left to their governance. The situation frequently is made worse by inadequate staffing and funding, which prevent most agencies from acquiring the expertise necessary for rational decision making. Despite these deficiencies, however, I believe that administrative regulation could be very useful in the computer-privacy arena.

The Locus of Regulatory Power

It is not immediately apparent who should be given regulatory power or what form it should take. Certain basic principles provide some guidance, however. Because of the national character of both the information industry and computer communications, control at the federal level seems essential. But it would be unwise to enact a legislative privacy directive that leaves each agency and bureau responsible for establishing rules governing its own information activities. This approach is likely to produce such significant variations in practice that little will be gained. It also seems axiomatic that overall regulatory power ought not be given to an agency that relies heavily on a flow of personal information. The debate over the proposed National Data Center[34] and revelations before congressional subcommittees concerning the intrusive activities of the Internal Revenue Service, the Post Office, and the Immigration and Naturalization Service make it abundantly clear that privacy values often get short shrift from agencies with a vested interest in gathering and using data.[35] Testimony indicating that agency personnel—admittedly few in number—systematically engage in mail-cover operations, electronic bugging, wiretapping, harassment of citizens, and other invasions of privacy demonstrates that governmental officials who deal with personal data often become too oriented toward the objectives of their own institutions or too vulnerable to pressures from other organizations (both inside and outside government) to be entrusted with primary responsibility for preserving the privacy of others. Consequently, most of the existing information agencies should be disqualified from a leadership role in formulating regulatory policy regarding the computer-privacy question.

Is there any existing organization that can be given responsibility for developing an administrative privacy scheme for information systems operated by the federal government, and perhaps those maintained by other organizations? The Census Bureau and the Office of Management and Budget spring to mind as possibilities. Even though the Census Bureau has an enviable security record,[36] it may have become so indoctrinated by practices that promote information acquisition that it would be difficult for the Bureau to formulate a balanced regulatory scheme for protecting privacy. It is hard to visualize the Census Bureau changing its present attitudes and becoming an ideal organization for developing rules that might have the effect of constricting the federal government's information-gathering activities.

As to the Office of Management and Budget, its supervision of federal reporting programs has been ineffectual from the perspective of individual privacy and the burdens imposed on citizens.[37] This is neither surprising nor particularly objectionable, in view of the institutional bias resulting from that office's primary fealty being to the White House. However, the Office's preoccupation with fiscal matters and governmental efficiency, as well as its unresponsiveness to Congress, does argue against giving it the responsibility for assuring that privacy is preserved. It also is worth recalling that both OMB and Census always have been oriented toward the federal scene and might not be entirely appropriate regulatory institutions if certain aspects of nonfederal information systems were to be brought under federal supervision.

Another candidate for the job is the Federal Communications Commission, which recognized the importance of the privacy issue some time ago and included the subject as one of the central concerns in its extensive inquiry into computer communications.[38] A relatively minor extension of the FCC's statutory jurisdiction would enable the agency to deal with a wide range of computer-privacy problems. As a matter of fact, the Commission undoubtedly has considerable flexibility under existing law to promulgate rules that would assure a significant level of communications security, especially in the computer-transmission field.

Entrusting the field of informational privacy to the FCC might prove to be less than ideal, however. There is some possibility that the Commission would find itself torn by an ideological conflict of interest, inasmuch as its primary concern is the efficient and useful exploitation of the nation's communications technology. In the context of regulating the telephone system, for example, economic considerations typically have predominated over efforts to insure the confidentiality of communications.[39] A similar emphasis emerged during the FCC's inquiry into data communications. Privacy received minimal attention in most of the responses filed by various organizations, especially in comparison to the treatment accorded the question whether regulation of computer systems is desirable.[40] Of course, this simply may reflect the parochialism of the communications industries, rather than the Commission's inability or unwillingness to deal with the privacy problem.

Yet, perhaps it is unwise to burden the FCC with primary responsibility for regulating a highly complex and multifaceted problem that will take it far outside its usual bailiwick. The Commission traditionally has dealt with problems associated with bandwidth allocation and with technical questions of transmission and communications facilities. An obligation to undertake comprehensive regulation in the computer-privacy arena would require the FCC to master entirely different subjects, such as single- and multilevel governmental information systems, computer manufacturing, and software development. The effect would be an extensive and potentially overwhelming expansion of its jurisdiction, one that it may not be prepared to handle, given its existing heavy workload. Moreover, the Commission has always assiduously avoided any detailed regulation of program or communication content. But precisely this type of involvement may be a vital ingredient of an effective scheme to preserve the privacy of individuals in the context of computer transmissions.

The Federal Trade Commission is another possible source of regulatory authority. It already has jurisdiction over unfair trade practices and deceptive advertising, which gives it considerable power to deal with abuses by credit bureaus, mail-list firms, communications and information companies, and mail and telephone solicitors, as well as a variety of information-extraction practices. Indeed, the FTC has already challenged the methods allegedly used by Metromedia Inc. to compile mailing lists, which allegedly involve sending out questionnaires and encouraging replies by suggesting that the respondent may win "fabulous gifts."[41] According to the FTC, those who respond are then put on mailing lists on the basis of what is revealed in their questionnaires. The Commission contends that it is misleading to fail to disclose that the purpose of the venture is to develop mail lists.

But as is true of the FCC, the Federal Trade Commission might find itself hard pressed in terms of expertise and staff if it were called upon to come to grips with the full spectrum of informational privacy issues generated by the new technologies. The FTC would be obliged to range far beyond its normal sphere of operations to do an effective job. Since the Commission probably already is overextended in terms of the relatively meagre resources at its disposal, it might not be wise to add the computer-privacy problem to its duties.

It therefore is quite possible that none of the existing federal bureaus, agencies, or departments has enough background or is sufficiently independent—in the sense of neither being obligated to various institutional "clients" nor being philosophically committed to the paramount importance of administrative efficiency— to be an effective guardian of individual privacy. If this is the case, the conclusion is inescapable: regulatory control must be lodged outside the existing administrative channels. As repugnant as it may sound in an era of expanding governmental involve-

ments, it may be necessary to establish a completely new institution—perhaps modeled after the semi-autonomous Government Accounting Office—that can operate under a set of legislative guidelines and establish policy for the protection of privacy.
If it were truly independent, the agency might regulate the
nature of the data that could be recorded and stored in various
systems, enforce a congressional standard of care for insuring
the accuracy of recorded information, and make certain that
all data centers employ the latest and most appropriate technological advances to protect the security of their files.

The notion of an independent information agency is not a
new one. Many of the congressional witnesses and commentators on the proposal to create a National Data Center, myself
included, stressed the importance of locating control of such an
organization outside the existing regulatory framework.[42] The
call for a new agency was forcefully echoed by Senator Ervin in
a November 1969 speech at the Wharton School of Finance and
Commerce. In this address, which had a jarring effect on many
computer companies, the Senator advocated the total regulation
of computer technology and had this to say concerning the
source of control.

> I see no existing agency which could assume these compli-
> cated and delicate problems. Those charged with regulating
> communications have built-in biases in their operating
> methods and their approaches to these problems, particularly
> the preservation of individual privacy.
>
> While I dislike adding to an already weighty bureaucracy,
> the problem is serious enough to warrant a separate agency.
> For this reason, therefore, I would support the creation of
> some separate agency to deal specifically with computer sys-
> tems.
>
> I believe we have learned enough over the past 50 years
> about the design and operations and problems of regulatory
> agencies to enable us to create one which has built-in pro-
> tections to assure that it serves the interests of the individ-
> ual citizen and not solely those of the industry it is supposed
> to regulate.

Senator Ervin pursued this approach by scheduling hearings on
federal data banks and the need for regulation late in 1970.

Certainly the possibility of creating an independent federal agency to regulate computerization and information handling is worthy of serious consideration. Perhaps we should start with a Study Commission on Informational Privacy to lay the foundation for such an agency.[43] If nothing else, a serious undertaking of this type would expose the various policy considerations and implications that lie beneath the surface of the multifarious informational activities currently going on in both the public and private sectors.

Functional Aspects of Effective Administrative Control

Any serious proposal to establish a regulatory scheme for a subject as sensitive as the privacy aspects of computer systems would be subjected to the vagaries of the legislative process and would be the target of the lobbyists for various industrial and information-using groups. Consequently, it might seem a somewhat sterile exercise for me to forecast the contours of a regulatory agency that may well never come into existence. Nonetheless, there are several necessary attributes that any administrative body must possess in order to be effective and it might be useful to suggest them in a somewhat impressionistic fashion.

A governmental organization that seeks to regulate significant aspects of a technology as dynamic and pervasive as the computer must draw upon a wide range of expertise for assistance. At a minimum, the agency should be staffed by people who are versed in the relevant scientific and technical disciplines, the ways of the business community, the social sciences, the communications and computer industries, and the law. The commissioners themselves should be drawn from various fields. It is essential that the agency maintain a close liaison with other governmental organizations as well as the data-using community in the private sector in order to stay abreast of the nation's information needs and to be in a position to recommend a revision of the regulatory scheme when necessary. Given these goals, possible models for our hypothetical agency are the Commission for the Review of Federal and State Laws Relating to Wiretapping and Electronic Surveillance, created by the Omnibus Crime Control Act of 1968[44] and the proposals to establish a Department of Consumer Affairs inside HEW.

One of the basic duties of an informational privacy agency

is the education of the data worshipers, the privacy paranoids, and the general public in order to achieve some common understanding both of society's data needs and the growing concern over privacy. A roughly analogous endeavor is the Census Bureau's effort to win popular acceptance for the 1970 census. At present there is anxiety about the specter of a fishbowl environment, which is matched by a comparable lack of sensitivity to the problem on the part of the information managers. Thus far there has been too little informed concern over this mutual lack of understanding to be translated into effective action to minimize the antagonism.

To further this educative function, it might be desirable for the agency to hold public hearings and symposia on a broad range of subjects, to undertake technical and social science research projects, and to act as a clearinghouse for information relating to activity in each of the many disciplines that touch upon computer technology and individual privacy. By use of these and other methods, the agency would be adopting the premise underlying the proposals to create a Technology Assessment Board.[45] It no longer is sufficient simply to respond to technological threats as they become acute. Our world has become so complex that it is necessary to anticipate the dislocations caused by scientific innovation to insure that the fruits of the technological revolution are employed in socially desirable ways.[46]

Another basic ingredient for evolving a rational regulatory policy in the computer-privacy area is that the agency must have authority to engage in rulemaking relating to the technical features, personnel qualifications, and administrative procedures to be employed by all data centers that handle significant quantities of personal information. If airplanes and pilots must be certified before being put into service, if automobiles are required to meet safety standards and their drivers obliged to obtain licenses, why should not computer systems and information managers be forced to meet and be pledged to honor requirements relating to personal privacy?

Without any question, the task of defining the agency's rulemaking power, and prescribing the attendant licensing authority it might need, would be one of the most controversial aspects of the effort to gain congressional approval for any proposal calling for administrative regulation. Voices are bound to be raised over whether the agency's regulatory authority should extend beyond the activities of federal agencies so as to include systems operated by state and local governments or private organizations. Similarly, the computer industry will oppose attempts to give the agency power to impose privacy protection standards on the manufacturing of hardware and transmission equipment as well as on software packages and programming formats.

Ideally, the agency's power should be broad enough to cover those activities of nonfederal information systems and the products of private business concerns that relate to individual privacy. But because of the political facts of life, it stands to reason that at least initially any rulemaking power probably will have to be exercised sparingly in these contexts and is likely to be considerably more circumscribed than the agency's power over federal data systems. However, once standards are established for governmental systems, users and manufacturers may begin to apply them to nonfederal systems without administrative coercion. Indeed, it would be highly desirable if self-regulation and the availability of model information systems at the federal level would obviate the need for a heavy commitment of agency time and effort in the nonfederal arena.

To implement the controls ultimately thought necessary for protecting informational privacy, our hypothetical federal agency will have to engage in several other activities, particularly in the public-relations field. One method of encouraging compliance with privacy guidelines is suggested by the extensive press coverage and public response to congressional hearings on the proposed National Data Center and the regulation of the credit-bureau industry. Apparently there is enough citizen concern about individual privacy to make the glare of public investigations and pronouncements a realistic source of pressure.

Of course, it would be illusory to believe that governmental and private groups always respond to press releases or attempts at persuasion. Despite the fact that two congressional subcommittees were holding hearings on the propriety of some of the 1970 census questions and the desirability of retaining the criminal sanctions for noncompliance, the Census Bureau, apparently with White House approval, ordered the printing of the 1970 census. The only concession made was that the language of some questions was altered and the number of people who received the longest census form was reduced from fifteen to twelve million.[47]

Along with public education and activities designed to generate "feedback" on existing information practices, the agency must establish a procedure for handling individual grievances. One obvious method would be to give it statutory authority to investigate, direct correction, and award appropriate relief for any abuses brought to its attention. Through the use of these powers, its ability to negotiate with the information managers, and its status as a governmental organization, the agency could play the role of a troubleshooter—an information ombudsman. Several European countries have employed the ombudsman device in various official and unofficial contexts for many years. Typically he is a high-level officer who is independent of the agencies he may criticize, has long tenure of office, and is given the power to investigate administrative practices. His sole job is to act on complaints from citizens.[48] This concept has caught on in the United States and several bills calling for the creation of ombudsmen to perform various functions within the federal government have been before Congress since 1963.

To discharge its role as a privacy protector, the agency should develop and rely heavily on measures that give the individual some degree of effective control over personal information relating to him. As has been indicated, perhaps the single most significant defect in the existing legal regime is its failure to provide the individual with a voice in the important transactions concerning his life history—transactions that often essentially are "private adjudications" and may profoundly affect a person's future economic and social well-being.[49]

The law's traditional dedication to ideals of fair play and due process indicate that any set of rules regulating the handling of personal information should accord the individual, or someone who can represent his interests adequately, the right to receive notice and an opportunity to be heard before important decisions are made concerning his informational profile.[50] This right should include the ability to rebut damaging evaluations and to demand that recorded personal information conform to minimal standards of accuracy.[51] In order to be meaningful, an administrative procedure for resolving conflicts must be expeditious and inexpensive. To establish a right of individual review and then sabotage it with pitfalls, technicalities, expense, and delay is to create a false expectation of remedial assistance that may be worse than not offering citizens any illusion of governmental protection.

The effectiveness of an information agency that has been created to protect individual privacy obviously depends upon its ability to avoid becoming a captive of the governmental units and private interests that will have a stake in the information networks and systems to be regulated. The tendency of the so-called independent agencies to be captured by the industries they supposedly stand vigil over is a disheartening, but not totally bleak, prior history from which to proceed. Perhaps Senator Ervin is right when he suggests that we have learned enough during the last fifty years to avoid the mistakes of the past. The basic hope is that with proper staffing and well-chosen lines of authority, an information agency may be able to achieve the degree of independence needed to perform its watchdog role. The Government Accounting Office seems to have achieved this objective.

The other extreme must be avoided as well. An information agency cannot be permitted to become an island unto itself, neither responsive nor responsible to anyone and populated by technocrats whose conduct is shielded by the alleged omniscience of the machines they manage. It must be accessible and responsible to everyone. Above all, the agency's activities and regulations must not be permitted to ossify. For the foreseeable future the key to effective governmental activity in the computer-privacy area will be to maintain sufficient flexibility and resiliency to adjust to the constant change that characterizes our technological and social environment.

VII
How to Live With the Computer WIthout Becoming Neurotic — Safeguarding the Privacy of Computerized Information

Young Rossum invented a worker with the minimum amount of requirements. . . . He rejected everything that did not contribute directly to the progress of work—everything that makes man more expensive. In fact he rejected man and made the Robot. My dear Miss Glory, the Robots are not people. Mechanically they are more perfect than we are, they have an enormously developed intelligence, but they have no soul.

—Karel Capek, *R.U.R.* (1923), 17

Regardless of how the law reacts to the threat to privacy posed by the electronic age, our ability to strike a balance between the rights of the individual and the need for societal efficiency will largely depend on the conduct of the computer professions. Guidelines laid down by judges and lawmakers are not self-enforcing. Strengthened rules of law relating to informational privacy will be effective only if data handlers respond to them by developing and utilizing appropriate privacy-protecting devices and procedures for controlling the use of computerized data and minimizing the risk of information abuse. And until the legal system energizes itself, we are wholly dependent on the good faith and foresight of the computer community. This requires more than *ad hoc* reactions to security crises as they occur; what is needed is a comprehensive treatment of every aspect of privacy at the time an information system's basic hardware and software configuration is planned.

1. Technical Methods of Protection—The Quest for Mechanical Security

Enough has been said in the last few years about the difficulty of building foolproof systems and of the tricks to subvert such systems.

. . . One thing that stands out . . . is that the bulk of the useful contributions . . . have come almost exclusively from those in the universities and the independent nonprofit organizations.

. . . .

I do not mean to disparage the work presently being done by the commercial sector of the computer industry. . . . As a matter of degree, one would have hoped that they pursued these issues diligently, and with less secrecy. This is an arena where silence is almost equivalent to irresponsibility, and some people act as if they wish to take the Fifth Amendment. . . . The moral, however, is that we may be making as much of a mistake in expecting the computer manufacturers to straighten out the privacy problems as we have made in expecting automobile manufacturers to design adequate smog-control devices of their own accord. . . .

—Paul Baran, Legislation, Privacy and EDUCOM,
*Bulletin of the Interuniversity Communications
Council (EDUCOM)*, Dec. 3, 1969, at 3

Unless computer manufacturers and users undertake to work systematically on improving file security, there is little chance of improving upon the existing state of affairs. But from the manufacturers' perspective, talking about the computer-privacy problem (let alone expending money to do something about it) is not likely to promote sales, especially since there are many other design problems that have yet to be solved. From the customers' viewpoint, elaborate technical safeguards are relatively expensive; as with automobile safety equipment, many users are unwilling to pay the cost for "extras" that do not directly improve the machine's performance. In addition, privacy-protecting procedures often consume precious computer capacity. One expert has predicted that security routines in time-sharing systems might occupy up to twenty percent of its memory capacity.[1] Even though future economies and increased machine speed and capacity will prove this estimate high, it is unrealistic to expect profit-conscious businessmen or government administrators laboring under limited budgets to undertake expensive measures to protect privacy out of self-interest or benevolence.

Fortunately, file security is essential to the effective operation of a wide spectrum of remote-access time-share systems.[2] Given this incentive, a variety of mechanical protection techniques of varying cost, complexity, and effectiveness have been developed, others presently are on the drawing boards, and additional schemes undoubtedly will soon be feasible. The choice of an appropriate protective scheme depends upon the character of the particular system's hardware and software, how much storage and transmission security its data base is likely to need, and the nature of both the user class and those who are likely to attempt to gain access to the information without authorization. The process of deciding how sophisticated a set of privacy safeguards is necessary often will be a difficult one because a large or complex system usually will contain information of differing degrees of sensitivity. When this is the case, different groups of people will have to be able to reach some, but not necessarily all, of the data and some parts of the data store will be more attractive to snoopers than others. In addition, since systems change their purposes and dimensions over time, it often is impossible to predict the character of future security problems at the initial stages of development.

Certain threats to the integrity of computerized information are relatively easy to counteract and if the system carries sensitive data, there is no excuse for not taking appropriate steps. For example, there is some evidence that computer equipment radiates when in operation and that by using eavesdropping techniques the emanations can be captured, reconstituted in their original machine-readable format, and then deciphered. To guard against this possibility, the physical surroundings of the central processor and the remote terminals can be shielded with protective materials, such as metalized paper, or the amount of radiation can be reduced by circuit suppressors and filters.[3] Procedures of this type already are being used to protect computer terminals in various United States embassies and communications centers around the world. A comparable technique might be desirable for safeguarding stored computerized data as well.[4]

In the case of remote-access systems carrying sensitive personal information, a high level of protection against wiretapping can be achieved by coding the data or using "scramblers" to garble them before transmission and installing complementary devices in the authorized terminals to reconstitute the signal.[5] These procedures also will prevent "piggybacking" or "infiltrating" the system by surreptitiously attaching a terminal to an authorized user's transmission line. If the scrambling or coding of data is employed, the number of people with access to the cryptography principles must be limited and the keys will have to be changed periodically. Coding has a number of tangential privacy protecting advantages. In particular, it facilitates identification of those trying to use the data base and, in complex systems, sophisticated coding provides the necessary flexibility to process and transmit information having variant levels of sensitivity.

One pragmatic consideration is that the cost of scrambling devices and the development of completely break-proof codes is quite high. It simply is economically impossible to use them in connection with every computer system. Moreover, at least for the foreseeable future, the art of tapping digital transmissions and converting the commandeered data stream into a comprehensible form will be an expensive endeavor that can be practiced by very few. As a result, only a handful of networks containing extremely valuable or very sensitive data runs any substantial risk of falling prey to the tapping activities of law-enforcement agencies, elements of organized crime, or industrial-espionage experts. For many systems, then, all that presently is necessary is either a modest level of scrambling to make it uneconomic for an eavesdropper to intercept computer transmissions, or a set of different codes to protect the data according to the amount of security needed for their various sensitivity levels.[6]

A system's security can be improved if information is arranged and stored on an hierarchical basis according to its sensitivity or accessibility. The primary value of this technique is that when data require different degrees of protection, hierarchical storage coupled with mechanical controls built into the hardware and software of the central processor can limit a particular user's ability to reach into certain computer files. For example, the working storage of a time-sharing system can be "partitioned" so that each user's "worker programs" have access only to a limited part of the computer's memory.[7] To support this scheme, the monitor or control program can be designed to include a series of "privileged instructions" that provide the only possible way of altering the program.[8] If any user's worker program attempts to alter the monitor program and invade a portion of the memory that is "off limits" to it, the program can inform the system's supervisory personnel and shut down the offending terminal.[9] The integrity of this procedure can be tested by periodically checking a master copy of the monitor program against the one that is in operation in order to see if it has been altered.[10] The program's effectiveness in protecting against unauthorized access also can be verified by using a diagnostic program to make periodic attempts to deceive the monitor.[11] As a final safeguard, the monitor program can be designed to clear the working memory of the computer after each user has finished running his program, thereby eliminating the risk of data being left accessible to a subsequent user.[12]

Another important security function for a well-designed monitor program is to determine the legitimacy of each terminal and operator that attempts to gain access to the data files. One workable method of identifying terminals is a "call-back" system, which requires a user at a remote console to use a terminal identification code number or password as a precondition to entering the files.[13] The computer then shuts down the terminal, checks its files to see if the code number or password is correct,[14] and reopens the terminal if everything is in order.[15] This checking procedure could be performed automatically by building a device into each authorized terminal that would emit a unique identifying signal as a preface to each communication from the terminal.]

Call-back procedures have their limitations, however. Code numbers and passwords can be broken through trial and error, although sufficiently long numbers or words make it mathematically more difficult and time-consuming, or by examining the console's typewriter ribbon. Moreover, this type of security system determines only whether the terminal is a member of the computer network; it offers no assurance that the individual at the console has the authority to be there. Nor does a call-back system necessarily provide any protection against an individual gaining access to "off-limits" files through a particular terminal.

Significantly greater security is achieved by a procedure that determines whether to grant or deny access to the files on the basis of user, rather than terminal, identification. However, an identification code number assigned to each user, no matter how complex, can be disclosed to friends or traded among users. These risks are considerable in a system in which the access keys open up different portions of the data store. Similarly, magnetically coded identification cards, even those designed to receive new invisible code numbers after each transmission,[16] can be lost, stolen, or exchanged. "Fail-safe" systems requiring several users to insert keys in a terminal before certain files are made available are better than single keys because the snooper is required to subvert a larger group of persons to gain access.[17] A terminal in use in the banking industry is protected by three locks and keys. Two keys enable tellers to unlock the terminal to gain access to the system for routine transactions. The third key, available only to managerial personnel, permits the terminal to be used for opening, closing, auditing, and summary transactions.

Another possibility is to install a closed-circuit television channel between the terminal and the central processor, which would permit visual identification of the user;[18] but this is a comparatively costly and cumbersome procedure that requires constant monitoring. In the long run, the most promising method of assuring accurate user identification may be automatic scanning of fingerprints or voiceprints, but these procedures are not yet available. Alternatively, perfection of some technique for measuring the user's physical characteristics—perhaps coupled with an "answer-back" system that requires him to respond to one or more randomly chosen questions by inputting additional identifying data—would afford a high enough level of system security.[19] It would protect against the stealing or exchanging of identifying input, although it would not prevent an authorized user from obtaining data and improperly disclosing them to people who have no legitimate right of access.

[Privacy-protecting techniques and devices will be more efficient and economical if they are incorporated into the original hardware and software design of a system than if they are added after it is in operation.[20] For example, it has been estimated that in the case of a system containing national-security information, it would cost an extra ten percent to add safeguards to an operating enterprise that were not included in the original design. In many cases, however, sufficient foresight is not being exercised and some system developers are even failing to distinguish between those data bases that contain sensitive information and those designed for statistical purposes.]

Despite the availability of various methods of insuring the physical integrity of computerized information, until recently security technology received little more than passing mention in the professional literature.[21] As has proven true of automobile seat belts, the problem is not whether protective devices are available or will work but whether they will be used. The crucial question is: How do you get information managers and users to THINK PRIVACY?

2. Procedural Methods of Improving Security

The history of American freedom is, in no small measure, the history of procedure.

—Mr. Justice Frankfurter, in
Malinski v. *State of New York,*
324 U.S. 401, 411 (1945)
(concurring opinion)

Privacy-oriented technical safeguards must be supported by workable regulations designed to prevent people from bypassing the security devices. These procedural rules must be comprehensible to everyone who might gain access to the data, cover every aspect of the system's data-handling activities that bears on information security, and be reinforced by realistic penalties for noncompliance.[22] Indeed, an individual's willingness to abide by the established regulations should be a basic attribute for employment by a system that contains personal data. Careful hiring practices and the proper philosophical direction during the training period can be extremely valuable in developing a cadre of systems personnel who are sensitive to privacy considerations.

Perhaps the single most important privacy-protecting procedure is the maintenance of a record of the system's operation. This can take the form of a log listing every authorized user of the data, the files each user has examined, and all significant events that take place within the central processor.[23] This log can be kept either by the operator of the central processor, by an automatic recording procedure built into the computer itself, or by both.[24] If the machine does the monitoring, it can be programmed to take note of attempts to circumvent the security devices. The resulting protector file should be audited periodically by security experts for signs of abuse and to evaluate the effectiveness of the system's overall protection program. If there is any indication of a user employing illegal access procedures, unusual activity in one file, attempts to add or erase entries in a file that is considered "off limits" to those procedures, or improper print-ing-out of a file, it should be thoroughly investigated.

Except in unusual cases, an individual on whom a system maintains personal data should be allowed periodic access to the logs and the audit records, as well as the information pertaining to him.[25] The cost of granting data subjects access for these pur-poses may prove to be substantial, particularly if the system is obliged to mail printouts to everyone on whom it has a dossier.[26] In the case of information held by a governmental agency, the printout might be included in one of the periodic communi-cations sent to most citizens. Some private data centers need not be required to make periodic mailings, as long as the individual is given a reasonable opportunity to examine his file. This pro-cedure has now been incorporated in Congress's regulation of credit bureaus.[27]

In addition to the expense of giving individuals an oppor-tunity to examine their files and the monitoring logs, there is the cost of processing the potential flow of squabbles over the accuracy of the system's files and the propriety of its information-handling practices. Moreover, certain types of data might lose some of their commercial or security value by being revealed to the file subject. Nonetheless, the right of an individual to be protected against governmental or private dissemination of erroneous, mis-leading, or privacy-invading information about him is so im-portant that an information system's freedom to use its data may have to be limited so that it is not exercised in an arbitrary or undesirable way.

One possible compromise might be to require data centers to inform people when files on them are first opened and then to designate particular times and places for individuals to examine their records, either in person or through remote-access terminals in the case of a geographically dispersed system. Data centers also might be obliged to develop a procedure for hearing pro-tests concerning data inaccuracies or improper disseminations, which would avoid numerous disputes being lodged in the courts. Unfortunately, inconvenience, expense, and human lethargy would deter many people from taking advantage of the oppor-tunity to check on their files. But even a modest number of in-quiries and an occasional successful challenge, would expose most procedural and technical weaknesses in an information system, which might well have the effect of leading to their correction and sensitizing personnel to the privacy question (or at least put them on notice that someone might be looking over their shoulder).

Computer experts seem to disagree on at least one important administrative aspect of security: whether or not the personnel operating the central processor should have any detailed knowledge about the design of the monitor program. One school of thought is that it is best if knowledge of the monitor program's intricacies and the right of physical access to it are limited to as small a group as possible. This means that the operators of the central processor should never be told how the monitor program works, and the program's designers should not be permitted to gain access to the monitor except when they are needed to modify it.[28] Another school of thought believes that it is desirable to have someone who is thoroughly familiar with the security procedures, the monitor program, and the principal weaknesses of the system on duty at the central processor at all times.[29] But even under this second approach, most specialists agree that it is best to minimize the number of people who can reach both the central processor and the monitor program. The relative suitability of these methods in a particular situation probably depends upon practical considerations, such as the relative costs of the two techniques, the demonstrated dependability and faithfulness of the operating personnel, the sensitivity of the information in the system, and the degree to which the monitor program contains novel features that can best be protected by secrecy.

To take the notion of reducing the number of people who might compromise the system's integrity one step further, custody over data that might be attractive to the snooping fraternity should be given to specially selected personnel and not be left in the care of the machine operators or those who typically handle less sensitive data. This hand-picked group should be schooled in the importance and techniques of security, and periodically act as "devil's advocates" by trying to circumvent the existing precautions to assess the integrity of the system's security.[30]

The notion of developing a special privacy-protecting group seems especially appropriate in the context of integrated information systems in order to guard against hyperactivity on the part of some users. But even in systems doing aggregate or statistical work on data obtained from large groups of individuals, it is useful to place the file linking the special identifying number on each questionnaire to the respondents' real names with a small number of people who are fully aware of their responsibility. In the case of very large data centers, it may even be desirable to designate someone as a privacy ombudsman whose primary function would be to insure that the system was operating in the safest mode possible and to hear any disputes or complaints involving its practices.

3. Controls on Input, Output, and Storage

" 'Tis so," said the Duchess: "and the moral of that is—'Oh, 'tis love, that makes the world go round!' "

"Somebody said," Alice whispered, "that it's done by everybody minding their own business!"

—Lewis Carroll, *Alice's Adventures in Wonderland* (paper ed., 1960), 85

No set of technological devices or security procedures, however extensive or carefully designed they may be, can assure the integrity and privacy of the content of an information system. A computer's data store essentially is a file, and whatever has been placed in it can be extracted or altered by someone who knows the appropriate pathway to follow.[31] Recorded information always is vulnerable to human and mechanical foibles; therefore, the most critical regulations for assuring a high level of data security are those dealing with the information that may be gathered, the ways in which it is manipulated, and the identity of the people to whom the data may be disclosed. These are the issues that raise the tough policy questions relating to *privacy,* and they should not be obscured by a preoccupation with the mechanics of insuring file *security*.

If informational privacy is to be protected effectively, it is necessary to screen data before they are recorded; total reliance on post-collection procedures may be too little, too late. Furthermore, extremely sensitive personal information—records of mental and certain types of physical illness—or inherently soft data—psychological test results and "efficiency" evaluations—should be kept out of the information flow to the extent possible. Unless there is a clear and compelling reason to preserve information of this type, it should be destroyed when the purpose for which it was generated has been achieved. Admittedly, this is contrary to our natural instincts but it seems essential if personal privacy is to be preserved. When the data must be retained, it should be done in a format and a location that will make them snooper-proof. Normally, this will rule out storage in large remote-access time-sharing systems.[32]

The importance of input controls has been recognized by one bill before Congress that seeks to classify certain types of information as too sensitive to be collected by government agencies and to make it unlawful for federal administrative agencies to "require or request" information concerning their employees' race or national origin, participation in political organizations, religious beliefs, sexual practices, and psychological test results.[33] The federal statute regulating credit bureaus also somewhat inhibits data-collection activities, although far less directly.[34]

When potentially damaging personal information must be preserved, it should be subjected to the special storage and access procedures suggested earlier.[35] Moreover, in the case of information of a sensitive character, each data subject should be told at the collection stage the uses to be made of the data and the dimension and character of the group that will have access to them. An individual who has the legal option of remaining silent can exercise that right in a meaningful manner only if the information extractor is honest with him at the time disclosure is requested and can be relied upon to make a good faith effort to protect the data subject's privacy.

The screams of outrage are almost audible as I write of limiting data gathering and computerization. Every governmental agency, commercial enterprise, and academic discipline to which I have ever broached this subject fiercely insists that it cannot survive, let alone flourish, unless it has unbridled access to information and unregulated freedom to use data as it sees fit. The urban planners assert they must know everything about everybody's housing. The credit bureaus claim they must watch the nickels and dimes each borrower spends lest some of them turn into deadbeats, and at every turn clinical psychologists try to interrogate subjects about their sexual experiences, life style, and daily habits in the great quest to unearth the inner workings of human behavior. If one takes all of these supplications seriously, it indicates there is more truth than jest to Oscar Wilde's remark that "private information is practically the source of every large modern fortune." But I have a strong feeling that many of our data addicts could survive on considerably less than our informationally affluent society has to offer. Indeed, there are reasons to doubt that they are utilizing the existing sources as effectively as possible. Consequently, professional associations must broaden their horizons and develop standards for information processing that will upgrade the existing practices and help remove some of the risks that currently inhere in transfers of personal data.[36] Individualized data stored in a large computer system should be tested by rigid standards of accuracy and objectivity.[37] Hearsay and *ex parte* evaluations, especially when provided by someone whose position ordinarily does not involve the preparation of personal reports, should be screened out or be accompanied by a warning as to the questionable quality of the data when forwarded to someone not intimately familiar with the source. In addition, the effects of time on information present special problems for the conscientious data handler. A significant portion of the personal information that finds its way into the files becomes more sensitive as it ages and the underlying events are forgotten by the general public; other types of data atrophy and become less important with the passage of time. For example, the record of an isolated past arrest may be extremely damaging if it is dredged up after the subject has made a fresh start, whereas most financial data pose less of a threat the older they become. Consequently, ancient information from law-enforcement agencies and the Department of Defense may have to be handled with greater care than data of comparable age from the Federal Housing Authority or banking institutions.[38] In particular, computer programming techniques ought to be employed to prevent the output of data that are incomplete or have not been brought up to date. Thus, an arrest record or a notation that a lawsuit has been instituted against the data subject always should be accompanied by a description of the disposition of the case.

The desirability of preserving recorded personal information should be re-evaluated periodically so that it does not petrify. In many cases it will be necessary for computer systems to establish formal procedures for determining when the value of preserving data is counterbalanced by its potential for injuring the individual. Inasmuch as it is relatively simple to purge stale data from a computer system,[39] regulations concerning the storage life of various types of information should be relatively easy to implement. The range of people who are permitted access to different types of data also must be constantly reappraised. There is no reason to assume that because someone was once permitted to see a particular individual's records that his status as an "authorized" user continues in perpetuity.

Controls are essential even in the context of statistical data centers. Input and storage procedures for protecting anonymity can help preserve the integrity of these centers and prevent them from being used for intelligence and surveillance purposes. In some cases, data must be handled in small aggregates rather than in individualized units; doing so will make it difficult to trace or isolate data pertaining to a particular person.[40]

Even in purely statistical work it often is necessary to identify individuals for the purpose of updating information or examining changes over time. To preserve the integrity of the data, it is essential to assign each respondent an arbitrary code and delete any identifying characteristics from the data before they are stored. Violations of the numbering system can be minimized if the data are divided into a "substantive deck" for normal statistical use, which would contain the data along with the arbitrary numbers, and an "identification deck," which would be used to link the individual to his code number in order to make a new entry in his data.[41] The two decks would then be separated. The American Council on Education has decided to follow this pattern in connection with a number of questionnaires it periodically sends to groups of college students. It is also keeping the file linking the names of the students to the identifying numbers outside the United States in the hope of immunizing it from subpoenas and inquisitive Council staff people.[42]

Modern sampling techniques also make it possible to reach statistically valid results without analyzing the data on every available respondent unit. As a result, it may not be necessary to question every member of a particular class or, even when it is desirable to survey an entire group, to analyze everyone's responses. Thus, in many situations involving the examination of personal information on large groups it should be possible to deter snoopers by using a random sample, thereby making it unlikely that a successful intrusion will yield a dossier on a particular person.[43] Unfortunately, in multipurpose statistical centers, such as the proposed National Data Center, the objective is to develop one body of data that will be useful for a wide variety of analytical projects.[44] This means that the underlying or original "sample" must be large enough and have a sufficient quantum of data about individuals to enable many researchers to analyze numerous variables.[45]

When extensive samples or entire populations are required for a large statistical data center, perhaps the most effective protection is a set of instructions in the control program that allows the computer to output data only in aggregates reflecting a sufficient number of individual respondents so as to make identification of individuals impossible.[46] For example, a computer can be programmed to make a judgment about the statistical legitimacy of a request for information and to reject inquiries that seek responses on an individualized basis or on too small a population.[47]

4. Managing the Information Managers

The procession advanced; one by one the eggs advanced; one by one the eggs were transferred from their test-tubes to the larger containers; deftly the peritoneal lining was slit, the morula dropped into place, the saline solution poured in . . . and it was the turn of the labellers. Heredity, date of fertilization, membership of Bokanovsky Group— details were transferred from test-tube to bottle. No longer anonymous, but named, identified, the procession marched slowly on . . . into the Social Predestination Room.

"Eighty-eight cubic metres of card-index," said Mr. Foster with relish, as they entered.

"Containing all the relevant information," added the Director.
. . . .

"So many individuals, of such and such quality," said Mr. Foster.
. . . .

"The Predestinators send in their figures to the Fertilizers."
"Who give them the embryos they ask for."
"And the bottles come in here to be predestined in detail."
—Aldous Huxley, *Brave New World*
(paper ed., 1968), 5–6

Effective technical and procedural safeguards, combined with input-output controls, although vital prerequisites to maintaining the security and factual reliability of computerized information, are not sufficient by themselves. Even the most sophisticated set of mechanical and administrative regulations can be undermined by people working within the system and by outsiders who gain access to it illicitly.[48] In the long run, those who live on intimate terms with data bases and the technology may prove to be an even more dangerous group than malicious or profit-seeking interlopers, despite their lack of personal interest in the informational content of the material in their care. Thus, it would be sheer folly to treat the technicians who design and operate computer systems as a brahmin caste whose every act or decision is presumed socially desirable and beyond review.

Yet to treat them as if they had no effect on policy would be equally erroneous. Computer and information specialists are not simply white-collar mechanics. They have begun to perform many disparate roles and to assume managerial functions that range far beyond the activities we normally associate with people in technical positions. In the future programmers and systems operators will be given responsibilities that completely transcend the mundane tasks of collating and disseminating data or overseeing machine operations. With greater frequency they will be called upon to participate in information analysis and the decision-making process. Today's computer expert may emerge as tomorrow's information policy maker because the volume and variety of electronically processed data will be too great, the methods of storing and manipulating the information too complex, and the technical language too arcane to enable scientifically naive executives and public officials to maintain effective control over the activities of the information systems within their own institutions.[49]

Eventually, the governance of data centers may fall into the hands of those we now jokingly refer to as "computerniks," creating a danger that policy will be formulated by information managers who are so entranced with operating sophisticated machines and manipulating large masses of data that they will not be sufficiently sensitive to privacy considerations.[50] This threat will be particularly difficult to control because computer people are necessary at those points in the information-handling process that are particularly critical to preserving data integrity and security. It therefore is imperative (1) that the new breed of technocrats be trained with an eye toward the wider responsibilities they will shoulder in the future, and (2) that traditional policy-making groups develop a sufficient appreciation for the information technologies so as to minimize their abdicating responsibility to computer specialists.

Concern about the growing importance of computer technicians has led to several suggestions to "professionalize" various jobs in the data-processing industry, so that those who deal with sensitive information will be made subject to an enforceable code of ethics.[51] This notion has several attractive features. Since we are at a relatively embryonic stage in the development of information technology, legislative or administrative intervention might be premature. Moreover, it is doubtful that governmental regulation—whether originated on the federal or state level—could provide a sufficiently elaborate or forward-looking set of principles to govern the wide variety of situations in which computer personnel are called upon to handle personal data. This was the conclusion reached by a distinguished panel that studied the related problem of insuring privacy in behavioral research.[52]

The inculcation of a professional commitment to personal privacy by requiring data processors and users to adhere to a widely recognized code of conduct may provide a far more effective long-term restraint on the custodians of personal information than would governmental fiat. Moreover, it may be that the basic philosophical question—what are the duties and responsibilities of those who handle information relating to their fellow man—is as much an ethical dilemma as a legal issue. If so, perhaps it is best left to be regulated by the practitioners and beneficiaries of the technology—at least as an initial matter.

Unfortunately, it may be unrealistic to expect self-regulation or the professionalization of computer personnel to solve the problem. Programming, system design, data analysis, and machine operation, as well as most of the other vocations that have been spawned by information technology, are quite new. In addition, they are constantly changing in character and their ranks are swelling rapidly.[53] We therefore are talking about a range of occupations and a corps of people that lack well-developed traditions and standards. Although free of the status-quo conservatism and vested interests that characterize (and often immobilize) older professions, such as medicine and law, it is questionable whether the atmosphere in the computer science field is congenial to self-regulation. This doubt is especially significant because a meaningful code of ethics almost certainly would require the elimination of particular activities that currently are in vogue and would necessitate the development of a well-defined set of socially oriented attitudes.[54]

What has appeared thus far is not encouraging. For example, the following "guidelines" were promulgated by the Council of the Association for Computing Machinery in November 1966:

> 1.1 An ACM member will have proper regard for the health, privacy, safety and general welfare of the public in the performance of his professional duties.
> 2.1 An ACM member will act in professional matters as a faithful agent or trustee for each employer or client and will not disclose private information belonging to any present or former employer or client without his consent.[55]

Without intending to be unduly harsh on this particular group, which at least has tried to formulate some professional canons, I must say that provisions of this type are platitudinous; they are somewhat like asking for a pledge of allegiance to milk, motherhood, and the American flag. Moreover, they do not appear to be supported by any enforcement mechanisms. But there is some hope for the future. At the 1970 ACM convention, several influential members of the organization called for the reform of the guidelines and greater awareness of the privacy question.

There are other factors inhibiting self-regulation. Unlike the physician or lawyer, the computer operator does not deal face to face with the people whose life histories he processes. (Indeed, many data handlers only deal with personal information sporadically.) The data subject is not present to engage his sympathies or serve as a reminder that the way in which he discharges his duties may have an important impact on human beings. On the contrary, in most cases the immediate object of the operator's sense of obligation is the system that employs him. Thus he may find it difficult to visualize himself as the protector of the amorphous agglomeration of individuals whose computerized files fall within his province, but whose actual existence is evidenced only by a string of binary digits or a sequence of magnetic impulses.

Too many information handlers seem to measure a man by the number of bits of storage capacity his dossier will occupy. This climate is not conducive to enlightened self-restraint or the nurturing of humanistic values.

Finally, it may well be that today's data managers are imbued with values that are fundamentally incompatible with a commitment to the preservation of individual privacy. It has been harshly suggested that computer designers and operators are so devoted to the scientific quest and efficiency that they are willing to pursue their objectives at the expense of privacy and other values; those who subscribe to this theory think that computerniks view individuals as little more than units of data that must be made to act predictably and function properly within their well-designed information systems.[56] This judgment is much too uncharitable and ignores the many knowledgeable and socially concerned people who have been midwives to the new technology and who are now leading the movement to bring a sense of social responsibility to its use. But the caricature is plausible enough to caution those charged with the task of enunciating and enforcing public policy that they must exercise continuing vigilance over the information managers. The path of blithely yielding power to them is too easy and too often followed by policy makers who act timidly out of blind deference to the "experts" or because of their own feeling of insecurity about the technology.

An alternative method of reducing the possibility that careless, insensitive, or dishonest technical personnel will cause injury is to encourage the users of computerized data to develop ethical standards governing their practices relating to personal information.[57] This approach has certain inherent limitations. As suggested earlier,[58] an effective privacy-protection scheme tries to minimize the amount of potentially dangerous material that is collected and preserved; a regulatory scheme that focuses entirely on the ultimate use of the data comes too late in the information cycle. Moreover, computer applications are so varied and personal information is employed for so many purposes, that comprehensive self-regulation by each user class seems unrealistic. It would be akin to asking everyone in society to behave, which is a piece of wishful thinking that is not likely to strike too many responsive chords. Uniformity also would be difficult to achieve because of the diffuse interests, activities, and attitudes of information users, who are said to include "doctors, lawyers, accountants, journalists, sociologists, political scientists, historians and anthropologists"[59] among others. It is doubtful that any two of these groups have similar views on how much or what type of information protection is necessary. Most user groups also are likely to be primarily concerned with statistical analyses, and any scheme that relies on self-regulation pitched at the median level of community activity probably will leave unregulated the practices of those intelligence or surveillance activities that are particularly inimical to personal privacy. And, as a practical matter, many professional associations do not have the resources, technological experience, or motivation to develop and enforce privacy-protecting codes without outside assistance. If user regulation is to have any meaningful impact, it is necessary to have some measure of central coordination and an apparatus for disseminating one group's experience and thinking on the privacy question to all users.

Notwithstanding this catalogue of difficulties, self-regulation and self-examination by every organization that uses or handles personal information is imperative and is certain to play an important role in any serious attempt to guard informational privacy. The very lack of traditions or calcified attitudes in the current generation of computer specialists and the diversity of outlook among different user groups might prove to be important assets in developing a fresh approach to the problem. But to capitalize on these conditions, the development of professional codes of ethics must be treated as an innovative and experimental process and viewed as a supplement to, rather than a substitute for, the efforts of other societal institutions that are attempting to formulate privacy-protecting policies.

Epilogue

Personal Privacy in the Computer Age

Bureaucracy is the only way to coordinate the complex functions of a modern economy and society and therefore cannot be dismissed with a curse. Yet it is also an enormous potential source of arbitrary, impersonal power which folds, bends, spindles and mutilates individuals but keeps IBM cards immaculate.

—Michael Harrington, *Toward A Democratic Left* (1968), 144

It may seem surprising, and perhaps distressing to some, that several of the suggestions I have offered for protecting the modest level of privacy we presently enjoy from the intrusive potential of computer technology involve extensive governmental intervention. But the need for a rational and comprehensive plan becomes obvious once the computer's ever-widening impact on our society and its permeation of our daily affairs is appreciated. With considerable justification, the emerging information transfer networks can be described as society's electronic equivalent to the biological central nervous system.[1] This analogy seems apt because of the computer's unprecedented ability to integrate the activities of social institutions, improve our capacity to respond to human problems, and maintain a massive store of aggregate or individualized information that is subject to instant recall. As such, the computer is capable of immense social good, or monumental harm, depending upon how human beings decide to use it. "Processed information about individuals could be the basis for a police state. . . . But on the positive side this information could and should compel government to take account of every single individual in the development of its policy. Just to exist will be to participate."[2] Given the significance of the new technology, a response from the national level seems desirable and, to me, quite natural.

258

And if some of the foregoing has seemed slightly alarmist in tone, that may be necessary to counteract the all-too-complacent attitude of many citizens toward the management of our affairs by astigmatic administrators in both government and the private sector. As e. e. cummings once observed, "progress is a comfortable disease."[3] The considerable benefits conferred on us by computer technology may opiate our awareness of the price that is being exacted in terms of personal freedom. It thus seems imperative to sound the klaxon as a warning that the computer may be precipitating a subtle realignment of power within our society as it begins to play a greater role in the decision-making processes of practically all of our significant governmental and nongovernmental institutions. As the importance of information increases, the central issue that emerges to challenge us is how to contain the excesses of this new form of power, while channeling its benefits to best serve the citizenry. If we really believe that personal privacy is fundamental to our democratic tradition of individual autonomy, and that its preservation is thought desirable, then my raising a voice against the trend toward a Dossier Society seems justified.

Perhaps the single most imperative need at this point in time is a substantial input of human resources to help solve the difficult problem of balancing privacy and efficiency. The experimental laboratories exist—the federal agencies and several private organizations can provide the necessary structural context in which to test the privacy-protecting capabilities of hardware, software, and various administrative procedures. There have been hopeful developments in several critical professions. For example, the scientific and business communities are becoming attuned to the issue, privacy-protection techniques appear to be receiving increased attention in the literature, and the National Academy of Sciences now has a Project on Computer Data Banks underway.

But I fear that my own profession—the law—is being somewhat laggard in coming to grips with the broader ramifications of the computer. Leading groups within the legal fraternity, such as the American Law Institute, the National Conference of Commissioners on Uniform State Laws, and the American Bar Association, have yet to energize themselves in any significant manner. If these associations remain inactive and fail to join forces with corresponding organizations in other disciplines, we probably will continue to stumble in the dark. There will be no one to blame but ourselves if we then discover that the mantle of policymaking is being worn by those specially trained technicians who have found the time to master the machine and have put it to use for their own purposes. "That it is to be a dictatorship of test tubes rather than of hobnailed boots will not make it any less a dictatorship."[4]

Selective Bibliography

This bibliography reflects the significant works consulted in the preparation of this book. Many references found in the notes are not reproduced here because of limitations of space and a desire to focus on the most important material. Additional research assistance is offered by a series of bibliographies prepared by Professor Michael A. Duggan of the University of Texas that appear in Volumes 7, 8, and 11 of *Computing Reviews* and two bibliographies prepared by Annette Harrison for the Rand Corporation of Santa Monica, California.

I. Books and Monographs

American Assembly, *Ombudsmen for American Government?* (1968).

M. Philipson, ed., *Automation: Implications for the Future* (1962).

Baran, "On Distributed Communications: IX Security, Secrecy, and Tamper-Free Considerations," Rand Corporation Memorandum RM-3765-PR (1964).

J. Bernstein, *The Analytical Engine* (paper ed., 1966).

H. Black, *Buy Now, Pay Later* (1961).

R. Boguslaw, *The New Utopians* (paper ed., 1965).

M. Brenton, *The Privacy Invaders* (1964).

E. Cahn, *The Sense of Injustice* (1949).

A. Clarke, *Profiles of the Future* (1962).

Computers and Communications—Toward a Computer Utility (1968).

R. W. Gerard, ed., *Computers and Education* (1967).

Computers and the Law (American Bar Association Standing Committee on Law & Technology, 2d ed. 1969).

M. Duggan, M. Irwin, & E. McCartin, eds., *The Computer Utility: Implications for Higher Education* (1970).

Conservative Research Department, *Computers and Freedom* (1968).

Z. Cowen, *The Private Man* (Boyer Lectures, 1969) (Australia).

L. Cronbach, *Essentials of Psychological Testing* (2d ed., 1960).

Crosson & Sayre, "Modeling: Simulation and Replication," in *The Modeling of Mind: Computers and Intelligence* 3 (1968).

S. Dash, R. Schwartz & R. Knowlton, *The Eavesdroppers* (1959).

C. Davidson & E. Koening, *Computers: Introduction to Computers and Applied Computing Concepts* (1967).

P. Drucker, *The Age of Discontinuity* (1968).

Loughary & Tondow, eds., *Educational Information System Requirements: The Next Two Decades* (1967).

Edwards, "Effect of the Electronic Age Upon Invasion of Privacy," in *American Bar Association Section of Individual Rights and Responsibilities, Monograph No. 1,* at 25 (1967).

J. Ellul, *The Technological Society* (paper ed., 1964).

V. Ferkiss, *Technological Man* (1969).

W. Gellhorn, *When Americans Complain* (1966).

M. Gross, *The Brain Watchers* (1962).

S. H. Hollingdale & G. C. Tootill, *Electronic Computers* (paper ed., 1965).

Information Support Program Budgeting and the Congress (1968).

H. Kahn & A. Weiner, *The Year 2000* (1967).

R. Kamlah, *Right of Privacy, 4 Erlanger Juristiche Abhandlungen* (1969) (Germany).

J. Kirkpatrick, R. Ewin, R. Barrett, & R. Katzell, *Testing and Fair Employment* (1968).

B. Ladd, *Crisis in Credibility* (1968).

R. Landers, *Man's Place in the Dybosphere* (1966).

J. Licklider, *Libraries of the Future* (1965).

E. Long, *The Intruders* (1967).

Man Machine Systems in Education (J. Loughary ed., 1966).

M. McLuhan, *The Gutenberg Galaxy* (1962).

M. McLuhan, *Understanding Media: The Extensions of Man* (paper ed., 1964).

M. McLuhan & Q. Fiore, *The Medium is the Massage* (paper ed., 1967).

Miller, "Potentialities of a Multi-Media, Inter-University Educational Network," in *CIBA Foundation Symposium on Communication in Science: Documentation and Automation* (1967).

National Council for Civil Liberties, *Privacy Under Attack* (1968) (England).

J. Von Neumann, *The Computer and the Brain* (1958).

A. Oettinger, *Run, Computer, Run* (1969).

S. Wheeler, ed., *On Record: Files and Dossiers in American Life* (1969).

D. Parkhill, *The Challenge of the Computer Utility* (1966).

Public Television—A Program for Action, The Report of the Carnegie Commission on Educational Television (paper ed., 1967).

A. Rapoport, "Technological Models of the Nervous System," in *The Modeling of Mind: Computers and Intelligence* 25 (paper ed., 1968).

J. Rosenberg, *The Death of Privacy* (1969).

T. Roszak, *The Making of a Counter Culture* (paper ed., 1969).

T. Shibutani, *Society and Personality* (1961).

Wedemeyer, "The Future of Educational Television in the U.S.A.," in G. Moir, ed., *Teaching and Television* 132 (1967).

E. Weiss, *The Marketing Implications of the Checkless Society* (1968).

Westin, "Civil Liberties and Computerized Data Systems," in *Computers, Communications and the Public Interest* (1971).

A. Westin, *Privacy and Freedom* (1967).

W. Whyte, *The Organization Man* (1956).

N. Wiener, *The Human Use of Human Beings* (paper ed., 1970).

C. Zwick, "A National Data Center," in *American Bar Association Section of Individual Rights and Responsibilities, Monograph No. 1,* at 33 (1967).

II. Periodicals

Allen, "Danger Ahead! Safeguard Your Computer," *Harvard Business Review,* Nov.–Dec. 1968, at 97.

Allen, "Time Sharing Takes Off," *Harvard Business Review,* March–April 1968, at 128.

Askin, "Police Dossiers and Emerging Principles of First Amendment Adjudication," 22 *Stanford Law Review* 196 (1970).

Barron, "Access to the Press—A New First Amendment Right," 80 *Harvard Law Review* 1641 (1967).

Bates, "Privacy—A Useful Concept?," 42 *Social Forces* 429 (1964).

Batt, "Law and the Bedroom," *Saturday Review,* Aug. 3, 1968, at 45.

Beaney, "The Right to Privacy and American Law," 31 *Law and Contemporary Problems* 253 (1966).

Behrens, "Computers and Security," 91 *Science News* 532 (1967).

Benn, "Where Power Belongs," *The Nation,* Aug. 26, 1968, at 136.

Bennett, "Secrets Are for Sharing," *Psychology Today,* Feb. 1969, at 31.

Bettelheim, "The Right to Privacy Is a Myth," *Saturday Evening Post,* July 27, 1968, at 8.

"Big Corporations Can Have Their Own CIA," *The New Republic,* Feb. 18, 1967, at 18.

Bigelow, "Legal and Security Issues Posed by Computer Utilities," 45 *Harvard Business Review,* Sept.–Oct. 1967, at 150.

Bloustein, "Privacy as an Aspect of Human Dignity: An Answer to Dean Prosser," 39 *New York University Law Review* 962 (1964).

Bloustein, "Privacy, Tort Law, and the Constitution: Is Warren and Brandeis' Tort Petty and Unconstitutional As Well?," 46 *Texas Law Review* 611 (1968).

Brennan, "The Supreme Court and the Meiklejohn Interpretation of the First Amendment," 79 *Harvard Law Review* 1 (1965).

Bright, "Educational Technology and the Disadvantaged Child," *Educational Technology,* June 30, 1967, at 7.

Brown, "Tomorrow's Many-Splendored Tune-In," *Saturday Evening Post,* Nov. 30, 1968, at 38.

Burck, "The Computer Industry's Great Expectations," *Fortune,* Aug. 1968, at 92.

Campbell, "How the Computer Gets the Answer," *Life,* Oct. 27, 1967, at 60.

Comment, "Privacy, Defamation, and the First Amendment: The Implications of *Time, Inc.* v. *Hill,*" 67 *Columbia Law Review* 926 (1967).

"Computer Encoding of Fingerprints," 93 *Science News* 494 (1968).

Cooper & Sobol, "Seniority and Testing Under Fair Employment Laws: A General Approach to Objective Criteria of Hiring and Promotion," 82 *Harvard Law Review* 1598 (1969).

Creech, "The Privacy of Government Employees," 31 *Law and Contemporary Problems* 413 (1966).

Creech, "Psychological Testing and Constitutional Rights," 1966 *Duke Law Journal* 332.

Daddario, "Technology Assessment—A Legislative View," 36 *George Washington Law Review* 44 (1970).

Daley & Newmann, "A General Purpose File System for Secondary Storage," 27 *AFIPS Conference Proceedings* 213 (1965).

Davis, "The Information Act: A Preliminary Analysis," 34 *University of Chicago Law Review* 761 (1967).

Davis, "Ombudsmen in America: Officers to Criticize Administrative Action," 109 *University of Pennsylvania Law Review* 1057 (1961).

Diebold, "The New World Coming," *Saturday Review*, July 23, 1966, at 17.

Dixon, "The Griswold Penumbra: Constitutional Charter for an Expanded Law of Privacy?," 64 *Michigan Law Review* 197 (1965).

Doppelt & Bennett, "Testing Job Applicants from Disadvantaged Groups," *Test Service Bulletin of the Psychological Corporation*, May 1967, at 2.

Dunn, "Policy Issues Presented by the Interdependence of Computer and Communications Services," 34 *Law and Contemporary Problems* 369 (1969).

Eckler, "Profit from 1970 Census Data," *Harvard Business Review*, July–Aug. 1970, at 4.

Fleming, "The Computer and the Psychiatrist," *New York Times*, §6 (Magazine), April 6, 1969, at 44.

Freed, "A Legal Structure for a National Medical Data Center," 49 *Boston University Law Review* 79 (1969).

Freed, "Legal Aspects of Computer Use in Medicine," 32 *Law and Contemporary Problems* 674 (1967).

Fried, "Privacy," 77 *Yale Law Journal* 475 (1968).

Gleason, "Computer Assisted Instruction—Prospects and Problems," *Educational Technology*, Nov. 15, 1967, at 7.

Goldberg, "The Owen J. Roberts Memorial Lecture: Can We Afford Liberty?," 117 *University of Pennsylvania Law Review* 665 (1959).

Graham, "Protection in an Information Processing Utility," 11 *Communications of the ACM* 365 (1968).

Guion, "Employment Tests and Discriminatory Hiring," *Industrial Relations*, Feb. 1966, at 20.

Guise, "The '69 Time-Sharing Gold Rush," *Datamation*, Aug. 1969, at 38.

Handler & Hollingsworth, "Stigma, Privacy and Other Attitudes of Welfare Recipients," 22 *Stanford Law Review* 1 (1969).

Handler & Rosenheim, "Privacy in Welfare: Public Assistance and Juvenile Justice," 31 *Law and Contemporary Problems* 377 (1966).

Hentoff, "The Secret Companions," *Evergreen,* Sept. 1970, at 55.

Hodge, "Those Irritating Junk Phone Calls," *The Washington Post—Potomac,* Nov. 23, 1969, at 11.

Hoffman, "Computers and Privacy: A Survey," 1 *Computing Surveys* 85 (1969).

"How Computers Help MDs Diagnose," *Bulletin Interuniversity Communications Council (EDUCOM),* April 1966, at 3.

Irwin, "Computers and Communications: The Economics of Interdependence," 34 *Law and Contemporary Problems* 360 (1969).

Irwin, "The Computer Utility: Competition or Regulation?," 76 *Yale Law Journal* 1299 (1967).

Jacob & Jacob, "Confidential Communications," *The New Law Journal,* Feb. 6, 1969, at 133.

Jordan, "Better Mousetrap?," *Forbes,* Oct. 1, 1967, at 67.

Josephson, "Book Review," 15 *University of California at Los Angeles Law Review* 1586 (1968).

Jourard, "Some Psychological Aspects of Privacy," 31 *Law and Contemporary Problems* 307 (1966).

Kalven, "Privacy in Tort Law—Were Warren and Brandeis Wrong?," 31 *Law and Contemporary Problems* 326 (1966).

Kalven, "The Reasonable Man and the First Amendment: Hill, Butts, and Walker," 1967 *Supreme Court Review* 267.

Kamisar, "The Wiretapping-Eavesdropping Problem: A Professor's View," 44 *Minnesota Law Review* 891 (1960).

Karst, "The Files: Legal Controls over the Accuracy of Stored Personal Data," 31 *Law and Contemporary Problems* 342 (1966).

Katz, "Motivational Determinants of Racial Differences in Intellectual Achievements," 2 *International Journal of Psychology* 1 (1967).

Katzell, "Psychological Investigation and the Right of Privacy," 17 *Virginia Law Weekly,* DICTA 109 (1964–66).

Korn, "Law, Fact, and Science in the Courts," 66 *Columbia Law Review* 1080 (1966).

Kramer & Livingston, "Cashing In on the Checkless Society," 45 *Harvard Business Review,* Sept.–Oct. 1967, at 141.

Lozowick, Steiner, & Miller, "Law and Quantitative Multivariate Analysis: An Encounter," 66 *Michigan Law Review* 1641 (1968).

Ludwig, "Peace of Mind in 48 Pieces vs. Uniform Rights of Privacy," 32 *Minnesota Law Review* 734 (1948).

Macy, "Automated Government—How Computers Are Being Used in Washington to Streamline Personnel Administration to the Individual's Benefit," *Saturday Review,* July 23, 1966, at 25.

Main, "Computer Time-Sharing—Everyman at the Console," *Fortune,* Aug. 1967, at 88.

Maron, "Large Scale Data Banks," 60 *Special Libraries* 3 (1969).

Mayer, "Computers on the Brain," *Esquire,* Jan. 1969, at 100.

Michael, "Speculations on the Relation of the Computer to Individual Freedom and the Right to Privacy," 33 *George Washington Law Review* 270 (1964).

Miller, "Considerations in Determining the Content of the 1970 Census," 4 *Demography* 744 (1967).

Miller, "The Credit Networks: Detour to 1984," *The Nation,* June 1, 1970, at 648.

Miller, "The National Data Center and Personal Privacy," *The Atlantic,* Nov. 1967, at 53.

Miller, "On Proposals and Requirements for Solutions," in "Symposium—Computers, Data Banks, and Individual Privacy," 53 *Minnesota Law Review* 211 (1968).

Miller, "Personal Privacy in the Computer Age: the Challenge of a New Technology in an Information-Oriented Society," 67 *Michigan Law Review* 1089 (1969).

Miller, "Psychological Testing: Can We Minimize Its Perils?," *Think,* May–June 1969, at 24.

Miller, "The Town Meeting Reborn," *Saturday Review,* July 23, 1966, at 34.

Morris, "What the Credit Bureaus Know About You," *Reader's Digest,* Nov. 1967, at 85.

Nimmer, "The Right to Speak from Time to Time: First Amendment Theory Applied to Libel and Misapplied to Privacy," 56 *California Law Review* 935 (1968).

Note, "Anthropotelemetry: Dr. Schwitzgebel's Machine," 80 *Harvard Law Review* 403 (1966).

Note, "Credit Investigations and the Right to Privacy: Quest for a Remedy," 57 *Georgetown Law Journal* 509 (1969).

Note, "The Freedom of Information Act: Access to Law," 36 *Fordham Law Review* 765 (1965).

Note, "Freedom of Information: The Statute and the Regulations," 56 *Georgetown Law Journal* 18 (1967).

Note, "From Private Places to Personal Privacy: A Post-Katz Study of Fourth Amendment Protection," 43 *New York University Law Review* 968 (1968).

Note, "Legal Implications of the Use of Standardized Ability Tests in Employment and Education," 68 *Columbia Law Review* 691 (1968).

Note, "The 1966 [sic] Freedom of Information Act—Early Judicial Interpretations," 44 *Washington Law Review* 641 (1969).

Note, "Privacy and Efficient Government: Proposals for a National Data Center," 82 *Harvard Law Review* 400 (1968).

Note, "Tort Aspects of Reflections on Credit," 14 *St. Louis University Law Journal* 283 (1969).

O'Brien, "The Bank of Tomorrow: Today," *Computers and Automation,* May 1968, at 26.

Okun, "Investigation of Jurors by Counsel: Its Impact on the Decisional Process," 56 *Georgetown Law Journal* 839 (1968).

Opler, "The Receding Future," *Datamation,* Sept. 1967, at 13.

Packard, "Don't Tell It to the Computer," *New York Times,* §6 (Magazine), Jan. 8, 1967, at 44, 89.

Paul, "Access to Rules and Records of Federal Agencies: The Freedom of Information Act," 42 *Los Angeles Bar Bulletin* 459 (1967).

Pemberton, "On the Dangers, Legal Aspects, and Remedies," in "Symposium—Computers, Data Banks, and Individual Privacy," 53 *Minnesota Law Review* 211 (1968).

Peters, "Security Considerations in a Multi-Programmed Computer System," 30 *AFIPS Conference Proceedings* 283 (1967).

Petersen & Turn, "System Implications of Information Policy," 30 *AFIPS Conference Proceedings* 291 (1967).

Pipe, "Privacy: Establishing Restrictions on Government Inquiry," 18 *American University Law Review* 516 (1969).

"Playing for Fun," *Playboy,* April 1969.

"Professional Conduct in Information Processing," 11 *Communications of the ACM* 135 (1968).

Project, "The Computerization of Government Files: What Impact on the Individual," 15 *University of California at Los Angeles Law Review* 1371 (1968).

Prosser, "Privacy," 48 *California Law Review* 383 (1960).

Pyle, "CONUS Intelligence: The Army Watches Civilian Politics," *Washington Monthly,* Jan. 1970, at 4.

Pyle, "CONUS Revisited: The Army Covers Up," *Washington Monthly,* July 1970, at 49.

Rider, "Legal Protection of the Manifestations of Individual Personality—The Identity-Indicia," 33 *Southern California Law Review* 31 (1959).

Ridgeway, "Computer-Tutor," *New Republic,* June 4, 1966, at 21.

Romnes, "Managing the Information Revolution," *Business Automation,* Aug. 1966, at 31.

Rovere, "The Invasion of Privacy (1)—Technology and the Claims of Community," 27 *American Scholar* 413 (1958).

Ruggles, "On the Needs and Values of Data Banks," in "Symposium—Computers, Data Banks, and Individual Privacy," 53 *Minnesota Law Review* 211 (1968).

Sarnoff, "No Life Untouched," *Saturday Review,* July 23, 1966, at 21.

Sawyer & Schechter, "Computers, Privacy, and the National Data Center: The Responsibility of Social Scientists," 23 *The American Psychologist* 810 (1968).

Schwartz, "The Legitimation of Electronic Eavesdropping: The Politics of 'Law and Order'," 67 *Michigan Law Review* 455 (1969).

Schwitzgebel, "Electronic Innovation in the Behavioral Sciences: A Call to Responsibility," 22 *American Psychologist* 364 (1970).

"See What the 'Data Banks' Know About You," *U.S. News & World Report,* April 8, 1968, at 82.

Semling, "The Computer-Communications Inquiry," *Modern Data Systems,* July 1968, at 48.

Sesser, "Big Brother Keeps Tabs on Insurance Buyers," *The New Republic,* April 27, 1968, at 11.

Shubik, "Information, Rationality, and Free Choices in a Future Democratic Society," *Daedalus,* Summer 1967, at 771.

Silver, "Privacy and the First Amendment," 34 *Fordham Law Review* 553 (1966).

Star, "The Computer Data Bank: Will It Kill Your Freedom?," *Look,* June 25, 1968, at 27, 28.

Stevens, "Now—The Automated Physical Checkup," *Readers Digest,* July 1966, at 95.

Suppes, "The Uses of Computers in Education," *Scientific American,* Sept. 1966, at 207.

Surface, "What Computers Cannot Do," *Saturday Review,* July 13, 1968, at 58.

Szuprowicz, "The Time-Sharing Users: Who are They?," *Datamation,* Aug. 1969, at 55.

Trillin, "Onward and Upward with the Arts: You Can't Wear Out a List," *The New Yorker,* Sept. 24, 1966, at 126.

Wade, "Defamation and the Right of Privacy," 15 *Vanderbilt Law Review* 1093 (1962).

Ware, "Security and Privacy in Computer Systems," 30 *AFIPS Conference Proceedings* 279 (1967).

Warren & Brandeis, "The Right to Privacy," 4 *Harvard Law Review* 193 (1890).

Westin, "Science, Privacy, and Freedom: Issues and Proposals for the 1970's," 66 *Columbia Law Review* 1205 (1966).

Westin, "The Snooping Machine," *Playboy,* May 1968, at 130.

"Why Ma Bell Chops up the Signals," *Business Week,* Jan. 13, 1968, at 82.

III. Reports and Miscellaneous Documents

Additional material is cited in the Table of Abbreviations for Certain Frequently Cited Government Documents appearing on pages 271–73.

Comments of Microwave Communications, Inc. (March 5, 1968) (submitted in connection with *In re Regulatory and Policy Problems Presented by the Interdependence of Computer and Communication Services and Facilities,* FCC Docket No. 16,979).

House Committee on Post Office and Civil Service, Statistical Activities of the Federal Government: Personnel, Equipment, and Contract Costs, H. Rep. Report *1130,* 88th Cong., 2d Sess. 31 (1964).

H. Rep. Report No. 1497, Clarifying and Protecting the Right of the Public to Information, and for Other Purposes, 89th Cong., 2d Sess. 10 (1966).

Ontario Law Reform Commission, *Report on Protection of Privacy in Ontario* (1968) (Canada).

Privacy and the Law, Report by Justice, British Section of the International Commission of Jurists (1970).

Protecting Privacy and the Rights of Federal Employees, Senate Report No. 534, 90th Cong., 1st Sess. 19 (1967).

"Report of the Committee on the Preservation and Use of Economic Data to the Social Science Research Council," (April 1965) (Ruggles Report).

"Report of the Task Force on the Storage of and Access to Government Statistics" (Kaysen Report).

Response of International Business Machines Corporation Before the FCC (submitted in connection with *In the Matter of Regulatory and Policy Problems Presented by the Interdependence of Computer and Communication Services and Facilities,* Docket No. 16,979) (March 5, 1968).

Senate Report No. 813, Clarifying and Protecting the Right of the Public to Information, and for Other Purposes, 89th Cong., 1st Sess. (1965).

Senate Report No. 1097, 90th Cong., 2d Sess. (1968).

Sperry-Rand UNIVAC Response to the Inquiry of the FCC (submitted in connection with *In re Regulatory and Policy Problems Presented by the Interdependence of Computer and Communications Facilities,* Docket No. 16,979).

"Statistical Evaluation Report No. 6—Review of Proposal for a National Data Center" (Dunn Report).

To Improve Learning, Report by the Commission on Instructional Technology (H. Rep. Comm. Print 1967).

United States Department of Justice, *The Attorney General's Memorandum on the Public Information Section of the Administrative Procedure Act* (1967).

Table of Abbreviations for Certain Frequently Cited Government Documents

The Federal Paperwork Jungle	House Committee on Post Office and Civil Service, The Federal Paperwork Jungle, H.R. Report No. 52, 89th Cong., 1st Sess. (1965).
Government Dossier	Subcommittee on Administrative Practice and Procedure of the Senate Committee on the Judiciary, Government Dossier, 90th Cong., 1st Sess. (Committee Print 1967).
Hearings on 1970 Census and Legislation Related Thereto	Hearings on the 1970 Census and Legislation Related Thereto, Subcommittee on Census and Statistics of the House Committee on Post Office and Civil Service, 91st Cong., 1st Sess., Serial No. 91-8 (1969).
Hearings on 1970 Census Questions	Hearings on 1970 Census Questions Before the House Committee on Post Office and Civil Service, 89th Cong., 2d Sess. (1966).
Hearings on Data Processing Management	Hearings on Data Processing Management in the Federal Government Before a Subcommittee of the House Committee on Government Operations, 90th Cong., 1st Sess. (1967).
Hearings on Government Agencies	Hearings on Invasions of Privacy (Government Agencies) Before the Subcommittee on Administrative Practice and Procedure of the Senate Committee on the Judiciary, 89th Cong., 1st Sess. (1965–1966).

Hearings on Retail Credit Company	Hearings on Retail Credit Company Before the Subcommittee on Invasion of Privacy of the House Committee on Government Operations, 90th Cong., 2d Sess. (1968).
Hearings on the Right of Privacy Act	Hearings on S. 928 (Right of Privacy Act of 1967) Before the Subcommittee on Administrative Practice and Procedure of the Senate Committee on the Judiciary, 90th Cong., 1st Sess. (1967).
Hearings on Statistical Programs	Hearings on the Coordination and Integration of Government Statistical Programs Before the Subcommittee on Economic Statistics of the Joint Economic Committee, 90th Cong., 1st Sess. (1967).
House Hearings on Commercial Credit Bureaus	Hearings on Commercial Credit Bureaus Before a Subcommittee of the House Committee on Government Operations, 90th Cong., 2d Sess. (1968).
House Hearings on the Computer and Invasion of Privacy	Hearings on the Computer and Invasion of Privacy Before a Subcommittee of the House Committee on Government Operations, 89th Cong., 2d Sess. (1966).
Privacy and Behavioral Research	Office of Science and Technology of the Executive Office of the President, Privacy and Behavioral Research (1967).
Privacy and the National Data Bank Concept	House Committee on Government Operations, Privacy and the National Data Bank Concept, H.R. Report No. 1842, 90th Cong., 2d Sess. (1968).

Senate Hearings on Computer Privacy

Hearings on Computer Privacy Before Subcommittee on Administrative Practice and Procedure of the Senate Committee on the Judiciary, 90th Cong., 2d Sess. (1968).

Senate Hearings on Credit Bureaus

Hearings on Credit Bureaus Before the Subcommittee on Antitrust and Monopoly of the Senate Committee on the Judiciary, 90th Cong., 2d Sess. (1968).

Senate Hearings on Fair Credit Reporting

Hearings on Fair Credit Reporting Before the Subcommittee on Financial Institutions of the Senate Committee on Banking and Currency, 91st Cong., 1st Sess. (1969).

Task Force Report: Science and Technology

The Institute for Defense Analysis, Task Force Report: Science and Technology (1967).

Prologue

1. A. Clarke, *Profiles of the Future* 265–79 (1962); M. McLuhan, *The Gutenberg Galaxy* 11–279 (1962); H. Kahn & A. Weiner, *The Year 2000,* at 88–98, 348–49 (1967); A. Westin, *Privacy and Freedom* 158–68 (1967); *House Hearings on the Computer and Invasion of Privacy* (statement of Vance Packard); "Playing for Fun," *Playboy,* April 1969, at 110, 174. See generally *Automation: Implications for the Future* (Philipson ed., 1962).

2. V. Ferkiss, *Technological Man* 227 (1969); Miller, "The National Data Center and Personal Privacy," *The Atlantic,* Nov. 1967, at 53. See generally *Newsweek,* July 27, 1970, at 15–20.

3. The computer's threat to personal privacy is beginning to attract attention in foreign countries also. See generally Z. Cowen, *The Private Man (Boyer Lectures, 1969)* (Australia); R. Kamlah, *Right of Privacy,* 4 *Erlanger Juristische Abhandlungen* (1969) (Germany); *Privacy and the Law, Report by Justice, British Section of the International Commission of Jurists* (1970); Conservative Research Department, *Computers and Freedom* (1968) (England); National Council for Civil Liberties, *Privacy Under Attack* (1968) (England); Ontario Law Reform Commission, *Report on Protection of Privacy in Ontario* (1968); *New York Times,* April 21, 1969, at 50, cols. 7–8.

Chapter 1 : The Cybernetic Revolution

1. For a concise history of the genesis and development of computers, see J. Bernstein, *The Analytical Engine* 50–80 (paper ed., 1966). See also C. Davidson & E. Koening, *Computers: Introduction to Computers and Applied Computing Concepts* (1967); J. Rosenberg, *The Death of Privacy* 81–110 (1969); S. Hollingdale & G. Tootill, *Electronic Computers* 15–73 (paper ed., 1965).

2. *Senate Hearings on Computer Privacy* 118. A more detailed description of the workings of the computer, in terms intelligible to the layman, may be found in Campbell, "How the Computer Gets the

Answer," *Life,* Oct. 27, 1967, at 60. For a simplified description of programming techniques, see J. Bernstein, supra note 1, at 3–17.

3. For a brief description of the different computer "generations," see Taylor, "Computer Systems," in *Computers and the Law* 40 (American Bar Association Standing Committee on Law & Technology, 2d ed. 1969).

4. Ream, "New Directions in Computer Utilization," in *Computers and Communications—Toward a Computer Utility* 3, 6 (1968).

5. A working model of a system for storing information on plastic tape in the form of minute craters burned by a laser beam is described in A. Westin, *Privacy and Freedom* 167 (1967). This process permits the storage of 645 million bits of data per square inch of tape, recorded at the rate of 12 million bits per second.

6. *Time,* Sept. 27, 1968, at 51.

7. Mayer, "Computers on the Brain," *Esquire,* Jan. 1969, at 100, 103, 145.

8. See Diebold, "The New World Coming," *Saturday Review,* July 23, 1966, at 17; Gerard, "Shaping the Mind: Computers in Education," in *Educational Information System Requirements: The Next Two Decades* 48, 60–62 (1967). See generally D. Parkhill, *The Challenge of the Computer Utility* 121–44 (1966).

9. Fano, "The Computer Utility and the Community," in *Computers and Communications—Toward a Computer Utility* 39 (1968).

10. See, e.g., M. McLuhan, *The Gutenberg Galaxy* 265–79 (1962).

11. This dialogue is taken from Fano, supra note 9, at 48.

12. The answers offered by the computer are erroneous past the fifth digit (for the smaller number) and past the sixth digit (for the larger). The error is apparently based upon an approximation of pi which is incorrect past the fourth decimal. (3.1415927, not 3.1415899, is the correct approximation to seven places). For reasons peculiar to ease of computer expression, the programmer may not have intended accuracy past the fourth decimal. For a presentation of the distressing view that man and machine ultimately will become indistinguishable, see R. Landers, *Man's Place in the Dybosphere* (1966).

Professor Layman E. Allen, Research Associate Prudence C. Abram, and the author have produced a computer-based dialogue to assist in teaching part of a first-year law school course in civil procedure. Although it was demonstrated at the 1968 annual meeting of the American Association of Law Schools and tested during March and April 1969 on approximately 125 first-year students at the University of Michigan Law School, it still must be considered experimental. Nonetheless, preliminary evaluation indicates a high level of receptivity on the part of the students and reasonable success in terms of many educational values. *New York Law Journal,* March 31, 1969, at 1, col. 1.

13. J. Bernstein, supra note 1, at 1–2. See also J. von Neumann, *The Computer and the Brain* (1958); N. Wiener, *The Human Use of Human Beings* (paper ed., 1967).

14. Stevens, "Now—The Automated Physical Checkup," *Readers Digest,* July 1966, at 95. See also Fleming, "The Computer and the Psychiatrist," *New York Times,* § 6 (Magazine), April 6, 1969, at 44; "How Computers Help MDs Diagnose," *Bulletin Interuniversity Communications Council (EDUCOM),* April 1966, at 3–6. The U.S. Public Health Service currently is making a detailed study of the problems of interconnecting the nation's hospitals into a single computer network. *New York Times,* June 18, 1968, at 47, col. 6. See also Freed, "A Legal Structure for a National Medical Data Center," 49 *Boston University Law Review* 79 (1969); Freed, "Legal Aspects of Computer Use in Medicine," 32 *Law and Contemporary Problems* 674 (1967); Sarnoff, "No Life Untouched," *Saturday Review,* July 23, 1966, at 21.

15. See generally Halstead, "Use of Computers in Preparing Tax Returns," in *Computers and the Law* 77 (American Bar Association Standing Committee on Law & Technology, 2d ed. 1969). The Internal Revenue Service, on the other hand, is using computers to detect inconsistencies in individual tax returns. *Hearings on Statistical Programs* 23 (statement of Professor Richard Ruggles).

16. Star, "The Computer Data Bank: Will It Kill Your Freedom?," *Look,* June 25, 1968, at 27, 28.

17. Computers also are being used by some religious leaders to develop statistics and attitudinarian profiles of their congregations. *Time,* March 29, 1968, at 92.

18. *Hearings on Statistical Programs* 3, 7 (1967) (statement of Dr. Edgar S. Dunn, Jr., Research Analyst, Resources for the Future, Inc.).

19. Even the Congress of the United States may be computerized. See *Wall Street Journal,* March 27, 1969, at 23, col. 2:

> House leaders are considering [a] computerized "information retrieval" system that would store and serve up data on legislation, the budget and other topics. The House Banking Committee installed a rudimentary version of such a system in January; it feeds information about banking legislation into a Library of Congress computer, which provides data via teletypewriter when the committee staff requests it.

Compare *H.Rep.* 17,046, 17,644, 91st Cong., 2d Sess. (1970); *H.Rep.* 404, 5522, 91st Cong., 1st Sess. (1969); *Information Support Program Budgeting and the Congress* (1968); Chartrand, "Computer Technology and the Legislator," in *Computers and the Law* 90 (American Bar Association Standing Committee on Law & Technology, 2d ed. 1969).

20. See, e.g., Irwin, "The Computer Utility: Competition or Regulation?," 76 *Yale Law Journal* 1299 (1967).

21. Main, "Computer Time-Sharing—Everyman at the Console," *Fortune,* Aug. 1967, at 88. See also Szuprowicz, "The Time-Sharing Users: Who are They?," *Datamation,* Aug. 1969, at 55.

22. See Mayer, "Computers on the Brain," *Esquire,* Jan. 1969, at 100, 103.

23. Bauer, "Computer/Communications Systems: Patterns and Prospects," in *Computers and Communications—Toward a Computer Utility* 13 (1968). See also Dunn, "Policy Issues Presented by the Interdependence of Computer and Communications Services," 34 *Law and Contemporary Problems* 369 (1969); Irwin, "Computers and Communications: The Economics of Interdependence," 34 *Law and Contemporary Problems* 360 (1969).

24. *House Hearings on the Computer and Invasion of Privacy* 121 (statement of Paul Baran, computer expert for the Rand Corporation).

25. Romnes, "Managing the Information Revolution," *Business Automation,* Aug. 1966, at 31. Compare Guise, "The '69 Time-Sharing Gold Rush," *Datamation,* Aug. 1969, at 38.

26. See "Why Ma Bell Chops up the Signals," *Business Week,* Jan. 13, 1968, at 82.

27. See Brown, "Tomorrow's Many-Splendored Tune-In," *Saturday Evening Post,* Nov. 30, 1968, at 38.

28. See generally D. Parkhill, *The Challenge of a Computer Utility* (1966); *Computers and Communications—Toward a Computer Utility* (1968); Irwin, supra note 20; "Cable TV Leaps into the Big Time," *Business Week,* Nov. 22, 1969, at 100. A comprehensive study of this subject was undertaken in a symposium held on May 5–7, 1969. The papers and proceedings have been published in a book entitled *The Computer Utility: Implications for Higher Education* (Duggan, McCartan & Irwin, eds., 1970).

29. Bigelow, "Legal and Security Issues Posed by Computer Utilities," 45 *Harvard Business Review,* Sept.–Oct. 1967, at 150, 151.

30. Michael, "Speculations on the Relation of the Computer to Individual Freedom and the Right to Privacy," 33 *George Washington Law Review* 270, 275 (1964). The government's record-keeping activities are described in *On Record: Files and Dossiers in American Life* 225–315 (Wheeler ed., 1969).

31. *S.* 2,838, 91st Cong., 1st Sess. (1969); *H.Rep.* 13,472, 13,518, 91st Cong., 1st Sess. (1969).

32. *S.* 2,986, 91st Cong., 1st Sess. (1969); *H.Rep.* 14,173, 14,174, 14,175, 91st Cong., 1st Sess. (1969); *H.Rep.* 15,440, 91st Cong., 2d Sess. (1970).

33. Ruggles, "On the Needs and Values of Data Banks," in "Symposium—Computers, Data Banks, and Individual Privacy," 53 *Minnesota Law Review* 211, 216 (1968).

34. The term "model" is generic, and encompasses a variety of techniques. Crosson & Sayre, "Modeling: Simulation and Replication," in *The Modeling of Mind: Computers and Intelligence* 3 (1968), subdivided models into (1) replications, which reproduce some physical aspect of the original; (2) formalizations, which are symbolic representations of an original system that can be analyzed by paper-and-pencil mathematical operations; and (3) simulations, which, in contrast to formalizations, produce not a general solution but rather a statistical description of a large number of particular solutions for the more important variables. The simulation is the kind of model that most frequently requires the use of an electronic computer. For a simplified discussion of the methodology involved in making this kind of computer analysis, see Lozowick, Steiner, & Miller, "Law and Quantitative Multivariate Analysis: An Encounter," 66 *Michigan Law Review* 1641 (1968). See also Michael, supra note 30, at 275–76. The computer also can be programmed to edit the raw data and discover inconsistencies that would go unnoticed in hand editing.

35. *House Hearings on the Computer and Invasion of Privacy* 199.

36. See *House Hearings on the Computer and Invasion of Privacy* 52, 59, 97–98 (statement of Raymond T. Bowman, Assistant Director for Statistical Standards, Bureau of the Budget).

37. *House Hearings on the Computer and Invasion of Privacy* 199.

38. *Task Force Report: Science and Technology* 71.

39. *Computerworld,* Aug. 27, 1969, at 1.

40. Sarnoff, "No Life Untouched," *Saturday Review,* July 23, 1966, at 21.

41. M. McLuhan, *Understanding Media: The Extensions of Man* 65 (paper ed., 1964).

42. M. McLuhan & Q. Fiore, *The Medium is the Massage* 63 (paper ed., 1967). See also id. at 12–24.

43. See generally Rovere, "The Invasion of Privacy (1)—Technology and the Claims of Community," 27 *American Scholar* 413 (1958).

Chapter 11 : The New Technology's Threat to Personal Privacy

1. See, e.g., Dixon, "The Griswold Penumbra: Constitutional Charter for an Expanded Law of Privacy?," 64 *Michigan Law Review* 197, 199 (1965); Kalven, "Privacy in Tort Law—Were Warren and Brandeis Wrong?," 31 *Law and Contemporary Problems* 326, 333 (1966). See generally A. Westin, *Privacy and Freedom* (1967).

2. Office of Science and Technology of the Executive Office of the President, *Privacy and Behavioral Research* 8–9 (1967). See also Beaney, "The Right to Privacy and American Law," 31 *Law and Contemporary Problems* 253, 254 (1966); Fried, "Privacy," 77 *Yale Law Journal* 475 (1968); Foreword by former Vice President Hubert H. Humphrey to E. Long, *The Intruders* vii (1967). The idea is hardly a new one; see Warren & Brandeis, "The Right to Privacy," 4 *Harvard Law Review* 193, 196 (1890): "The common law secures to each individual the right of determining, ordinarily, to what extent his thoughts, sentiments, and emotions shall be communicated to others."

3. See Bloustein, "Privacy as an Aspect of Human Dignity: An Answer to Dean Prosser," *New York University Law Review* 962, 988 (1964).

4. See, e.g., *House Hearings on Commercial Credit Bureaus; Senate Hearings on Computer Privacy; Hearings on Statistical Programs; House Hearings on the Computer and Invasion of Privacy.*

5. See Karst, " 'The Files': Legal Controls over the Accuracy of Stored Personal Data," 31 *Law and Contemporary Problems* 342, 343 (1966); Comment, "Copyright Pre-emption and Character Values: The Paladin Case as an Extension of Sears and Compco," 66 *Michigan Law Review* 1018, 1035–36 (1968).

6. *House Hearings on the Computer and Invasion of Privacy* 94 (statement of Edgar S. Dunn, Jr., research analyst, Resources for the Future, Inc.).

7. Allen, "Danger Ahead! Safeguard Your Computer," *Harvard Business Review,* Nov.–Dec. 1968, at 97, 100.

8. Petersen & Turn, "System Implications of Information Policy," 30 *AFIPS Conference Proceedings* 291 (1967).

9. Id. at 298. See also *Sperry-Rand UNIVAC Response to the Inquiry of the FCC, J-15* (submitted in connection with *In re Regulatory and Policy Problems Presented by the Interdependence of Computer and Communications Facilities,* Docket No. 16,979) (undated) [hereinafter *UNIVAC Brief*]: "There are many devices on the market today

which make it possible to pick up intelligence from a [computer] communications terminal and record the content of messages."

10. For a general discussion of security in time-sharing systems, see Ware, "Security and Privacy in Computer Systems," 30 *AFIPS Conference Proceedings* 279 (1967). See also Hoffman, "Computers and Privacy: A Survey" 1 *Computing Surveys* 85 (1969).

11. See, e.g., A. Oettinger, *Run, Computer, Run* 162–63, 173–77 (1969); Surface, "What Computers Cannot Do," *Saturday Review,* July 13, 1968, at 58.

12. *UNIVAC Brief* at H & I–11 to H & I–12.

13. Petersen & Turn, supra note 8, at 298.

14. Ware, supra note 10, at 281.

15. Ibid.

16. See *Computerworld,* July 29, 1970, at 1. The surveillance implications of computer technology are discussed on pages 38–46.

17. Similarly, consider the effect of the hypothetical dossier on an uninformed reader if it described Mr. William F. Rickenbacker, whose "crime" consisted of refusing to answer part of the 1960 census questionnaire on the ground that it was illegal and invaded his privacy. See *United States* v. *Rickenbacker,* 309 F.2d 462 (2d Cir. 1962), certiorari denied, 371 U.S. 962 (1963).

18. *Task Force Report: Science and Technology* 76.

19. The federal courts have upheld the validity of the New York statute. See *Thom* v. *New York Stock Exchange,* 306 F.Supp. 1002 (S.D.N.Y. 1969), affirmed, 425 F.2d 1074 (2d Cir. 1970), certiorari denied, 398 U.S. 905 (1970). See also *Computerworld,* Feb. 18, 1970, at 12.

20. See Karst, supra note 5, at 356.

21. Psychological testing is discussed at pages 90–105.

22. One of the pitfalls of sharing information based upon noncomparable categories or premises is that it often leads people to make unknowing comparisons between apples and oranges. Indeed, the noncomparability of most information is a major impediment to the creation of an integrated federal statistical system. See, e.g., *Hearings on Statistical Programs* 3:

In general, the bodies of data [collected by federal agencies] do not mesh according to any overall system and there is much inflexibility which often prevents fitting the micro data to behavioral models. Reasons for the incompatibility include the following:

(1) differing definitions, classifications, and timing of respondent reports when uniformity is needed;

. . . .

(3) differing qualities of data and inconsistent documentation. The difficulties in obtaining comparable statistics even when the categories are uniform are discussed in *Hearings on Statistical Programs* 12.

23. E. Long, *The Intruders* 54 (1967).

24. Id. at 54–55. For the most comprehensive discussion to date of the impact of science on problems of proof, see Korn, "Law, Fact, and Science in the Courts," 66 *Columbia Law Review* 1080 (1966). See also B. Botein, *The Trial of the Future* (1963).

25. See, e.g., M. McLuhan & Q. Fiore, *The Medium Is the Massage* 12 (paper ed., 1967); Address by former Supreme Court Justice Arthur J. Goldberg, "The Owen J. Roberts Memorial Lecture: Can We Afford Liberty?," Feb. 20, 1968, at 4, reprinted in 117 *University of Pennsylvania Law Review* 665 (1959). See also "Symposium—Computers, Data Banks, and Individual Privacy," 53 *Minnesota Law Review* 211 (1968).

26. See pages 5–7.

27. Pyle, "CONUS Intelligence: The Army Watches Civilian Politics," *Washington Monthly*, Jan. 1970, at 4, 5.

28. *Computerworld*, Feb. 25, 1970, at 1. Events following the disclosure of the Army's activities are described in Pyle, "CONUS Revisited: The Army Covers Up," *Washington Monthly*, July 1970, at 49. See also Hentoff, "The Secret Companions," *Evergreen*, Sept. 1970, at 55; *New York Times*, June 28, 1970, at 1.

29. *House Hearings on the Computer and Invasion of Privacy* 119–35 (testimony of Paul Baran, computer expert with the Rand Corporation).

30. Star, "The Computer Data Bank: Will It Kill Your Freedom?," *Look*, June 25, 1968, at 27, 28 (emphasis added).

31. "Big Corporations Can Have Their Own CIA," *The New Republic*, Feb. 18, 1967, at 18.

32. "See What the 'Data Banks' Know About You," *U.S. News & World Report*, April 8, 1968, at 82.

33. Sullivan, "Wiretapping and Eavesdropping: A Review of the Current Law," reprinted in *Hearings on the Right of Privacy Act*, part 1, at 62–63. A technical description of the pen register may be found in *Hearings on Government Agencies, part* 2, at 954–61.

34. *Hearings on Government Agencies* 67. The legality of mail cover operations has been upheld in *United States* v. *Schwartz*, 283 F.2d 107 (3d Cir. 1960), certiorari denied 364 U.S. 942 (1961), and *United States* v. *Costello*, 255 F.2d 876, 881–82 (2d Cir.), certiorari denied, 357 U.S. 937 (1958). See generally E. Long, supra note 23, at 102–08.

35. News Release, Sept. 29, 1969.

36. See *Senate Hearings on Computer Privacy* 72 (statement of the author); Freed, "Legal Aspects of Computer Use in Medicine," 32 *Law and Contemporary Problems* 674, 691 (1967); Miller, "The National Data Center and Personal Privacy," *The Atlantic,* Nov. 1967, at 53; Schwitzgebel, "Electronic Innovation in the Behavioral Sciences: A Call to Responsibility," 22 *American Psychologist* 364 (1970).

37. See, e.g., Fleming, "The Computer and the Psychiatrist," *New York Times,* § 6 (Magazine), April 6, 1969, at 45. See also Michael, "Speculation on the Relation of the Computer to Individual Freedom and the Right to Privacy," 33 *George Washington Law Review* 270, 281 (1964). The actual use of these techniques is described in Berry, "Project Brain Control," reprinted in 111 *Cong. Rec.* 16,181, 16,182 (July 9, 1965):

> ESB [electrical stimulation of the brain] has . . . been used experimentally to treat mental patients. At Tulane University . . . a select group of chronic mental cases were equipped with self-stimulators. Buttons on a special belt activated electrodes in their brains. Whenever a patient felt depressed, he pushed the button. ESB, washing away anxiety, helped restore a more cheerful mood. In cases where patients had severe psychotic seizures, ESB turned uncontrollable rage into euphoria.

38. See Note, "Anthropotelemetry: Dr. Schwitzgebel's Machine," 80 *Harvard Law Review* 403, 407 (1966). See also Miller, "On Proposals and Requirements for Solutions," in "Symposium—Computers, Data Banks, and Individual Privacy," 53 *Minnesota Law Review* 211, 226–27 (1968).

39. Some of the limitations on total surveillance are pointed out in V. Ferkiss, *Technological Man* 166–67 (1969).

40. Sarnoff, "No Life Untouched," *Saturday Review,* July 23, 1966, at 21.

41. E. Cahn, *The Sense of Injustice* 151 (1949).

42. Kamisar, "The Wiretapping-Eavesdropping Problem: A Professor's View," 44 *Minnesota Law Review* 891, 892 (1960).

43. E.g., Bennett, "Secrets Are for Sharing," *Psychology Today,* Feb. 1969, at 31.

44. Handler & Hollingsworth, "Stigma, Privacy and Other Attitudes of Welfare Recipients," 22 *Stanford Law Review* 1, 2 (1969).

45. A. Westin, supra note 1, at 34. See also P. Drucker, *The Age of Discontinuity* 255–56 (1968); T. Shibutani, *Society and Personality* 213–28, 239–48, 270–76 (1961); Bates, "Privacy—A Useful Concept?," 42

Social Forces 429 (1964); Jourard, "Some Psychological Aspects of Privacy," 31 *Law and Contemporary Problems* 307 (1966).

46. Michael, supra note 37, at 277.

47. *House Hearings on the Computer and Invasion of Privacy* 145.

48. Wagner, "Records and the Invasion of Privacy," reprinted in 111 *Cong. Rec.* 10,821, 10,823 (May 18, 1965). See also T. Shibutani, supra note 45, at 239–47.

49. *House Hearings on the Computer and Invasion of Privacy* 12 (statement of Vance Packard).

50. *Senate Hearings on Computer Privacy, part* 2, at 289.

51. *New York Times,* Nov. 4, 1968, § 1, at 27, col. 5.

52. "That New Black Magic," *Time,* Sept. 27, 1968, at 42.

53. "Sticky Ticket Wicket," *Time,* March 2, 1970, at 16.

54. E.g., M. Frayn, *The Tin Man* (paper ed., 1965); R. Heinlein, *The Moon is a Harsh Mistress* (paper ed., 1966); O. Johannesson, *The Tale of the Big Computer* (1968); D. Jones, *Colossus* (1966).

55. E.g., E. Burdick, The 480 (1964); T. Tyler, *The Man Whose Name Wouldn't Fit* (paper ed., 1968).

56. Compare K. Capek, *R.U.R.* (1923).

57. E.g., *Hot Millions* (described in Dickon, "Hot Millions and the Computer Ethic," *Careers Today,* Feb. 1969, at 12; *2001: A Space Odyssey; The Computer Wore Tennis Shoes.*

58. E.g., Hayakawa, "Solemn Thoughts on the Second Industrial Revolution," 23 *ETC: A Review of General Semantics* 7–8 (1966). See also Auden, "The Unknown Citizen," in *Modern Poetry* 206–07 (2d ed. paper, 1961); Lamport, "A Sigh for Cybernetics," in *Scrap Irony* 15 (1961).

59. E.g., Kerr, "Push Button 'A' for Laugh 'B'," *New York Times,* Sept. 29, 1968, at D1, col. 1.

60. Katzell, "Psychological Investigation and the Right of Privacy," 17 *Virginia Law Weekly,* DICTA 109–10 (1964–66).

61. *Potomac Electric Power Company* v. *Washington Chapter of Congress of Racial Equality,* 210 F.Supp. 418 (D.D.C. 1962). See generally Michael, supra note 37, at 284–85.

62. *Time,* Feb. 21, 1969, at 39; *New York Times,* Feb. 12, 1969, at 3, col. 3.

63. Shubik, "Information, Rationality, and Free Choices in a Future Democratic Society," *Daedalus,* Summer 1967, at 771, 777. See also Sherill, "Instant Electorate," *Playboy,* Nov. 1968, at 155; Miller, "The Town Meeting Reborn," *Saturday Review,* July 23, 1966, at 34.

64. Miller, "Privacy Implications of Instructional Technology—A Preliminary Overview" 27–29 (undated) (unpublished paper prepared for the Study on Instructional Technology). See also pages 105–22. But compare Bettelheim, "The Right to Privacy Is a Myth," *Saturday Evening Post,* July 27, 1968, at 8.

65. *Saturday Review,* April 13, 1968, at 77–78. See also Maron, "Large Scale Data Banks," 60 *Special Libraries* 3 (1969).

Chapter III : The Changing Face of Information Handling—Privacy in the Crucible

1. *The Federal Paperwork Jungle* 12–13.

2. See generally Macy, "Automated Government—How Computers Are Being Used in Washington to Streamline Personnel Administration to the Individual's Benefit," *Saturday Review,* July 23, 1966, at 25; "The Design of a Federal Statistical Data Center" in *House Hearings on the Computer and Invasion of Privacy,* Appendix C, at 288.

3. "Review of Proposal for a National Data Center" in *House Hearings on the Computer and Invasion of Privacy,* Appendix 2, at 260–64. See also id. at 199, 201; *Senate Hearings on Computer Privacy* 28–29.

4. See generally "Committee on Scientific and Technical Information of the Federal Council for Science and Technology," *Proceedings of the Forum of Federally Supported Information Analysis Centers* (1967). The need for the development of an overall information policy on the federal level is discussed by the chairman of COSATI in A. Aines, "The Quest for National Policies for Information Systems" (Feb. 18, 1969) (unpublished mimeo).

5. See Ruggles, "On the Needs and Values of Data Banks," in "Symposium—Computers, Data Banks, and Individual Privacy," 53 *Minnesota Law Review* 211, 217–18 (1968).

6. The proposal to create a federal data center was advanced in a series of three reports: "Report of the Committee on the Preservation and Use of Economic Data to the Social Science Research Council" (April 1965) (Ruggles Report), reprinted in *House Hearings on the Computer and Invasion of Privacy* 195–254; "Statistical Evaluation Report No. 6—Review of Proposal for a National Data Center" (Dunn Report), reprinted in *House Hearings on the Computer and Invasion of Privacy* 254–94; "Report on the Task Force on the Storage of and Access to Government Statistics" (Kaysen Report), reprinted in *Senate Hearings on Computer Privacy* 25–37. See generally J. Rosenberg, *The Death of Privacy* 22–40 (1969).

7. See Sawyer & Schechter, "Computers, Privacy, and the National Data Center: The Responsibility of Social Scientists," 23 *The American*

Psychologist 810, 813 (1968). See also Pipe, "Privacy: Establishing Restrictions on Government Inquiry," 18 *American University Law Review* 516 (1969).

8. See generally *House Hearings on the Computer and Invasion of Privacy; Senate Hearings on Computer Privacy; Senate Hearings on Computer Privacy, part 2;* 112 *Cong. Rec.* 19,961 (Aug. 18, 1966).

9. See, e.g., *Labor*, April 13, 1968, at 8, col. 1; *New York Times*, July 28, 1966, § C, at 18, col. 1; id., July 27, 1966, § M, at 33, col. 4.

10. See, e.g., "Chains of Plastic," *Newsweek*, Aug. 8, 1966, at 27; "A Government Watch on 200 Million Americans?," *U.S. News & World Report*, May 16, 1966, at 56; Miller, "The National Data Center and Personal Privacy," *The Atlantic*, Nov. 1967, at 53.

11. Miller, "Personal Privacy in the Computer Age: The Challenge of a New Technology in an Information-Oriented Society," 67 *Michigan Law Review* 1089 (1969); "Symposium: Computers, Data Banks, and Individual Privacy," 53 *Minnesota Law Review* 211 (1968); Note, "Privacy and Efficient Government: Proposals for a National Data Center," 82 *Harvard Law Review* 400 (1968); Project, "The Computerization of Government Files: What Impact on the Individual?," 15 *University of California at Los Angeles Law Review* 1371 (1968).

12. See *House Hearings on the Computer and Invasion of Privacy* 52, 59, 97–98.

13. Dunn, "The Idea of a National Data Center and the Issue of Personal Privacy," reprinted in *Hearings on Statistical Programs* 32, 35.

14. Compare *Senate Hearings on Computer Privacy* 74.

15. *Privacy and the National Data Bank Concept* 14.

16. Id. at 11.

17. Id. at 6.

18. Zwick, "A National Data Center," in American Bar Association, *Section of Individual Rights and Responsibilities, Monograph No. 1*, at 32 (1967).

19. *The Federal Paperwork Jungle* 18.

20. The following is typical of the asserted differences between the two types of systems. It appears in *House Hearings on the Computer and Invasion of Privacy* 92–93 (statement of Edgar S. Dunn, Jr., research analyst, Resources for the Future, Inc.):

The distinction is basic. Intelligence systems generate data about individuals as individuals. They have as their purpose "finding out" about the individual. . . .

. . . .

[A] statistical system is busy generating aggregates, averages, percentages, and so forth that describe relationships. No information about the individual is generated.

No information about the individual needs to be available to anyone under any circumstances for the statistical information system to perform its function.

21. See *House Hearings on the Computer and Invasion of Privacy* 112, 142; *Senate Hearings on Computer Privacy* 67–68.

22. *House Hearings on the Computer and Invasion of Privacy* 61. See also remarks of Representative Gallagher on *H.Rep.* 7659 (authorizing a mid-decade census), 113 *Cong. Rec.* 10,383 (Aug. 10, 1967): "[N]o matter what name the Census Bureau gives to its 'information system,' what it is actually creating is a very complete and thorough National Data Bank."

23. Pub. L. 89,306, 79 Stat. 1127, § 111(b)(1)(1965). See also § 111(g).

24. *Hearings on Data Processing Management* 54–55.

25. Pub. L. 89–306, 79 Stat. 1128, § 111(f) (1965).

26. *Hearings on Data Processing Management* 72 (statement of A. V. Astin, Director of the National Bureau of Standards). See also id. at 25 (statement of Phillip S. Hughes, Deputy Director of the Bureau of the Budget).

27. Statement on Behalf of the Customer Interest of the Executive Agencies of the United States 9–27 (submitted in connection with *In re Regulatory and Policy Problems Presented by the Interdependence of Computer and Communications Services and Facilities, FCC Docket No. 16,979)* (March 5, 1968).

28. See pages 21, 150–51.

29. Johnson, "Computers and the Public Welfare—Law Enforcement, Social Services and Data Banks," in *Computers and Communications—Toward a Computer Utility* 173, 187–88 (1968).

30. The Budget Bureau's powers were summarized in Subcommittee on Economic Statistics of the Joint Economic Committee, 90th Cong., 1st Sess., *Report on the Coordination and Integration of Government Statistical Programs* 8 (Joint Comm. Print 1967).

31. *Hearings on Data Processing Management* 5.

32. *H.Rep.* 8809, 91st Cong. 1st Sess. (1969).

33. See, e.g., *Senate Hearings on Computer Privacy* 5 (statement of Carl Kaysen, Director, Institute for Advanced Studies, Princeton University).

34. *The Federal Paperwork Jungle* 98.

35. Id. at 14.

36. 5 U.S.C. § 139 (1964).

37. *The Federal Paperwork Jungle* 14–15.

38. Id. at 39.

39. House Committee on Post Office and Civil Service, *Statistical Activities of the Federal Government: Personnel, Equipment, and Contract Costs, H.Rep. Report* 1130, 88th Cong., 2d Sess. 31 (1964).

40. *The Federal Paperwork Jungle* 94–95.

41. Id. at 87.

42. *Government Dossier* 8.

43. *The Federal Paperwork Jungle* 36.

44. Id. at 33.

45. Okun, "Investigation of Jurors by Counsel: Its Impact on the Decisional Process," 56 *Georgetown Law Journal* 839, 852–53 (1968).

46. See pages 43–45.

47. *Government Dossier* 8.

48. See Bureau of the Budget, "Report of the Task Force of the Storage of and Access to Government Statistics," reprinted in *Senate Hearings on Computer Privacy* 25, 27–28.

49. See, e.g., Packard, "Don't Tell It to the Computer," *New York Times,* § 6 (Magazine), Jan. 8, 1967, at 44, 89.

50. *The Federal Paperwork Jungle* 39.

51. Id. at 64.

52. Id. at 41.

53. See, e.g., *Senate Hearings on Computer Privacy* 42–43 (statement of Charles J. Zwick, Assistant Director of the Bureau of the Budget); *House Hearings on the Computer and Invasion of Privacy* 49–50 (statement of Raymond T. Bowman, Assistant Director for Statistical Standards, Bureau of the Budget). See also Ruggles, "On the Needs and Values of Data Banks," in "Symposium—Computers, Data Banks, and Individual Privacy," 53 *Minnesota Law Review* 211, 217–18 (1968).

54. *House Hearings on Commercial Credit Bureaus* 89 (statement of Henry C. Jordan, President of Credit Data Corp.).

55. *The Federal Paperwork Jungle* 49–52.

56. Id. at 47.

57. The growth of credit buying is documented in H. Black, *Buy Now, Pay Later* (1961). Each month approximately eight billion dollars worth of credit is extended in the United States. *Time,* Dec. 20, 1968, at 79.

58. See, e.g., Michael, "Speculation on the Relation of the Computer to Individual Freedom and the Right to Privacy," 33 *George Washington Law Review* 270, 275 (1964).

59. See, e.g., *House Hearings on Commercial Credit Bureaus* 125–26.

60. See generally *Senate Hearings on Credit Bureaus; House Hearings on Commercial Credit Bureaus; Hearings on Retail Credit Company.*

61. See, e.g., Sesser, "Big Brother Keeps Tabs on Insurance Buyers," *The New Republic,* April 27, 1968, at 11. See also Morris, "What the Credit Bureaus Know About You," *Reader's Digest,* Nov. 1967, at 85; *Wall Street Journal,* Feb. 1, 1968, at 1.

62. *Hearings on Retail Credit Company* 21.

63. *The Washington Post,* July 21, 1969, at A5.

64. *Hearings on Retail Credit Company* 32 (testimony of W. Lee Burge, President of Retail Credit Company).

65. The distinction between "credit reporting agencies" such as the Retail Credit Company, and "credit bureaus" serving retail merchants, such as the ACB, is discussed in *House Hearings on Commercial Credit Bureaus* 104–05. However, the distinction is far from sharp. For example, a wholly owned subsidiary of Retail Credit Company controls sixty credit bureaus, *Hearings on Retail Credit Company* 1, while the ACB makes its files accessible to more than 1,400 collection agencies, *Senate Hearings on Credit Bureaus* 23.

66. See, e.g., *Senate Hearings on Credit Bureaus* (statements of Henry C. Jordan, President of Credit Data Corporation, and T. Monty Skiles, Director, Industry Relations of Associated Credit Bureaus, Inc.); *House Hearings on Commercial Credit Bureaus* 87–88.

67. *CBS Evening News,* March 17, 1969, reprinted in 115 *Cong. Rec.* 8308–09 (daily ed. March 17, 1969) [hereinafter *CBS News*].

68. Id. at S3009.

69. Associated Credit Bureaus, Inc., *Credit Bureau Guidelines To Protect Consumer Privacy,* § C.

70. *CBS News* at S3009.

71. Id.

72. *House Hearings on Commercial Credit Bureaus* 11.

73. See, e.g., *Time,* Dec. 20, 1968, at 79; *The National Observer,* March 3, 1969, at 1, col. 1.

74. *Hearings on Retail Credit Company,* Appendix, 47. W. Lee Burge, President of Retail Credit Company, sought to justify his com-

pany's clause as a way of protecting his company's sources of information. Id. at 14–16.

75. See, e.g., *House Hearings on Commercial Credit Bureaus* 110 (statement of John L. Spafford, Executive Vice President of the Associated Credit Bureaus of America).

76. M. Brenton, *The Privacy Invaders* 35 (1964).

77. See *House Hearings on Commercial Credit Bureaus* 93, 147 (testimony of Henry C. Jordan, President, Credit Data Corporation).

78. Id. at 74; cf. id. at 111.

79. Id. at 87.

80. Id. at 83–84. See also Jordan, "Better Mousetrap?," *Forbes,* Oct. 1, 1967, at 67.

81. See *Sperry-Rand UNIVAC Response to the Inquiry of the FCC* (submitted in connection with *In re Regulatory and Policy Problems Presented by the Interdependence of Computer and Communications Facilities,* Docket No. 16,979), A–9: "A real-time system is one which provides the ability to obtain information in time to affect events as they occur."

82. *House Hearings on Commercial Credit Bureaus* 109.

83. According to Harold S. Geneen, president of IT&T: "[IT&T] is currently accelerating its programs for the establishment of an international system of data processing service centers, supplementing existing operations in England, Sweden, Germany, and France." John J. Spafford, Executive Vice-President of ACB added: "This system will combine the most advanced communications and computer technologies through the use of 'third-generation' computers, standards communications lines, and a variety of typewriter like or visual display terminals." Credit News Bureau press release, Sept. 20, 1968.

84. Western Union has acquired an interest in a firm that proposes to transmit credit information by common carrier and International Telephone and Telegraph Company has designed a computer system for the ACB. *House Hearings on Commercial Credit Bureaus* 149; Credit News Bureau press release, Sept. 20, 1968. See also Irwin, "The Computer Utility: Competition or Regulation?," 76 *Yale Law Journal* 1299, 1302 (1967).

85. See, e.g., *Standard Sanitary Mfg. Co. v. United States,* 226 U.S. 20 (1912).

86. See "Money Goes Electronic in the 1970's," *Business Week,* Jan. 13, 1968, at 54, 74; 115 *Cong. Rec.* E2613 (daily ed., April 2, 1968).

87. See, e.g., *Senate Hearings on Computer Privacy, part 2,* at 327–33 (statement of Paul Armer, Associate Head, Computer Sciences De-

partment, the Rand Corporation); O'Brien, "The Bank of Tomorrow: Today," *Computers and Automation,* May 1968, at 26; "Electronic Money," *Forbes,* April 1, 1967, at 42; Kramer & Livingston, "Cashing In on the Checkless Society," 45 *Harvard Business Review,* Sept.–Oct. 1967, at 141; E. Weiss, *The Marketing Implications of the Checkless Society* (1968).

88. See Karst, " 'The Files': Legal Controls over the Accuracy and Accessibility of Stored Personal Data," 31 *Law and Contemporary Problems* 342, 375 (1966).

89. See, e.g., A. Westin, *Privacy and Freedom* 165 (1967); Westin, "The Snooping Machine," *Playboy,* May 1968, at 130.

90. *House Hearings on Commercial Credit Bureaus* 50. See also Trillin, "Onward and Upward with the Arts: You Can't Wear Out a List," *The New Yorker,* Sept. 24, 1966, at 126.

91. Credit News Bureau press release, November 20, 1967.

92. *New York Times,* July 30, 1968, at 41, col. 1. Compare *Lamont v. Commissioner of Motor Vehicles,* 269 F.Supp. 880 (S.D.N.Y.), affirmed per curiam, 386 F.2d 449 (2d Cir. 1967); 39 U.S.C. § 4009 (Supp. III, 1965–67) ("Prohibition of pandering advertisements in the mail").

93. Hodge, "Those Irritating Junk Phone Calls," *The Washington Post—Potomac,* Nov. 23, 1969, at 11.

94. See generally M. Brenton, supra note 76, at 45; E. Long, *The Intruders* 50–51 (1967). See also A. Westin, *Privacy and Freedom* 160 (1967); Star, "The Computer Data Bank: Will It Kill Your Freedom?," *Look,* June 25, 1968, at 27.

95. M. Brenton, supra note 76, at 30.

96. See, e.g., *House Hearings on Commercial Credit Bureaus* 7–10, 121–24. See also *Hearings on Retail Credit Company* 22–23, 39 (testimony of W. Lee Burge, President of Retail Credit Company).

97. This explanation was offered by an ACB official in *House Hearings on Commercial Credit Bureaus* 133:

> Credit bureaus consider it a responsibility in the interest of good government to assist government investigations with information that may be helpful. Some of these agencies are interested in identifying information rather than credit information. If the bureau file shows a former address, a former employer, or other clue to pertinent history, the agency investigator uses the lead to continue his investigation. We believe that this substantially reduces the expenditure of time and money by the various agencies.

Both Retail Credit Company and Hooper-Holmes Bureau cooperate with government investigatory efforts. *Hearings on Retail Credit Company* 22–23; Sesser, supra note 61, at 11.

98. See, e.g., *House Hearings on Commercial Credit Bureaus* 91.

99. Thus far TRW Credit Data's efforts to resist government subpoenas have not been successful. *United States* v. *Davey*, 426 F.2d 842 (2d Cir. 1970).

100. Credit News Bureau press release, Nov. 30, 1967.

101. Ibid.

102. News release, March 20, 1969.

103. Hodge, supra note 93, at 11.

104. *House Hearings on Commercial Credit Bureaus* 115.

105. *Computerworld,* Dec. 24, 1969.

106. S. 823, 91st Cong., 1st Sess. (1969); see 115 *Cong. Rec.* S1163–69 (daily ed., Jan. 31, 1969). See also 114 *Cong. Rec.* S10,029 (daily ed., Aug. 2, 1968). Broad hearings on the original bill were held on May 19–23, 1969. *Senate Hearings on Fair Credit Reporting.*

107. *Senate Hearings on Fair Credit Reporting* 377.

108. *H.Rep. Report* 16340, 91st Cong., 2d Sess. (1970). Hearings were held in March, 1970, with the usual cast of characters testifying.

109. Compare Note, "Credit Investigations and the Right to Privacy: Quest for a Remedy," 57 *Georgetown Law Journal* 509, 529 (1969): "An Oklahoma statute [Okla. Stat. Ann. tit. 24, §§ 81–85 (1965)] is the only legislation, state or federal, which specifically deals with the credit bureau problem." Bills have been introduced in several states during the past few years. See, e.g., Mich. House Introductory No. 4839 (1970); N.Y. Sen. Introductory No. 338, N.Y. Assembly Introductory No. 570 (1968); *Des Moines Register,* April 14, 1969, at 10, col. 1. See also Gibson & Sharp, *Privacy and Commercial Reporting Agencies,* Legal Research Institute, University of Manitoba (1968); infra note 110.

110. Calif. Civil Code §§ 1750 et seq. (1970); Mass. Gen. Laws, ch. 93, §§ 44–47 (1969); N.Y. Sess. Laws, ch. 300 (1970).

111. See pages 71–72.

112. ACB, Inc., *Credit Bureau Guidelines To Protect Consumer Privacy,* § E(1)(b) (emphasis added).

113. Id. at § E(1)(c).

114. Id. at § A(2).

115. See pages 239–57.

116. The subject is discussed generally in D. Goslin, *The Search for Ability* (1963).

117. M. Gross, *The Brain Watchers* (1962); Barton, "Pseudo Psyches," *American Mercury,* Oct. 1956, at 5.

118. See generally J. Kirkpatrick, R. Ewen, R. Barrett & R. Katzell, *Testing and Fair Employment* (1968); Cooper & Sobol, "Seniority and Testing Under Fair Employment Laws: A General Approach to Objective Criteria of Hiring and Promotion," 82 *Harvard Law Review* 1598, 1637–49 (1969); French, "The Motorola Case," *Industrial Psychologist*, Aug. 1965, at 20; Guion, "Employment Tests and Discriminatory Hiring," *Industrial Relations,* Feb. 1966, at 20.

119. See Cooper & Sobol, supra note 118, at 1649–69; Note, "Legal Implications of the Use of Standardized Ability Tests in Employment and Education," 68 *Columbia Law Review* 691, 706–34 (1968).

120. See Doppelt & Bennett, "Testing Job Applicants from Disadvantaged Groups," *Test Service Bulletin of the Psychological Corporation*, May 1967, at 2; Katz, "Motivational Determinants of Racial Differences in Intellectual Achievements," 2 *International Journal of Psychology* 1–12 (1967).

121. See generally L. Cronbach, *Essentials of Psychological Testing* (2d ed. 1960).

122. See generally E. Ghiselli, *The Validity of Occupational Aptitude Tests* 34–36, 49–51 (1966); D. Super & J. Crites, *Appraising Vocational Fitness* 106 (rev. ed. 1962).

123. See pages 39–46.

124. The extent of the use of psychological testing in industry and government is described in A. Westin, supra note 94, at 135–45.

125. *Protecting Privacy and the Rights of Federal Employees, Senate Report No. 534,* 90th Cong., 1st Sess. 20 (1967).

126. M. Gross, supra note 117, at 12–49.

127. See D. Goslin, supra note 116, at 171–91. See also J. Gardner, *Excellence* (1961); M. Young, infra note 128.

128. T. Goslin, supra note 116, at 55–56. M. Young, *The Rise of the Meritocracy* (1958), is a fictionalized account of a society in which undue reliance is placed on I.Q. tests.

129. W. Whyte, *The Organization Man* 192 (1956).

130. See generally A. Westin, supra note 94, at 259–68.

131. *Protecting Privacy and the Rights of Federal Employees, Senate Report No. 534,* 90th Cong., 1st Sess. 19 (1967). See also Ridgeway, "The Snoops: Private Lives and Public Service," *New Republic,* Dec. 19, 1964, at 13; Zola, "Adventures of a Test Taker," *National Review,* Jan. 12, 1965, at 21.

132. See generally D. Goslin, supra note 116, at 55–94.

133. See M. Gross, supra note 117, at 286–87.

134. See generally Office of Science and Technology of the Executive Office of the President, *Privacy and Behavioral Research* (1967).

135. See Miller, "Psychological Testing: Can We Minimize Its Perils?"*Think*, May–June 1969, at 24. See also pages 120–22.

136. See pages 38–46.

137. M. Gross, supra note 117, at 239–40.

138. See pages 239–57.

139. See J. Licklider, *Libraries of the Future* (1965); *Man Machine Systems in Education* (Loughary ed. 1966); *Computers and Education* (Gerard ed. 1967); *Educational Information System Requirements: The Next Twi Decades* (Loughary & Tondow eds., 1967).

140. See Bright, "Educational Technology and the Disadvantaged Child," *Educational Technology,* June 30, 1967, at 7. See generally *To Improve Learning, Report by the Commission on Instructional Technology* (H.Rep. Comm. Print 1970).

141. See Suppes, "The Uses of Computers in Education," *Scientific American,* Sept. 1966, at 207, 218. See also Gerard, "Shaping the Mind: Computers in Education," in *Educational Information System Requirements: The Next Two Decades* 48, 56–63 (Loughary & Tondow eds., 1967).

142. Reported in J. Rosenberg, *The Death of Privacy* 57 (1969).

143. See Girard, "Shaping the Mind: Computers in Education" in *Educational Information System Requirements: The Next Two Decades* 48, 60–62 (Loughary & Hondow, eds., 1967).

144. Suppes, supra note 141, at 207.

145. Tondow, "The Nature of Educational Information," in *Educational Information System Requirements: The Next Two Decades* 9, 11 (Loughary & Tondow eds., 1967).

146. See Opler, "The Receding Future," *Datamation,* Sept. 1967, at 13. See also Gleason, "Computer Assisted Instruction—Prospects and Problems," *Educational Technology,* Nov. 15, 1967, at 7.

147. See generally A. Oettinger, *Run, Computer, Run* 178–214 (1969).

148. Even the much publicized Stanford University-Brentwood School experiment in grade school level computer-assisted instruction has a rather limited scope both in terms of the number of students affected and the range of material presented by machine. See A. Oettinger, supra note 147, at 183–85; Silberman, "Technology is Knocking at the Schoolhouse Door," *Fortune,* Aug. 1966, 120–25.

149. Oettinger, "The Myths of Educational Technology," *Saturday Review,* May 18, 1968, at 77. See also A. Oettinger, supra note 147, at 185–95.

150. *To Improve Learning,* supra note 140, at 21.

151. See generally Loughary, "Educational System Requirements and Society," *Educational Information System Requirements: The Next Two Decades* 1–8 (Loughary & Tondow eds., 1967).

152. *Educational Technology Act,* S. 1189, 91st Cong., 1st Sess. (1969). See also *H.Rep.* 4843, 8659, 8838, 91st Cong., 1st Sess. (1969).

153. See Gerard, supra note 141, at 59–60.

154. See Suppes, supra note 141, at 219–20. The current condition of record-keeping in the nation's schools is described in *On Record: Files and Dossiers in American Life* 29–93 (Wheeler ed., 1969).

155. See pages 5–7.

156. See Ridgeway, "Computer-Tutor," *New Republic,* June 4, 1966, at 21.

157. See generally Flemming, "Confidentiality and Educational Information," in *Educational Information System Requirements The Next Two Decades* 120, 124–27 (Loughary & Tondow eds. 1967).

158. See Flemming, supra note 157.

159. See pages 239–57.

160. See *Marmo v. New York City Board of Education,* 56 Misc.2d 517, 289 N.Y.S.2d 51 (Sup.Ct. 1968); *Van Allen v. McCleary,* 27 Misc.2d 81, 211 N.Y.S.2d 501 (Sup.Ct. 1961). See also *Johnson v. Board of Education of City of New York,* 31 Misc.2d 810, 220 N.Y.S.2d 362 (Sup.Ct. 1961).

161. Wedemeyer, "The Future of Educational Television in the U.S.A., in *Television and Teaching* 132, 140 (Moir ed., 1967).

162. See, e.g., Licklider, "Televistas: Looking Ahead Through Side Windows," *Public Television—A Program for Action, The Report of the Carnegie Commission on Educational Television* 201–25 (paper ed., 1967) (supplementary paper); *To Improve Learning,* supra note 140, at 19–26, Appendix A.

163. See generally Wedemeyer, supra note 161, at 146.

164. Weltman, "Teaching and Television—ETV Explained," in *Television and Teaching* 100, 101–02 (Moir ed., 1967).

165. Compare M. Brenton, *The Privacy Invaders* 165–67 (paper ed., 1964).

166. Mitzel, *National Observer,* Nov. 29, 1965.

167. See pages 52–53.

168. See Ridgeway, supra note 156, at 21 (quoting Dr. Robert D. Tschirgi).

169. Wedemeyer, supra note 161.

170. See Hill, "Technology and Television," in *Public Television —A Program for Action, The Report of the Carnegie Commission on Educational Television* 193–200 (paper ed., 1967) (supp. paper).

171. See generally Allen, "Time Sharing Takes Off," *Harvard Business Review*, March–April 1968, at 128; Burck, "The Computer Industry's Great Expectations," *Fortune,* Aug. 1968, at 92; Dearden, "Computers: No Impact on Divisional Control," *Harvard Business Review,* Jan.–Feb. 1967, at 99; Brady, "Computers in Top-Level Decision Making," *Harvard Business Review,* July–Aug. 1967, at 67.

172. See, e.g., Freed, "A Legal Structure for a National Medical Data Center," 49 *Boston University Law Review* 79 (1969); Freed, "Legal Aspects of Computer Use in Medicine," 32 *Law and Contemporary Problems* 674 (1967); Sarnoff, "No Life Untouched," *Saturday Review,* July 23, 1966, at 21; Stevens, "Now—The Automated Physical Checkup," *Reader's Digest,* July 1966, at 95.

173. A number of colleges and universities have recognized the advantages of maintaining joint computer facilities and sharing data bases. See, for example, the description of a nonprofit corporation formed by Harvard University and the Massachusetts Institute of Technology for the purpose of establishing a joint telecommunications system based on shared computer facilities in *New York Times,* July 7, 1968, § 2, at 52, col. 4. The Interuniversity Communications Council (EDUCOM), another nonprofit corporation, also is designed to promote the application of the new communications technology to education. See also Miller, "Potentialities of a Multi-Media, Inter-University Educational Network," in *CIBA Foundation Symposium on Communication in Documentattion and Automation* 235–52 (1967).

174. See the description of the FBI's computerized National Crime Information Center on pages 147–48. The Law Enforcement Assistance Administration of the Justice Department is considering a proposal to create a national computer system devoted to information on organized crime. The system would contain data supplied by police departments, information on real estate transactions from recorders' offices, and records of state and local tax license fees. *Chicago Daily News,* April 19, 1969, at 1, col. 3 (state weekend ed.).

175. See, for example, the description of California's efforts to establish a statewide data-processing system in Project, "Computerization of Government Files: What Impact on the Individual?," 15 *University of California at Los Angeles Law Review* 1371, 1401–10 (1968).

See also "Symposium—Computers, Data Banks, and Individual Privacy," 53 *Minnesota Law Review* 211, 234–35 (1968) (description of the New York State Identification and Intelligence System by Professor Richard Ruggles); *Wall Street Journal,* April 9, 1969, at 1, col. 6 (description of Maryland State Employment Service computerized "job bank"); pages 146–52.

176. See, e.g., "A City Where Computers Will Know About Everybody," *U.S. News & World Report,* May 15, 1967, at 78.

Chapter 1 v : Through the Microscope Darkly—The Handling of Personal Information by the Federal Government: Current Practice

1. U.S. Constitution, art. 1, § 2.

2. See generally *Hearings on 1970 Census Questions.*

3. See Steinberg, "Government Records: The Census Bureau and the Social Security Administration," in *On Record: Files and Dossiers in American Life* 225–42 (Wheeler ed., 1969); Miller, "Considerations in Determining the Content of the 1970 Census," 4 *Demography* 744 (1967). See also Eckler, "Profit from 1970 Census Data," *Harvard Business Review,* July–Aug. 1970, at 4.

4. 115 *Cong. Rec.* H859 (daily ed., Feb. 6, 1969). See generally Pipe, "Privacy: Establishing Restrictions on Government Inquiry," 18 *American University Law Review* 516 (1969).

5. 13 U.S.C. §§ 221–224 (1964).

6. See, e.g., *United States* v. *Rickenbacker,* 309 F.2d 462, 463–64 (2d Cir. 1962), certiorari denied, 371 U.S. 962 (1963). Compare *United States* v. *Moriarity,* 106 F. 886, 390–92 (C.C.S.D.N.Y. 1901). The prosecution of Mr. Rickenbacker seems to have resulted from both his failure to honor the census and his authorship of an article attacking the Bureau's practices. See Rickenbacker, "The Fourth House," *National Review,* May 21, 1960, at 325.

7. *Hearings on the 1970 Census and Legislation Related Thereto* 53–54.

8. This point was discussed by several of the witnesses before the Senate Subcommittee on Constitutional Rights during its hearings on Senator Ervin's bill, S. 1791, in April 1969. See generally *Hearings Before Subcommittee on Census and Statistics of the House Committee on Post Office and Civil Service,* 90th Cong., 1st Sess. (1967); 114 *Cong. Rec.* H4053–75 (daily ed., May 21, 1968).

9. Id. See also 113 *Cong. Rec.* at H13,429–31 (daily ed., Oct. 16, 1967) (remarks by Congressman Betts).

10. See, e.g., *Wall Street Journal,* March 27, 1970, at 1, col. 4. See generally Louviere, "The Ruckus over the Census," *The American Legion Magazine,* July, 1969, at 5.

11. *Detroit News,* March 23, 1969, at 8A, col. 1.

12. See, e.g., *Hearings on 1970 Census Questions* 70 (statement of Morris B. Abram, President, American Jewish Committee); id. at 3 (statement of Representative Cornelius Gallagher). The following is typical of the attempt to defend the question.

> Many commercial and welfare interests can be served by statistics about religious affiliation. In industrial and commercial circles it is well known that markets are influenced by the religious affiliation of prospective customers. Market analyses . . . would be more complete—and better suited to the needs of the citizenry—if they incorporated projections based on statistics on religious affiliations.

Id. at 45–46 (statement of the Most Reverend Paul F. Tanner, General Secretary, National Catholic Welfare Conference).

13. See, e.g., *H.Rep.* 20, 91st Cong., 1st Sess. (1969), which would limit criminal penalties to refusals to answer questions involving name and address, relationship to head of household, sex, date of birth, marital status, and visitors in the home at the time of the census. See also *S.* 494, 90th Cong., 1st Sess. (1969); 113 *Cong. Rec.* H16,231–32 (daily ed., June 19, 1967).

14. Among the witnesses were three law professors, including the author, and a number of citizens said to be "representative of thousands from every walk of life who have complained to Congress about unwarranted invasion of their personal privacy and about increased harassment by government agencies in their everlasting quests for information." Office of the Senate Constitutional Rights Subcommittee, press release, April 14, 1969. The hearings have now been published.

15. *H.Rep.* 12884, 90th Cong., 1st Sess. (1969). The bill was the result of extensive hearings entitled *1970 Census and Legislation Related Thereto,* held by the House Subcommittee on Post Office and Civil Service, 91st Cong., 1st Sess., Serial No. 91–8 (1969). Another by-product of the hearings was the establishment of a Blue Ribbon Advisory Panel to study the census and make recommendations. The Panel is heavily dominated by data users, which led Congressman Betts to charge that it was "stacked." The author was appointed to the Panel following that speech.

16. See, e.g., Ruggles, "On the Needs and Values of Data Banks," in "Symposium—Computers, Data Banks, and Individual Privacy," 53 *Minnesota Law Review* 211, 218–19 (1968).

17. See *Hearings on 1970 Census and Legislation Related Thereto* 210–11.

18. See, e.g., *House Hearings on the Computer and Invasion of Privacy* 51–56; *Hearings on 1970 Census Questions* 27–28.

19. Hirsch, "The Punchcard Snoopers," *The Nation,* Oct. 16, 1967, at 369.

20. See Miller, "On Proposals and Requirements for Solution," in "Symposium—Computers, Data Banks, and Individual Privacy," 53 *Minnesota Law Review* 224, 230 (1968).

21. 13 U.S.C. § 9(a) (1964).

22. 13 U.S.C. § 214 (1964).

23. See pages 21–22.

24. 13 U.S.C. § 8(a) (1964).

25. 13 U.S.C. § 8(b) (1964).

26. 13 U.S.C. § 8(c) (1964). The prohibition on detrimental use extends only to material appearing in the three censuses enumerated in section 8(a). *St. Regis Paper Co.* v. *United States,* 368 U.S. 208, 215 (1961).

27. See *Hearings on the 1970 Census Questions* 29 (statement of Dr. A. Ross Eckler, Director, Bureau of the Census).

28. In *Edwards* v. *Edwards,* 239 S.C. 85, 121 S.E.2d 432 (1961), the defendants in an inheritance dispute contended that the plaintiffs' use of census records as evidence was detrimental to their interests. The South Carolina Supreme Court rejected this construction of the Census Act.

29. 368 U.S. 208 (1961).

30. 13 U.S.C. § 9(a)(3) (1964).

31. 368 U.S. at 218.

32. The Census Bureau normally codes and edits the data, sends one copy to the requesting agency, and retains the raw data and one copy of the coded data. See *Survey of New Beneficiaries: Report Compiled in Response to a Letter from Senator Ervin* of Feb. 28, 1969, at 3 (prepared by Robert M. Ball, Commissioner of Social Security).

33. Senator Ervin has introduced a bill designed to remedy intrusive federal data-gathering activities. *S.* 1791, 91st Cong., 1st Sess. (1969). The bill was the focal point of the April, 1969 hearings of the Subcommittee on Constitutional Rights. See note 14, supra.

34. See *Report of the Committee on Ways and Means on H.Rep. 16311, H.Rep. Report No. 91–904,* 91st Cong., 2d Sess. 20 (1970).

35. 14 U.S.C. § 3507 (1968). This power is subject to several exceptions, the most notable of which encompasses "the obtaining or releasing of information by the Internal Revenue Service." Id.

36. 44 U.S.C. § 3508(b) (1968).

37. 44 U.S.C. § 3508(a) (1968).

38. *Privacy and the National Data Bank Concept* 14–15.

39. Id. at 15.

40. Treasury Regulation § 301.6103(a)–1(f) (1964):

[I]f the head of an executive department . . . or of any other establishment of the Federal Government, desires to inspect, or to have
some other officer or employee of his department or establishment
inspect, a return . . . in connection with some matter officially
before him, the inspection may, in the discretion of the Secretary
of the Treasury or the Commissioner of Internal Revenue or the
delegate of either, be permitted upon written application. . . .

See also Treasury Regulation §§ 301.6103(a)–1(e) (1960), 301.6103(a)–
1(g) (1960), 301.6103(a)–100–107 (1961). See generally *Wall Street
Journal,* April 21, 1970, at 1, col. 6.

41. 255 F.2d 876, 882–84 (2d Cir.), certiorari denied, 357 U.S. 937,
rehearing denied, 358 U.S. 858 (1958).

42. See pages 239–57.

43. See, e.g., *Senate Hearings on Computer Privacy* 49–66 (plan for
a regional economic data bank for the St. Louis region).

44. See Project, "The Computerization of Government Files:
What Impact on the Individual?," 15 *University of California at Los
Angeles Law Review* 1371, 1401–10 (1968) (proposals for a state data-
processing system in California). See generally *Hearings on Govern-
ment Electronic Data Processing Systems Before the Subcommittee on
Census and Statistics of the House Committee on Post Office and Civil
Service,* 89th Cong., 2d Sess. 231–36 (1966) (statement of Dr. Thomas C.
Rowan, Vice President, Systems Development Corporation); Pennsyl-
vania Senate Bill No. 239 (1969) (state police computerized data bank).

45. See, e.g., "What the 'Data Banks' Know About You," *U.S. News
& World Report,* April 8, 1968, at 82 (Santa Clara County, California);
"A City Where Computers Will Know About Everybody," *U.S. News
& World Report,* May 15, 1967, at 78 (New Haven, Connecticut); *Sen-
ate Hearings on Computer Privacy, part 2,* at 303–25 (Washington, D.C.).

46. Internal Revenue Code of 1954, § 6103(b)(2). See generally
Clurman & Provorny, "Publicity and Inspection of Federal Tax Returns," 46 *Taxes* 144 (1968).

47. Treasury Regulation § 301.6103(a)–1(d) (1965).

48. CCH 1969 Standard Federal Tax § 5209.576.

49. *Cong. Rec.* E2656 (daily ed., April 3, 1968).

50. Internal Revenue Code of 1954, § 7213. This section also provides that federal employees convicted of wrongful disclosure are to be discharged from their jobs.

51. See pages 27–28 Clurman & Provorny, supra note 46.

52. For a description of the New York State Identification and Intelligence System, see *House Hearings on the Computer and Invasion of Privacy* 146–81.

53. *Computerworld,* Nov. 12, 1969.

54. See *Task Force Report: Science and Technology* 35–36. New York City currently is using a system of computer-assisted dispatching of patrol cars, called "SPRINT" (Special Police Radio Inquiry Network), *New York Times,* Dec. 29, 1967, § 7, at 53, col. 1. Project SEARCH (System for the Electronic Analysis and Retrieval of Criminal Histories), which is a joint venture of several states and the Law Enforcement Assistance Administration, is fast approaching an operational status.

55. *New York Times,* Jan. 15, 1968, § 1, at 27, col. 4.

56. *Computerworld,* Feb. 11, 1970, at 6, 7. New Jersey's efforts are discussed on pages 200–02.

57. *Task Force Report: Science and Technology* 72–74.

58. *House Hearings on the Computer and Invasion of Privacy* 182–83.

59. See pages 40–41, 62–63.

60. See pages 5–7.

61. Family Assistance Act, *H.Rep.* 16,311, 91st Cong., 2d Sess. (1970), § 452.

62. See, e.g., *Public Law* 90–550 (1968); *Public Law* 90–575, § 504(a) (1968).

63. See, e.g., *H.* 815, 75th General Assembly of the State of Missouri; *H.* 92 (Minnesota Legislature, introduced Jan. 15, 1969); *H.* 1138, 1st Sess., 32d Legislature of the State of Oklahoma.

64. *Hearings on Data Processing Management* 24–25 (statement of Phillip S. Hughes, Deputy Director of the Bureau of the Budget).

65. *Task Force Report: Science and Technology* 74–75.

66. Of particular importance is the United States Supreme Court's decision in *Time, Inc.* v. *Hill,* 385 U.S. 374 (1967). The impact of Hill and related cases is discussed on pages 190–209.

67. 5 U.S.C. § 552 (Supp. III, 1965–1967). See generally Davis, "The Information Act: A Preliminary Analysis," 34 *University of Chicago Law Review* 761 (1967); Paul, "Access to Rules and Records of Federal Agencies: The Freedom of Information Act," 42 *Los Angeles Bar Bulletin* 459 (1967); Sky, "Agency Implementation of the Freedom of Information Act: What It Means to Tax Practitioners," 27 *Journal Taxation* 130 (1967); Note, "The Freedom of Information Act: Access to Law," 36 *Fordham Law Review* 765 (1968); Recent Statute, 80 *Harvard Law Review* 909 (1967); Note, "The Information Act: Judicial Enforcement of the Records Provision," 54 *Virginia Law Review* 466 (1968).

68. *General Services Administration* v. *Benson,* 415 F.2d 878 (9th Cir. 1969).

69. *Martin* v. *Neuschel,* 396 F.2d 759 (3d Cir. 1968).

70. *Epstein* v. *Resor,* 421 F.2d 930 (9th Cir. 1970).

71. The fundamental conflict between these two objectives is perhaps best illustrated by the following excerpt from the Statement of President Johnson on Signing Public Law 89–487 (the Freedom of Information Act) on July 4, 1966, reprinted in United States Department of Justice, *The Attorney General's Memorandum on the Public Information Section of the Administrative Procedure Act ii* (1967) [hereinafter *Attorney General's Memo*]:

A citizen must be able in confidence to complain to his Government and to provide information. . . .

Fairness to individuals also requires that information accumulated in personnel files be protected from disclosure. . . .

. . . .

I have always believed that freedom of information is so vital that only the national security, not the desire of public officials or private citizens, should determine when it must be restricted.

72. The Act "does not authorize withholding of information . . . except as specifically stated" in nine exceptions. 5 U.S.C. § 552(c) (Supp. III, 1965–67). See *Benson* v. *General Services Administration,* 289 F.Supp. 590 (W.D. Wash. 1968), affirmed, 415 F.2d 878 (9th Cir. 1969). See also § 552(a)(3) of the Act and *Epstein* v. *Resor,* 421 F.2d 930 (9th Cir. 1970).

73. 5 U.S.C. § 552(b) (Supp. III, 1965–1967).

74. Davis, supra note 67, at 798.

75. Ibid.

76. See *General Services Administration* v. *Benson,* 415 F.2d 878 (9th Cir. 1969); *Consumers Union of United States, Inc.* v. *Veterans Administration,* 301 F.Supp. 796 (S.D.N.Y. 1969).

77. 5 U.S.C. § 552(a)(3) (Supp. III, 1965–1967); see *Skolnick* v. *Parsons*, 397 F.2d 523 (7th Cir. 1968).

78. Davis, supra note 67, at 765–66.

79. *Attorney General's Memo* 28.

80. *Consumers Union of United States, Inc.* v. *Veterans Administration*, 301 F.Supp. 796 (S.D.N.Y. 1969).

81. Id. at 806.

82. *NLRB* v. *Clement Brothers Co.*, 407 F.2d 1027 (5th Cir. 1969). See also *Barceloneta Shoe Corp.* v. *Compton*, 271 F.Supp. 591 (D.P.R. 1967).

83. See *Attorney General's Memo* 28: "Following the statutory plan, the district court would presumably issue an order directed to the agency, which, under the language of the statute, is the only party defendant." The memorandum does not discuss the possibility that the party whose privacy was threatened by disclosure might be able to intervene in the action. The real problem, of course, is lack of notice to the party whose personal data are being sought.

84. Davis, supra note 67, at 807.

85. 5 U.S.C. § 552(b) (Supp. III, 1965–1967).

86. *Grumman Aircraft Engineering Corp.* v. *Renegotiation Board*, 425 F.2d 578 (D.C. Cir. 1970). See generally Davis, supra note 67, at 797–99.

87. 5 U.S.C. § 552(a)(2) (Supp. III, 1965–1967).

88. 5 U.S.C. § 552(b)(4) (Supp. III, 1965–1967).

89. *Attorney General's Memo* 32. See also Davis, supra note 67, at 802–03, in which the author contends that a literal construction of this provision leads to the conclusion that "[t]he Act is a nullity with respect to all commercial or financial information, and with respect to all non-commercial and non-financial information which is privileged or confidential" (emphasis removed).

90. *Senate Report No. 813, Clarifying and Protecting the Right of the Public to Information, and for Other Purposes*, 89th Cong., 1st Sess. 9 (1965): "[Exemption four] is necessary to protect the confidentiality of information which . . . would customarily not be released to the public by the person from whom it was obtained. . . . It would . . . include information customarily subject to the doctor-patient, lawyer-client, lender-borrower, and other such privileges." The *House Report* is substantially similar, and also states that the exemption includes "information which is given to an agency in confidence, since a citizen must be able to confide in his government. Moreover, where the Government

has obligated itself in good faith not to disclose documents or information which it receives, it should be able to honor such obligations." *H.Rep. Report No. 1497, Clarifying and Protecting the Right of the Public to Information,* 89th Cong., 2d Sess. 10 (1966). See also *General Services Administration* v. *Benson,* 415 F.2d 878 (9th Cir. 1969). At present, there are nearly 100 statutes regulating access to information held by the Government. *H.Rep. Report No. 1497,* supra, at 10. See also *Attorney General's Memo* 31–32.

91. 5 U.S.C. § 552(b)(3) (Supp. III, 1965–1967).

92.. In Note, "Freedom of Information: The Statute and the Regulations," 56 *Georgetown Law Journal* 18, 37 (1967), this possibility is described as "one of the greatest loopholes in the bill."

93. See, e.g., *Wall Street Journal,* March 27, 1970, at 1, col. 1.

94. See, e.g., *Bristol-Myers Co.* v. *FTC,* 424 F.2d 935 (D.C. Cir. 1970).

95. Compare Staff of the Subcommittee on Administrative Practice and Procedure of the Senate Committee on the Judiciary, 90th Cong., 2d Sess., *The Freedom of Information Act (Ten Months' Review)* (Committee Print, 1968).

96. See Note, "The 1966 [sic] Freedom of Information Act—Early Judicial Interpretations," 44 *Washington Law Review* 641 (1969).

97. This procedure was apparently contemplated by Congress. See *Attorney General's Memo* 28; *H.Rep. Report No. 1497, Clarifying and Protecting the Right of the Public to Information, and for Other Purposes,* 89th Cong., 1st Sess. 9 (1965). For an example of regulations governing such administrative appeals, see 15 *Code of Federal Regulations* § 60.11 (1968) (Census Bureau); 14 *Code of Federal Regulations* §§ 1206.800–.805 (1968) (National Aeronautics and Space Administration).

98. See *New York Times,* June 10, 1968, § 1, at 22, col. 4. See also *Wall Street Journal,* Oct. 23, 1968, at 1, col. 4.

99. Davis, supra note 67, at 803.

100. See, e.g., *Cooney* v. *Sun Shipbuilding & Drydock Co.,* 288 F.Supp. 708 (E.D. Pa. 1968); *Clement Brothers Co.* v. *NLRB,* 282 F.Supp. 540 (N.D. Ga. 1968); *Barceloneta Shoe Corp.* v. *Compton,* 271 F.Supp. 591 (D.P.R. 1967). See also *Talbott Construction Co.* v. *United States,* 49 F.R.D. 68 (E.D. Ky. 1969).

101. See, e.g., *Bristol-Myers Co.* v. *FTC,* 424 F.2d 935 (D.C. Cir. 1970); *Ackerly* v. *Ley,* 420 F.2d 1336 (D.C. Cir. 1969); *American Mail Line, Ltd.* v. *Gulik,* 411 F.2d 696 (D.C. Cir. 1969); *Tuchinsky* v. *Selective Service System,* 294 F.Supp. 803 (N.D. Ill. 1969), affirmed, 418 F.2d 155 (7th Cir. 1969); compare *Martin* v. *Neuschel,* 396 F.2d 759 (3d Cir. 1968).

102. See, e.g., *General Services Administration* v. *Benson,* 415 F.2d 878 (9th Cir. 1969).

103. 5 U.S.C. § 552(a)(3) (Supp. III, 1965–1967).

104. *Olmstead* v. *United States,* 277 U.S. 438 (1928).

105. 47 U.S.C. § 605 (1964).

106. See generally S. Dash, R. Schwartz & R. Knowlton, *The Eaves-droppers* (1959); L. Hall, Y. Kamisar, W. LaFave & J. Israel, *Modern Criminal Procedure* 334–402 (3d ed. 1969); A. Westin, *Privacy and Freedom* 69–89 (1967); Kamisar, "The Wiretapping-Eavesdropping Problem: A Professor's View," 44 *Minnesota Law Review* 891 (1960).

107. Compare *Silverman* v. *United States,* 365 U.S. 505 (1961), with *Goldman* v. *United States,* 316 U.S. 129 (1942).

108. See Mr. Justice Harlan's dissenting opinion in *Desist* v. *United States,* 394 U.S. 244 (1969).

109. 82 Stat. 197 (1968) [hereinafter *Act*].

110. For a discussion of the vast number of state and federal crimes that will support a grant of eavesdropping authority under title III, see Schwartz, "The Legitimation of Electronic Eavesdropping: The Politics of 'Law and Order'," 67 *Michigan Law Review* 455, 481–82 (1969). See also id. at 486–95.

111. *Senate Report No. 1097,* 90th Cong., 2d Sess. 182 (1968) [hereinafter *Senate Report No. 1097*]. See generally Theoharis & Meyer, "The 'National Security' Justification for Electronic Eavesdropping: An Elusive Exception," 14 *Wayne Law Review* 749 (1968).

112. See Schwartz, supra note 110, at 477–80. See also *Hearings on Senate Resolution 190 Before Subcommittee on Administrative Practices and Procedures of Senate Committee on the Judiciary,* 90th Cong., 1st Sess. (1967); *Task Force Report: Organized Crime, President's Commission on Law Enforcement and Administration of Justice* 92 (1967).

113. Dissenting opinion in *Olmstead* v. *United States,* 277 U.S. 438, 470 (1928).

114. See Schwartz, supra note 110, at 498–508. See also Spritzer, "Electronic Surveillance by Leave of the Magistrate: The Case in Opposition," 118 *University of Pennsylvania Law Review* 169 (1969); "Effect of the Electronic Age Upon Invasion of Privacy," *American Bar Association Section of Individual Rights and Responsibilities, Monograph No. 1,* at 25–41 (1967).

115. Approximately five per cent of the total communications channel mileage currently consists of data communications. *Sperry-Rand*

UNIVAC Response to the Inquiry of the FCC, H & I–2 (submitted in connection with *In re Regulatory and Policy Problems Presented by the Interdependence of Computer and Communications Facilities,* Docket No. 16,979). However, the annual volume of data communications is doubling every two years. *Comments of Microwave Communications, Inc.,* at 3 (March 5, 1968) (submitted in connection with *In re Regulatory and Policy Problems Presented by the Interdependence of Computer and Communications Services and Facilities,* FCC Docket No. 16,979). An official of the American Telephone and Telegraph Company has predicted that it will not be long until the volume of information carried by data communication will exceed that carried by voice transmissions. *UNIVAC Brief* at H & I–3 to H & I–5.

116. Act § 2510(4) (emphasis added).

117. 47 U.S.C. § 605 (1964). Section 605 was amended by sections 803 of the Crime Control Act.

118. E.g., *Rathbun* v. *United States,* 355 U.S. 107 (1957); *Goldstein* v. *United States,* 316 U.S. 114 (1942); *Nardone* v. *United States,* 308 U.S. 338 (1939); *Weiss* v. *United States,* 308 U.S. 321 (1939); *Nardone* v. *United States,* 302 U.S. 379 (1937).

119. *United States* v. *Dote,* 371 F.2d 176, 180 (7th Cir. 1966):

The dial telephone system does not generally require human intervention to connect two telephone's. The telephone company was not therefore the intended recipient of the signal. The "intended recipient" was the telephone of another subscriber. . . . Ultimately, the intended human recipient of the signal was the subscriber called.

Also of interest is the following passage from *Senate Report No.* 1097, at 90:

Other forms of surveillance are not within the proposed legislation. . . . An examination of telephone company records by law enforcement agents . . . would be lawful because it would not be an "interception." (United States v. Russo, 250 F.Supp. 55 (E.D. Pa. 1966)). The proposed legislation is not designed to prevent tracing of phone calls. The use of a "pen register," for example, would be permissible. But see United States v. Dote, 371 F.2d 176 (7th 1966). The proposed legislation is intended to protect the privacy of the communication itself and not the means of communication.

See also *Goldstein* v. *United States,* 316 U.S. 114 (1942).

120. The conflict between state and federal wiretapping laws has long been a difficult problem for the courts. See, e.g., *Lee* v. *Florida,* 392 U.S. 378 (1968); *Pugach* v. *Dollinger,* 277 F.2d 739 (2d Cir. 1960),

affirmed per curiam, 365 U.S. 458 (1961); Recent Development, "Inadmissibility of Wiretap Evidence in State Courts," 1968 *Duke Law Journal* 1008. See generally *Berger* v. *New York*, 388 U.S. 41, 45–49 (1967).

121. See generally *Katz* v. *United States*, 389 U.S. 347 (1967); *Berger* v. *New York*, 388 U.S. 41 (1967); Schwartz, supra note 110.

122. Act § 251(2)(c). Section 2511(a)(d) sharply limits the availability of the consent exception when the eavesdropping is done by a private person.

123. See generally Schwartz, supra note 110, at 495–96.

124. Act § 2510(5)(a)(i).

125. The telephone companies' ability to control "foreign attachments"—the linking of customer-supplied equipment to the national telephone network—is a subject of heated controversy. A series of recent decisions has sharply limited the carriers' monopoly over transmitting devices. See *In re American Tel. & Tel. Co.*, 15 F.C.C.2d 605 (1968) ("Foreign Attachment" tariff revisions in AT&T Tariff, FCC Nos. 259, 260, 263); *In re Use of Carterfone Device in Message Toll Telephone Service*, 13 F.C.C.2d 420 (1968). However, whatever the ultimate resolution of the legal issues, it seems clear that the communications carriers will still supply a substantial number of the devices used in data transmissions.

126. One example of an essential carrier-supplied communications device that may be vulnerable to eavesdropping is a modem (modulation/demodulation), which is a mechanism that is generally required to convert data signals into a format that is suitable for transmission.

127. Act § 2518(10).

128. Act § 2510(11).

129. *Senate Report No. 1097*, at 91, 163, 173.

130. Act § 2520.

131. See Schwartz, supra note 110, at 484–86.

132. See, e.g., pages 63–64, 83, 149.

133. See *On Lee* v. *United States*, 343 U.S. 747, 755 (1952); Pitler, "The Fruit of the Poisonous Tree Revisited and Shepardized," 58 *California Law Review* 579, 586–88 (1968).

134. In *Alderman* v. *United States*, 394 U.S. 165 (1969), the Supreme Court held that under the Fourth Amendment a party who was merely the subject of an illegally seized conversation does not have standing to suppress evidence taken from the illegal interception.

135. *Senate Report No. 1097*, at 91, merely states that the language "is intended to reflect existing law" and cites several cases.

136. 362 U.S. 257 (1960). The legislative history also cites the lower court decision in *Mancusi* v. *De Forte*, 392 U.S. 364 (1968), which the Supreme Court had not decided when the Senate Report was written. In Mancusi, the Supreme Court held that since the papers seized at the petitioner's office were the property of his employer, his claim of standing to suppress the fruits of the search would have to be based on the language of the Fourth Amendment proclaiming the "right of the people to be secure in their . . . houses." 392 U.S. at 367. The Court then cited the Jones decision and concluded that the "capacity to claim the protection of the Amendment depends not upon a property right in the invaded place but upon whether the area was one in which there was a reasonable expectation of freedom from governmental intrusion." 392 U.S. at 368.

137. 362 U.S. at 261.

138. 394 U.S. 165, 208–09 (1969).

139. 394 U.S. at 176–77.

140. 394 U.S. at 175–76 n. 9.

141. Act § 2518(5).

142. See *New York Times,* June 5, 1969, at 27, col. 1. See also Navasky, "The Government and Martin Luther King," *The Atlantic,* Nov. 1970, at 43; Spritzer, supra note 114, at 190–91.

143. See Smith, "The Mob," *Life,* Sept. 8, 1967, at 91.

144. See page 65.

145. Conceivably, a tap on a trunk line connecting a primary and a back-up central unit of a computer system could result in interception of the entire store of data in the system.

146. See A. Westin, *Privacy and Freedom* 125 (1967); Schwartz, supra note 110, at 466–68.

147. Act § 2518(5). Wiretaps over long periods of time have been common. See Schwartz, supra note 110, at 461–63.

148. For a discussion of the weaknesses in the judicial supervision provided by the Act, see Schwartz, supra note 110, at 483–86.

Chapter v : The Law Relating to Privacy—A Thing of Threads and Patches

1. Kalven, "Privacy in Tort Law—Were Warren and Brandeis Wrong?," 31 *Law and Contemporary Problems* 326, 327 (1966).

2. 4 *Harvard Law Review* 193 (1890).

3. See Prosser, "Privacy," 48 *California Law Review* 383, 383–86 (1960).

4. Warren & Brandeis, "The Right to Privacy," 4 *Harvard Law Review* 193, 196 (1890).

5. *Prince Albert* v. *Strange,* 2 De G. & Sm. 652, 64 Eng. Rep. 293 (V.C. 1849).

6. See Bloustein, "Privacy As an Aspect of Human Dignity: An Answer to Dean Prosser," 39 *New York University Law Review* 962 (1964), for an analysis of the Warren-Brandeis thesis.

7. *Roberson* v. *Rochester Folding Box Co.,* 171 N.Y. 538, 64 N.E. 442 (1902). Earlier cases testing the proposed right to privacy include: *Manola* v. *Stevens,* N.Y.Sup.Ct. 1890, reported in *New York Times,* June 15, 18, 21, 1890; *MacKenzie* v. *Soden Mineral Springs Co.,* 27 Abb.N.C. 402, 18 N.Y.S. 240 (1891); *Marks* v. *Jaffa,* 6 Misc. 290, 26 N.Y.S. 908 (1893); *Schuyler* v. *Curtis,* 147 N.Y. 434, 42 N.E. 22 (1895); *Corliss* v. *E. W. Walker Co.,* 64 F. 280 (D.Mass. 1894); *Atkinson* v. *John E. Doherty & Co.,* 121 Mich. 372, 80 N.W. 285 (1899).

8. N.Y.Sess. Laws 1903, ch. 132, §§ 1–2. Now, as amended in 1921, N.Y. Civil Rights Law §§ 50–51.

9. *Pavesich* v. *New England Life Ins. Co.,* 122 Ga. 190, 50 S.E. 68 (1905).

10. See Prosser, supra note 3.

11. *Ettore* v. *Philco Television Broadcasting Corp.,* 229 F.2d 481, 485 (3d Cir. 1956).

12. Prosser, supra note 3.

13. See Bloustein, supra note 6, in which the author argues that there is in reality a single tort for invasion of privacy rather than four categories or separate torts. See also Kalven, supra note 1.

14. See *Restatement (Second) Torts* § 652A (Tent. Draft No. 13, 1967). See also W. Prosser, *Torts* § 112, at 833–44 (3d ed. 1964).

15. *Pavesich* v. *New England Life Ins. Co.,* 122 Ga. 190, 50 S.E. 68 (1905).

16. *Eick* v. *Perk Dog Food Co.,* 347 Ill.App. 293, 106 N.E.2d 742 (1952).

17. *Hinish* v. *Meier & Frank Co.,* 166 Or. 482, 113 P.2d 438 (1941).

18. *De May* v. *Roberts,* 46 Mich. 160, 9 N.W. 146 (1881).

19. *Hamberger* v. *Eastman,* 106 N.H. 107, 206 A.2d 239, 11 A.L.R. 3d 1288 (1964).

20. *Pearson* v. *Dodd,* 410 F.2d 701 (D.C. Cir. 1969), certiorari denied, 395 U.S. 947 (1969).

21. Id. at 704.

22. See *Katz* v. *United States,* 389 U.S. 347 (1967), in which the Supreme Court applied the "expectancy" approach to electronic eavesdropping.

23. 25 N.Y.2d 560, 307 N.Y.S.2d 647, 255 N.E.2d 765 (1970).

24. In Dean Bloustein's view, the mass publication requirement is based on the premise that "[u]nless there is a breach of a confidential relationship . . . the indignity and outrage involved in disclosure of details of a private life, only arise when there is a massive disclosure. . . ." In short, "[t]he damage is to an individual's self-respect in being made a public spectacle." Bloustein, supra note 6, at 981.

25. *Brents* v. *Morgan,* 221 Ky. 765, 299 S.W. 967, 55 A.L.R. 964 (1927).

26. *Biederman's of Springfield, Inc.* v. *Wright,* 322 S.W.2d 892 (Mo. 1959).

27. Bloustein, supra note 6, at 980. In this situation, the author concludes, the wrong "is not the disclosure itself, but rather the disclosure in violation of a relationship of confidence. Disclosure, whether to one person or many, is equally wrongful as a breach of the condition under which the information was initially disclosed." Prosser, supra note 3, at 393, is in substantial accord.

28. Implying the duty would have the desirable effect of removing a latent anomaly in the confidential-relationship theory. The anomaly arises from the fact that the confidentiality of a relationship depends upon the reasonable expectations of the party asserting an invasion of privacy; thus, an organization that is powerful enough *vis-à-vis* the individual to coerce or entice information from him while giving him notice of the fact that it will not keep the information in confidence could drastically reduce the scope of personal privacy. Josephson, "Book Review," 15 *University of California at Los Angeles Law Review* 1586, 1597–99 (1968).

Apparently the English courts have been more alert than their American counterparts to the unique dangers of handling personal information, and more willing to imply a confidential relationship. See, e.g., Jacob & Jacob, "Confidential Communications," *The New Law Journal,* Feb. 6, 1969, at 133.

29. Batt, "Law and the Bedroom," *Saturday Review,* Aug. 3, 1968, at 45. See also Rider, "Legal Protection of the Manifestations of Individual Personality—The Identity-Indicia," 33 *Southern California Law Review* 31 (1959).

30. See pages 90–105 for a discussion of psychological testing in the computer age.

31. Warren & Brandeis, supra note 4, at 215–16.

32. Warren & Brandeis, supra note 4, at 214–19. See pages 185–87 for a discussion of the application of the consent defense to the computer area.

33. W. Prosser, *Torts* § 110, at 809 (3d ed. 1964). See also Note, "Credit Investigations and the Right to Privacy," 57 *Georgetown Law Journal* 509, 513–19 (1969); *Watwood* v. *Stone's Mercantile Agency, Inc.,* 194 F.2d 160, 161 (D.C.Cir.), certiorari denied, 344 U.S. 821 (1952).

34. *House Hearings on Commercial Credit Bureaus* 147; William J. Mangan, General Manager of Credit Bureau of Greater Boston, Inc., Statement Before a Public Study Session on the Procedures and Practices of Credit Bureaus, Consumers' Council, Boston, Mass., Oct. 15, 1968, at 5 (unpublished mimeo).

35. See, e.g., *House Hearings on Commercial Credit Bureaus* 93 (statement of H. C. Jordan, President of Credit Data Corporation).

36. *Brents* v. *Morgan,* 221 Ky. 765, 299 S.W. 967, 55 A.L.R. 964 (1927); *Biederman's of Springfield, Inc.* v. *Wright,* 322 S.W.2d 892 (Mo. 1959).

37. *Banks* v. *King Features Syndicate,* 30 F.Supp. 352 (S.D.N.Y. 1939).

38. *Melvin* v. *Reid,* 112 Cal.App. 285, 297 Pac. 91 (1931).

39. *Sidis* v. *F–R Publishing Corp.,* 113 F.2d 806 (2d Cir. 1940).

40. Id. at 807.

41. Id. at 809.

42. *Restatement (Second) Torts* § 652D, comment b (Tent. Draft No. 13, 1967). See also W. Prosser, *Torts* § 109 (3d ed., 1964); Bloustein, supra note 6, at 979–80.

43. See the discussion of *Time, Inc.* v. *Hill,* 385 U.S. 374 (1967), on pages 190–99.

44. See pages 185–87 for a discussion of the defenses of consent and waiver.

45. The fact that the two theories have overlapped significantly in practice is discussed in Wade, "Defamation and the Right of Privacy," 15 *Vanderbilt Law Review* 1093 (1962). See also *Hazlitt* v. *Fawcett Publications, Inc.,* 116 F.Supp. 538 (D. Conn. 1953); *Spahn* v. *Julian Messner, Inc.,* 23 App.Div.2d 216, 260 N.Y.S.2d 451 (1965), vacated and remanded, 387 U.S. 239, original decision adhered to, 21 N.Y.2d 124, 233 N.E.2d 840, 286 N.Y.S.2d 832 (1967); Kalven, supra note 1, at 339–41; Prosser, supra note 3, at 398–401, 422–23. But compare Nimmer, "The Right To Speak from Times to Time: First Amendment Theory Applied to Libel and Misapplied to Privacy," 56 *California Law Review* 935, 958 (1968):

Defamation protects a man's interest in his reputation. Reputation is by definition a matter of public knowledge. . . . The right of privacy protects not reputation, but the interest in maintaining the privacy of certain facts. Public disclosure of such facts can create injury regardless of whether such disclosure affects the subject's reputation.

46. *Martin* v. *Johnson Publishing Co.,* 157 N.Y.S.2d 409 (1956).

47. See Wade, supra note 45, for a discussion of the advantages of suing in privacy rather than in defamation.

48. See Kalven, supra note 1, at 339–41.

49. See Warren & Brandeis, supra note 4, at 216–17.

50. Warren & Brandeis, supra note 4, at 218. See also *Reitmeister* v. *Reitmeister,* 162 F.2d 691 (2d Cir. 1947); *Jenkins* v. *Dell Publishing Co.,* 143 F.Supp. 952 (W.D. Pa. 1956), affirmed, 251 F.2d 447 (3d Cir. 1958).

51. *Metter* v. *Los Angeles Examiner,* 35 Cal.App.2d 304, 95 P.2d 491 (1939).

52. *Gill* v. *Hearst Publishing Co.,* 40 Cal.2d 224, 253 P.2d 441 (1953).

53. Compare *Lopez* v. *United States,* 373 U.S. 427, 452 (Justice Brennan, dissenting):

[The suggestion that the right of privacy is lost by the auditor's consent to the electronic transcription of the speaker's words] invokes a fictive sense of waiver wholly incompatible with any meaningful concept of liberty of communication. If a person must always be on his guard against his auditor's having authorized a secret recording of their conversation, he will be no less reluctant to speak freely than if his risk is that a third party is doing the recording. . . . In a free society, people ought not to have to watch their every word so carefully.

See also *Osborn* v. *United States,* 385 U.S. 323, 347 (1966) (Justice Douglas, dissenting); Greenawalt, "The Consent Problem in Wiretapping and Eavesdropping," 68 *Columbia Law Review* 189 (1968).

54. See, e.g., *Miranda* v. *Arizona,* 384 U.S. 436, 468 n. 37 (1966) [quoting P. Devlin, *The Criminal Prosecution in England* 32 (1958)]: "[T]here is still a general belief that you must answer all questions put to you by a policeman, or at least that it will be the worse for you if you do not."

55. See generally Handler & Rosenheim, "Privacy in Welfare: Public Assistance and Juvenile Justice," 31 *Law and Contemporary Problems* 377 (1966). See also *Privacy and Behavioral Research* 18:

Free consent may be compromised by the subject's external circumstances. . . . The gravest invasions of privacy are likely to occur among the weakest and most helpless segments of the population—children, the very poor, the very sick, those who do not speak the language, and minority groups.

56. See, e.g., *Senate Report No. 534* (to accompany S. 1035), 90th Cong., 1st Sess. 5 (1967). See also Creech, "The Privacy of Government Employees," 31 *Law and Contemporary Problems* 413 (1966).

57. *Privacy and Behavioral Research* 4, 18.

58. *The Federal Paperwork Jungle* 36.

59. *House Hearings on Commercial Credit Bureaus* 28. See also the discussion at pages 88–89 of the ACB Guidelines.

60. Compare *Privacy and Behavioral Research* 4.

61. *Ellsworth* v. *Martindale-Hubbell Law Directory, Inc.*, 69 N.D. 610, 289 N.W. 101 (1939).

62. Id. at 622, 289 N.W. at 105.

63. See W. Prosser, *Torts* § 125 (3d ed. 1964).

64. 28 U.S.C. §§ 1346, 1402, 1504, 2110, 2401, 2402, 2411, 2412, 2671–2680.

65. See pages 199–205 for a discussion of constitutional safeguards for privacy.

66. 385 U.S. 374 (1967).

67. See pages 171–72.

68. 385 U.S. at 388.

69. *Ibid.*

70. 326 U.S. 254 (1964). See generally W. Lockhart, Y. Kamisar & J. Choper, *Constitutional Law: Cases-Comments-Questions*, Ch. 12, § 7 (3d ed. 1970).

71. Nimmer, supra note 45, at 958. See also *Time, Inc.* v. *Hill*, 385 U.S. 374, 411 (1967) (Justice Fortas, dissenting); Kalven, "The Reasonable Man and the First Amendment: Hill, Butts, and Walker," *1967 Supreme Court Review* 267, 284: "The logic of New York Times and Hill taken together grants the press some measure of constitutional protection for anything the press thinks is a matter of public interest."

72. N.Y. Civil Rights Law §§ 50–51.

73. See pages 183–85 for a discussion of the false light privacy action.

74. 385 U.S. at 383 n. 7.

75. Warren & Brandeis, supra note 4, at 214–19.

76. One commentator has argued that defamatory or reputation injuring statements are of inherently greater public interest than privacy invading statements. Nimmer, supra note 45. In *Grove* v. *Dun & Bradstreet, Inc.*, 308 F.Supp. 1068 (D.C. Pa. 1970), constitutional protection was given to the publication of a credit report that had been circulated to a limited number of subscribers who had requested it. The court's opinion betrays a total unawareness of the consequences.

77. See pages 199–205 for a discussion of constitutional safeguards for privacy.

78. See pages 40–41, 46–53 for a discussion of some of the many psychological and political aspects of a loss of privacy.

79. 385 U.S. at 387–91.

80. See, e.g., Bloustein, supra note 6; Brennan, "The Supreme Court and the Meiklejohn Interpretation of the First Amendment," 79 *Harvard Law Review* 1 (1965); Comment, "Privacy, Defamation, and the First Amendment: The Implications of *Time, Inc.* v. *Hill*," 67 *Columbia Law Review* 926 (1967).

81. *Valentine* v. *Christensen*, 316 U.S. 52 (1942).

82. Sarnoff, "No Life Untouched," *Saturday Review*, July 23, 1966, at 21. See also *The National Observer*, Oct. 17, 1966, at 1.

83. Russel, "Playing for Fun," *Playboy*, April, 1969, at 110, 174; Brown, "Tomorrow's Many-Splendored Tune-In," *Saturday Evening Post*, Nov. 30, 1968, at 38, 78.

84. In *Time, Inc.* v. *Hill*, Justice Harlan advocated using the concept of a "marketplace of ideas" or "independent [public] interest" in the subject of the publication as a test for the operation of First Amendment privileges, 385 U.S. at 407–08. But compare Kalven, "The Reasonable Man and the First Amendment: Hill, Butts, and Walker," *1967 Supreme Court Review* 267, 300:

> For centuries it has been the experience of Anglo-American law that the truth never catches up with the lie, and it is because it does not that there has been a law of defamation. I simply do not see how the constitutional protection in this area can be rested on the assurance that counterargument will take the sting out of the falsehoods that the law is thereby permitting. And if this premise is not persuasive, the whole Harlan edifice trembles.

85. Kalven, supra note 84, at 283–84. But compare Bloustein, "Privacy, Tort Law, and the Constitution: Is Warren and Brandeis' Tort Petty and Unconstitutional As Well?," 46 *Texas Law Review* 611, 625–26 (1968).

86. See *Pearson* v. *Dodd,* 410 F.2d 701 (D.C. Cir. 1969), certiorari denied, 395 U.S. 947 (1969).

87. 376 U.S. 254 (1964).

88. See *Rosenblatt* v. *Baer,* 383 U.S. 75, 85 (1966).

89. Id. at 89 (Justice Douglas).

90. *Barr* v. *Matteo,* 360 U.S. 564 (1959).

91. 385 U.S. at 385 n. 9. See also the concurring and dissenting opinion of Justice Harlan at 404: "No claim is made that there was any intrusion upon the Hills' solitude or private affairs in order to obtain information for publication. The power of the State to control and remedy such intrusion for newsgathering purposes cannot be denied. . . ."

92. *Dietemann* v. *Time, Inc.,* 284 F.Supp. 925 (C.D. Cal. 1968).

93. *Hearings on Government Statistical Programs* 28 (statement of Professor Richard Ruggles).

94. See pages 20–23.

95. In *Pearson* v. *Dodd,* 410 F.2d 701 (D.C.Cir. 1969), certiorari denied, 395 U.S. 947 (1969), it was held that newspaper reporters who had published information they knew had been obtained by an unauthorized intrusion into the plaintiff's files were not guilty of invasion of privacy. The court reasoned that the intrusion and the publication aspects of the tort "should be kept clearly separate." Id. at 705. Applying this analysis, the court concluded that the publication was within the ambit of the First Amendment privilege and, since the reporters had not been parties to the intrusion, they were not held liable in tort:

> If we were to hold appellants liable for invasion of privacy on these facts, we would establish the proposition that one who receives information from an intruder, knowing it has been obtained by improper intrusion, is guilty of a tort. In an untried and developing area of tort law, we are not prepared to go so far.

Id. at 705. Since the plaintiff's employees who had originally intruded into his files were not parties to the action, the court did not reach the question of whether they would be able to assert the newspaper's First Amendment privilege. Apparently the reporters did not advance this argument, but rather contended that the employees' disclosure was privileged because of a public policy in favor of exposing wrongdoing. Id. at 705 n. 19.

96. *NAACP* v. *Alabama,* 357 U.S. 449, 462 (1958).

97. Id. at 460.

98. *Gibson* v. *Florida Legislative Investigation Committee,* 372 U.S. 539, 546 (1963). See also *District 12, UAW* v. *Illinois State Bar Ass'n,* 389 U.S. 217 (1967).

99. *NAACP* v. *Alabama,* 357 U.S. 449 (1958). See also *Bates* v. *City of Little Rock,* 361 U.S. 516 (1960). The principle has been applied whether the organization is forced to reveal the names of its members, as in *NAACP* v. *Alabama,* or the individual is compelled to reveal all organizations of which he has been a member, as in *Shelton* v. *Tucker,* 364 U.S. 479 (1960).

100. *Anderson* v. *Sills,* 106 N.J.Super. 545, 256 A.2d 298 (1969). See also Askin, "Police Dossiers and Emerging Principles of First Amendment Adjudication," 22 *Stanford Law Review* 196 (1970).

101. Id. at 562–66, 256 A.2d at 310–13.

102. Id. at 558, 256 A.2d at 305.

103. See pages 40–41, 62–63, for discussion of the Army's data bank.

104. *Anderson* v. *Sills,* 56 N.J. 210, 265 A.2d 678 (1970). A strikingly more sympathetic judicial attitude is expressed in *Menard* v. *Mitchell,* 430 F.2d 486 (D.C. Cir. 1970), which involved a request to expunge an FBI file.

105. See pages 41–42, 44–45 for a description of governmental mail cover operations and airline reservation surveillance.

106. 390 U.S. 17 (1968).

107. Id. at 20 n. 2.

108. Id. at 21.

109. Id. at 25. See also *Stanley* v. *Georgia,* 394 U.S. 557 (1969).

110. See *United States* v. *Robel,* 389 U.S. 258 (1967); *Keyeshian* v. *Board of Regents of University of State of New York,* 385 U.S. 589 (1967); *Shelton* v. *Tucker,* 364 U.S. 479 (1960); *Schware* v. *Board of Bar Eaminers of State of New Mexico,* 353 U.S. 232 (1957); *Law Students Civil Rights Research Council, Inc.* v. *Wadmond,* 299 F.Supp. 117 (S.D.N.Y. 1969).

111. *Wolf* v. *Colorado,* 338 U.S. 25, 27–28 (1949).

112. *Olmstead* v. *United States,* 277 U.S. 438, 478 (1928). See *Berger* v. *New York,* 388 U.S. 41 (1967), for a more recent expression of the protection afforded to privacy by the Fourth Amendment.

113. See, e.g., *Katz* v. *United States,* 389 U.S. 347, 353 (1967) ("[W]e have expressly held that the Fourth Amendment governs not only the seizure of tangible items, but extends as well to the recording of oral statements overhead without any 'technical trespass under . . . local property law.' "); *Berger* v. *New York,* 388 U.S. 41 (1967). See also

Warden v. *Hayden,* 387 U.S. 294, 304 (1967); Schwartz, "The Legitimation of Electronic Eavesdropping: The Politics of 'Law and Order,'" 67 *Michigan Law Review* 455, 475–76 (1969) ("Privacy is invaded at the point when the information in [testimonial communications like conversations and letters] is obtained by one not entitled to it, and this can easily be by aural or visual perception. . . . Where privacy is invaded by seeing or listening, the search and seizure are identical and simultaneous. . . ."); Note, "From Private Places to Personal Privacy: A Post-Katz Study of Fourth Amendment Protection," 43 *New York University Law Review* 968, 974 (1968) ("The essence of a search is the gathering of nonpublic information; this is as effectively accomplished by the reception of visual stimuli as by actual, physical penetration. . . ."). But see the strong dissents of Justice Black in Katz, 389 U.S. at 364–74, and Berger, 388 U.S. at 78–81, concluding that the Fourth Amendment applies only to tangible property.

114. *Katz* v. *United States,* 389 U.S. 347, 350 n. 5 (1967).

115. *Griswold* v. *Connecticut,* 381 U.S. 479 (1965).

116. Id. at 484.

117. 390 U.S. at 25.

118. See, e.g., *United States* v. *Kalish,* 271 F.Supp. 968, 970 (D.P.R. 1967). See also *McGovern* v. *Van Riper,* 137 N.J. Eq. 24, 43 A.2d 514 (1945).

119. Compare *Aptheker* v. *Secretary of State,* 387 U.S. 500 (1964); *Edwards* v. *California,* 314 U.S. 160 (1941).

120. See generally J. Cohen, *The Criminal Process in the People's Republic of China, 1949–1963,* at 19–20, 106–08 (1968).

121. See Josephson, supra note 28, at 1596. In recent eavesdropping cases the Supreme Court seems to have recognized the special threat of technology and has enunciated expansive general principles to protect a person's legitimate expectations concerning his privacy. See *Katz* v. *United States,* 389 U.S. 347, 352 (1967), a case involving a police wiretap on a public telephone. See also Note, supra note 113, at 968, 981.

122. Bloustein, supra note 6, at 984. See also Ludwig, "Peace of Mind in 48 Pieces vs. Uniform Rights of Privacy," 32 *Minnesota Law Review* 734, 748–50 (1948), in which the author argues that the scope of privilege recognized in actions for invasion of privacy has varied according to the characteristics of the medium of publication.

123. See Karst, "'The Files': Legal Controls over the Accuracy and Accessibility of Stored Personal Data," 31 *Law and Contemporary Problems* 342, 350 (1966). See also Silver, "Privacy and the First Amendment," 34 *Fordham Law Review* 553, 566 (1966).

124. See, e.g., *Osborn* v. *United States,* 385 U.S. 323, 343 (1966) (Justice Douglas dissenting).

125. Josephson, supra note 28, at 1599.

126. See generally *Hearings on 1970 Census Questions; House Hearings on the Computer and Invasion of Privacy; Senate Hearings on Computer Privacy; House Hearings on Commercial Credit Bureaus; Senate Hearings on Credit Bureaus; Hearings on Retail Credit Company.*

127. *Pearson* v. *Dodd,* 410 F.2d 701 (D.C.Cir.), certiorari denied, 395 U.S. 947 (1969).

128. *Nader* v. *General Motors Corp.,* 25 N.Y.2d 560, 307, N.Y.S.2d 647, 255 N.E.2d 765 (1970).

129. The British are considering passing legislation that would create a tort action for invasion of privacy. See *A Report by Justice: Privacy and the Law* (Joint Chairmen of Committee—Mark Littman and Peter Carter-Ruck), and the proposed Right of Privacy Act 1970.

130. 385 U.S. 374, 411–12 (1967).

131. *Commonwealth* v. *Wiseman,* 249 N.E.2d 610 (Mass. 1969).

132. Id. at 618–19.

Chapter v i : The Quest for a New Legal Framework

1. A. Westin, *Privacy and Freedom* 324–25 (1967).

2. Shils, "Privacy and Power," reprinted in *Senate Hearings on Computer Privacy* 321, 347.

3. See *Katz* v. *United States,* 389 U.S. 347 (1967); *Berger* v. *New York* 388 U.S. 41 (1967). But compare *Alderman* v. *United States,* 394 U.S. 165, 194 (1969) (Justice Harlan, concurring and dissenting): "[T]he right to conversational privacy is a personal right, not a property right."

4. See, e.g., *Zimmermann* v. *Wilson,* 81 F.2d 847, 848 (3d Cir. 1936). See also *Brex* v. *Smith,* 146 A. 34, 36 (N.J. Ch. 1929): "There is an implied obligation . . . on the bank, to keep [records of deposits and withdrawals] from scrutiny until compelled by a court of competent jurisdiction to do otherwise. The information contained in the records is certainly a property right."

5. See generally *Haelen Laboratories, Inc.* v. *Topps Chewing Gum, Inc.,* 202 F.2d 866 (2d Cir.), certiorari denied, 346 U.S. 816 (1953); Nimmer, "The Right of Publicity," 19 *Law and Contemporary Problems* 203 (1954). But compare *Miller* v. *Commissioner,* 299 F.2d 706 (2d Cir. 1962), which demonstrates the range of potential absurdities that could result from treating personal information as property.

6. Warren & Brandeis, "The Right to Privacy," 4 *Harvard Law Review* 193, 200–01 (1890). See pages 170–72.

7. See pages 175–76.

8. *Pearson* v. *Dodd,* 410 F.2d 701 (D.C. Cir.), certiorari denied, 395 U.S. 947 (1969).

9. See, e.g., *Ettore* v. *Philco Television Broadcasting Corp.,* 229 F.2d 481, 484–85, 493–95 (3d Cir.), certiorari denied, 351 U.S. 926 (1956); Ludwig, "Peace of Mind in 48 Pieces vs. Uniform Right of Privacy," 32 *Minnesota Law Review* 734, 759–62 (1948); Comment, "Copyright Preemption and Character Values: The Paladin Case as an Extension of Sears and Compco," 66 *Michigan Law Review* 1018, 1029–31 (1968).

10. See, e.g., *S.* 543, 91st Cong., 1st Sess. § 301(a) (1969).

11. "Developments in the Law—Competitive Torts," 77 *Harvard Law Review* 888, 932 (1964).

12. 248 U.S. 215 (1918).

13. Id. at 236. See also the dissenting opinion of Justice Brandeis. Id. at 250.

14. See "Developments in the Law—Competitive Torts," *supra* note 11, at 946. The continued viability of the misappropriation tort in the context of commercial values that border on the copyright or patent domain is open to serious question in light of the Supreme Court's decisions in *Sears, Roebuck & Co.* v. *Stiffel Co.,* 376 U.S. 225 (1964) and *Compco Corp.* v. *Day-Brite Lighting, Inc.,* 376 U.S. 234 (1964). This should not affect the problem under discussion, however.

15. See Westin, "Civil Liberties and Computerized Data Systems," in *Computers, Communications and the Public Interest* (1971).

16. *Senate Hearings on Computer Privacy, part* 2, at 310–11. For the full text of the agreement, see id. at 312–17. See generally Brooks, "The Role of the Data Bank in UPO" (May 25, 1967) (mimeo).

17. See, e.g., 1 G. G. Bogert & G. T. Bogert, *The Law of Trusts and Trustees* § 111, at 562–63 (2d ed. 1965); 1 A. Scott, *The Law of Trusts* §§ 74–77 (3d ed. 1967).

18. The trust provision by which the United Planning Organization, the donor-recipient, reserves the power to seek judicial enforcement of the terms of the agreement is set out in *Senate Hearings on Computer Privacy, part* 2, at 315.

19. *S.* 1791, 91st Cong., 1st Sess. (1969). Congressman Betts has introduced a comparable bill in the House. *H.Rep.* 10,566, 91st Cong., 1st Sess. (1969).

20. See page 135.

21. See pages 130–31.

22. See page 22.

23. See pages 161–68.

24. See pages 152–61.

25. See, e.g., *H.Rep.* 7214, 91st Cong., 1st Sess. (1969); *H.Rep.* 889, 91st Cong., 1st Sess. (1969); *H.Rep.* 20, 91st Cong., 1st Sess. (1969); *H.Rep.* 15,627, 90th Cong., 2d Sess. (1968); *S.* 1035, 90th Cong., 1st Sess. (1967).

26. See, e.g., *H.Rep.* 20, 91st Cong., 1st Sess. (1969).

27. See pages 85–88, 158–59. State legislation has been rendered largely superfluous by the enactment of the Fair Credit Reporting Act.

28. *S.* 782, 91st Cong., 1st Sess. (1969). An earlier version appeared as *S.* 1035, 90th Cong., 1st Sess. (1967). See also *Senate Report No.* 534, 90th Cong., 1st Sess. (1967).

29. *H.Rep.* 7214, 91st Cong., 1st Sess. (1969).

30. Id. § 552(a)(5).

31. *An Act to Provide for Data Surveillance*, Bill 182, 28th Ontario Legislature, 2d Session (1968–69).

32. *The Personal Records (Computers) Bill*, House of Lords (1969).

33. See B. Ladd, *Crisis in Credibility* 221–27 (1968).

34. See generally *House Hearings on the Computer and Invasion of Privacy; Senate Hearings on Computer Privacy; Senate Hearings on Computer Privacy, part 2.*

35. See generally *Hearings on Constitutional and Administrative Problems of Enforcing Internal Revenue Statutes Before the Subcommittee on Administrative Practice and Procedure of the Senate Committee on the Judiciary*, 90th Cong., 2d Sess. (1968); *Hearings on Government Agencies.*

36. See Ruggles, "On the Needs and Values of Data Banks," in "Symposium—Computers, Data Banks, and Individual Privacy," 53 *Minnesota Law Review* 211, 218–19 (1963). See also pages 135–36.

37. See page 62.

38. "Federal Communications Commission Notice of Inquiry," Docket No. 16,979, reprinted in *Senate Hearings on Computer Privacy* 87.

39. See generally *Hearings on Government Agencies, part 5*, at 2364–75, 2380–86, *part 6.*

40. Semling, "The Computer-Communications Inquiry," *Modern Data Systems*, July 1968, at 48–52.

41. See *Wall Street Journal*, April 10, 1970, at 6, col. 4.

42. Note, "Privacy and Efficient Government: Proposals for a National Data Center," 82 *Harvard Law Review* 400, 404 (1968). See also *Senate Hearings on Computer Privacy* 79–80 (statement of the author); Ruggles, supra note 36, at 219; Zwick, "A National Data Center," in *American Bar Association Section of Individual Rights and Responsibilities, Monograph No. 1,* at 33 (1967).

43. Congressman Gallagher has introduced a Resolution calling for the establishment of a Select Committee on Technology, Human Values and Democratic Institutions, which could serve this function.

44. 82 Stat. 197 (1968). Variations on this general theme can be found in *Senate Hearings on Computer Privacy* 41–42; *House Hearings on Commercial Credit Bureaus* 49; *Privacy and the National Data Bank Concept* 8–9. See also the proposal for a commission to study copyright and the new technologies, in title II of S. 543, 91st Cong., 1st Sess. (1969).

45. *H.Rep.* 6698, 90th Cong., 1st Sess. (1967).

46. See, e.g., Daddario, "Technology Assessment—A Legislative View," 36 *George Washington Law Review* 44 (1970).

47. *Wall Street Journal,* April 18, 1969, at 1, col. 3.

48. *Hearings on S. 1195 Before the Subcommittee on Administrative Practice and Procedure of the State Committee on the Judiciary,* 90th Cong., 2d Sess. 22 (1968). See generally American Assembly, *Ombudsmen for American Government?* (1968); Gellhorn, *When Americans Complain* (1966); Davis, "Ombudsmen in America: Officers to Criticize Administration Action," 109 *University of Pennsylvania Law Review* 1057 (1961).

49. *House Hearings on the Computer and Invasion of Privacy* 26–27 (testimony of Professor Charles Reich).

50. Compare the concurring opinion of Justice Black in *Joint Anti-Fascist Refugee Committee* v. *McGrath,* 341 U.S. 123, 143 (1951). See also *House Hearings on the Computer and Invasion of Privacy* 28 (testimony of Professor Charles Reich); *House Hearings on Commercial Credit Bureaus* 14 (testimony of Professor Alan Westin); Creech, "Psychological Testing and Constitutional Rights," 1966 *Duke Law Journal* 332, 362–64; *H.Rep.* 7214, 91st Cong., 1st Sess. (1969).

51. See, e.g., *Hearings on Commercial Credit Bureaus* 14 (testimony of Professor Alan Westin). Even in the context of the mass circulation media, in which First Amendment considerations are clearly strongest, it has been argued that a state still might impose a duty to print retractions or corrections of damaging news items. Barron, "Access to the Press—A New First Amendment Right," 80 *Harvard Law Review* 1641, 1659 (1967). Further analogical support for a right to cor-

rect potentially damaging data items can be found in 39 U.S.C. § 4009 (Supp. III, 1965–1967), which provides that the individual has a right to compel anyone who mails "pandering advertisements" to remove his name from the mailing list.

Chapter VII : How to Live With the Computer Without Becoming Neurotic—Safeguarding the Privacy of Computerized Information

1. Behrens, "Computers and Security," 91 *Science News* 532 (1967).

2. See, e.g., Kramer & Livingston, "Cashing In on the Checkless Society," 45 *Harvard Business Review*, Sept.–Oct. 1967, at 141, 143, in which it is suggested that two of the major technical problems preventing the implementation of a "checkless-cashless society" based on computer systems are "[c]hoosing and applying a numbering to identify system users" and "[p]erfecting security protection systems and devices for preventing accidental or fraudulent transactions."

3. See, e.g., *Sperry-Rand UNIVAC Response to the Inquiry of the FCC, J–22 to J–23* (submitted in connection with *In re Regulatory and Policy Problems Presented by the Interdependence of Computer and Communications Facilities, Docket No. 16,979*) [hereinafter *UNIVAC Brief*].

4. A. Westin, *Privacy and Freedom,* 324 (1967); Petersen & Turn, "System Implications of Information Privacy," 30 *AFIPS Conference Proceedings* 291, 294–95 (1967).

5. *Senate Hearings on Computer Privacy* 78 (statement of the author); *UNIVAC Brief* at J–22: "This kind of protection can be provided in several degrees ranging from quite simple, which an expert would not find difficult to decipher, to the almost unbreakable."

6. The subject of computer cryptography is discussed in Baran, "On Distributed Communications: IX Security, Secrecy, and Tamper-Free Considerations," *Rand Corporation Memorandum RM–3765–PR* (1964).

7. See *Response of International Business Machines Corporation Before the FCC, I–68* (submitted in connection with *In the Matter of Regulatory and Policy Problems Presented by the Interdependence of Computer and Communications Services and Facilities, Docket 16,979*) (March 5, 1968) [hereinafter *IBM Brief*].

8. See generally Graham, "Protection in an Information Processing Utility," 11 *Communications of the ACM* 365 (1968).

9. *UNIVAC Brief* at J–28.

10. *IBM Brief* at I–69 to I–70.

11. *UNIVAC Brief* at J–27; *IBM Brief* at I–70.

12. *IBM Brief* at I–68 to I–69.

13. See Daley & Newmann, "A General Purpose File System for Secondary Storage," 27 *AFIPS Conference Proceedings* 213–29 (1965).

14. *IBM Brief* at I–65.

15. *UNIVAC Brief* at J–23 to J–24.

16. See Kramer & Livingston, supra note 2, at 144.

17. *IBM Brief* at I–64 to I–65.

18. Id. at I–66.

19. *UNIVAC Brief* at J–25. See also "Computer Encoding of Fingerprints," 93 *Science News* 494 (1968). Community Systems Foundation of Ann Arbor, Michigan, is now testing a system that identifies users by a combination of physical characteristics and responses to questions asked the user.

20. *House Hearings on the Computer and Invasion of Privacy* 126 (statement of Paul Baran).

21. In 1966, computer expert Paul Baran testified: "As one who has for many years been interested in the problems of preserving privacy in interconnected computer-communications systems, I have been unable to find [a] large body of literature [on security devices]. . . ." *Hearings on 1970 Census Questions* 5. Some valuable work has been done since this statement was made. See generally Hoffman, "Computers and Privacy: A Survey," 1 *Computing Surveys* 85 (1969).

22. See Peters, "Security Considerations in a Multi-Programmed Computer System," 30 *AFIPS Conference Proceedings* 283, 284 (1967).

23. *Senate Hearings on Computer Privacy* 78 (statement of the author); A. Westin, supra note 4, at 324; Peters, supra note 22, at 284.

24. Peters, supra note 22, at 284.

25. *Senate Hearings on Computer Privacy* 77 (statement of the author); Ruggles, "On the Needs and Values of Data Banks," in "Symposium—Computers, Data Banks, and Individual Privacy," 53 *Minnesota Law Review* 211, 219 (1968).

26. *Senate Hearings on Computer Privacy* 77 (statement of the author).

27. See pages 85–88.

28. *UNIVAC Brief* at J–30 to J–31.

29. Peters, supra note 22, at 284.

30. Allen, "Danger Ahead!—Safeguard Your Computer," 46 *Harvard Business Review*, Nov.–Dec. 1968, at 97, 101; Peters, supra note 22, at 285.

31. See *Senate Hearings on Computer Privacy* 119 (testimony of Dr. Emanuel R. Piore, Vice President of International Business Machines Corp.); *House Hearings on the Computer and Invasion of Privacy* 128 (testimony of Paul Baran of the Rand Corporation).

32. See generally Douglas, "The Computerized Man," 33 *Vital Speeches* 700 (1967).

33. *S.* 1035, 90th Cong., 1st Sess. (1967).

34. See pages 85–88. See generally Pipe, "Privacy: Establishing Restrictions on Government Inquiry," 18 *American University Law Review* 516 (1969).

35. See pages 239–48.

36. Compare Karst, " 'The Files': Legal Controls over the Accuracy and Accessibility of Stored Data," 31 *Law and Contemporary Problems* 342, 361 (1966); Sawyer & Schechter, "Computers, Privacy and the National Data Center: The Responsibility of Social Scientists," *American Psychologist,* Nov. 1968, at 810, 813.

37. See *Senate Hearings on Computer Privacy* 77 (statement of the author); Sawyer & Schechter, supra note 36, at 816.

38. See, e.g., *House Hearings on the Computer and Invasion of Privacy* 278.

39. See, e.g., *House Hearings on Commercial Credit Bureaus* 89 (testimony of Henry C. Jordan, President, Credit Data Company).

40. *Senate Hearings on Computer Privacy* 44 (statement of Charles J. Zwick, Assistant Director of the Bureau of the Budget).

41. *Senate Hearings on Computer Privacy, part* 2, at 310. See also Pemberton, "On the Dangers, Legal Aspects, and Remedies," in "Symposium—Computers, Data Banks, and Individual Privacy," 53 *Minnesota Law Review* 211, 224 (1968).

42. See *Computerworld,* March 4, 1970, at 1.

43. *Senate Hearings on Computer Privacy* 44 (statement of Charles J. Zwick, Assistant Director of the Bureau of the Budget); *Hearings on Statistical Programs* 10; Note, "Privacy and Efficient Government: Proposals for a National Data Center," 82 *Harvard Law Review* 400, 413 (1968).

44. See pages 22, 56–57.

45. Compare Note, supra note 43, at 413–14.

46. See, e.g., Lozowick, Steiner, & Miller, "Law and Quantitative Multivariate Analysis: An Encounter," 66 *Michigan Law Review* 1641, 1650 n. 13 (1968).

47. *House Hearings on the Computer and Invasion of Privacy* 94.

48. See, e.g., *Senate Hearings on Computer Privacy* 119 (testimony of Dr. Emanuel R. Piore, Vice President of International Business Machines Corp.).

49. Michael, "Speculations on the Relation of the Computer to Individual Freedom and the Right to Privacy," 33 *George Washington Law Review* 270, 279–80 (1964). See also Baran, "Communications, Computers and People," 27 *AFIPS Conference Proceedings* 45 (1965).

50. See R. Boguslaw, *The New Utopians* 97–98 (paper ed., 1965). See also *Senate Hearings on Computer Privacy* 75 (statement of the author).

51. See, e.g., Karst, supra note 36, at 362–63.

52. *Privacy and Behavioral Research* 7, 14.

53. See, e.g., *Hearings on Data Processing Management* 149. See generally President's Science Advisory Committee, *Computers in Higher Education* (1967), reprinted in *Hearings on Data Processing Management* 255–337.

54. It is somewhat ironic that one credit bureau that is moving toward computerization is attempting to protect its files against unauthorized use by periodically administering lie detector tests to its employees. See Drattel, "Corralling Credit Data," *Business Automation,* Feb. 1968, at 40.

55. See "Professional Conduct in Information Processing," 11 *Communications of the ACM* 135 (1968).

56. R. Boguslaw, supra note 50, at 97–98, 202–04. See also T. Roszak, *The Making of a Counter Culture* (paper ed., 1969).

57. See Westin, "Science, Privacy, and Freedom: Issues and Proposals for the 1970's," 66 *Columbia Law Review* 1205, 1218 (1966); *Privacy and Behavioral Research* 28–29.

58. See pages 248–50.

59. Westin, supra note 57, at 1218.

Epilogue

1. Compare M. McLuhan, *Understanding Media: The Extensions of Man* 304 (paper ed., 1964). See also Rapoport, "Technological Models of the Nervous System," in *The Modeling of Mind: Computers and Intelligence* 25 (paper ed., 1968).

2. Benn, "Where Power Belongs," *The Nation,* Aug. 26, 1968, at 136, 137.

3. *100 Selected Poems* by E. E. Cummings 89 (paper ed., Grove Press 1959).

4. J. Ellul, *The Technological Society* 434 (paper ed., 1964).

Index

Abacus, 8
Agencies, government:
  information transfers, 142
  statute authorizing, 142–44
Alderman v. *United States,* 166
American Airlines: flight reservation computer, 42
American Civil Liberties Union, 41, 149
American Council of Education, 251
American Medical Association, 136
Anderson v. *Sills,* 200–02
Appropriation theory, 173–75
Army, U.S.:
  data gathering authority, 62
  records, 150
  surveillance by, 40
  See also Investigative Records Repository
Associated Credit Bureaus of America:
  communications link, 75–76
  guidelines, 89
  practices, 83
  television report, 71–72
Association for Computing Machinery:
  guidelines, 255
Atomic Energy Commission, 55
Audiovisual technology:
  computer-assisted instruction, privacy comparison, 117
  consent requirement, 119–20
  educational experiments, 118
  future potential, 117–18

Bales, Stephen G., 3
Batch processing, 17
Bernstein, Jeremy, 15
Betts, Jackson (Congressman):
  census reform, 128, 134
Biederman's of Springfield, Inc. v. *Wright,* 177
Binary code, 11
Binet, Alfred, 91
Birth number, 4
Bit, 11, 19
Boole, George, 11
Brandeis, Louis D.:
  Harvard Law Review article, 170, 172
  property theory, 213
  public disclosure theory, 177
  right to be let alone, 204
Brave New World, 39
Brents v. *Morgan,* 177

Call-back system, 243
Census Act:
  criticism of, 137
  protection under, 136
Census Bureau, 20, 55, 58:
  criminal sanctions, 129–30
  data uses, 128
  regulatory agency, 230
  surveys, other agencies, 140
  See also Decennial census
Census Reform Bill, 135, 137
Central Personality Bureau, 102
Cincinnati-Hamilton County Crime Information Center, 148
Clarke, Sir Arthur, 2
COBOL (Common Business Oriented Language), 13

327